THE
GOLDEN
DREAM

THE
GOLDEN
DREAM

Seekers of El Dorado

ROBERT SILVERBERG

OHIO UNIVERSITY PRESS

Athens

First Ohio University Press paperback edition printed 1996

02 01 00 99 98 97 96   1 2 3 4 5

Library of Congress catalog card number 66-30498

Text designed by Guy Fleming

Printed in the United States of America

"Shadow," said he, "where can it be—
This land of Eldorado?"

"Over the Mountains of the Moon,
Down the Valley of the Shadow,
    Ride, boldly ride,"
    The shade replied,—
"If you seek for Eldorado!"

—Poe

Contents

[1]

THE GILDED MAN

OF CUNDINAMARCA

HE QUEST FOR EL DORADO WAS AN ENTER-
prise of fantasy that obsessed the adventurers of Europe for more than a century.
Tales of a golden kingdom and of a golden
king, somewhere in the unexplored wilderness of South America, spurred men on to
notable achievements of endurance, chiv-
alry, and—too often—crime. Nothing halted the pursuers of
the golden dream, neither snow-capped mountains nor blazing plains, neither the thin air of lofty plateaus nor the green
intricacy of steaming tropical jungles. They marched on,
killing and plundering, suffering incredible torments, often
traveling—as one chronicler put it—*con el alma en los dien-
tes*, with their souls between their teeth.

They did not find El Dorado. The stuff of dreams
cannot easily be transmuted into solid reality. The seekers
sought, and their deeds constitute a monument to futility as
well as an epic of high adventure.

Yet there was a kernel of truth within the fantasy. This
is where the quest began, a third of the way through the
sixteenth century: with a glittering story that journeyed
down from the high tableland of Bogotá to dazzle the *conquistadores.*

The tale came out of Cundinamarca, "the land of the condor," now the Andean highlands of the Republic of Colombia. No white man had then penetrated that remote inland plateau, although the Spaniards had gained a foothold in bordering lands. There were Spanish settlements along the coasts of what now are Venezuela and Colombia; Spaniards had mastered the proud Incas of Peru; they had nibbled at the shores of Guiana. But as late as 1535 Cundinamarca was *terra incognita*. On that great plateau, more than 7500 feet above sea level, it was possible that a high civilization of spectacular wealth, comparable to the civilizations of Peru and Mexico, might still await the lucky explorer.

This was the legend out of Cundinàmarca:

At a lake called Guatavitá on the Bogotá plateau, a solemn ceremony was held each year to reconsecrate the king. On the appointed day the monarch came forth, removed his garments, and anointed his body with turpentine to make it sticky. Then he rolled in gold dust until covered from head to foot with a gleaming coat.

Gilded and splendid, the king arose and proceeded to the shores of Lake Guatavitá while all the multitudes of his subjects accompanied him, celebrating with music and jubilant songs. The king and his nobles boarded a canoe and paddled to the middle of the mountain-rimmed lake. There he solemnly hurled offerings of gold and emeralds into the water; and at the climax of the ceremony the gilded man himself leaped from the canoe and plunged in to bathe. At the sight of that flash of brightness, the crowd on shore sent up a mighty cheer. Soon the king emerged and returned to shore, and a festival of dancing and drinking and singing began.

A gilded man—*el hombre dorado*—ruling over a nation so wealthy that it could afford to coat its monarch's skin with gold! That fabled plunge kindled the imagination of many a gold-seeker. Already the treasuries of the Incas and the Aztecs had yielded wealth so immense as to unbalance the economy of Europe and set in motion a formidable inflation. Not content, the gold-seekers looked now for the land of the gilded man of Cundinamarca.

The legend underwent mutations. *El dorado*, the gilded man, became El Dorado, the kingdom of gold. The location of that kingdom shifted in steady progression eastward across South America during the century of pursuit, migrating from Colombia to the basin of the Amazon to the jungles of Guiana as each site in turn failed to fulfill its glistening promise. The original El Dorado, where the annual rite of the gilded chieftain actually had been performed, was discovered early in the quest; but since it did not conform to the hopes of its discoverers, the seekers continued to search.

It was a time of quests. Men had searched for Prester John, the Christian king of Asia; they had looked for the lost continent of Atlantis, for King Solomon's mines at Ophir, for the Seven Cities of Cíbola, for the Fountain of Youth, for the Holy Grail, for the domain of the women warriors, the Amazons. Often gold had been the mainspring of the search, as in the instance of the Río Doro of Africa, the River of Gold that Arab merchants described. Gold in plenty was found during that age of exploration, but rarely did it coincide with the site of one of the grand romantic quests. The golden cities of Cíbola turned out to be the mud pueblos of the Zuni; Prester John, that king of rubies and diamonds, was tracked to a Mongol tent in a grim steppe; and El Dorado became a trap that unmanned even the most valiant.

But the joy of a quest is in the questing. The kingdom of the gilded man lay always over the next mountain, beyond the next turn in the river, past the next thicket of the jungle. Each successive adventurer was aware of the perils and

[5]

pitfalls of the quest, and knew the grim fate of his predecessors; yet the pull of El Dorado was relentless. The record of earlier failure only served to intensify the hunger of the new generations of explorers. As Sir Walter Raleigh, the last and most tragic of the Doradists, wrote in 1596, "It seemeth to me that this Empire is reserved for her Majesty and the English nation, by reason of the hard success which all these and other Spaniards had in attempting the same." [1]

The ceremony of an Indian tribe became the magnet of doom for hundreds of bold men. A will-o'-the-wisp, a fantasy, a golden dream—a chieftain transformed into a shining statue—the bright gleam of his diving body—El Dorado, the realm of gold—it was an obsessive quest from which there was no turning back, no reprieve for those condemned to follow its fruitless trails.

2

Gold is a beautiful metal and a useful one. It is dense and heavy, with a satisfying feeling of mass. It has a splendid yellow gleam which is virtually imperishable, for gold is not a chemically active metal and therefore not subject to rust. Its unwillingness to combine with other elements made it easily accessible to primitive man; when smelting was unknown, such metals as iron were unattainable but nuggets of pure gold could be found in many parts of the world.

Gold is malleable. It can be hammered or drawn into attractive shapes. The Egyptians and Sumerians recognized the beauty and utility of gold and fashioned it into jewelry six thousand years ago. Before the concept of currency was known, gold was desired above all other metals and must have been a choice barter item.

Gold is scarce. That added to its value. Scarce but not *too* scarce, easy to fabricate, beautiful, durable, massy, divisible into small units without impairment of value, gold quickly established itself as a high prize. Eventually the idea arose of coining it into pieces of uniform weight; the traditional birthdate of coinage is about 700 B.C. in the kingdom of Lydia in Asia Minor. Iron, copper, lead all served as the basis of currency in some lands, and their deficiencies were demonstrated. Silver won great acclaim, and much of Europe preferred the silver standard well into modern times. But gold was always the master metal. Hercules went in quest of the golden apples of the Hesperides. Phoenician miners quarried gold in Spain and fetched it to the Levantine coast to grease the wheels of commerce. King Solomon sent treasure-fleets down the Red Sea to Tarshish and Ophir. "Men now worship gold to the neglect of the gods," Propertius complained in his *Elegies*, two thousand years ago. "By gold good faith is banished and justice is sold."

Propertius had good reason to grumble. Few nations pursued gold as assiduously as Rome. The Romans were the inheritors of Alexander's Greek empire, and Alexander had taken possession of the Persian hoard, and the Persians were successors to Babylonia, Egypt, and Assyria. All that shining treasure cascaded down to the regime of the Caesars. The Romans worked the mines of Spain to virtual exhaustion, and their coffers bulged accordingly. The high point of their prosperity came in the reign of Augustus. At his death, in 14 A.D., the Roman gold supply may have been as great as 500,000,000 ounces.

That matchless treasury was gradually dissipated. Roman gold flowed eastward in exchange for such goods as Chinese silks, deflating the Roman economy considerably, but much more damage was done by the barbarian incursions that cut Rome off from the lands where gold was mined. The yellow metal disappeared into private hands, was carried off by Goths and Vandals to become jewelry, or simply vanished. By 800 A.D., the total recoverable gold supply of Europe—the basis of currency—was less than a tenth of what it had been in the time of Augustus Caesar. The lack of gold, and a corresponding shortage of silver, hampered trade and kept prices low in relation to the purchasing power of precious metals.

The slow awakening of Europe in medieval times coincided to some extent with the revival of the gold supply. Old mines were reopened, new ones discovered; and as seamen grew more bold, it became possible to replenish the treasuries of Europe by venturing abroad. In the thirteenth century, Marco Polo and other Venetians reached as far as China, but that was a false dawn of commerce. It was nearly two centuries later that Prince Henry the Navigator of Portugal goaded his captains to journey ever farther down the western coast of Africa, until at last in 1488 Bartolomeu Dias rounded the Cape of Good Hope and showed that a sea route to India lay ahead. Dias fell short of the goal, but nine years later Vasco da Gama sailed completely around Africa and reached India, opening a glamorous new trade route that gave Portugal a short interlude of world dominance.

While the Portuguese went east for gold, the Spaniards went west. They found a new world brimming with the yellow metal and changed the path of history. The story of El Dorado is largely a Spanish story, and its starting point is the year 1492.

That year merits its place among history's exalted dates for several reasons. It was, of course, the year in which a stubborn Genoese seaman named Cristoforo Colombo persuaded the Spanish Queen to finance a westward voyage that brought him to the Indies. More than that, it was the year that Spain as a nation took form, and without that event there would have been no voyage of Columbus, no conquest of the Americas, and probably no quest for El Dorado.

Spain lies closer to Africa than any other European

state, and in the eighth century had fallen victim to that spectacular surge of Arab militarism that erupted across the Christian world. For centuries thereafter the Iberian Peninsula was an outpost of Islam. The enlightened Moors brought their universities to Spain, their doctors and poets and astronomers, and in a rude and ignorant Europe the Moslem kingdoms of Spain became the channel by which learning entered. The overthrown Christian rulers of Spain had taken refuge in the mountains of Asturias, and maintained a shaky independence there. Gradually the Moors yielded ground as resurgent Spanish Christians pressed them from the north in a seemingly endless war of reconquest.

There was no real unity in Spain during the *reconquista*. Geographically, Spain is a broken land, divided by mountain chains and lacking the navigable rivers that can bind a nation together. Thus Christian Spain became a patchwork of small kingdoms that vied for dominance— Castile, Aragon, Navarre, León, and others. Now and again one kingdom attained brief supremacy, but the general picture was one of restless little states vying for power while moving in and out of complex dynastic alliances and somehow prosecuting the common war against the Moors. The Spaniards themselves referred to their peninsula until quite recent times as *las Españas*, "the Spains," and not as "Spain."

A complex mixed society of Christians and Moors took form in the thirteenth and fourteenth centuries as a result of the shifting alliances of "the Spains." By the middle of the thirteenth century the conquest of the Moorish-held territories had proceeded to the point where most of the Moslems were concentrated in the kingdom of Granada along the Mediterranean coast. Granada acknowledged the supremacy of the Christian kingdom of Castile in western Spain. To the east, the kingdom of Aragon extended its sway over what was left of Moorish Spain. The two kingdoms of Aragon and Castile emerged as the leading powers of the land and the Moors remained in their part of the peninsula mainly by tolerance of their Christian overlords.

A significant marriage in 1469 indicated the ultimate destiny of "the Spains." Prince Ferdinand, heir to the throne of Aragon, wed Princess Isabella, the heiress to the throne of Castile, and by 1479 they had come to power in their respective kingdoms. Though Aragon and Castile remained separate states, they were joined at last by a bond of marriage, and the dynastic link gave the pair of monarchs control over most of the peninsula.

During the period of uncertainty while the youthful Ferdinand and Isabella were coming to their thrones, the Moors of Granada had chosen to withhold their customary tribute. In 1482, the joint rulers commenced a final war against the Spanish Moors—the last crusade of Europe. Village by village, Granada was conquered and drawn into full Christian power. The war lasted a decade. On January 2, 1492, the city of Granada itself fell to the Catholic kings, and the rulers of Castile and Aragon now ruled all of Spain. It was a propitious time for Columbus to come before Isabella and offer her Cathay.

Ferdinand and Isabella maintained the separateness of their states. Ferdinand's Aragon, the smaller kingdom, was a limited monarchy with a strong parliament—the *Cortés*—and its government was stable and orderly. Isabella's Castile, upon her accession, had been loosely run, infested with corrupt officials and haughty nobles who indulged in private wars; it received a thorough overhauling at Isabella's hands, and she emerged as Castile's absolute monarch. By imposing the total supremacy of the Castilian crown she shaped the pattern for the conquest of the Americas.

3

Awkwardly, two huge continents turned out to lie between Spain and Asia. Columbus made his landfall in the Bahamas on October 12, 1492, and persuaded himself that he had found the outlying islands of the Indies. It was not so, and gradually the immensity of the unknown western territory made itself apparent. So, too, did the New World's riches demonstrate themselves.

On Saturday, October 13, Columbus recorded in his journal the details of his first contact with the islanders: "Many of these people, all men, came from the shore . . . and I was anxious to learn whether they had gold. I saw also that some of them wore little pieces of gold in their perforated noses. I learned by signs that there was a king in the south, or south of the island, who owned many vessels filled with gold." [2]

The first gleam was encouraging. But Columbus was after bigger game. He did not plan to search immediately for the southern land of gold, "for I must endeavor to reach Cipangu quickly."

He pioneered that pleasant institution, the Caribbean cruise. Asking everywhere for news of the Great Khan, he sailed from island to island. On October 28 he landed at Cuba, an island big enough to be his dreamed-of Cipangu; but the natives told him to keep going if he would find the true home of gold. He sailed on through blue water and tropical warmth, but his men grew restless. Late in November his lieutenant, Martín Pinzón, took the *Pinta* and went off on a private voyage to the land of gold. A few days later Columbus discovered Hispaniola, the island now shared by Haiti and the Dominican Republic, where gold abounded. The chastened Pinzón returned, empty-handed, to learn that he had missed the great moment. In January, 1493, Columbus went back to Spain to bring the glad tidings to Isabella. He could not claim that he had found Cathay or Cipangu, but certainly he had found gold.

Queen Isabella, well pleased by the news, claimed the Indies as the direct and exclusive possessions of the Castilian crown, as was her right, and thereafter all ventures to the New World were conducted under license from the throne of Castile. In 1493, Pope Alexander VI confirmed the Castilian right of discovery by obligingly dividing the world between Spain and Portugal. The Pope drew a line from pole to pole, a hundred miles west of the Azores. All that lay east of that line was granted to Portugal for exploitation; the land to the west was Spain's.

Spanish activities at first were confined to the West Indies, centering about the settlement that Columbus planted on Hispaniola. It was known, in a vague way, that the isles found by Columbus were flanked by two gigantic land masses, neither of which was Asia. The Spaniards settled down to the occupation of the West Indies and the destruction of their native inhabitants, but gradually the lust for wealth drew them to the mainland.

Columbus first glimpsed the mainland of South America on his third voyage, in 1498. He found evidence of gold on the coast of what shortly would be called Venezuela. That name was given two years later when a former companion of Columbus, Alonso de Ojeda, explored over a thousand miles of the northern coast of South America from Guiana to Colombia. He thought that the islanded coast reminded him of "a queer little Venice"—*Venezuela*. One of his navigators, Amerigo Vespucci, also contributed to the growing terminology of the New World; in a mysterious way his first name became attached to the western continents themselves.

Ojeda found gold on the Venezuelan coast, and pearls

as well. The best pearls and the lion's share of the gold went into the Spanish royal treasury, for all this land belonged to Castile, and by Castile's laws the monarch took a bullion royalty of two thirds the value. (In practice this proved too much to extort from the explorers; between 1500 and 1504, the royal share was successively reduced by petition of the American settlers to a half, a third, and a fifth. There it remained, and the "royal fifth," the *quinto reál*, was demanded by Spanish officials until the eighteenth century.)

The reconnaissance proceeded rapidly. In 1500, Rodrigo de Bastidas, a notary from Seville, explored the region around the Isthmus of Panamá on foot and came away with gold in abundance. About the same time, Christoval Guerra and Pedro Alonso Niño guided a rotted caravel along the Venezuelan coast and returned to Spain with gold and a multitude of pearls. They reported that gold was scarce among the Indian tribes of the eastern part of South America's northern coast, but was more abundant farther to the west, toward the Isthmus. Vincente Yañez Pinzón went in the other direction, past the Equator and down the coast of Brazil as far as the mouth of the Amazon, but he was ruined by shipwreck and came home with only a few survivors.

On his last expedition in 1502, Columbus called first at Santo Domingo, Hispaniola, where he met a fleet of thirty ships about to depart for Spain laden with West Indian gold. The veteran explorer warned of storms but the Spaniards would not heed him, and hurricanes sent twenty ships to the bottom, one of them carrying a nugget of gold said to weigh 36 pounds. Columbus himself waited out the storm and then went on to Jamaica, Cuba, and Honduras. He moved southward along the eastern coast of Central America, collecting a considerable quantity of gold. The Indians told him of a wealthy and civilized nation lying nine days' march overland to the west, on the Pacific shore, but they also told him that the western coast was "ten days' journey from the Ganges," so Columbus evidently was hearing what he chose to hear. No European yet had crossed that narrow strip of land that divides the great oceans. Columbus sought in vain for some navigable strait that would bring him to the western coast of Central America. Finding none, he returned to Jamaica, poverty, and a year of sickness and hunger. By 1504 he was back in Spain just as his patron, Queen Isabella, was dying. Columbus, gouty and deprived of the benefits of his discovery, survived her by eighteen months. After his first great voyage, his life had been a sequence of misadventures, and other men reaped the harvest of the Indies.

It was a cruel harvest, not only of gold and pearls but of the bodies and souls of men. The ruthless behavior of the Spaniards toward the natives of the New World was an unhappy accompaniment to the expansion of Spanish power. The historian William H. Prescott, a New England puritan at heart, criticized Spanish harshness this way in his classic *History of the Conquest of Peru* in 1847: "Gold was the incentive and the recompense, and in the pursuit of it [the Spaniard's] inflexible nature rarely hesitated as to the means. His courage was sullied with cruelty, the cruelty that flowed equally—strange as it may seem—from his avarice and his religion. . . . The Castilian, too proud for hypocrisy, committed more cruelties in the name of religion than were ever practiced by the pagan idolater or the fanatical Moslem." [3] Prescott could not resist drawing the contrast between the cruel "children of Southern Europe" and his own forebears, "the Anglo-Saxon races who scattered themselves along the great northern division of the western hemisphere. . . . They asked nothing from the soil, but the reasonable returns of their own labor. No golden visions threw a deceitful halo around their path and beckoned them onward through seas of blood to the subversion of an unoffending dynasty."

The Spaniards have few apologists, though recent historians have attempted to countervail the "black legend" of Spanish atrocity by insisting that they were, at least, no more cruel than anyone else of their time. R. B. Cunninghame Graham, in his *The Conquest of New Granada* (1922), points out that "Spaniards then, as now, were the most individualistic people on the earth. Thus fortified, both by religious and by racial pride, holding their faith with fierce intensity, they felt they had a mission to fulfill, laid on them from on high. Gold was not always their chief aim, as Protestant historians aver, although they loved it, wading ankle-deep in blood in its pursuit. When all is said and done, they were much like ourselves, not knowing, and not caring much to know, where their greed ended and their faith began." [4]

They were tough men from a rugged land. Those who went to the New World were warriors, all sentimentality burned from them by the Spanish sun. They swore by Christ, but not the loving Christ of the Gospels; they saw no contradiction in spreading the worship of Jesus by the sword, if necessary, nor did they hesitate to enslave men they deemed lacking in souls. Some Spaniards clearly embraced terror for its own sake; others used it as an instrument of policy; still others, and they were few, recoiled from bloodshed except in the last resort. The fact stands that the Spaniards were more ruthless in their treatment of the natives than their great rivals, the English; and we will see English voyagers turning that fact to their own advantage. The best that can be said for the average *conquistador* is that he was as unsparing with his own life as with the lives of others. Sir Walter Raleigh, who had little reason to love the Spaniards, managed high praise for their "patient virtue" in his *History of the World:*

"We seldom or never find any nation hath endured so many misadventures and miseries as the Spaniards have

done in their Indian discoveries. Yet persisting in their enterprises, with invincible constancy, they have annexed to their
kingdom so many goodly provinces, as bury the remembrance of all dangers past. Tempests and shipwrecks, famine, overthrows, mutinies, heat and cold, pestilence, and all
manner of diseases, both old and new, together with extreme
poverty, and want of all things needful, have been the enemies, wherewith every one of their most noble discoveries, at
one time or other, hath encountered. Many years have
passed over some of their heads in the search of not so many
leagues: Yea, more than one or two have spent their labor,
their wealth, and their lives, in search of a golden kingdom,
without getting further notice of it than what they had at
their first setting forth." [5]

Valor and vainglory, murderous cruelty and rocklike
endurance—these were the marks of the Spaniards as they
spread out into South America. A harsh light plays over
their exploits. They were fed on romantic dreams of chivalry
and on the somber inflexibility of the Inquisition, and out of
this brew of fantasy and militant intolerance they took the
nourishment of empire. For their crimes, their bravery is
their only absolution. They stand indicted by one of their
own people, the saintly Bartolomé de las Casas, "the apostle
of the Indies," who wrote in 1542 of the destruction worked
on the Indians of the West Indies:

"Upon these lambs so meek, so qualified and endowed
of their Maker and Creator, as hath been said, entered the
Spanish . . . as wolves, as lions, and as tigers most cruel of
long time famished: and have not done in those quarters
these forty years past, neither do at this present, ought else
save tear them in pieces, kill them, martyr them, afflict them,
torment them, and destroy them by strange sorts of cruelties
never neither seen, nor read, nor heard of the like . . . so
far forth that of above three millions of souls that were in the

probable existence of a rich empire on the western coast of South America, and in time that empire would be revealed to be no myth at all, but the Peru of the Incas. However, it happened that a different golden realm was the first to fall.

Spaniards commanded by Juan de Grijalva set out from Cuba in 1518 on a voyage of reconnaissance. They landed on the Caribbean coast of Mexico, which was a land unknown to them. Some Spaniards had been shipwrecked off Yucatán in 1511 and had fallen into the hands of the Mayas, but nothing had been heard from them at the time Grijalva sailed. Besides, his landing was made at an entirely different part of Mexico.

The strangers' stay was short, but it aroused great interest among the Mexicans. Only a generation before, a tribe known as the Aztecs had succeeded in imposing its authority over most of central Mexico. The Aztecs ruled in splendor from their inland capital of Tenochtitlán, at the present-day site of Mexico City; but their king, the moody, superstitious Moctezuma II, was troubled by a prophecy that bearded white-skinned gods would come one day out of the eastern ocean to relieve him of his kingdom. Grijalva and his men were mistaken for these divine visitors. Moctezuma hastened to send loads of jewelry, precious stones, capes of feathers, and elegant articles of bright gold as gifts. Grijalva returned to Cuba laden with treasure.

Diego de Velásquez, a veteran of Columbus' voyages, now ruled Cuba. He was irritated with Grijalva for not having ventured farther inland, and chose a different man to go back to Mexico on a mission of conquest. He selected Hernando Cortés, a lively, even flamboyant, Spaniard of unswerving courage. Cortés quickly assembled a picked party. Velásquez was unnerved by the young Spaniard's show of ambition and tried to revoke the appointment; but in 1519 Cortés set out with a fleet of eleven ships, 500 men, thirteen musketeers, thirty-two crossbowmen, sixteen horses, and seven cannons hardly larger than toys.

The implausible story of Cortés' achievement is well known. With this tiny army he marched successfully across Mexico and brought the invincible Aztecs quickly to defeat. He had many advantages: the charismatic nature of his own leadership, the willingness of vassal Indian tribes to ally themselves with the Spaniards against the Aztecs, and the services of a slave girl named Malinal, or Dona Marina, who was his interpreter. Cortés had rescued one of the Spaniards shipwrecked off Yucatán in 1511, and he spoke the Mayan language; so did Malinal, who learned her Spanish from him. Thereafter she was the go-between through whom Cortés could communicate his precise wishes to the natives of Mexico.

As Cortés marched westward toward Tenochtitlán, the frightened Moctezuma attempted to placate him with rich gifts. Aztec ambassadors met the invaders laden with treasure. Bernal Díaz, one of Cortés' soldiers and probably the most reliable chronicler of the conquest, left this description of the gifts of Moctezuma:

"The first article presented was a wheel like a sun, as big as a cartwheel, with many sorts of pictures on it, the whole of fine gold, and a wonderful thing to behold. . . . Then another wheel was presented of greater size made of silver of great brilliancy in imitation of the moon with other figures on it, and this was of great value as it was very heavy. . . . Then we were brought twenty golden ducks, beautifully worked and very natural looking, and some ornaments like dogs, and many articles of gold worked in the shape of tigers and lions and monkeys, and ten collars beautifully worked and other necklaces; and twelve arrows and a bow with its string, and two rods like staffs of justice, five palms long, all in beautiful hollow work of gold. Then there twenty years, one Spaniard was offering 10,000 golden pesos—perhaps a million dollars in modern purchasing power—for an ordinary saddle-horse, and he found no sellers.

Atahuallpa still languished a prisoner. In a rash moment, Pizarro allowed a belligerent faction among his men to bring him to trial on charges of idolatry, polygamy, treason against the Spaniards, the murder of his half-brother Huascar, and other absurd charges. Swiftly he was sentenced to death, and executed on August 29, 1533. Instantly the treasure-trains still en route to Cajamarca halted. The bearers of gold for the ransom hurled their burdens into rivers and lakes. Among the lost items, so it was said, was a chain of gold 700 feet long, weighing several tons. The casual treachery of the Spaniards had cost them heavily in gold, and it cost them the peace of Peru as well, for while Atahuallpa alive was a helpless puppet, Atahuallpa dead was the martyred symbol of revolt. It now became necessary for the Spaniards to follow their easy and bloodless conquest with a series of taxing military campaigns before Peru was finally subdued.

The *Casa de Contratación* at Seville enjoyed a steady stream of gold. Between 1516 and 1520 it had recorded imports totalling 993,000 *pesos de oro*—the last output of the dwindling West Indian mines, and the first dividends from Panamá. From 1521 to 1525, only 134,000 *pesos de oro* arrived. The first impact of Cortés' conquest of Mexico was felt in the statistics for 1526–30, which showed a new high figure of 1,038,000 *pesos de oro*. The totals for 1531–35 reflect the yield both of Mexico and Peru: 1,650,000 *pesos de oro*. In another five years, the harvest had risen steeply: 3,937,000 *pesos de oro* between 1536 and 1540.

Spain was enriched by the Indies, although, as we will see, all this wealth brought little prosperity to the homeland.

The statistics compiled at Seville showed a rising trend, but yet the golden flow itself diminished rapidly once the treasures of temples and palaces were looted. It was easy to grab golden objects that had been accumulated over generations; prying new supplies of gold from the earth took more time. Between 1493 and 1530, more than 98% of the treasure received at Seville was gold. Then the scales tipped, and between 1531 and 1550 more than 85% of what came in was silver, far less valuable by the ounce. At the peak of Spanish imperialism—1591–95—the New World would produce treasure to the value of 35,185,000 *pesos de oro*, but 98.5% of this would be in silver.

Mexico and Peru were not enough, then. Their treasuries were cleaned of gold, and the natives, weakened by disease and sullen from mistreatment, had little incentive to dig more for their Spanish masters. Yet the Americas were Spanish imperialism—1591–95—the New World would repay its finders as Mexico had repaid Cortés and Peru Pizarro?

The legends of golden kingdoms persisted. Balboa and Solís and Cabot had sniffed out the wealth of Peru, and Pizarro had found it. Now came new stories, tales of the gilded man of Cundinamarca, El Dorado, he who coated his skin in precious dust. The rumors of Peru had proved to be no fantasies. The quest for El Dorado commenced in earnest, with the shining examples of Cortés and Pizarro to serve as spurs for the brave.

THE GERMAN

CONQUISTADORES

HE NEED FOR MONEY MOTIVATED THE NEXT phase of the opening of South America, a phase roughly contemporaneous with Pizarro's conquest of Peru but far less rewarding. The problems of an emperor, the ambitions of a banking house, and the spread of a new and troublesome disease all had a share in the exploratory maneuvers that brought Europe the first word of El Dorado.

The problems of Emperor Charles V dated from January 12, 1519, when his grandfather Maximilian, the Holy Roman Emperor, died. For centuries the imperial title had been in the hands of the Habsburg family, of whom Charles was now the chief heir. But actually the throne was elective. Seven European princes held the power of choosing the new Emperor; and the electors could be bought.

Maximilian had dreamed of uniting all the thrones of Europe under Habsburg power by interlocking marriages. By wedding his son Philip to the heiress of Ferdinand and Isabella, he had made the kingdoms of Spain Habsburg possessions. There were five children of that marriage, and all would make royal marriages that eventually would weave

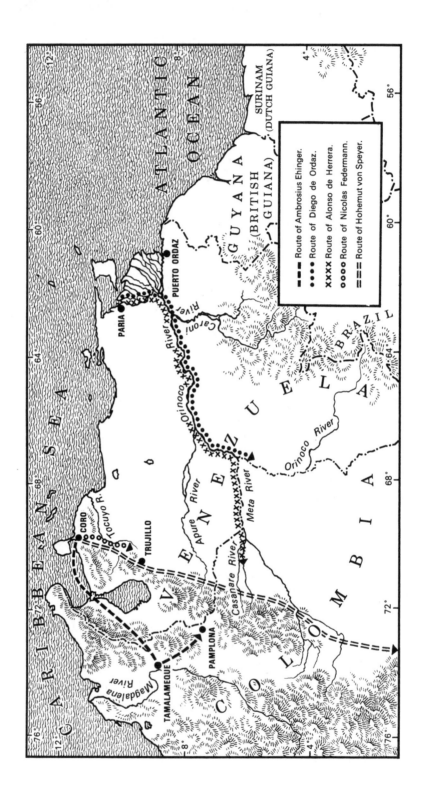

France, Hungary, Portugal, Denmark, and even England into the dynastic web for varying spans of time. The key to Maximilian's plan was giving the Holy Roman Empire itself —essentially, Germany and Austria—to his grandson Charles. The chief rival to the nineteen-year-old Charles was Francis I, King of France.

Francis one day would be Charles' prisoner, and shortly afterward Charles' brother-in-law; but in 1519 he felt that he had an opportunity to become the universal European ruler of whom Maximilian had dreamed. He put himself forward as a candidate for election. The third man in the race, Henry VIII of England, stood little chance. Charles and Francis set about buying up electors. They emptied their treasuries, and when the coffers were bare they began mortgaging their estates. Their resources were strained to the limits, and the seven electors tallied the bids in a mood of icy calculation. Charles had an overwhelming advantage: he held the support of the rich banking houses of Germany. The house of the Welsers loaned him 143,000 gold florins. When that proved to be insufficient, the bank of the Fuggers advanced Charles 543,000 florins more, and an Italian bank put up another 65,000. At Frankfurt, on June 28, 1519, by unanimous vote, Charles was chosen to be the Holy Roman Emperor Charles V.

It was an expensive victory, and now the debts had to be settled. In 1519 Charles did not yet have the revenues of Mexico and Peru at his command. To the Fuggers, the biggest creditors, he surrendered rich mining concessions in the Tyrol; that did not quite balance the account, so in 1525 he turned over to them the income that he drew from the holdings of three wealthy knightly orders of Spain. The Welsers had to wait longer for their notes to be redeemed. In 1527 Charles gave them Venezuela.

The Emperor thus departed from the policy of his

grandparents, Ferdinand and Isabella, who might hire foreigners as pilots and captains, but who granted territory only to Spaniards. Isabella had reserved the New World for men of Castile; after her death, Ferdinand had opened it to his subjects of Aragon. Now Charles permitted the Welsers to become proprietary lords of Venezuela in perpetuity, with the right of nominating governors. Although Spain would retain title to the land, the German bankers could send at their own cost 300 men to Venezuela, could found two towns and three fortresses, and were to pay the usual royal fifth on all treasure obtained. The *capitulación*, signed in March, 1528, also dealt with the Indians. Charles declared, "I give you license and faculty . . . to take as slaves those Indians who are rebels, after admonishing and requiring them . . . and you may take and purchase those who are already truly slaves, paying the usual fifth on slaves." [21] Two Welser agents, Heinrich Ehinger and Jerome Seyler, signed the contract on behalf of the bankers.

For the house of Welser it was the best that could be obtained, since Charles could not possibly repay his debt in cash. The Welsers were content. They were among the most ambitious and prosperous of the new class of bourgeois bankers in Europe; since founding their bank in 1473, they had extended their interests to many parts of the world. Clearly they hoped to recoup their investment in Charles' throne by harvesting gold and slaves in their portion of the New World.

The Welsers had another reason to see profit in Venezuela. It seemed a likely place to obtain the drug known as *guaiac*, and guaiac was the specific for syphilis, so a supply of it might well be more valuable than mere gold.

The history of syphilis is a cloudy one, but apparently it was unknown in Europe before the voyage of Columbus. The crew of the *Pinta* seem to have brought the pox back with them from the New World in 1493, and it traveled rapidly. There was an outbreak in Barcelona that year, and another in England, where it was dubbed "the French disease." It reached Germany under that name in 1495; but the French, who picked it up in Italy that summer, called it the *mal de Naples*, the Neapolitan disease. To the Italians it was the *mal francese*. In 1496 the Poles reported attacks of "the German disease," three years later the Russians accused the Poles of infecting them, and by 1512 the natives of the East Indies and much of Asia were muttering about "the Portuguese disease."

Under any name, syphilis was grisly. The private secretary of the Emperor Maximilian described it in an official account: "Many of those poor fellows were covered from head to foot with vile running sores and looked so repulsive that their own comrades would not go near them. Others had certain parts of their bodies, namely their foreheads, necks, chests, etc., covered with hard scales like the gnarled lumps found on a tree-trunk. In their pain, the poor devils would tear off these scabs with their fingernails, revealing the purulent flesh underneath. Others had warts and wens in such numbers that they could not be counted, and when these excrescences broke open they gave off a putrid stench that was not to be borne." [22]

Many remedies were proposed, some of them merely worthless, others positively damaging to the sufferer. One that found an immediate success was guaiac, the wood of the guaiac tree, or lignum vitae. This is an extremely heavy, attractive wood found in Florida, the West Indies, and along the northern coast of South America. Nicholas Monardes, a Spanish physician born in 1493, told of the discovery of guaiac's healing properties in his book on the natural history of the Americas, published in 1574 and Englished three years later by John Frampton under the title, *Joyfull Newes out of the Newe Founde Worlde:*

"A Spaniard that did suffer great pains of the Pox,

which he had by the company of an Indian woman, but his servant being one of the Physicians of that country [Hispaniola] gave unto him the water of Guaiacan, wherewith not only his grievous pains were taken away that he did suffer: but healed very well of the evil, with the which many other Spaniards, that were infected with the same evil were healed, the which was communicated immediately, with them that came from hence, hither to Seville, and from thence it was divulged throughout all Spain, and from thence through all the world. . . ."[23] According to Monardes, the guaiac came from "a great tree, of the greatness of an oak: he doth cast out many boughs, the rind it doth cast from it being dry, great, and full of gum." This "rind" was to be pulverized and steeped in water for medicinal purposes.

One of the first to publish news of this remedy was the German scholar Ulrich von Hutten, in 1515. Certainly the Welsers knew the book of Ulrich von Hutten, and were alert to the commercial possibilities of importing guaiac. In time his cousin Philipp von Hutten came onto their payroll and went to Venezuela as their administrator, though what he was pursuing was not guaiac but the gold of El Dorado.

2

In theory, the northern coast of South America had been incorporated into the neat political structure of Spain's overseas empire as early as 1520. The Spaniards had built an elaborate governmental system, dividing their newly found territories into a number of kingdoms, presidencies, viceregencies, and governorships. Overseeing the entire structure were the *audiencias*, or "Royal Audiences," administrative lawcourts with the right of review over the viceroys. The first of these was founded in Santo Domingo on Hispaniola, and others followed in Mexico and Panamá;

had not only buried hundreds of their comrades in the wilderness but who had returned to civilization without the gold they had set out to gain.

3

While Ehinger had been conducting his frustrating, fierce, and ultimately fatal search for the undiscovered golden empire, a similar endeavor was under way far to the east. It was led by Diego de Ordaz, one of the most valiant of the captains of Cortés during the conquest of Mexico.

Ordaz had distinguished himself in many ways during Cortés' campaign; even though he had originally belonged to the faction of Cortés' enemy, Diego de Velásquez of Cuba, and had been regarded for a while by Cortés as a potential traitor, Ordaz had made himself an important figure in the conquest. Cortés valued him for his chivalry, for his courage under fire, and for his gallant bearing. Of all the exploits of Ordaz in Mexico, the one that gained him the most fame was his ascent of the volcano Popocatepetl. Accompanied by nine Spaniards and a few Indians, Ordaz clambered through the thick forests on the lower slopes of the mountain, untroubled by the subterranean rumblings and other fearsome hints of internal combustion. At 13,000 feet, the Indians refused to continue through a zone of dwarfed vegetation into the track of lava and volcanic earth ahead, and Ordaz and his Spanish comrades went on without them. They attained the region of perpetual snow, and then came to the crater itself, but the suffocating blasts of gases and sparks from the mountain's interior forced them to turn back before entering the crater. Ordaz did collect some samples of sulfur and some huge icicles, which he displayed upon his return to his awed countrymen in the tropical encampment at the base of the mountain. A full report of the ascent was forwarded to the Emperor Charles V, who graciously permitted the Ordaz family to include a burning mountain in its coat-of-arms thereafter.

Ordaz had not climbed Popocatepetl merely because it was there; he had hoped to find a source of sulfur to provide powder for the Spanish muskets. Cortés, however, decided that it would be simpler to import the powder from Spain than to get it by scaling the volcano.

Mexico had given Ordaz fame, but apparently not wealth. He returned to Spain after the conquest and petitioned Charles V for the license to plant a settlement of his own in South America. The eastern coast of the continent had been explored in a sketchy fashion; Vespucci had possibly sailed past it in 1499 and more definitely in 1501 on behalf of Spain, and Vincente Pinzón, who had captained the *Niña* on Columbus' first voyage, had examined the Brazilian coast as far south as the mouth of the Amazon in 1499. A few months after Pinzón's voyage, a Portuguese fleet under Pedro Alvares Cabral reached Brazil by accidentally sweeping too far to the west while bound round Africa for the Indies. Cabral had landed on the Brazilian shore at a place where South America bulges so far out to the east that it fell on the Portuguese side of the Pope's boundary line in the Atlantic. This laid the foundation for the future Portuguese empire in Brazil, but there were no Portuguese settlements there until 1531.

Diego de Ordaz, in 1530, asked Charles V to grant him the right to colonize the region around the mouth of the Amazon. This was substantially north of the territory claimed by Portugal. The license was granted: Ordaz was given the title of *adelantado* and was permitted to occupy the land from the Amazon estuary as far west as the border of the Welser tract. Subject to paying the royal fifth, the income of this vast domain was to be his. He used his

Mexican gains to finance the outfitting of three ships, and sailed from Spain with about 500 men late in 1530. A fourth ship with a hundred men joined the expedition at the Canary Islands.

The Amazon estuary is gigantic; the river, greatest in the world, pours into the sea through many outlets, some of them so broad that they seem like seas themselves. One island in the estuary is larger than Switzerland. The current is violent, and the river flows with such force that fresh water surges into the Atlantic more than a hundred miles off shore. Ordaz' first impression upon landing in this region of titanic geography was encouraging; he met Indians who carried "emeralds as big as a man's fist." They told him "that on going up during a certain number of suns toward the west, he would find a rock of green stone." [25] It was a mountain of emerald, then, and not an empire of gold, that originally launched Ordaz on his quest into the interior of South America.

The attempt to enter the river was a failure. Storms and shoals sent three of the four vessels to the bottom almost as soon as the estuary was reached. Ordaz managed to get his own flagship out of the swampy coastal shallows, and allowed the prevailing currents to carry him northwestward around the curve of South America. He studied the coast of Guiana with an eye toward finding a river entry there, but did not halt until, to his surprise, he found himself arriving at a Spanish port in eastern Venezuela, near the mouth of the Orinoco River.

It was Paria, the garrison town founded a short while before by Antonio Sedeño after the failure of his attempt to settle the island of Trinidad. Sedeño, a wealthy landowner of Puerto Rico, had hoped to grow even wealthier by exploiting Trinidad. Arriving there late in 1530, he tried to pacify the natives with worthless trinkets, which they cheerfully accepted. But they drove him out once he had exhausted his supply of beads and cheap hatchets, and with fifty men he dug in on the mainland at Paria.

Ordaz had no knowledge of Sedeño's outpost on the coast until he came upon it while looking for a safe harbor. The two men were not pleased to meet one another. Sedeño's royal license extended only to Trinidad, while the mainland fell under the grant of Ordaz; but Sedeño held Paria by right of prior possession, at least. Ordaz attacked the fort and compelled Sedeño's garrison to submit. Then, using Paria as his base of operations, he began to assemble a new fleet.

One taste of the Amazon estuary had been enough for Ordaz. He did not care to venture into that monstrous many-mouthed river again, not even for the sake of a mountain of emerald. His survey of the coast of Guiana and Venezuela had led him to believe that his best route to the treasures of the interior would be up a river that was also of great size, but not quite so intimidating as the Amazon: the Orinoco, which flows north and then east across much of Venezuela.

He built seven new galleys at Paria and set off up one of the numerous mouths of the Orinoco with 280 men. Threading a path through the thickly jungled and confusing waterways of the delta proved to be not much less of a challenge than entering the Amazon, but this time Ordaz' boats were specially designed with a shallow draft for river navigation, and there were no disasters. He was the first European to enter the Orinoco, and thus the first to sample its hardships: the powerful current, the maze of its many channels, the torrential rains of its basin, the heat, the flash floods, the fevers.

The little vessels moved cautiously. In the rainy season of 1531 the river was high and rapid, and it was no easy matter to proceed against its flow. The Indians of the delta supplied provisions willingly; those a little farther inland had to be compelled by force of arms to bring food to the Spaniards. At no time, however, did Ordaz engage in the gratuitous atrocities that Ehinger was perpetrating just then nearly a thousand miles to the west. The Spaniards halted for a while at the village of Carao, near the point where the River Caroni meets the Orinoco—a place that would later play a major part in the quest for El Dorado. Then they journeyed upstream to the confluence of the Orinoco and the Meta.

The Indian guides that Ordaz had acquired advised him to leave the Orinoco at that point and proceed up the Meta. It was in fact a river that could take him to the eastern *cordillera* of the Andes and the tableland of Cundinamarca, which Ehinger was then approaching from the north. There, according to Ordaz' Indians, was the province of a populous and civilized nation ruled by "a very powerful prince with one eye" and possessing "animals less than stags, but fit for riding like Spanish horses." Since Pizarro's conquest of Peru was still in its early stages, Ordaz knew nothing of llamas; but surely the Indians were describing these pack-animals of the Andes to him, and retailing the stories they had heard of the civilization of the Colombian highlands.

The tales of the gold to be had at the source of the Meta tempted Ordaz. But now it was coming into the dry season, and the Meta did not look navigable to him. It would have been necessary to leave the boats and proceed westward overland, and Ordaz did not want to do that. An accident of interpretation decided the matter: one of the Indians pointed along the Orinoco, which by now trended south instead of west, and made a sound that the Spaniards took to be an imitation of the hammering of goldsmiths. The Spaniards resolved to continue up the Orinoco. Shortly they came to the cataracts of Ature, where, as the Indian had tried to tell them, their boats would be smashed on the rocks. It was necessary to turn back.

Having no choice, they tried now to navigate the Meta toward the promised western land of gold and llamas. But the dry season indeed made the river too shallow even for their small boats. Ordaz came back downstream, determined to return equipped for an overland trek into the Meta district another time.

The journey back to Paria was a trying one. The full heat of summer baked the explorers, and illness plagued them. Ordaz, his temper frayed by hardship, countenanced a slaughter of Indians at one point that was worthy of Ehinger, and many of his own men were repelled by the deed. Gloomy and weakened, Ordaz arrived at Paria in 1532 after an exploration of more than a thousand miles—the first European entry into the basin of the Orinoco. It had been a difficult trip, and its only immediate yield was the unverified story of a land of gold that could be reached westward along the Meta. Even with the dim geography of 1532, Ordaz realized that this land was not Peru, whose location relative to Venezuela was reasonably well comprehended. Coming in from the east, he had picked up news of Cundinamarca just as Ehinger had done on his approach from the north.

The remainder of Ordaz' story is melancholy. Intending a second inland venture, he sent an advance party of men under his lieutenant, Alonso de Herrera, to the town of Cumaná, several hundred miles west of Paria. Cumaná was then the only other Spanish settlement on the Venezuelan coast, aside from the Welser town of Coro. Eight days after Herrera's departure, Ordaz followed him there, leaving a small garrison behind to hold Paria.

His reception at Cumaná was unfriendly: a volley of cannonballs. The startled Ordaz was informed that Herrera and his men were under arrest and had been taken to the island of Cubagua, off the Venezuelan coast, where the Spaniards had for some years maintained a headquarters for the commerce in pearls and slaves. Ordaz crossed to Cubagua himself and learned that the dispossessed master of Paria, Antonio Sedeño, had intrigued against him at the Spanish court. The terms of Ordaz' royal grant had entitled him to colonize the land from the Brazilian coast to the limits of the Welser leasehold, and on this basis he had pushed Sedeño out of Paria. But Sedeño had discovered that the *capitulación* Ordaz held also specified that his grant extended only two hundred leagues along the coast from the Amazon estuary. Paria lay well outside that boundary, even though it was still some distance east of the Welsers' line. Sedeño thus was able to argue that he had come upon territory that lay between the grants of Ordaz and the Welsers. The Spanish government agreed with him, and ruled that Ordaz was a trespasser at Paria. Cubagua was also held to lie in Sedeño's territory.

Ordaz protested hotly that Sedeño himself had no valid claim since his license allowed him only Trinidad, and not any mainland property at all. In 1533 he sailed for Spain to argue his case before the Council of the Indies, after the *Audiencia* at Santo Domingo refused to issue a decree deciding between the rival claims. On the voyage Ordaz died, possibly having been poisoned by a minion of Sedeño, and his career came to an inglorious end. Sedeño himself soon was enmeshed in a quarrel with the governor of Cubagua over local supremacy and was imprisoned.

While the men of the Venezuelan coast were engaged in these legal broils, one of Ordaz' lieutenants was safely arriving at the Spanish court to plead against Sedeño. He was Gerónimo D'Ortal, a persistent man who managed to get title to Paria as the successor to his late captain. The court had already awarded Paria to Sedeño, but somehow D'Ortal successfully pressed Ordaz' claim and had the earlier ruling reversed—a common enough occurrence at a time when Spain was attempting to exert direct rule over a distant empire about which little was known.

D'Ortal returned to Venezuela later in 1533, just in time for the falling out between Sedeño and his erstwhile supporters of Cubagua. The people of Cubagua had released Sedeño from prison, and he had gone to Trinidad, but was harried by the Cubaguans until he returned to Puerto Rico. Brooding there, he resolved to support D'Ortal against the people of Cubagua.

Another who had obtained his freedom was Ordaz' faithful second-in-command on the Orinoco journey, Alonso de Herrera. When D'Ortal landed at Paria he found it under the control of Herrera and about thirty men. D'Ortal and Herrera were tempted by the treasure they hoped could be found in what was now being called "the land of Meta"—the unknown kingdom that lay somewhere west of the confluence of the Meta and Orinoco rivers. Together they planned the voyage that Ordaz had hoped to take.

D'Ortal sent Herrera, with a hundred thirty men and ten ships, to the Orinoco delta to begin the exploration. He himself chose to wait at Paria until the arrival of new *conquistadores* who were en route from Spain; then he would follow Herrera to Meta. Late in 1533 Herrera set out for the Orinoco.

The story of Herrera's journey comes to us from the chronicler Gonzalo Fernandez de Oviedo, who devoted much space in his vast *Natural e General Historia de las Indias* of 1547 to the story of El Dorado. Oviedo describes Herrera as a man who "knew much better how to kill Indians than to govern them," but says that he was regarded affectionately by his fellow Spaniards, who gladly followed him through the most severe privations. Beginning at Paria, they sailed up the Orinoco to a point just below the confluence with the Caroni, and stayed there for thirteen months while building flat-bottomed boats for river travel. A twenty-day journey brought them to the mouth of the Meta, which had been in low water on Ordaz' visit three years earlier but now was in full flood at the height of the rainy season. Indeed, the river was so high that the boats had to be towed upstream by men hauling on ropes from the shore. Some of the time they slogged through muddy thickets, the rest they waded in waist-deep water, and in forty days they succeeded in advancing only sixty miles up the Meta. Oviedo declares, "I do not believe that any of those who took part in this expedition would have taken so much trouble to get into Paradise." [26] But at length came a point at which not even towing was possible. The river had burst its banks and had converted its valley to an enormous flood plain; most of the natives had fled to higher land, and the countryside had become a chain of lagoons.

Herrera was determined to go on at all costs. He was possessed by that strange fever that had no cure, and he spared neither himself nor his men. They left their boats and tried to make their way across the flooded plains. Rain was constant; the clothing rotted from their bodies as they huddled in their camps. Without Indians to guide them, the Spaniards could do no more than force aimlessly onward toward the west. When an Indian woman who spoke an understandable dialect was captured, she told of a large village ahead, but warned that the cannibalistic inhabitants would surely devour Herrera's party. Angered by her mockery and obvious lies, Herrera had her hanged, "in thanks for her work," says Oviedo, "and since he was groping around, as it were, in the dark, he thought he might find the way better by means of this kind of holy torch, or by this good act. No wonder that an equally speedy and still sadder death fell upon him and others." [27]

Some fifty miles from the place where they had left their boats, the country began to look more favorable. The land was higher and the dry stretches between the flooded lagoons were larger. The Indian settlements seemed prosperous, with fields of corn and other plants. Herrera noted that in one town the Indians dined on the flesh of dogs. The Spaniards halted at a village to collect provisions, both for themselves and for a group of sick men who had been left behind to tend the boats. At night the Indians attacked. They were driven off, but Herrera and three others were wounded by poisoned arrows, and all the horses but one were killed. Herrera died a painful death; released from his command, the men promptly abandoned the quest for the land of Meta and turned back.

The river that had been such a fearsome enemy on the upstream trek now served the haggard survivors well as they returned. They whisked along on the crest of the flood and in fourteen days were back at the Orinoco. With equal speed they let themselves be swept by that river to the sea, and in 1535 the straggling remnants of Herrera's party appeared in Paria after an absence of eighteen months. They had gone through the Orinoco basin as far as the plains of eastern Colombia, something no Europeans had ever done before, and they had reinforced earlier knowledge by gaining new tales of the elusive and unattainable western land of gold. But, like the men of Ehinger, they had returned empty-handed and leaderless, very much the worse for their exploit.

The Spaniards in the Cumaná-Cubagua-Paria region clung tightly to the golden dream of the land of Meta. Many expeditions were projected. In 1534, the Royal Audience at Santo Domingo notified the Council of the Indies under date of January 30—while Herrera was still wandering in Meta —that "according to altitudes and measurements" taken by navigators and explorers, the realms of gold were located "directly opposite this island [Hispaniola] and the island of San Juan [Puerto Rico], entering directly southward, lying on both sides of the equator." [28] The Council authorized an expedition of 400 men to find the golden land after "consulting with the navigators many times," but nothing came of the plan.

However, D'Ortal did go through with his expedition in 1535, with the usual result. Having learned of the troubles of the Herrera expedition, D'Ortal tried something new: approaching Meta by land from the north, instead of coming in from the east via the Orinoco. He found an unexpected ally in Sedeño, but was harried by the men of Cubagua, who regarded both of them as threats to their continued prosecution of the lucrative trade in pearls and slaves. After several false starts, D'Ortal and Sedeño set out together, but quarreled on the way. They separated; Sedeño met his death in the interior, while D'Ortal continued south until his path was crossed by the Orinoco. He prepared to make a river journey into Meta, but his men rebelled against his leadership. One group wandered away, and we will meet them again as members of a Welser expedition. The others made D'Ortal a captive and took him back to the coast, where the Cubaguans put him on trial and imprisoned him for sixteen months. When he was released, we learn from Oviedo, D'Ortal was purged of all wish to explore the land of Meta, and was eager to marry and live a more sedate life. "As his purpose was a good one," Oviedo notes, "God gave him a good wife, a respectable and virtuous widow of suitable age, who had means . . . enough for him to live decently in our city of Santo Domingo on the island of Hispaniola, with more security and fame than could come to him in all these wars, or in hunting the fabulous riches of Meta, of which no one knows anything to this day, or can find the way there without its costing yet more human lives and leading to other troubles." [29]

4

Gerónimo D'Ortal was thus one of the few seekers of El Dorado who met a peaceful end. Not for him was the fate of such turbulent questers as Herrera or Ehinger.

Ehinger, in his obsession with the mysterious golden land, had almost totally neglected his duties as the Welsers' governor in Venezuela. He had absented himself from Coro from mid-1529 to mid-1530, and in 1531 had departed once more on what proved to be his final adventure. During Ehinger's first journey to the interior, the Welsers despatched a new force of men to Venezuela, and among them was Nicolaus Federmann, a young German who shortly would be deeply involved in the search for the kingdom of gold.

Federmann was as attractive a figure in the story of El Dorado as Ehinger was sinister and brutal. He was just twenty-four when the Welsers chose him, in 1529, to command their second expedition to Venezuela. He came from a wealthy family, and was an active, energetic man who, like Ehinger, boasted a flowing red beard. The Welsers put him in charge of a division of soldiers and twenty-four German miners. Toward the end of 1529 his ship called at Hispaniola, and by the following March Federmann was in Coro. He was unable to present his credentials to Governor Ehinger, though, since Ehinger was then somewhere west of Maracaibo and presumed dead.

Shortly after Federmann's arrival, three more Welser ships docked at Coro. They brought a Welser agent named Hans Seissenhoffer, a man of sufficient authority to make himself governor in Ehinger's place. Seissenhoffer gave young Federmann the second highest post in the colony, and invested him with authority greater than that of any of the Spaniards then in Welser service—an act that caused some friction between Federmann and the veteran Spanish officers.

Had Ehinger returned and found Seissenhoffer supplanting him, there might have been a violent collision between the two Welser agents. However, Seissenhoffer opportunely died just before Ehinger's unexpected return from the wilderness. Federmann thus acknowledged Ehinger as the governor without hesitation.

Ehinger's grueling journey had weakened his health. After a brief stay at Coro, he sailed to Santo Domingo to recover his strength and to raise money for his second expedition, leaving Federmann in charge. Perhaps life in Coro was intolerably dull, or perhaps Federmann simply had the restlessness of youth, for he quickly abandoned his responsibility to go exploring. He declares in his autobiography, *A Charming and Agreeable Account of the First Trip of Nicolaus Federmann the Younger of Ulm to the Indies*, "Finding myself in the city of Coro with a number of men who were unoccupied, I determined to undertake a campaign into the interior toward the south or the Southern Sea, in the hope of finding something profitable." [30]

That amiable statement indicates the state of geographical knowledge in 1530: Federmann believed that South America was an island of moderate size, and that he could reach the Pacific by marching due south from the Venezuelan coast for no great distance. Magellan's voyage down the entire eastern flank of the continent seemingly had no impact on this delusion. No one had any clear idea of the distance separating Peru in the west from Brazil in the east, nor did anyone seem to recognize the existence of vast tracts of territory in western South America between Panamá and Peru.

Federmann left Coro on September 12, 1530, with 110 Spaniards on foot, sixteen mounted men, and a hundred Indian porters. Like all those who looked for the golden land during this phase of the quest for El Dorado, he had no specific goal in mind; he sought a place that lay somewhere south of Venezuela and east of Peru, but of the actual topography he had not the remotest notion. Marching through northwestern Venezuela, Federmann came to the Río Tocuyo south of Coro, crossed it, and went in search of a rumored tribe of pygmies a yard high. Drifting in a generally southwesterly direction but remaining east of the Lake of Maracaibo at all times, Federmann began to ascend the rugged foothills of the Sierra de Mérida, getting about as far as the present-day city of Trujillo. The raids of hostile Indians discouraged him from further progress.

He had covered perhaps one third the distance from Coro to the land of El Dorado, but of course he was moving at random with no knowledge at this time of the ceremony of the gilded chief of Cundinamarca. The march gained him some 3000 *pesos de oro*, and from the Indians he also acquired the inevitable glowing stories of the country rich in gold still farther toward the west. By March of 1531, Federmann was back in Coro. The main value of his six-month march was the preparation it afforded him for the much more extensive journey of exploration that lay a few years in his future.

Soon after Federmann's return to Coro, Ehinger set out on the quest that would bring him death in a wild and remote Colombian valley. Federmann, who had sailed back to Europe, was in Spain when news came of Ehinger's fate. He lost no time applying to the Welsers for the vacant governorship of Venezuela, and it was granted despite his youth. However, Federmann had offended some influential Spanish officers during his brief period of authority in Coro in the spring of 1530, and they protested against the appointment. After some delicate negotiations, Federmann was recalled as governor even before he had reached Venezuela. Another man was given the post, Federmann being named second-in-command.

Ehinger's successor as governor of the country was Georg Hohemut, a knight of the commercial town of Speyer. The Spaniards, who had converted "Welsers" into *Belzares* and "Ehinger" into *Alfinger*, found Georg von Speyer's surname of "Hohemut" too barbaric for their palates. They used his knightly title instead, referring to him always as *Jorge de Spira*. Hohemut himself adopted that as his signature in the decrees he issued from Coro, and he is known to the Spanish chroniclers as *Spira*, *Speyer*, or *Espira*.

Speyer—or Hohemut—landed at Coro in 1534. Federmann recognized his authority with good enough grace, considering his own sharp disappointment at not having the governorship; perhaps it had occurred to him that he was much younger than the new governor, and might get the post eventually after all. In any case Federmann had nothing to gain by showing a glum face to Hohemut, on whose favors he would depend for his future advancement. They got along well. Hohemut's first problem was a boundary dispute: a valley that lay west of the Lake of Maracaibo was claimed by the government of Santa Marta, although it seemed clearly to fall under the Welser grant of Venezuela. Hohemut sent Federmann into the disputed valley with a small force of troops, ordering him to hold it against the claim of Santa Marta. The assignment was agreeable to Federmann, for on his expedition of 1530–31 he had learned to his own satisfaction that the land of gold did not lie south of Coro, and thus had to be located in the west. Once he had made the boundary safe against the men of Santa Marta, he could always proceed a little farther to the west and search for the enigmatic kingdom.

Hohemut, too, had his dreams of gold. Early in 1535 he began to assemble his own expedition. By this time, Ordaz had long since carried out his reconnaissance of the Orinoco basin, and Herrera's surviving men had made their limping retreat to Paria. The stories of the "land of Meta" had traveled westward along the Venezuelan coast from Paria and Cumaná to Coro. Hohemut concluded—evidently without discussing the point with Federmann—that golden Meta lay south of Coro. On May 13, 1535, the German set out in that direction after having sent a small advance party a short time before.

Retracing the path Federmann had taken in 1530, Hohemut crossed the Río Tocuyo and by July came to an Indian settlement near the modern town of Barquisimeto. Four and a half years earlier, Federmann had obtained gold from the natives there, but now Hohemut encountered his vanguard in hasty retreat from the attack of warlike tribesmen. The attackers, however, were quickly subdued by Hohemut's main force of three hundred infantry and one hundred cavalry, and the expedition made its way farther south.

The heat and humidity of the lowlands forced Hohemut to alter his route when he was only a few days' journey past the scene of the battle. Fever swept his forces, and only a hundred foot soldiers and thirty horsemen were strong enough to go on. It was necessary to get out of the malarial lowlands as quickly as possible. To the east the rivers were flooding, so Hohemut made a southwesterly turn. This put him back on Federmann's earlier track along the eastern foothills of the Sierra de Mérida. Some of his men recovered, but many had to be sent back to Coro, about five hundred miles to the north.

The German Conquistadores

With a hundred fifty infantrymen and forty-nine horsemen Hohemut continued steadily into the unknown southwest. By all accounts, he was a wise and moderate leader, and yet he plunged onward with the fervor of such gold-seeking fanatics as Ehinger and Herrera, venturing ever farther into unexplored country under the guiding illusion that a realm of gold would somehow turn up if he kept going long enough. The examples of Peru and Mexico danced before him; for by now, Pizarro the swineherd was on the golden throne of Atahuallpa.

Shifting the path from due south to southwesterly made the journey more bearable, but hardly comfortable. The roadless mountains of the Sierra de Mérida proved too difficult for the horses, so Hohemut had to keep to the plains, where innumerable obstacles also confronted him. This was a land of many streams, all converging toward the Orinoco, and when the rains came these minor tributaries turned to dreadful torrents. In wet weather, the explorers had to crawl through flooded marshes and drowned prairies; in the dry season, the heat was cruel and the countryside drab and discouraging.

Hohemut sent raiding parties into the mountains to take corn and salt from the hill tribes, and in fair weather the Spaniards lived on the numerous deer of the plains. But when the rains came, the deer vanished, and the only available food was roots and leaves. An experiment in building canoes to traverse the flooded country was not a success. Jaguars trailed the Spaniards on their line of march, pouncing on the horses and even killing one of Hohemut's men.

Still the trek continued, month after month. Hohemut was finding no gold and gaining no definite information about the fabled rich civilization of Meta, but he drove his small band forward in the stubborn conviction that something would turn up. Coro, far to the north, seemed now like a poorly remembered dream to men who had camped in the open for an entire summer and an entire winter. On February 2, 1536, Hohemut came to the Río Apure, a large northern tributary of the Orinoco. Proceeding to the southwest for another hundred miles, he reached the Río Casanare, which flows into the Meta. He was now as far to the south as Herrera had gone in 1534, but was hundreds of miles farther west. In the mountain country just beyond the Casanare, Hohemut encountered the friendly Zaquitios Indians, who told him that just on the other side of the mountains lay a grassy plateau on which dwelled a tribe rich in gold, who kept tame sheep. They spoke of a chieftain named Caziriguey, whose city had a great temple filled with objects of gold. The Indians pointed westward, toward Cundinamarca, the Bogotá plateau. No European had yet entered that region, although in 1532 Ehinger had come unknowingly to its northeastern border before turning back.

The Zaquitios offered to guide Hohemut to a mountain pass that led to the plateau country. According to Oviedo, "This information gratified, strengthened, and encouraged the Spaniards so much that all the hardships they had endured were forgotten, and the way lying before them appeared as safe and easy as the streets of Valladolid and Medina del Campo." [31] But the pass proved impossible to locate. While Hohemut and his men prowled the foothills of the great eastern *cordillera* looking for a way across, they were set upon by hostile Indians. The guides fled. In a two-hour battle, the Spaniards repelled their attackers, but Hohemut conceded that it was unsafe to remain in the vicinity. Wearily they resumed the march to the south along the slope of the mountains in search of a westward pass.

They now were trespassing on the country of the Uaupés, a powerful and well-organized Indian tribe of agriculturists and river fishermen. These Indians came to battle with their bodies painted black, protected by large shields of tapir skin; their habit of becoming half intoxicated before a skirmish, though, made their spears and arrows less effective than they might otherwise have been. Hohemut's cavalry and musketry kept the Uaupés at a safe distance, but torrential rains proved a much more troublesome foe. The eternal downpour sent flash floods rolling down out of the mountains to the west, often compelling the Spaniards to make camp for days at a time. Occasional contact with Indians more friendly than the Uaupés kept the hopes of a golden conquest alive; Hohemut learned that he was near the source of the Meta, which had become a magical talisman of a name to the gold-seekers, and the accounts of the wealthy plateau-dwellers on the far side of the mountains grew more exact.

It seemed impossible to cross those mountains, however. Since the rains would not relent, Hohemut retreated to the country of the Zaquitios, where he had left several dozen sick men before entering the land of the Uaupés. He was disturbed to learn that those men had given up and gone back to Coro. Now a hundred forty men remained in Hohemut's party, and forty-four horses. After resting for a while, Hohemut ordered a second thrust into the territory of the Uaupés.

This *entrada* was more successful. The source of the Meta was attained, and here the Uaupés were more friendly. They had gold and silver, and once more tantalized Hohemut with their tales of a golden kingdom on the other side of the western mountains. Hohemut also discovered that white men in boats had tried to come up the Meta several years before—the ill-fated Herrera expedition.

The cliffs of the *cordillera* remained unapproachable. At the urging of a lieutenant named Estevan Martín, Hohemut decided to keep going south. They fought their way through several unfriendly Indian tribes and crossed the Río Guaviare. One of Hohemut's men took an astrolabe reading and calculated their latitude as 2°40′ N. By now they were well south of Cundinamarca, and practically at the borders of present-day Ecuador—but they still had not found any route across the mountains that lay to their west. When Estevan Martín offered to lead a survey party up the Río Caqueta, Hohemut agreed; but Martín was set upon by Chogues Indians and slain. The main party then ascended the Caqueta and avenged the death of Martín, but when Hohemut reached the source of the river he found himself staring hopelessly up at the mountain wall once again. There did not seem to be a pass anywhere. The men were exhausted, and Hohemut's own resolve was weakening.

On August 10, 1537, having marched from the Venezuelan coast to a point one degree of latitude north of the Equator, Hohemut admitted defeat and ordered the return to Coro to commence. For twenty-seven months he had followed the route of his fantasy, with no tangible results, and now the prospect of war with the Chogues was too much to face. Only fifty of Hohemut's men were fit for service; the rest were shambling invalids. Back they went, through the country of the Uaupés, through the province of the Zaquitios, past the source of the Meta, past the Río Casanare, a hasty withdrawal that took a third of the time it had taken to go in the opposite direction. When he reached the Río Apure, where he had camped early in 1536, Hohemut received bewildering news from the Indians: his lieutenant Federmann had been there two months before, they said. Since Hohemut had ordered Federmann into northwestern Venezuela to occupy the disputed valley, he did not understand what his red-bearded countryman could possibly be doing hundreds of miles southeast of his proper position. Was it a relief expedition? Or had Federmann given his governor up for lost and gone on some project of his own?

Hohemut hastened back to Coro, which he reached on

May 27, 1538, three years and two weeks after his departure. He had traversed 1500 miles, much of it previously unexplored, visiting the western tributaries of the Orinoco, the plains of Colombia, and even the northwestern branches of the Amazon. The geographical harvest was immense, but of gold Hohemut had acquired only 5518 *pesos de oro*. He had demonstrated more clearly than Ehinger, Ordaz, or Herrera that the home of the golden kingdom was on a grassy plateau that lay southwest of Venezuela and north of Peru, but he had not succeeded in scaling the mountain wall that blocked the eastern access to the plateau.

Hohemut did not find Federmann at Coro when he returned. To his amazement and distress, the governor learned that Federmann had taken advantage of his absence to launch his own enterprise almost immediately after the departure of the Hohemut expedition. With what can be interpreted either as high good spirits or as utter treachery, Federmann had doubled back from his assignment in the west and in 1536 had set out for the land of Meta. No one in Coro had any idea of his present whereabouts.

Worn out by his own exertions, Hohemut did not leave Coro again, although early in 1540 he began to think of making a second expedition to the golden kingdom. His plans were still incomplete when death took him that year. Some accounts say he died peacefully, others that he was killed by Spaniards attempting a *coup d'état* against Welser rule.

Before he died, however, Georg Hohemut had learned the story of Federmann's recent adventures. The young lieutenant was still alive. He had wandered for three years in the wilderness—and then he had found the route to the plateau. Nicolaus Federmann had reached the land of El Dorado.

But he had not been the first European to get there.

[3]

THE CONQUEST OF

NEW GRANADA

HE EXTRAORDINARY ADVENTURE OF NICO-laus Federmann began with an act of insubordination and culminated in a wholly improbable series of coincidences. It led to the discovery of El Dorado and then to the repudiation of that discovery, because the reality was not the equal of the myth. A kind of monstrous implausibility surrounds the entire episode.

Late in 1534, after his arrival at Coro, Georg Hohemut sent Federmann across the Lake of Maracaibo to protect a borderline valley against incursions by the men of Santa Marta. That small, squalid outpost on the coast of Colombia had never looked with pleasure toward the Welser-operated settlement of Coro to its east, and the friction between Santa Marta and Coro was high. Soon after dispatching Federmann to the west, Hohemut himself had set out on his three-year journey to the south, leaving Coro in May of 1535.

Federmann's activities during 1535 are uncertain, and so are the motives that led him away from his post of command. Apparently he did go to the valley Hohemut had assigned him to protect, but did not remain there long. Instead he returned to Coro some time late in 1535 and began to assemble men for an expedition to follow Hohe-mut's path.

That Federmann should have gone south in search of the golden kingdom seems surprising, for he had done just that in 1530–31 without any success. He knew that the land of gold, if it existed at all, lay to the west of those impassable mountains whose eastern slope he had followed on his first expedition. Hence he might well have considered continuing west across the upper limb of South America and making his southward turn on the far side of the *cordillera*.

But that would have been a shameless trespass on the government of Santa Marta, and perhaps Federmann hesi-tated to risk open war with those unruly Spaniards. So he set out once more on what was becoming a well-beaten track, south from Coro, in the spring of 1536. He was accompa-nied by four hundred men.

Hohemut had been gone for nearly a year at that time, and possibly Federmann's original motive for following the track of his chief was to bring him provisions and reinforce-ments. He may indeed have told his own men that they were going to the relief of the Hohemut party. However, Feder-mann very shortly was taking good care not to meet or overtake the governor's expedition. He kept his route some-what east of Hohemut's as he traveled. The first stage of the journey took Federmann through familiar country: the marshy land near the shores of the Lake of Maracaibo, with the eastern *cordillera* of the Andes standing on the right to guide him. Then, to avoid a collision with Hohemut, Feder-mann began his eastward veer into the *llanos*, or grassy plains, of the Orinoco basin.

It was difficult country. R. B. Cunninghame Graham, who spent much of his life in South America and traveled Federmann's route shortly before the First World War, wrote that the *llanos* "stretch out like a sea. Rivers innumerable that have no name on any map cut them in all directions, and marshes intersect them, whose paths are known but to the wandering Indians and the rude herdsmen of the plains. Great canebrakes, so tall that a man on horseback disappears completely in them, spring up on the rivers' banks, and clumps of the Moriche palm, slender and feathery as ostrich plumes, are scattered here and there. Even today the traveller who loses his direction perishes. He wanders up and down until his horse is either eaten by a tiger, escapes at night, or falls down dead from sunstroke and fatigue. Then the doomed man wanders round in a circle, till at last he sits down with his back against a palm-tree, and is found months afterward a skeleton, his flesh devoured by the wild beasts, or a dry mummy shrivelled by the sun." [32]

Somehow maintaining his bearings in this labyrinth even though he no longer had a view of the Andes to direct him, Federmann led his men on a zigzagging southward course through the *llanos*. He reached the Orinoco somewhere east of its junction with its tributary the Apure, and there he encountered a ragged band of Spaniards who had broken away from the expedition of Gerónimo D'Ortal the year before, in 1535. Federmann incorporated these men into his own company.

After roaming the *llanos* for a year Federmann turned west again and crossed the Río Meta. The efficient Indian communications system kept him informed of Hohemut's whereabouts; Federmann learned in the summer of 1537 that his chief had gone far to the south, but was giving up and coming back. Taking particular care not to cross Hohemut's path, Federmann began to march south along the foothills of the *cordillera*—the same enterprise that had just defeated Hohemut. (When he reached the Apure on his northward march late in 1537, Hohemut got his first inkling of what Federmann was doing.)

Having successfully bypassed a meeting with Hohemut, Federmann began to search for a pass over the *cordillera*. He spent all of 1538 in this pursuit. Indians narrowed his forces to little more than two hundred men. Their clothes rotted away in the rain, and they fashioned crude garments from animal skins. Their beards were long, and they let their hair grow thick and shaggy to protect them from the sun. Their remaining horses, gaunt and weary, had lost their shoes and now clopped unshod over the rocky paths. During the rainy seasons, Federmann camped and waited; he went about his exploration as though he fully intended to devote a lifetime to it, if necessary. Now he challenged the ice-crested mountains, and now he fell back to wander without purpose in the plains. After he had been on the march for three years, Federmann summoned his forces for another attempt to force the *cordillera*. Some time early in 1539 he came to the Indian town of Pasacote and discovered the long-sought-for mountain route, the pass of Suma Paz.

The hardships of the passage were immense. Thirteen thousand feet above sea level, the bedraggled explorers traced their way along a trail that wound from one frightful precipice to another. In places the pass simply disappeared, and the men had to scramble over cold rock faces, hauling their horses up with ropes. At last, after a terrible struggle, Federmann and his party came over the *cordillera* and found themselves at the edge of the broad, grassy savannah of the Bogotá plateau.

Ahead—somewhere—lay the golden land. And now the route would be an easy one.

While he permitted his depleted men to rest, Federmann sent one of his officers, Pedro de Limpias, ahead with a few companions to scout the territory. The ragged, unkempt Limpias, clad only in his tattered deerskin, rode off on a bony horse to see what was to be seen.

He had not gone far when he made a surprising and dismaying discovery. Camped nearby was a band of men— not Indians, but Spaniards out of Santa Marta. Limpias introduced himself to them as an advance rider from the expedition of Captain Don Nicolaus Federmann, of German extraction, lieutenant-general to Don Jorge Espira (Hohemut), Governor of Venezuela for the Welsers in the name of the Emperor Charles V. Then he returned to Federmann with the staggering news that they had all been forestalled. After three years of fearful suffering they had reached the fabled plateau, only to find it full of rival Spaniards.

2

During the years when Coro and Paria had been the chief bases for ventures into the South American interior, the town of Santa Marta had played little part in the epic of exploration. This settlement, on the Colombian coast, lay far to the west of the more active Venezuelan towns, and its growth was hampered by internal turmoil. Bad luck had dogged Santa Marta since its founding by Rodrigo de Bastidas in 1525. The tough and efficient Bastidas soon was murdered by one of his own lieutenants; subsequent administrators gave the city up as hopeless, and it quickly degenerated into a miserable and decaying town. After ten years, Santa Marta had only one building of stone; the rest were thatched mud hovels. The settlers led lives of poverty and despair. There was no gold to be had at Santa Marta, which occupied a coastal position at the head of a nearly landlocked bay. Twenty miles inland a mountain range that reached heights of seventeen thousand feet cut the town off from the interior.

The Spaniards who had come to Santa Marta were soldiers, not farmers. They had intended to fight their way to the inland provinces and compel the Indians to supply them with gold. But the Indians proved too tough to defeat, and the snowy *sierra* was an impenetrable wall. Discouraged, the men of Santa Marta relapsed into dull melancholy, not even attempting to farm their land but forcing the natives to provide them with food and clothing.

This collapsing settlement became in 1535 the responsibility of Don Pedro Fernández de Lugo, who gave up an hereditary post as governor of the peaceful, lovely Canary Islands to take on the thankless role of *adelantado*, or governor, of Santa Marta. Perhaps someone misled Don Pedro about the prospects and present condition of Santa Marta; possibly he willingly victimized himself, accepting the illusory hope that Santa Marta would deluge him with gold. In any event, Lugo assembled an expedition of cavaliers as hopeful as he was of Santa Marta's riches, and in 1535 sailed from the port of Tenerife, bound for South America. Some twelve hundred men accompanied him—not the usual rabble of an American expedition, but an assortment of well-placed grandees and wealthy young men.

After a sea passage of forty days, Lugo's fleet arrived at Santa Marta. The handsome cavaliers, brilliant in their plumed helmets and finely polished breastplates, descended on the beach and strutted proudly before the town. Then a delegation came out from Santa Marta to meet them: a few disreputable-looking men in filthy garments of Indian-woven skins. They introduced themselves as the town council of Santa Marta. One man who looked like a mule-driver greeted Don Pedro de Lugo and informed him that he was Don Antonio Bezos, the interim governor of the city.

The startled Spaniards proceeded to Santa Marta, which they found to be a wretched and dismal place, tense with civil feuds and racked by hunger. The new colonists, aghast at the sight, began at once to succumb to dysentery and tropical fevers, and Lugo saw immediate ruin in store for him. He had planned to pay the crews of his fleet from the treasury of Santa Marta, but the town was without resources. Mutiny threatened. Lugo decided on bold steps to save the situation: a war of pacification against the Indians of the vicinity, and an expedition to the interior to find gold with which to pay the sailors.

With a thousand of his best men, Lugo invaded a nearby Indian town that was thought to have much gold. He drove off the inhabitants, suffering heavy losses, but found nothing of value in the town. Then, dividing his forces, he attacked other towns in a simultaneous thrust, and the raids yielded 15,000 *pesos de oro* in golden images. This sum Don Pedro turned over to this son Alonso, instructing him to take it back to Santa Marta and use it to pay the fleet. Alonso de Lugo had other plans. The *adelantado*'s son commandeered one of the vessels anchored at Santa Marta and quietly slipped off to Spain with the treasure. Infuriated, Don Pedro sent a ship after him, but Alonso reached Spain first. He was imprisoned briefly after being denounced by his father's emissary. Using the purloined gold, Alonso bribed his way to freedom and won the affections of a young lady of an influential family, whom he married. That gave him a voice at court, and he made good use of it in later years.

Don Pedro was shaken by his son's defection which made his position at Santa Marta all the more precarious. A man in extreme straits, he chose an extreme remedy: an expedition into the unknown interior to find gold. The only possible route was up the Río Magdalena. The men of Santa Marta had explored a short distance up the Magdalena, but most of its length was a mystery. In 1531 Ehinger had reached the upper Magdalena by cutting diagonally across from Venezuela; the lower reaches had never been entered by Europeans.

Ehinger and Hohemut, the Welser governors at Coro,

had not hesitated to leave their city for years at a time on jungle adventures. Pedro de Lugo, however, preferred to remain at his post and send a trusted lieutenant on the hazardous trip up the Magdalena. The man he chose was Gonzalo Jiménez de Quesada, who became one of the central figures of the Spanish conquest of South America as a result.

Quesada—for so he is always called, though his surname actually was Jiménez—was born about 1500 in the city of Córdova, and grew up in the former Moorish capital of Granada. His father, the licentiate Jiménez, was a lawyer, and his mother, Doña Isabel de Quesada, was of noble blood. According to Fray Pedro Simón, whose *Noticias Historiales de las Conquestas de Tierra Firme en las Indias Occidentales* of 1627 is the chief documentary source for much that follows, young Quesada entered his father's profession, and became "consummate in grammar and in the law, in which he graduated, and began to practice in the same court as his father." [33] The practice of law did not keep him from developing skill at arms or from becoming an adept horseman. Granada had been the scene of the climactic battle that crushed Moorish Spain in 1492, and veterans of that great struggle had settled in numbers in the city. Quesada grew up among these old soldiers and doubtless learned much from them.

There were no further wars to fight in Spain, but adventurous Spaniards could look to the Indies. Quesada was not minded to pass his life in the lawcourts of Granada. When Don Pedro de Lugo was organizing his expedition to Santa Marta in 1535, he invited the young lawyer to accompany him as chief magistrate of the settlement. Evidently Quesada demonstrated his unusual abilities of leadership during the first tense months at Santa Marta, for it was to him that Lugo turned to lead the expedition that seemed like the colony's only hope of salvation.

The party of reconnaissance was divided into two sections. Quesada and most of the men were to march overland along the western bank of the Magdalena for some forty leagues to the town of Tamalameque, Ehinger's camping place in 1531. Meanwhile the bulk of the expedition's baggage and about a third of the troops would be traveling up the river aboard brigantines, decked boats suitable for river navigation. The two parties would join forces at Tamalameque.

Five brigantines were hastily constructed, mainly by pressing Indians into forced labor. The boats were victualed and the men were assembled. On April 6, 1536, the expedition was ready to set out. (Federmann was just about ready at that time to leave Coro on his expedition.) The men of Santa Marta gathered at the shore to hear Don Pedro de Lugo confer his commission on Quesada, solemnly naming him "general both of the infantry and of the cavalry of the army that is ready to set out on the discovery of the sources of the great River Magdalena." [34]

Quesada's party included 620 foot-soldiers and 85 horsemen. With him went most of the men who had left Spain for Santa Marta with such high hopes the year before. Two hundred men were on board the brigantines, under the general command of an officer named Ortun Velásquez de Velasco. A high mass was celebrated; then the brigantines put out to sea, and Quesada, mounted on a fine charger, led his men westward toward the Magdalena.

3

Quesada's route took him through the hot, desolate desert wastes of the province of Chimila. From the first day, his expedition was harassed by hostile Indians, who lurked in thickets and behind rocks to shower the marching Spaniards with poisoned arrows. The glistening steel armor so highly prized by the *conquistadores* had been left behind in Santa Marta, for Quesada had shrewdly chosen to outfit both his men and his horses in cotton quilts.

Quilted armor was something the Spaniards had learned about during Cortés' conquest of Mexico. It was much lighter than clanking metal plates, and so was infinitely more suitable for jungle travel, while it had also proven highly effective in blocking Indian arrows. Fray Pedro de Aguado, a priest who accompanied Quesada, set down a good account of the quilted armor in his *Historia de Venezuela*, written about 1570 but not published until 1906:

"Out of sacking or light linen cloths they make a kind of surcoat that they call a coat of arms. These fall below the knee, and sometimes to the calf. They are all stuffed with cotton, to the thickness of three fingers. The layers of cotton are quilted between folds of linen and sewed with rough thread made in the country, and every thread is strongly knotted. . . . The sleeves are made in the same fashion. . . . Of the same cotton they also make a breastplate and a helmet, though some make these of tapir's or ox hide, formed like a skull cap. . . . In the same manner and of the same cotton and linen they make armor for the horse that guards his face and chest, and covers him in front. Fixed to the saddle is another covering over his croup that falls down over his legs. A mounted man armed in this way, upon his horse caparisoned in the same fashion, looks the most hideous and monstrous thing that it is possible to see." [35]

It took a week to march through barren Chimila to the mouth of the Magdalena. Then came the real struggle: hacking a path southward through the roadless jungle, thick with vines and studded with sharp thorns. Men with machetes hewed the way, and sometimes Quesada himself lent a hand at the work to raise morale. Alligators and jaguars lurked on the banks of the river, but the Spaniards found the mosquito a more irritating foe. Sweating and feverish, they clawed their way upstream to Tamalameque, expecting to find the brigantines waiting there for them. The flotilla had not arrived. Quesada pitched camp against the river in some puzzlement. Days went by; the rainy season began, and the Magdalena swelled ominously toward flood stage. Living now in a virtual swamp, the Spaniards suffered from a variety of diseases, and were menaced constantly by the Indians. Provisions dwindled. Gunpowder was diminishing. Where were the brigantines?

Their voyage had been disastrous. Reaching the Magdalena's mouth, they had found it in full spate: a rushing flood of yellow water surged into the sea, carrying with it the trunks of massive trees and the tangled networks of stripped underbrush. The flimsy vessels were rudely buffeted as they attempted to enter the flooding river. A storm carried them past the mouth, nearly to the small town of Cartagena, which had been founded in 1532. Three of the five brigantines were lost off the big island of Salamanca, and their few surviving crewmen made their way through the forest to Cartagena. The other two boats were driven ashore but managed to get afloat and escape, too badly damaged to risk the voyage up the river.

Lugo ordered the immediate repair of the damaged brigantines. While this was being done, three other vessels were quickly constructed and sent to Quesada under command of an officer named Juan Gallegos. These slowly made their way up the Magdalena while the perplexed Quesada waited for some news of his support party.

Quesada had moved upstream to a town called Chiriguana, where he encountered some Spaniards who had deserted from Ehinger in 1531 and had spent five years in the jungle. They offered to guide him; and since Quesada had abandoned hope of getting the support flotilla, he accepted the offer. For all their jungle experience, Ehinger's renegades promptly got everyone lost. They wandered in uninhabited country for twelve days, living off fat, placid deer, and came ultimately to an Indian village that had been devastated by Ehinger. The Indians were understandably chary of contact with another band of Europeans, but Quesada managed to make contact with them and learned that he was still near Tamalameque. They guided him back to that village. He sent a scouting party ahead to find a river route.

After twenty days spent in building canoes, Quesada set out to join his advance camp. They paddled warily in the rapid river with the horses tethered to the light canoes by their halters. The region seemed one vast swamp, and the forlorn town of Santa Marta must have grown luxurious in nostalgia to the mildewed explorers as they pressed onward. Quesada halted again; this time he was cheered to see the overdue brigantines of Juan Gallegos finally coming into view.

It was three months since he had had any contact with Santa Marta. The boats brought provisions and letters—some bread, some Castilian wine, news of the coast. What Quesada did not learn, because it had happened after Gallegos' departure, was that Don Pedro de Lugo had died, heartbroken over his son's treachery and exhausted by the climate. Santa Marta had relapsed into confusion, and Quesada's expedition had already passed out of mind. There could be no hope of further reinforcements. Santa Marta would leave the explorers to their fate.

Knowing nothing of that, Quesada delivered a stirring address of encouragement to his men and they prepared to plunge onward into the steaming, swampy valley of the Magdalena. *Macheteros* wielding keen blades went first, chopping a path through the vegetation. The problem was to march parallel to the river without getting engulfed in the flooded banks, and that often meant taking detours that brought the Spaniards perilously far from the river that was their only guide. Quite often they found themselves bewildered by a maze of crisscrossing streams, having no idea of the route back to the Magdalena; but each time, they managed to find the river again.

One of the several chroniclers of this expedition was Juan de Castellanos, who set down the story of the golden quest in a compendious volume of doggerel, *Elegias de Varones Illustres de Indias*, published in 1589 after he had given up soldiering for the priesthood. "Quesada saw," wrote Castellanos, "his numerous troops diminished by fevers and sores from the plagues of travel, ticks, bats, mosquitoes, serpents, crocodiles, tigers [jaguars], hunger, calamities, and miseries with other ills which pass description. . . . Jerónimo de Insa, captain of the *macheteros*, advances breaking through thickest woods and bridging the swamps and creeks, consuming the whole torrid days in incredible labors, so that with innumerable ink the fifth part could not be told." [36]

The Spaniards died "like bugs," to use a Castilian simile. The Indian porters, sagging under their burdens, perished by the dozens. The horses suffered greatly, and to spare these valuable beasts the Spaniards loaded their gear on their own backs. A jaguar devoured one man; an alligator seized another. Through the forest flitted Indians armed with spears and poison-tipped arrows. Of Quesada's original force of more than seven hundred men, only two hundred nine still lived by the fourth month of the march.

There were no towns in the jungle that could be raided for provisions, and game was scarce. Such food as was taken had to be consumed immediately or it would spoil. The Spaniards were reduced to such unsavory fare as anteaters and bats; several horses disappeared under mysterious circumstances and quite likely were eaten, and the chroniclers even offer dark hints of cannibalism among Quesada's men. After eight months of such travail, death seemed inevitable to all, for the jungle was endless and it would be impossible for the hungry, weakened men either to go much farther or to survive the long return journey to Santa Marta.

Quesada maintained command by a mixture of firmness and tolerance, heading off the possibility of mutiny. When a man openly killed his horse for meat, Quesada had him executed as an example to the others, and no one murmured; but generally he won support by less stringent measures. Just when the limits of endurance had been reached, and Quesada and his men were half mad from misery and exhaustion, a turning point came. One of the brigantines had proceeded up the river ahead of the slow-moving land party, and the lookout reported seeing a town perched on a high red bluff.

It was sundown when this news was brought to Quesada. Though night was falling with tropical suddenness, he resolved to explore the town himself without waiting for the dawn. He ordered three canoes to be equipped and chose seven companions, including his brother, Hernán Pérez de Quesada. In the darkness the fragile crafts set out on the high, violent river. They traveled all night. By the first light of morning they saw the town, some thirty houses in a clearing overhanging the Magdalena. It was all but deserted, for the natives, well remembering the cruelties of Ehinger, had fled at the first sign of the brigantines the night before.

Bizarrely, it appears that the Spaniards ransacked the town in search of gold before they bothered to hunt for food. No gold was to be had, but there were fields of ripening corn. Quesada and his companions ate sparingly, knowing the dangers of gorging themselves after their long starvation, and sent word back to the main body of the expedition to come at once.

Six days later the army arrived. Quesada carefully parceled out food to each man. The village—which a few captured Indians told them was called Tora—became their base while a scouting party went up the river.

The scouts returned in three weeks with no cheering report. The territory ahead, they said, was without settlements or cultivated land, and the forests seemed to grow more dense the farther they proceeded. The dejected Spaniards were paying the price for Ehinger's savagery, for he had worked such devastation here on his visit six years earlier that the district had been abandoned. As las Casas noted in his account of the sufferings of the natives, those who came from Santa Marta in Ehinger's tracks "with the self same holy intention to discover the same sacred golden palace" had found the country "so burned, dispeopled, and spoiled, having been before most notably peopled, and most fertile . . . that themselves as very tyrants and savage beasts as they were, wondered and stood astonished to see the tracks of the destructions so lamentable, wheresoever he had passed." [37]

Without a series of Indian villages from which food could be obtained, Quesada's party was in a serious plight. The men were so weak that several had been slain by alligators as they tottered to the bank of the river to drink. They had no provisions and no guides. One of Quesada's most devoted associates was bold enough to suggest that they retreat to Tamalameque to rest and refit, sending to Santa Marta for reinforcements and new ships. Tamalameque, properly developed, would serve as a base for a second thrust along the upper Magdalena, it was argued.

Quesada responded as reasonably as though this were a legal debate in a Granadan courtroom, mustering his evidence against a retreat. They could not hope for support from Santa Marta, for that city's resources were limited, he pointed out. They had little chance even of surviving the withdrawal to Tamalameque. The only hope was to go on; for in the village of Tora they had found linen mantles of exquisite workmanship, obviously the product of some highly civilized Indian people not too far distant. They had come this far; they had to continue. Without a murmur, the men capitulated and there was no retreat.

Another scouting party was organized. Quesada delegated as its leader the man who had petitioned for a withdrawal, Juan de San Martín. This able captain took twelve men in three canoes to explore the Río Opón, a large river descending from the mountains east of the Magdalena's valley. On the second day of the reconnaissance, the Spaniards came upon a canoe manned by three Indians, who speedily fled. In the canoe were fine woven cloths dyed purple, and several blocks of hard white salt wrapped in banana leaves. The Indians of Tamalameque had also had such salt, which they said they obtained by trade from a nation in the south. The salt in this canoe seemed evidence that the civilized realm must be near.

Going a little farther ahead, San Martín spied three huts on shore, which proved to be full of cakes of salt. They were warehouses for Indian traders, evidently. Leaving three men to guard the huts, he marched inland with the other nine, and after a dozen miles burst through the jungle into a large plain with a clear road cut through it. He followed this for forty miles. Mountains became visible, and before them lay cultivated fields and several large villages.

San Martín did not risk entering the villages. He obtained more salt and cotton cloth from several deserted huts and hurriedly retraced his steps. On the way back the scouts were attacked by Indians just before dawn, but beat them off and succeeded in taking a prisoner, an alert, intelligent native named Pericón who would later serve Quesada usefully as an interpreter.

With Pericón in tow, San Martín and his comrades entered the main camp, wearing feather crowns and Indian cloth mantles and carrying cakes of salt. Jubilantly they shouted the news that *tierra buena*, "a good land," lay near at hand. The Spaniards went into a wild dance of joy and passed the rest of the day cleaning their weapons and readying themselves for the march. They set out at dawn toward the mountains on the left bank of the Opón.

The Opón was too narrow for the brigantines to break out their sails, and so the boats had to be rowed upstream while the army marched along the banks. Abruptly, several days out from Tora, a flash flood swept down on them. The Spaniards clambered into trees to save themselves, and their baggage was swept away. They lost all their provisions, and their gunpowder was ruined. When the last of the corn from Tora was gone, they boiled their scabbards and belts into broth and ate that.

Twenty days passed before the entire suffering force reached the cultivated fields of San Martín had seen. They found that the corn had been harvested a short time before and the fields were empty. Two dogs were captured, though, and converted to stew. Quesada made camp and waited for the brigantines, which had been battered by the flash flood and had made a poor trip up the Opón.

It was impossible for the brigantines to go farther up the narrow, shallow river. Quesada decided to send his sick men back to Santa Marta aboard the boats, proceeding the rest of the way solely by land. The sufferers were loaded onto the brigantines, and their commander, Juan Gallegos, promised Quesada that he would return in exactly a year's time, bringing reinforcements. As it happened, though, Gallegos' downstream journey was hellish, and many men were slain through the treachery of an Indian guide who betrayed the Spaniards into an ambush. Gallegos himself lost an eye in the fight, and eventually reached Santa Marta with one brigantine and twenty men. Feeling that he had disgraced himself, he abandoned Santa Marta and went to Peru, where he served valiantly during the civil wars of the *conquistadores* of that country.

When he had seen Gallegos off, Quesada and his remaining 166 men set out to cross the broad plain San Martín had discovered. In two days they were in hilly country. Rain began to fall—not the warm rain of the tropical lowlands, but a harsh, chilling drizzle. Still, the Spaniards were relieved to be passing out of the humid river valley. Following steep Indian trails they wound their way upward into the mountains, shivering in the cold and engulfed in an unpleasant perpetual mist.

Two officers named Juan de Cespedes and Lazaro Fonte went out on a scouting mission with the Indian Pericón and a detachment of men. They crossed through a region of many small towns, each with its belt of cultivated fields. At one village they captured the chief, calmed him with presents of bells, beads, and knives, and discussed, via Pericón, the geography of the district. Where, the Spaniards wanted to know, was the rich country that the cakes of salt came from? Not far, the chief replied; one had to cross some barren land just ahead and traverse some steep mountains, and there was the realm of salt. Cespedes and Fonte persuaded the chief to guide them, harnessing him in a leather collar and leash to discourage a sudden escape. He led them through the hills without any false moves, until the two Spaniards stood at the edge of a great plateau.

They did not explore it, however, since Quesada had ordered them to return within twenty days, and that time was nearly up. They reversed their path, Fonte and some of the Spaniards remaining in the village of the friendly chief, Cespedes hurrying back to Quesada's camp. In twelve days of marching, the main body of the Spaniards joined Fonte at the Indian village and assembled for the trek onto the plateau.

Quesada reviewed his forces. He still had the 166 men who had remained after the departure of the brigantines, and, astonishingly, 62 horses had survived all the rigors of the journey. It was January, 1537. Nearly ten months had passed since the departure from Santa Marta, but to the Spaniards it must have seemed ten centuries.

While Quesada's men were gathered on the cool plain, readying themselves for the next phase of their adventure, an enormous band of Indians descended on them. "The whole valley seemed to boil with Indians," one chronicler wrote. The battle went on all day and into the night. Quesada broke camp and led his men into more open country, and when the Indians followed they were subjected to a full-fledged cavalry charge that put them to rout.

There were no more obstacles. The Spaniards went forward onto the plateau of Cundinamarca. Here dwelt the Indians known as the Chibchas, of whom so many hazy fables had been transmitted into the surrounding regions. Here was the home of the gilded man, El Dorado.

4

Many of the Spaniards, deluded by the legends they had heard so long, maintained that the kingdom of the Chibchas rivaled in richness and in complexity of civilization the great empires of the Incas and the Aztecs. This was not the case, though it was painful for some of the chroniclers to admit it. The Chibchas—or the Muiscas, as they sometimes were called—were far above the lowland Indians in culture as well as in altitude. But their state was not a Peru, nor was it a Mexico, and those who looked for such splendors on the Cundinamarca plateau were fated to be disappointed.

The sophisticated Incas and Aztecs had stone cities, elaborate religious and political organizations, and advanced engineering abilities. They knew the secrets of astronomy and of the calendar. Networks of superb roads linked the far-flung provinces of the Incas, while the Aztecs had made central Mexico prosperous with a stunning array of canals, causeways, and dams. All these things were beyond the capabilities of the Chibchas.

What heightened the mystery of the Chibchas was their geographical isolation. They occupied a circumscribed and almost unapproachable highland area, less than a hundred fifty miles long from north to south and about forty miles wide, surrounded by lofty mountain barriers and almost endless plains.

Colombia is a region of great physical diversity; most of the country is *tierra caliente*, the tropical lowlands of heat and humidity, but three rugged Andean *cordilleras* divide the interior into distinct zones, running up from the south and losing themselves in the hot flood plain of the Caribbean coast. East of the easternmost *cordillera* lies the jungled region of the Orinoco and Amazon basins. West of the westernmost *cordillera* is the rain forest of Colombia's Pacific coast. The three mountain chains are interleaved by the valleys of two great rivers, the Magdalena and the Cauca. The broadest of the *cordilleras* is the eastern one, which rises precipitously from the Orinoco plains, then flattens into the plateau of Cundinamarca or Bogotá, and drops sharply on the west to the valley of the Río Magdalena. On this plateau the Chibchas had settled. Ehinger and Hohemut had tried in vain to find a route to the plateau from the eastern side of the *cordillera;* Federmann had succeeded, only by driving his men through a pass so inhospitable that it has almost never been used since his time. Quesada, coming up the Magdalena, had found his way onto the plateau from the western side.

On this high plateau, more than 7500 feet above sea level, the temperate climate imposed limits on Chibcha agriculture. Unable to rely on the prolific fertility of the lowlands, the Indians of chilly Cundinamarca were compelled to do their best with what they had, and their relatively advanced cultural position may give some support to the theories of those who, following Arnold Toynbee, see human progress as a process of challenge and response. In a region where the temperature never rose much above 66° or fell much below 50°, the Chibcha farmers were confined to a narrow range of highland crops, and any staples they could not grow had to be obtained through trade with their lowland neighbors.

The main Chibcha crop was a thick tuber that the Spaniards had never seen before. Castellanos, the soldier of Quesada who turned priest and chronicler in later years, described the "scanty flowers of a dead purple color" of this strange plant, and praised its "farinaceous roots of pleasant flavor, much prized by the Indians and a delicacy even to the Spaniards." [38] It was the potato. The Chibchas grew a variety of other edible tubers, but they had to depend on commerce to bring them grain, fruits, fish, and even the cotton from which they wove their fine garments.

Luckily they had a major natural resource at their disposal: salt springs that yielded a rich supply of this necessary commodity. The lowlands folk had no salt source of their own. The large white cakes of Chibcha salt were important items of trade, and were marketed all over Colombia to jungle dwellers who valued it for its taste and for its preservative qualities. The Chibchas also had an abundance of emeralds which were prized in the lowlands. And from the raw cotton obtained by trade they produced cloth garments for export. Like any modern nation that has industrial skill but little in the way of natural resources, the plateau people were quick to seize on the advantage of buying cheap produce from primitive neighbors and selling finished goods back to them at healthy profits. That the Chibchas were able to produce a surplus of cloth for export is a tribute to the nutritive value of the potato, since a tribe living on a bare-subsistence level of agriculture cannot spare any hands for manufacturing surplus goods.

The trade routes were clearly defined. International markets were held on specified days at accessible points along the Río Magdalena, and the Chibchas brought their salt, emeralds, and woven fabrics to exchange for the tropical produce and raw materials of the lowlands. But the plateau dwellers did not import only fruits, grain, and cotton. They also imported gold.

This was a source of great grief to the Spaniards, when the incomprehensible fact finally came home to them that the very worshippers of El Dorado did not have any gold of their own in their kingdom. The tableland of Cundinamarca was wholly lacking in precious metals. The gold of the Chibchas came from the lowlands in the form of gold dust; the jungle people were happy to trade the attractive but useless metal for such more desirable commodities as salt and cloth.

Since metal was not native to their region, the Chibchas never became metallurgists to match the Incas or the Aztecs. Although the workmanship of their gold objects dazzled Quesada's Spaniards, the Chibchas actually were quite backward in the handling of metal. They could not compare with the smiths of Ecuador, for example, who had developed an intricate technique for handling platinum. Platinum, with a melting point above 3000°F., remained unworkable in Europe until the nineteenth century because no furnace could reach such temperatures; in pre-Columbian Ecuador, metalworkers found a way of mixing platinum grains with gold dust, and heating and hammering the mixture into a homogeneous mass without actually ever melting the platinum. In Mexico and Peru, elegant methods were used for extracting copper and tin from a variety of ores in small charcoal-fired cylindrical smelting furnaces. In Panamá and Costa Rica, relatively primitive cultures learned to fashion extremely delicate jewelry from gold.

By comparison, the Chibchas were awkward metallurgists who learned their skills late, borrowing from coastal people. Their chief metal was an alloy of gold and copper known as *tumbaga*, which they worked either by hammering or by the wax-model casting process of *cire perdue*. The copper gave the gold strength; the Colombian metalworkers in time discovered that the sheen of the gold could be preserved even after alloying through the technique of "pickling." This was a process of quenching a heated *tumbaga* object in an acid bath of plant juices; the acid ate away the outer layer of copper oxide that formed during the heating, and each successive pickling increased the proportion of gold to copper in the surface of the object without removing the hard copper in its core.

Considering their geographical disadvantages, the Chibchas had done well for themselves. They were agriculturally self-supporting, and maintained a dense population of over a million on their plateau; they were reasonably adept craftsmen, expert in weaving and pottery; and their exports of salt, emeralds, and manufactured goods brought them the gold and foodstuffs they lacked. They lived in substantial villages, with large communal buildings of wood and thatching, not even remotely the equal of the splendid stone cities of Mexico and Peru but imposing enough by the standards of surrounding tribes.

About sixty years before the arrival of the Spaniards, the Chibchas had formed a consolidated political structure of a bipolar sort, focused around two chieftains whose relation was one of uneasy cooperation bordering on outright rivalry. The main chief bore the title of *zipa*, and ruled from the town of Muequetá. At the time of Quesada's appearance, the reigning *zipa*'s name was Bogotá, and the Spaniards, following a common habit of theirs, gave his name first to his town and then to the entire region. The present city of Bogotá stands on the site of the former Chibcha capital of Muequetá.

The *zipa* Bogotá was the grandson of the Chibcha chief who had imposed a kind of unity on the plateau about 1470. According to the Chibcha records found by Quesada, their formal history began in that year when the first *zipa*, Saguamachica, overcame most of the neighboring tribes. After a reign of twenty years, Saguamachica was succeeded by Nemequené, his son, and Nemequené in turn by his son, Bogotá.

The other Chibcha chief bore the title of *zaque*. Nominally he was subordinate to the *zipa*, but in practice he was virtually independent and ruled a domain of his own from his capital city. At the time of the Spanish invasion, the reigning *zaque*'s name was Tunja; the name of his capital was lost, and is known only by its erroneous Spanish designation, which was also Tunja. A Colombian city of that name exists today some miles northeast of Bogotá.

The *zipa* had never quite been able to subdue the *zaque*, but existed in a state of perpetual cold war with him, sometimes taking a more harmonious approach when external enemies threatened the Chibcha state. Dangers lay on all sides: to the west were wild, fierce cannibals, the Panches, raiders of the Magdalena valley, and to the north were other savage tribes. Since these Indians were scattered and primitive, they could harass the Chibchas but never could mount a serious invasion. From time to time marauding bands of Panches were driven off by armies sent out jointly by the *zipa* and the *zaque;* at other times, the rival leaders concentrated on strengthening their networks of alliances with various satellite tribes tributary to each.

Chibcha religious practice was more complex than that of their neighbors, and indicates some influence from the high civilization of Peru. That the Chibchas possibly were migrants from Peru has been suggested by their language, which was similar to the Quechua spoken in Peru, and also by some features of their theology. The Chibcha creation myth told how in the beginning all was darkness, until a flock of black birds burst forth to bring light to the world. Soon after that first of all days, a beautiful woman called Bachué came up from the lake of Iguaqué leading a small boy, and when he grew to manhood he married Bachué and fathered upon her all the human race.

The people of the plateau lived in ignorant barbarism until a tutelary god named Bochica came to their highlands from the east—a natural route of approach if he had come from Peru. Bochica, described as a bushy-bearded old man of a race different from that of the plateau-dwellers, was credited with being the child of the sun. He taught the arts of agriculture, metalworking, and weaving, showing the Chibchas how to form communities and live a civilized life. The grateful people toasted him with *chicha,* a thick intoxicant made from fermented corn, and in time their festivals of celebrations turned into bacchanals of outrageous drunkenness.

Bochica grew weary of the excesses of his adopted people and resolved to destroy them. He turned two rivers loose on the plain to form a vast lake. A few of the Chibchas escaped the deluge and fled to the mountains. These survivors appealed for mercy to Bochica, who appeared before them on a rainbow and announced that he had relented. Throwing down a golden rod, he therewith broke through the rocky wall that formerly had enclosed the plateau. The water drained away through the waterfall of Tequendama, leaving only a few small and useful lakes.

The Chibcha religion consisted mainly of a recapitulation of the events of creation and the founding of civilization. Large temples made of cane and thatched with palm leaves were dedicated to the sun and the moon, but a number of lakes and caves were also considered sacred and contained small shrines. At all sacred places idols of wood, stone, cotton, and particularly gold were worshipped, and offerings of emeralds and precious metals were made to them. A priestly class, the *jeques*, operated the temples. Training for a *jeque* involved several years of seclusion, fasting, and sexual abstinence. During the religious observances, incense was burned and the priests often stupefied themselves with hallucinogenic drugs. Captured warriors of the uncivilized neighboring tribes sometimes were offered as human sacrifices to the sun.

The most important Chibcha cult involved ceremonies held in a twenty-day pilgrimage cycle at five sacred lakes— Guatavitá, Guasca, Siecha, Teusacá, and Ubaque. The subjects of the *zipa* began their pilgrimage at Ubaque and moved toward Guatavitá, and those of the *zaque* traveled in the opposite direction. The ceremonies were held to propitiate snake gods living in the lake, and apparently were bound up with such characteristic religious goals as the continued fertility of Chibcha fields and Chibcha wombs. Each lake was regarded as the seat of a particular divinity, who had to be placated with offerings of gold and emeralds thrown into the water.

From the point of view of the Spaniards, the major element of these lake rituals was the ceremony of the *dorado*, held at Guatavitá. Apparently this festival had been suppressed about 1500 by order of the *zipa*, but its picturesque qualities were so vivid that the accounts of the rite continued to reverberate outward like shock waves for a generation thereafter, coming to the ears of Ehinger and Ordaz, of Federmann and Quesada, of all those who sought for the land of the gilded chief.

The Guatavitá rite was the one in which a naked Chibcha chief coated himself with sticky resin and rolled in gold dust until he gleamed like a human statue, then leaped into the lake. The Indians about Guatavitá had celebrated this function for generations upon the inauguration of each new chieftain, and it seems that the early *zipas* of the unified Chibchas may have continued the rite on an annual basis for a while before abolishing it.

What was its purpose?

Since the gold that decorated the body of the *dorado* was imported, the ceremony was in a way a celebration of the superiority of the Chibchas over their uncivilized neighbors, for it showed that the Chibchas not only could obtain gold from them but could afford to squander it in the lake. More than mere conspicuous consumption was involved in the Guatavitá ritual, though. Some anthropologists have suggested that it was a "solemn act of expiation for the sins of the people" [39] analogous to an annual ritual of the Incas known as the *situa*.

The *situa* is known to us from many accounts, of which

the best is found in the *Royal Commentaries* of the Spanish-Inca halfbreed historian, Garcilaso de la Vega. He describes it as a rite in which the Inca capital of Cuzco and its environs "were purged of all diseases and any other ills the inhabitants might be suffering from." It began at dawn, with the participants rubbing their heads and bodies with a raw dough that had been kneaded with human blood drawn from children by non-fatal bloodletting. Then:

"As soon as the sun appeared, the inhabitants of the entire city ·threw themselves prone on the ground and implored the god-star to banish all their ills, both interior and exterior. They next breakfasted on the other bread, that contained no human blood. Then a richly clad Inca appeared at the gate of the fortress. This was the messenger of the sun. In his hand he carried a lance, trimmed with a border of multicolored feathers than ran through gold rings from the blade to the end of the shaft. . . . He ran down the slope of the Sacsahuaman hill, brandishing his lance, until he reached the middle of the main square, where he was awaited by four other Incas of royal blood, carrying lances and, like himself, in war dress. Then, touching the weapons of his four brothers with his own, he ordered them, in the name of the sun, to go to the four corners of the city and banish disease.

"They immediately started running along the four royal roads that lead from there to the four parts of the world. As they approached, all the citizens came out on their doorsteps and shook their clothing, with loud cries and exclamations of joy, as though to rid them of dust. They next passed their hands over their faces, their arms and their bodies, as though they were washing themselves, in order to cast into the street all the diseases in their houses, in the direction of God's herald who would bear them away from the city. . . .

"A similar ceremony took place the following night to

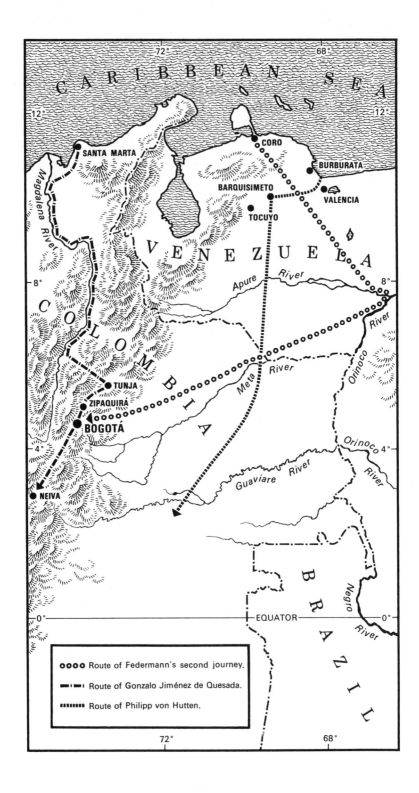

○○○○	Route of Federmann's second journey.
━ ╺ ━ ╺	Route of Gonzalo Jiménez de Quesada.
▪▪▪▪▪▪▪	Route of Philipp von Hutten.

banish all nocturnal ills from the city. Now the lances were replaced by great straw torches, round in shape and slow burning . . . which the Indians brandished as they ran through the streets and on out into the countryside. There, far from the city, they threw the extinct torches into a stream, along with the water in which they had washed themselves the preceding night, in order that, from stream to stream, the last ills of the city should be carried away till they reached the sea.

"Thus the people, the houses and the entire city having been purified by means of fire and sword, there next took place in Cuzco a great festival, that lasted an entire quarter of the moon. To thank the sun, lambs and sheep were sacrificed, and there was carousing, night and day, with continued singing and dancing, in the people's homes as well as on the public squares." [40]

Instead of Inca nobles anointing themselves with raw dough, a Chibcha chief dusting himself with powered gold; instead of a populace thrusting torches into a stream, a gilded king diving into a lake; then a festival, to celebrate the renewal of the year and the purification of the commonwealth. Possibly this was in fact the purpose of the rite of the *dorado*. At the core of the Chibcha observance, though, there glittered a unique image, that of the gilded man; and that image held a fatal brilliance that drew legions of questing Europeans to their doom.

5

Quesada and his 166 men, having endured the humid torments of the Magdalena jungle and having weathered the exertions of the climb to the cool plateau, stood now, in January of 1537, at the approach to the Chibcha land. They had tracked the fantastic figure of the gilded man to its source.

As he prepared for his invasion of Cundinamarca Quesada delivered a speech to his men which, if Padre Simón's reported version is at all accurate, must have been nearly unique among the Spanish conquerors. "We are now in a settled and well-populated country," Quesada is alleged to have declared. "Let no one show violence to any man. We must have confidence in God, and carry matters with a light hand. Thus shall we gain the sympathy of those we meet, for after all they are men like ourselves, if perhaps not so civilized, and every man likes to be treated with civility. So will these Indians. Therefore we must not take from them that which they do not want to give. By following this plan, they will give us what we require, whereas by harsh treatment we shall force them to withhold even necessities. After all, even the ground we tread upon is theirs, by natural and divine right, and they allow us as a favor to be here, and owe us nothing." [41]

It was a remarkable attitude for a Spaniard of that era to espouse; yet, as Quesada's later conduct shows, he adhered to it as much as was practicable. Although he destroyed the Chibcha state and dispossessed its inhabitants, he did it in a polite and kindly manner. (But consider, though, that las Casas refers to Quesada as a "tyrant" and devotes some pages to a list of atrocities perpetrated at his orders or with his tacit approval.)

The invaders proceeded across the plateau with the Indians fleeing at their approach. At a town called Sorocotá the Spaniards made their first discovery of the potato. At Tinca, a town on a rocky outcropping overlooking the Magdalena far below, they found the venerable trail leading to the Chibcha capital of Muequetá. They filed through a narrow gorge and the Indians dwelling on the slopes above them took the bearded strangers for gods; in the belief that the Spaniards were cannibals, the natives tossed young children down on which the new gods could feast. It was with the greatest difficulty that Quesada persuaded the Indians that his host did not need to be placated in this way. Through the interpreter Pericón, Quesada conveyed some notions of Christianity and announced that he had come to improve the spiritual lot of the people of the plateau.

They took this news complacently. However, the *zipa* Bogotá had learned of the invasion and was not gratified by Quesada's announced purpose. Bogotá's troops fell upon Quesada's rear guard, which consisted chiefly of sick and wounded men. Quesada sent reinforcements under Cespedes to the rear, and these cavalrymen took advantage of the flatness of the plateau to administer a heavy setback to the Chibchas. Bogotá's men scattered.

It was now March of 1537. The Spaniards had reached the salt-mining town of Zipaquirá. At Quesada's orders, they approached the palisaded settlement in orderly fashion, making no hostile moves. The people of Zipaquirá received the Spaniards peaceably, and pointed the way toward Muequetá, where, they hinted, an abundance of gold and emeralds could be had.

The *zipa* Bogotá, who had led the unsuccessful attack against Quesada from a golden litter, had taken refuge in the nearby town of Cajicá. The Spaniards beseiged it, and it fell in eight days. Bogotá slipped away after having buried all the treasure he had with him; but the golden litter fell into Quesada's hands and inflamed the avarice of his men. They were persuaded now that they were on the verge of the conquest of a great civilization, and that Bogotá was a king to rank with Moctezuma and Atahuallpa. A search of Cajicá failed to produce any other treasure.

The Spaniards remained for a while at Cajicá, where some of Quesada's scholarly priests began to collect information about Chibcha customs. Their compilations are our only sources of information about the natives of Cundinamarca. The Spaniards learned that major crimes were punishable by death; that women suspected of adultery were forced to eat hot peppers until the pain made them confess or until the length of time they endured the torment proclaimed their innocence; that defaulting debtors were presented with jaguar cubs by the *zipa*, and were obliged to keep them tied before their doors, fed and cared for, until the debt was settled. All this was of interest to the Spaniards, as was the observation that the wives of chiefs had the privilege of beating them when they had done wrong. Quesada himself observed a local leader tied to a post and being beaten by his several wives for drunkenness. But ethnology was secondary for the Spaniards to the quest for treasure. Although they had been absent from Santa Marta for more than a year, they must still have occasionally recalled that the purpose of their expedition was to bring back gold to help Don Pedro de Lugo pay the colony's bills.

Word came to Quesada that the chief of the town of Chiá had fled his home after burying gold and emeralds in a secure hiding place. Quesada moved on to Chiá and passed Easter there in a fruitless search for the gold. He also attempted to open negotiations with the fugitive *zipa* Bogotá, but the ruler would have no dealings with him, so the exasperated Quesada took the step that he had hoped to avoid: he invaded Muequetá, Bogotá's capital.

The city was empty when the Spaniards arrived. Once more the populace had fled after stripping their houses of all treasure. The angry Spaniards roamed through the bare rooms of Muequetá in bitter frustration. They captured a few Indians and put them to the torture, but none would reveal the location of a scrap of Chibcha gold.

Quesada made Muequetá his base of operations. Bogotá's soldiers emerged from hiding and harassed the Spaniards from a safe distance, firing blazing arrows over the palisades into the thatched roofs of the huts the Spaniards occupied. Unwilling to impose his authority on Cundina-marca by force, Quesada continued to send messages to Bogotá with naïve persistence, imploring the *zipa* to surrender peacefully to benevolent Spanish rule in the name of the Emperor Charles V.

Bogotá remained silent. Quesada hesitated to flush him from his hiding place, and while awaiting the *zipa*'s capitulation sent scouting parties to explore the plateau. One group, led by San Martín and Cespedes, went westward to the territory of the Panches, the tall, agile cannibals who were the hereditary foes of the Chibchas. While venturing down a narrow mountain pass, the Spaniards in their quilted cotton armor were attacked by five thousand Panches, but burst through them into an open plain where their cavalry could be employed. The Panches were routed.

Meanwhile Quesada had captured some of Bogotá's men and had questioned them about the location of the emerald mines. They admitted that the mines lay to the west, not far from the country of the Panches. Possibly their willingness to provide this information stemmed from Bogotá's hope of involving the Spaniards with those deadly cannibals. Since Cespedes and San Martín had broken the strength of the Panches, Quesada was quick to send another expedition, under an officer named Pedro Valenzuela, to find the mines.

Valenzuela's first halting-place was at Guatavitá. The Spaniards slept beside the lake of the *dorado* ceremony and never would be closer to the fount and origin of their gilded fantasy. But they did not yet know that this particular lake was the lake of El Dorado, and so they made no attempt to search its waters for gold, but moved on the next day. At a town called Chocontá, on the frontier of the *zipa*'s territory, forty Spaniards went into convulsions from eating the berries of a tree that the Spaniards called the *borrachera*, the "tree of drunkenness." When they had recovered, they crossed unknowingly into the domain of the *zipa*'s great rival, the *zaque* Tunja, but did not pass near Tunja's capital, where they would have found gold in plentiful supply. They went on out of Chibcha country and located the emerald mines, which Valenzuela discovered would be difficult to work. Gathering up a few stones, the Spaniards began their return journey.

At the emerald mines, Valenzuela told Quesada, he had caught a glimpse from a high point of vast, grassy plains in the distance. Quesada sent San Martín out to investigate them. San Martín passed through the town of Sogamoso, where a large Chibcha temple of the sun stood, and collected some gold. Still another scouting party led by one Hernando Vanegas came back with an equally modest supply of gold, but also with some exciting information. A disgruntled Indian who had quarreled with his chief had approached Vanegas, offering to lead him to a great city where immense wealth could be obtained.

This was the first that the Spaniards had learned of the *zipa*'s rival, the *zaque*, and of his city of Tunja. Quesada himself led the march against Tunja, carrying it out with such stealth that the *zaque* was taken by surprise. For once the Spaniards entered a Chibcha city before the natives had had a chance to hide their treasure. It was two hours to sundown when Quesada appeared at the gates of Tunja. A few Indians emerged, looking uneasily at the Spanish horses, for they had never seen such creatures before. Quesada formally requested entry. The Tunjans requested him to wait until morning, because an unexpected visit at night would alarm their *zaque*, who was, they said, old and feeble. Quesada had had enough experience with vanishing

Chibcha monarchs by now, and refused to wait. As the sun set, the Spaniards forced their way into Tunja over the opposition of excited and alarmed defenders who shouted and blew war whistles but did not put up any real struggle.

The dying rays of the sun presented a fantastic sight. From nearly every house hung thin plates of gold, blood-red in the twilight, swaying in the breeze and tinkling softly like Aeolian harps. No melody could have been sweeter to the Spaniards than the gentle clink of these golden sheets. The houses were spacious, surrounded by stockades; and those of the notable citizens were further decorated by towering varnished poles, bright red in color. Quesada led his men through this wonderland to the dwelling of the *zaque*. It was locked with strong cord and surrounded by armed guards. But the guards melted away in awe as Quesada approached with drawn sword. He hacked at the cords and opened the gate himself. Then, with ten followers, he entered the inner courtyard and sought the throne chamber.

The *zaque* was on a wooden throne, flanked by courtiers who wore golden breastplates and crowns of plumes. He was an old man of enormous corpulence, with a gnarled beak of a nose, fierce eyes, and a look of formidable authority. The ponderous *zaque* sat calmly before Quesada and remained silent as the Spaniard's interpreter relayed a discourse on the greatness of Charles V and on the importance of accepting the teachings of Jesus. Quesada extended an offer of alliance to the *zaque*, expressing a willingness to confirm him in possession of his own lands if he would merely become a vassal of the Emperor Charles.

It may have seemed to the *zaque* that his guests were mad, but it did not occur to him that they might be dangerous. He heard Quesada out and pleasantly invited him to retire to a nearby house for the night; the next day, Tunja suggested, Quesada might come again and discuss this matter of an alliance in greater detail. Quesada, who had only fifty men against the thousands of Tunja, feared some trick. As Cortés and Pizarro had amply proven, safety in such circumstances was best attained by making the Indian king a prisoner. With a nod to his nearest lieutenant, Quesada advanced toward the throne to seize the fat *zaque.*

For the first time it struck Tunja that he was in peril. He rose to his full and majestic height and thundered a command to his armed retinue to slay the insolent intruders. The Indians converged on Quesada with leveled lances, but feared to strike. In that fatal moment of hesitation the gates were thrown open and several of Quesada's men burst into the throne room on their horses. The Indians dissolved in confusion as the magnificent beasts reared high above them. The war cries of the Spaniards cut through the shrill screams of hundreds of Chibchas in and about the palace, and abruptly the melee around the throne halted and Quesada could be seen. He was grasping the *zaque* firmly and threatening him with his sword.

The corpulent king surrendered, and the men of Tunja ratified the conquest by putting down their arms. Fifty Spaniards had taken a mighty city without suffering a scratch. Not releasing the *zaque,* Quesada led him to the courtyard and put him under Spanish guard, instructing his men to treat him with courtesy and to allow his ministers to have free access to him.

Then the Spaniards were turned loose to loot the town. They ran down one street and up the next, stripping away the sheets of gold whose bright sheen the Chibchas found so lovely and whose wind-stirred tinkle seemed so musical. One man stumbled upon a bag containing gold to the value of 8000 *pesos de oro;* another found a reliquary containing the bones of some earlier *zaque,* with a weight of 6000 golden pesos. From each house came emeralds, gold, emeralds, gold. A flushed Spaniard, his eyes bright with the joy of plundering, rushed up to Quesada, who sat quietly beside his conquered *zaque*, and blurted out in happiness, "Peru, Sir General, Peru! This is another Peru!"

6

That first wild night in Tunja it seemed that a new Peru had indeed been found. Tunja was a city of gold. Every man's ears carried heavy golden rings; emeralds as big as walnuts were common items of jewelry; the priests were weighted down by golden pendants and plumed diadems of feathers embedded in gold; the tinkling sheets of gold dangled from the front of every house. All night the ransacking went on, and a mound of treasure grew in the palace courtyard so high that a man could not see over its top. The count in the morning tallied 200,000 golden pesos —two hundred pounds—of pure gold, 18,000 pesos of silver, 37,000 pesos of golden objects alloyed with copper, and 1815 emeralds, along with countless fine mantles, shields, gold-inlaid weapons, and handsome beads. Much more was lost when the Tunjans heaved their choice treasures over the walls during the night to confederates outside the city.

As though this were not enough, some of Quesada's men persuaded their leader to request the *zaque* to ransom himself after the fashion of Atahuallpa with yet more gold. Quesada made the request, but received a somber glare. No ransom would be paid. "My body is in your hands, do with it what you choose," he told Quesada, "but no one shall command my will!" [42]

Quesada was impressed by the *zaque*'s resolution, and this most atypical of *conquistadores* dropped the ransom request at once. He ordered the king's release without further payment, and let it be known that he was to be treated with the respect due his rank. It was a noble gesture, and it cost Quesada nothing in the way of authority, for the *zaque* was a broken man and died of his brooding a few weeks afterward.

Eighty of Tunja's subjects were chained together to carry the booty as the Spaniards moved on to what they hoped would be a succession of golden conquests. Only slowly would they learn that their "new Peru" was merely a gilded façade, and that there would be no mines of gold to be found in Cundinamarca; once they had robbed the Chibcha cities of such gold as they held, no more was to be had on the plateau. And as the Spaniards passed from town to town, the Chibchas melted from sight like spring snowflakes, taking their gold with them. There was little further loot.

One chief, a man named Tundama, held his ground and gave battle. In the fray Quesada was clubbed from his horse, but one of his soldiers helped him to remount, and Tundama's forces were defeated, yielding some plunder to the Spaniards. Returning to Tunja, Quesada soon was on the track of a new fantasy: he learned of a valley called Neiva, near the Magdalena, which supposedly boasted a temple standing on pillars of solid gold. Neiva lay in the hot lowlands, and could be reached only by a strenuous march across a barren and frigid plateau twelve thousand feet high, but Quesada left his brother Hernán in command at Tunja and took fifty men to search for Neiva.

The trip was doubly taxing: first the painful crossing of the plateau, and then the descent from chill into the sweltering *tierra caliente* once more. Neiva proved to be a fertile and lovely valley, but it harbored no golden temple, only a few deserted huts. As Quesada prepared for the return to Chibcha country, there came a surprise: an Indian swam across the Magdalena, which was three-fourths of a mile in width there, and staggered into the Spanish camp with a heavy bundle on his head. It contained heart-shaped plates of gold, which he had brought as a gift to the godlike strangers. Quesada was not unmindful of the irony of the situation, for his men were exhausted by the journey, and after their months on the plateau were weak with fevers contracted in the humid valley. They might very well die of their fatigue before they ever saw Muequetá again, but at least they would die carrying gold.

The trip back was grueling, but the Spaniards survived it and gathered at Muequetá for a division of the loot that had been taken thus far. The royal fifth was set aside: 40,000 golden pesos. Each infantryman received 520 *pesos de oro*—perhaps $500,000 in modern purchasing power— and each cavalryman was awarded a thousand. The officers drew two thousand pesos apiece. Quesada apportioned 14,000 pesos to himself, and 18,000 for Don Pedro de Lugo. Later, when he learned of Lugo's death, Quesada appropriated the *adelantado's* share himself, rather than allow it to be inherited by Don Pedro's worthless son Alonso. This cost him some trouble afterward.

Most of the Chibcha country now had been conquered; but the *zipa* Bogotá remained at large, making his headquarters in an impregnable marsh an hour's journey from Muequetá. While never leaving the marsh himself for fear of capture, the *zipa* sent out guerrilla raiders who were causing Quesada difficulties. Two of these raiders were captured by Quesada and tortured to reveal the location of Bogotá's secret fortress. One died rather than say anything, but the other weakened, and guided the Spaniards into the marsh. They came to a well-fortified stockade manned by several thousand loyal Indians who fled as Quesada's men burst upon them.

The fate of the *zipa* is a matter for dispute. Padre las Casas, the historian of Spanish cruelty, provides a gaudy scene in which Quesada put the captured king to torture in hope of extorting a golden ransom, complete with "burning suet on his naked belly," "the strappado with cords," "bolts upon his feet," and the rack, with "the tyrant [Quesada] coming up and down now and then, willing him to have his death given him by little and little, if he made not ready the gold." [43] But Padre Simón, whose account of Quesada's expedition seems quite trustworthy, says simply that Bogotá was accidentally slain by a Spanish crossbowman as he attempted to escape. That appears more likely, for there is little reason for Quesada to have tried to get a ransom from Bogotá after declining to wring one from Tunja, and the zipa would have been far more useful to the Spaniards as a puppet captive than as a corpse.

There proved to be just one golden vessel in the marsh stronghold of the zipa. Quesada returned to Muequetá, where he received an unexpected visitor: a Chibcha warrior named Sagipá, who said that he had been chosen as the new zipa. Sagipá was in great peril, for his lands were menaced on one side by an outburst of the Panches, and on the other by the chief of Chiá, a rival claimant to the throne of the late Bogotá. He requested an alliance with the Spaniards, whom he regarded as invincible.

Quesada was taken by Sagipá's princely bearing as well as by his grasp of practical politics, and concluded an alliance on the spot. The new zipa became a vassal of Charles V, and the lawyer Quesada at last had the legal basis for his conquest that he had desired so long. Quesada's cavalry joined Sagipá's army in a campaign of pacification against the Panches.

They were more troublesome now than when San Martín had invaded them a few months before. In the first skirmish Sagipá's men were routed and ten Spaniards were wounded. Quesada, who had studied military tactics well, employed the old device of the feigned retreat to draw the Panches into a position of vulnerability. He sent Sagipá's army forward into the rocky ravines of the Panches to counterfeit a quick defeat; then, as the Chibchas fled in deliberate panic, the Panches pursued them into an open plain, where Quesada's horsemen shattered them. The next day they sued for peace and swore allegiance to the *zipa*, their hereditary enemy.

It seemed that Sagipá would be a useful puppet. But shortly Quesada discovered that the claim of the chief of Chiá to the Chibcha throne was indeed valid, and that Sagipá was a usurper. Some legalistic compulsion drove Quesada to arrest his ally. Sagipá was charged not only with usurpation but with the theft of Bogotá's treasure. When he failed to produce the gold that he had allegedly secreted, he was tortured to death—a shameful blot on Quesada's otherwise relatively admirable record.

The fate of the chief of Chiá is uncertain, but in any event no more *zipas*, legitimate or not, were chosen in Cundinamarca. Quesada was the absolute master of the plateau. He intended now to return to Santa Marta with his gold, and then to go to Spain to apply for the governorship of the country he had conquered. First, though, some administrative details had to be dealt with. In August of 1538, Quesada formally claimed the land in the name of Charles V and put Indian laborers to work building on the site of the Chibcha capital of Muequetá the first Catholic church of the new city of Santa Fe de Bogotá. Quesada thus founded what has become simply the city of Bogotá, capital of the present-day republic of Colombia. To the plateau in general he gave the name of the New Kingdom of Granada, after the city where he had been reared, and Colombia was generally known as New Granada until 1861.

On August 6, 1538, mass was celebrated in Bogotá for

the first time. Quesada now prepared for his journey to the coast and then to Spain. But before he set out his soldiers brought him news of a tribe living on the western bank of the Magdalena whose temple, the House of the Sun, contained far more gold than all of Tunja. They begged Quesada to lead them on an expedition to this temple, and Quesada, having learned nothing from the fool's errand that took him to Neiva, agreed to make the march into the *tierra caliente* again.

While this project was being planned, one of Quesada's closest associates turned against him: Lazaro Fonte, the able scout who had first found the route onto the Cundinamarca plateau. Fonte declared that Quesada had pocketed valuable emeralds that should have gone into the royal fifth. Quesada, who had kept a scrupulous account of the Emperor's share, was infuriated by the charge, which does indeed seem to have been unfounded. He arrested Fonte, arraigned him on a countercharge of having hidden some emeralds himself, and sentenced him to death. The Spaniards were aghast at this harsh treatment of a popular officer, and some suggested that the very vindictiveness of the punishment might betray Quesada's own guilty conscience. They implored Quesada to pardon Fonte.

The general weakened. The sentence was commuted to banishment: Fonte was to dwell in Pasca, a frontier town where the Indians still were restless under Spanish rule. Presumably Quesada thought that Fonte would be murdered when he arrived there. But an Indian girl had become Fonte's mistress, and she accompanied him to Pasca and asked the chief of the town to admit him. The exiled Pasca and his Chibcha paramour took up residence in the Indian town with the blessing of the chief.

With the matter of Lazaro Fonte out of the way, Quesada once again began to assemble the expedition that was to search for the rumored House of the Sun. Now came another interruption, even more jarring than the defection of Fonte. An Indian messenger arrived in Bogotá with word that a party of Spaniards was approaching Cundinamarca. They had come out of the Cauca valley and across the unknown heights of the central *cordillera*, and then had descended into the valley of the Magdalena, resting for a while at that same fertile vale of Neiva where Quesada had been given the heart-shaped plates of gold. Now they were preparing to ascend the plateau of Cundinamarca. The Indian described these men as well dressed and well equipped.

The strangest episode in the quest for El Dorado was about to unfold. Quesada could not now look for golden temples, nor could he make his overdue journey to Santa Marta, not until the question of this rival party of Spaniards was explored. With great misgivings and not a little fear, Quesada sent his brother Hernán forth to meet the advancing forces of Sebastián de Belalcázar.

7

Belalcázar was a striking figure among the Spaniards in the new world: a man of unsurpassed courage, ambition, and cruelty. Tempestuous and self-willed, he functioned as a law unto himself, hewing to some inner code of morality that allowed him to lie, cheat, or kill when necessary, not for bloodshed's sake but for the sake of enhancing the empire of Spain and the power of Sebastián de Belalcázar.

That was not really his name. Like Quesada, who was really a Jiménez, and like New Mexico's Coronado, who was really a Vásquez, Belalcázar is known to history by a name that was not his surname. As Germán Arciniegas puts it in his biography of Quesada, *The Knight of El Dorado*, "Throughout the whole conquest of America one never knows who is who. Names are always being changed about.

. . . Sebastián de Belalcázar, for example, was named Sebastián Moyano, but historians wrote reams of paper, saying, some, that he was called Belalcázar, and others, Benalcázar. As a matter of fact, he was probably not a Moyano at all but a García. Let the reader go to Quito, Popayán, or Cali, however, and tell residents that the founder of their city was named García Moyano, and they will laugh in his face, if they do not stone him to death."

He who was to become Belalcázar was born at the village of that name in the Spanish province of Estremadura, which produced many of the *conquistadores*. His father was a woodman, and the boy Sebastián went about the little town to sell the wood from the back of a donkey. The story goes that the donkey became stuck in mud one day and refused to move. Sebastián, then about fourteen, grew exasperated and struck the animal with such force that he killed it. Out of fear of his father's wrath he ran off to the port of Cádiz and joined the fleet that Pedrarias Davila was assembling bound for Panamá. He did not give his name, and so was known only as "Sebastián from Belalcázar," which became his style in the Americas.

Young Belalcázar reached Panamá in 1514. He was there to witness the downfall of Balboa and to hear tales of golden kingdoms on the South American mainland. The boy attracted attention one day when Pedrarias and a large force of Spaniards had become lost in a jungle; provisions were running low, and no landmarks could be sighted, when Sebastián scaled a tree and spied a campfire in the distance, far beyond the range of the eyes of the older men. He led them to it, and it proved to be the camp of some friendly Indians who guided the Spaniards back to Darien. Pedrarias, impressed by Belalcázar's keen sight and also by a maturity beyond his years, marked him for future importance. So did Pizarro, who while still in the service of Pedrarias was making his own plans for the conquest of Peru. The first major exploit of Belalcázar in manhood was a successful campaign in Nicaragua. He helped to found the city of León there and governed it for a few years. Then Pizarro and his *compadre* Diego de Almagro invited Belalcázar to join them in the invasion of Peru. Belalcázar was a member of that small band of Spaniards that confronted the legions of Atahuallpa at Cajamarca in late 1532. Atahuallpa was taken, and soon his cell at Cajamarca was filling with golden ransom. In the summer of 1533 Atahuallpa was executed; shortly afterward Pizarro left Cajamarca on a southward march to subdue the hinterlands of Peru.

Belalcázar did not accompany him on this expedition. Pizarro had an important assignment for him: the command of the garrison at the city the Spaniards called San Miguel, the only port of entry to Peru. It was of vital importance to secure this base on the coast, and Belalcázar was despatched with 150 men to hold it while Pizarro moved south.

In October of 1533, after he had been at San Miguel only a short while, Belalcázar was drawn from his duty by a private enterprise of treasure-seeking. Emissaries from a tribe known as the Cañari, which had been subject to the Incas, came to him to ask for help. It seemed that an Inca general, Rumiñavi, had fled into Ecuador after the downfall of Atahuallpa, and had established a tyranny over the natives. The Cañari invited Belalcázar to deliver them from the tyrant. They played on the Spaniard's greed by tempting him north with tales of the great wealth of the Ecuadorian capital, Quito.

Although he was betraying Pizarro's trust, Belalcázar set out without authorization to overthrow Rumiñavi and conquer Quito. With 104 men, both horse and foot, and a large auxiliary force of friendly Indians, he marched northward through the Andes onto the tableland where Quito is situated. Rumiñavi met him with thousands of men, but the Spaniards received aid from the oppressed Cañari and other local tribesmen, and after some months of fierce campaigning the combined efforts of Spanish cavalry and native hordes carried the victory. Rumiñavi set fire to Quito and fled into a remote mountain refuge, taking with him as much of the city's treasure as he could carry and burying the rest. Belalcázar entered Quito as a conqueror early in 1534. He found the city ruined and without gold.

Indian laborers restored the despoiled city, and Belalcázar renamed it San Francisco del Quito in honor of the name-saint of Pizarro. That was the extent of his genuflection toward his distant general, however. Belalcázar ruled in Quito as though Ecuador, the northernmost province of the dismembered Inca empire, were his own fief.

His sovereignty over Ecuador was challenged later in 1534 by another free-lance conqueror, the brilliant, handsome, wholly callous Pedro de Alvarado, who nine years before had branched away from Cortés in Mexico to subjugate Guatemala. Alvarado took Guatemala in a campaign of singular criminality, and ruled it with a royal grant from Spain. However, it lacked enough gold to please him, and he launched a venture in South America upon learning of the success of Pizarro and Almagro in Peru. Searching for his own golden land, Alvarado disembarked on the Ecuadorian shore after a 1500-mile voyage from Guatemala and looted a coastal town, obtaining much treasure. As they marched inland, Alvarado's men suffered the hardships of entering a tropical lowland, and had to abandon their booty for lack of strength to carry it. At length they approached the Quito tableland which Belalcázar had conquered ten months earlier.

News of Alvarado's invasion reached Pizarro and

Almagro at the Inca capital of Cuzco. Oddly, they had no idea that their own lieutenant, Belalcázar, had already invaded Quito himself, but they knew that Alvarado must be halted in his trespass on territory that belonged to them by right of conquest over the Incas. Almagro hurried north to San Miguel to confer with Belalcázar, and was considerably startled to learn that that officer had abandoned his post months before to go to Ecuador. The grizzled and elderly Almagro immediately followed Belalcázar's route and met him at the Ecuadorian city of Riobamba. The confrontation was a tense one; but Belalcázar argued that he had had no disloyal intent in making his unauthorized conquest, and joined his army to that of Almagro.

Finding himself faced with the combined forces of Almagro and Belalcázar, and knowing that he had no legal claim to Ecuador, Alvarado allowed himself to be bought off. In August, 1534, he sold his ships and weapons to Almagro for 100,000 *pesos de oro* and withdrew. Almagro confirmed Belalcázar as the governor of Quito—in Pizarro's name—and rode off toward Cuzco with Alvarado, who had decided on a holiday in the Peruvian capital.

Belalcázar had survived a ticklish situation, and it must have been no easy matter for him to face down the ferocious old Almagro when accused of abandoning San Miguel. Now, however, Belalcázar was ruler in Quito with the grudging consent of his superior officers. He commenced an ambitious program of construction and treasure-hunting. Palaces and temples were ripped apart in search of any gold they might contain, then were laboriously rebuilt by the Indians at Belalcázar's command. The Cañari, who had invited him as a liberator, now groaned under a yoke far more terrible than that of the deposed Rumiñavi. Belalcázar marched up and down the land of Ecuador, unearthing less gold than he had hoped to find.

Although he sent word of his activities to Pizarro, Belalcázar acted at all times in Quito as ruler in his own right. But Pizarro in Peru had something more tangible than mere power to possess; he had gold. Belalcázar had not found the wealth he coveted in conquered Quito. Some time in 1535, however, there came to him an Indian out of Colombia who waved before Belalcázar's eyes the dazzling, irresistible lure of El Dorado. The chronicler Castellanos gave this account in his lengthy verse relation of the conquests:

An alien Indian, hailing from afar,
Who in the town of Quito did abide,
And neighbor claimed to be of Bogotá,
There having come, I know not by what way,
Did with him [Belalcázar] speak and solemnly announce
A country rich in emeralds and gold.

Also among the things which them engaged
A certain king he told of who, disrobed,
Upon a lake was wont, aboard a raft,
To make oblations, as himself had seen,
His regal form o'erspread with fragrant oil
On which was laid a coat of powdered gold
From sole of foot unto his highest brow,
Resplendent as the beaming of the sun.

Arrivals without end, he further said,
Were there to make rich votive offerings
Of golden trinkets and of emeralds rare
And divers other of their ornaments;
And worthy credence these things he affirmed;
The soldiers, light of heart and well content,
Then dubbed him El Dorado, and the name
By countless ways was spread throughout the world.[44]

It was not the first time, of course, that an Indian had related details of the Lake Guatavitá ceremony to Spaniards. But the tales heard by Ehinger and Herrera and Federmann and Quesada had come at second or third hand. This man actually came from the plateau of Cundinamarca, and could describe the ritual as it really had been performed.

Apparently Belalcázar himself coined the title *El Dorado* for the gilded man, by analogy with such nicknames for Spanish kings as *El Bravo, El Cruel, El Impotente, El Sabio*. Padre Simón credits him with the invention, at any rate, and it seems likely that Belalcázar was capable of it, since for all his lowly origin and bellicose nature he was a literate man with some knack for clever phrases. So in Quito in 1535 the legend of El Dorado at last assumed its complete form. This was no hazy rumor wrung from forest tribesmen by an unreliable interpreter, but a full and detailed account of a gilded king and of a golden kingdom, and the poetic image of El Dorado blazed with blinding light in Belalcázar's brain.

Like most Spaniards of the day, he was peculiarly susceptible to such romantic fantasies. The active presses of Spain had poured forth a quantity of books of travel and adventure, both real and fancied, and these were enormously popular among the *conquistadores*. A century later, Cervantes would base the entire structure of his *Don Quixote* on the ability of such romances of chivalry as *Amadis of Gaul* and *Sergas de Esplandián* to unhinge the reason of a knight of La Mancha; and in fact Cervantes knew that those very novels had done much to disrupt the rational processes of the hard-bitten conquerors of the New World.

In the mind of the *conquistador* a caldron of dreams stewed and bubbled at all times. Tales of golden temples in distant lands, of Amazon warriors, of deserts where the sands sparkled with gems, of monsters and chimeras, drifted from the printed page to the receptive mind and then into a sort of potential reality that was ever on the brink of being fulfilled. A few Spaniards with the cursed gift of literacy could infect an entire flotilla of adventurers with these illusory visions. The most popular romance of all, the one that was the undoing of poor Don Quixote, was *Amadis of Gaul*, written by one Garci-Rodríguez de Montalvo some time after 1492, and first published at Zaragoza in 1508. This novel related the adventures and transcendental love of Oriana, the daughter of King Lisuarte of Great Britain, and Amadis, the secret child of King Perion of Gaul. Amadis had Moses-like been put in a floating ark and had drifted to Scotland, to be reared at the royal court.

The plot of *Amadis of Gaul* is picaresque—an almost infinite series of exotic adventures by which Amadis proves himself worthy of a knight-errant's title and of the hand of the fair Oriana—and its vision of far lands and strange beasts was irresistible to many generations of Spaniards. It was bitterly attacked as a corruptor of the minds of youth, and in 1531 the Spanish Queen officially banned exports of *Amadis* and other secular works to Mexico, a ban evidently not observed, since five years later it was banned once more. In Spain itself a parliamentary bill of 1555 demanded the suppression of "such false and foolish books as *Amadis*," declaring, "Notorious is the harm done and being done to youths, maidens, and other people in these realms by the reading" of such works.[45] But by then the damage was done.

Sergas de Esplandián, a sequel to *Amadis* by another hand, also did its share of corruption. This long-winded work included an episode in which a tribe of Amazon women appears, led by its Queen, Calafia. The Amazons, hailing from "the islands of California," had come to do battle on the side of the Moslems against the Christian rulers of Constantinople, and their doughty queen challenged both

Amadis and Sergas in single combat before being vanquished. Chapter 157 of this work declared:

"Know ye that on the right hand of the Indies there is an island called California, very close to the Earthly Paradise, and inhabited by black women without a single man among them, for they live almost in the manner of Amazons. They are robust in body with stout, passionate hearts and great strength. The island itself is the most rugged with craggy rocks in the world. Their weapons are all of gold as well as the trappings of the wild beasts which they ride after taming, for there is no other metal on the whole island. They dwell in well-formed caves." [46]

Some of this was derived from tales told by Columbus' men, for the flow of fantasy moved in two directions. The wealth of Queen Calafia's realm seemed real enough to Cortés, who went in search of it up the Pacific coast after his conquest of Mexico, and became the discoverer of those shores that bear the name of California today. In the same way, the Indian's tale of El Dorado carried for Belalcázar the compulsion of reality, and at once his fertile mind embroidered upon the authentic ceremony of a man gilded with metallic dust and produced an infinitely rich kingdom to the north of Ecuador.

The Indian informant told him that the province of El Dorado was called "Cundirumarca," and lay no more than twelve days' journey from Quito. Restless, Belalcázar set out at once, but the journey was destined to last many more days than twelve. The swarthy, narrow-eyed Belalcázar left Quito in 1536, taking with him hundreds of Spaniards and a retinue of thousands of Indian bearers, and appointing a deputy to look after his interests in Ecuador. At the time of his departure, Quesada was getting under way from Santa Marta, and Federmann was about to leave from Coro. So it happened that three expeditions converged on Cun-

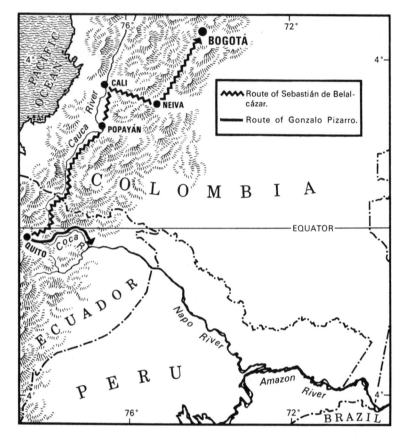

dinamarca simultaneously, one from the north, one from the northeast, and one from the south.

While Federmann roamed in the trackless savannahs of the Orinoco basin and Quesada was making his hellish trip up the Magdalena, Belalcázar was approaching El Dorado in a far more comfortable manner. He first crossed out of what is now Ecuador into what is now Colombia— which in that day meant leaving the province of Quito and entering the province of Popayán. Ahead of him, the Andes split into the three northward-running *cordilleras*, with the valleys of the great rivers, the Cauca and the Magdalena, separating them. No Europeans had ventured into this country from any direction. Not even the Incas had managed to extend their vast empire this far north.

A chief named Popayán ruled over the region of the same name although there was no organized state. Belalcázar found an array of scattered tribes, cannibalistic and uncivilized, who raised simple crops and mined some gold to trade to the Chibchas on the plateau north of them. It was impossible for Belalcázar to proceed to Cundinamarca until he had conquered Popayán. This he did easily enough, invading the weak villages with his musket-wielding cavalry and with a horde of specially trained and highly ferocious dogs of war. The natives fled before this terrifying assault, and by destroying their cultivated fields Belalcázar speedily reduced them to a condition of famine and then to total collapse. To consolidate this victory he founded the city of Popayán late in 1536 as his first base in the conquered land.

After a while he continued northward, choosing the route down the Cauca—that is, the western route. Some sixty miles north of the city of Popayán, Belalcázar set up another base, which is now the large city of Cali. After establishing Cali in 1537, he selected 200 infantrymen and 100 cavalrymen and a strong force of Indians and pressed northward in quest of the golden realm of El Dorado.

Belalcázar's ambitious activities had caused some distress in Peru. Pizarro, already enmeshed in the feuds that were to erupt in civil war and destroy him a few years later, saw his lieutenants breaking away from him on all sides. His old partner Almagro was now his enemy, while the once-trusted Belalcázar seemed to be wholly independent in the north. Hearing tales of terrible devastation and depopulation in the region around Quito, Pizarro sent one of his officers to take command of that city and arrest Belalcázar. Belalcázar had already gone into Colombia; Pizarro's deputy, Lorenzo de Aldana, took control of Quito, introduced measures to protect the natives, and then followed Belalcázar northward. Aldana halted at Popayán and took steps to alleviate the famine caused by Belalcázar's techniques of conquest. He reached Cali next, to find that Belalcázar had eluded him again. At Cali, Aldana encountered several hundred ragged men who had set out from the recently founded Colombian coastal city of Cartagena on an expedition down the Pacific coast. These men joined Aldana's forces. Among them was a young soldier named Pedro de Cieza de León, who became one of the most important historians of the subsequent events in western South America.

Aldana and a lieutenant named Jorge Robledo concentrated on expanding Spanish control over southern Colombia, and made no attempt to follow Belalcázar into the unknown northern country. Belalcázar was marching on, through 1537 and all of 1538, into progressively more difficult country. He hoped to reach and conquer El Dorado, carry off its gold, and continue northward until he came to the coast, where he could take ship at Cartagena or Santa Marta for Spain. Once in Spain he planned to petition the court for the governorship of Popayán as well as that of Quito; but governorships and court visits seemed only like remote dreams to the marching Spaniards now.

Progress was slow, for Belalcázar had not chosen to travel lightly. Along with his giant dogs and his thousands of Indian bearers he also had a huge herd of swine, to provide food for the marchers no matter what their circumstances. As the jungle thickened, Belalcázar's forces were increasingly harried by Indians armed with poisoned arrows. Cieza de León describes these attacks:

"It must not be thought that the wounds were very great, but with the poison on the arrows it was only necessary to make a prick and bring out a drop of blood, when quickly the poison reached the heart and the victim, overcome by great nausea, biting his own hands, and abhorring life, longed to die. So fierce was the flame of that poison that it consumed the entrails, the vital spirit fled and the victims seemed to be distraught, crying out like madmen; next there was a terrible spasm and they expired." [47]

Twenty of the Spaniards were hit by these arrows in the first onslaught. Nineteen died. Cieza de León tells us, "The survivor's name was Diego López, and the reason he did not die was that he and his companion named Trujillo were standing in a river when he was wounded in the calf of the leg, and before the poison could penetrate he cut the flesh sharply with the hook with which he was fishing. Then taking out a knife, he gave it to his companion, and told him to cut away, without mercy, all the flesh round the place where he was wounded, and not to delay, because he was beginning to have the same symptoms as those who had died of their wounds. His companion promptly cut away the flesh before the poison had time to enter the system. In that way this Spaniard saved his life, but lost the calf to his leg." [48]

Belalcázar fought his way across the western *cordillera*, passing from zones of tropical heat to zones of wintry chill, and at last descended into the Magdalena valley. At the beginning of 1539 he made camp at Neiva, where he could look up at the plateau of El Dorado. And there, to his great chagrin, Belalcázar discovered that Spaniards from another part of the continent had beaten him to the conquest of Cundinamarca.

8

Hernán Pérez de Quesada, the brother of the conqueror, knew that his little band did not cut a very satisfactory figure as it advanced toward Belalcázar's camp. The men of Santa Marta were roughly dressed in the skins of jaguar and deer; their powder had nearly run out; the cross-bowmen had few bolts. The newcomers from the south were clad in silk and scarlet cloth, and wore steel helmets and elegant plumes. As Hernán de Quesada marched toward Neiva, one of his Indian guides picked up some arrows lying on the ground and identified them as arrows of Peru, different from the local kind. Nearing Belalcázar's camp, Quesada's men dug in quietly in the thick canebrake beside a river. One of Belalcázar's scouts, riding that way, stumbled over a concealed man and hurried to the camp, shouting, "To arms, the enemy is here!"

Twenty of Quesada's horsemen took their mounts and rode toward the encampment. Belalcázar sent cavalry of his own to meet them. But there was no clash; when each side saw that the other was Spanish, they halted and made introductions. Belalcázar was cautious, but offered tents to Quesada's men, and the two groups spent the night peacefully if warily.

In the morning Belalcázar explained that he was one of the conquerors of Peru, who had mastered Quito and then had worked his way northward in search of Cundinamarca and its gilded king. Hernán de Quesada tactfully informed Belalcázar that the conquest of Cundinamarca was complete, and that his brother Gonzalo ruled at Santa Fe de Bogotá. The soldiers of each leader muttered among themselves of a test of arms to see which party of Spaniards should possess the land, but all was tranquil among the high command. Belalcázar offered arms, horses, and his pigs as gifts to Hernán de Quesada, who reciprocated with golden plates and Chibcha cloth. In a mood of good cheer the combined forces ascended the plateau and made their way toward Bogotá. Their advance was a slow one, for Belalcázar was driving 300 pregnant sows; but the men of Santa Marta, who had tasted no bacon for three years, were quite willing to accommodate their pace to that of the live-stock.

Gonzalo de Quesada had remained at Bogotá while his brother was going to meet Belalcázar. Before Hernán's return, Gonzalo de Quesada received a message from Lazaro Fonte, the officer whom he had sent to live in exile among the Indians. Fonte had not lost his loyalty to the general who had tried to sentence him to death, apparently, for on a piece of deerskin he inscribed the information, "My Lord, I have had certain news that a band of Spaniards is at hand. They are coming from the plains. They are close by and will arrive here tomorrow. Let your worship determine quickly what measures to take." [49]

Quesada was appalled to learn that a second band of strangers was encroaching on his territory. The thought came to him that these two independent groups might join forces against him; to head off such a possibility, he galloped eastward with his best horsemen to the town where Fonte lived. There was a quick and touching reunion. Quesada embraced the man with whom he had had such a deadly quarrel, and retracted the sentence passed upon him. As Quesada and Fonte conferred, the advance guard of the newly arrived Spaniards appeared. The unkempt, ghostly figure of Pedro de Limpias came before Quesada on a horse that might have been the prototype of Quixote's gaunt Rosinante, and presented the compliments of Captain Don Nicolaus Federmann.

The weird triple meeting on the plateau of Cundinamarca was now complete. Quesada, Federmann, and Belalcázar shortly were together at Bogotá, each having wandered through unexplored jungle for several years only to come together in the land of El Dorado in the same month of February, 1539. Quesada had looked with envy on the handsomely equipped men of Belalcázar, clad in their lavish silks, but now he in turn drew the envy of Federmann, whose tattered army was in a miserable state after its long jungle stay and its brutal crossing of the *cordillera*. By all odds the strangest touch of this strange meeting was that each army numbered exactly 166 men—an improbable detail worthy of the author of *Amadis of Gaul*.

For several days the three commanders joined in feasting and contests of sport at Bogotá. Belalcázar's swine were slaughtered in gay abandon, and the newcomers to the plateau tasted their first potatoes, and perhaps the Spaniards celebrated their eerie meeting with bowls of native *chicha* as well. Then came more serious moments. Quesada, who regarded himself as the master of the plateau, still feared a combination of the other two to unseat him. But Federmann and Belalcázar were not of that stripe. They both could be ruthless when the occasion merited it, but neither cared to abuse Quesada's hospitality by attacking him. An odd cordiality and affability marked their discussions.

Perhaps the irregular nature of the positions of all three had something to do with their willingness to cooperate. Belalcázar had marched north in defiance of Pizarro, who had sent men to apprehend him. Federmann had taken his three-year jaunt in disregard of his responsibilities to Governor Hohemut of Venezuela. Quesada himself seems to have forgotten his obligations to Don Pedro de Lugo, for he had long overstayed himself in Cundinamarca while presumably Lugo was in sore need of the gold he had sent Quesada to find. Quesada, Belalcázar, and Federmann could all be certain of unpleasant receptions if they ever returned to the bases from which they had set out.

Any possible friction between the three was averted by a gift of 4000 *pesos de oro* to Federmann, who had no wealth to show for his many adventures. Then, in the course of three months of hunting and festival, the future of New Granada—Cundinamarca—was arranged. Belalcázar, who was the most serious threat to Quesada's power, would not make any claim to the plateau. His generosity was motivated, perhaps, by the discovery that the legend of El Dorado had not been backed with much gold, for by now it was understood that all the gold of Cundinamarca had been imported and no mines were to be found. Federmann, pocketing the gold Quesada had given him, also waived any claim he might make. It was agreed that the three would sail to Spain together so that the Emperor could parcel out to them the governorships of all the newly discovered lands.

In May of 1539 the three discoverers of El Dorado entered the final act of this comedy of conquest. A ship had been built to take the generals down the Magdalena to Cartagena, where they would embark for Spain. Quesada formally named his brother Hernán to rule in his place, and then, laden with gold and emeralds, he and Belalcázar and Federmann mounted their horses and rode to the banks of the Magdalena to set sail. With Indians heaving at the oars, the generals moved downstream on their homeward journey, the best of friends.

The river trip was interrupted once by a portage around a waterfall, and once by an Indian attack that was beaten off by soldiers of Belalcázar's entourage. In fourteen days—such was the beauty of sailing downstream—they were in the port of Cartagena on South America's Caribbean coast, and were regaling the settlers with tales of El Dorado. The three generals were the sensations of the moment, and told their stories again and again. Quesada had long since been given up for dead, while Belalcázar of Peru and Federmann of Venezuela were unknown in this Colombian town.

Quesada now learned of the death of Don Pedro de Lugo soon after his departure from Santa Marta three years before. He did not return to Santa Marta, with which he had had no contact all this while, fearing that Lugo's successor as governor might try to strip him of his share of the takings. Nor did Federmann attempt to revisit Coro, which might have been embarrassing. By August, the three were in Cuba, and a pleasant Atlantic crossing brought them swiftly to Europe. There the oddly assorted trio parted company.

Federmann was in a bitter mood, angry not with the heroic Quesada but with Ehinger and Hohemut, who had come so close to El Dorado without attaining it. While still in the West Indies in the summer of 1539 he wrote to a friend charging them with cowardice and ineffectiveness, for "they might otherwise—the one eight years, the other three years before—have secured the wealth which now the people of Santa Marta have taken." He added, "The stories about Meta are not wholly false, for that river does rise in the mountains that border the plain; and the House of Meta which was sought for so long is the Temple of Sogamosa, the holy objects in which the people of Santa Marta have now carried away in sacks." [50] When he reached Spain, Federmann tried to receive some preferment from Charles V for his discoveries, but nothing was forthcoming. In 1540 he learned of the death of Hohemut, and applied for the governorship of Venezuela. But the Welsers were not minded to be generous to a man who had abandoned his post for three years to hunt for phantom empires. If Federmann had been the first to find El Dorado, he might have fared better; as it was, the Welsers berated him and gave the Venezuelan job to another man. After writing his autobiography, Federmann disappeared into obscurity. He never returned to South America.

Belalcázar was favorably received at court. Despite or perhaps because of his quarrel with Pizarro—whose bloody exploits had come to disturb the Emperor Charles V— Belalcázar was granted the governorship of the province of Popayán. He returned in 1541 and found Popayán under the administration of Jorge de Robledo, one of Pizarro's officers. Robledo accepted service under Belalcázar, and for several years they worked together harmoniously. During the civil wars of the *conquistadores* in Peru, Belalcázar took up arms against the Pizarro faction, was captured in battle, and was brought wounded before a brother of Pizarro, who spared his life. Returning to his own province, Belalcázar discovered that Robledo had turned against him and was attempting to supersede him in the government. Showing none of the mercy that had just been shown to him, he arrested Robledo and hanged him in 1544. Robledo had influential friends at the Spanish court, and at their urging Belalcázar was recalled to Spain to stand trial for the execution. He fell ill at Cartagena and died there, his last days shrouded by legal charges and bitter accusations.

Quesada's career after Cundinamarca was a mottled one. Instead of going at once to Madrid to apply to the Emperor for title to New Granada, he inexplicably lingered for months in Lisbon, where he encountered Hernando Pizarro, brother of Peru's conqueror, and spent much of his gold on a prolonged spell of gambling and wining with Pizarro—something that seems out of Quesada's character. By the time he finally reached the court in 1540, carrying with him a box containing the royal fifth from New Granada's conquest, Quesada's enemies had turned the Emperor against him.

Chief among these foes was Alonso de Lugo, the scapegrace son of Don Pedro. Five years earlier he had fled to Spain with Santa Marta's gold and made a high marriage. Now he used his influence at court to claim the governorship not merely of Santa Marta, by right of inheritance, but of New Granada as well, which he said Quesada had conquered on his father's behalf! Since a thousand miles separated the hot lowland town of Santa Marta from the cool plateau that now was called New Granada, the claim to join both of them under one government did not seem well founded. But the worthless Alonso had an array of documents that gave him at least the appearance of a valid case, and Quesada's delay in reaching court was fatal to his own interests. Had he arrived while Belalcázar was there, he might have fared better, for Charles V was fond of Belalcázar and might have heeded his words in favor of Quesada. Belalcázar was gone, though, when Quesada arrived. In a monstrous miscarriage of justice, the Emperor listened to both sides and awarded both Santa Marta and New Granada to Alonso de Lugo.

Quesada's three years of struggle had gained a new American kingdom for Spain, but nothing for himself. He left his homeland in disgust and traveled through Europe, settling for a while in France and in Flanders, and writing a number of autobiographical books, none of which survive. The Council of the Indies put him on trial *in absentia* for his murder of the *zipa* Sagipá, sentencing him to a fine that does not seem to have been paid. Eventually, after nine years of wandering, Quesada returned to Spain and petitioned the court for some employment in New Granada. He was granted the title of Marshal of Bogotá, with no duties or authority attached, and early in 1550 landed at Cartagena. From there he made his way south to New Granada, where he was welcomed warmly by the people of the thriving settlement he had founded a dozen years before. He lived in honorable poverty there, respected by all. And, as we will see, his involvement with El Dorado did not come to an end with the melancholy failure of his conquest of New Granada. Gonzalo Jiménez de Quesada had found the country of the gilded man, but he had not found the true source of gold of which he dreamed. He was of the legion of the obsessed, and he joined in the universal delusion that saw El Dorado pursued to every corner of the New World.

[4]

EL DORADO OF
THE OMAGUAS

FTER THE THREE GENERALS HAD SAILED for Spain, Hernán Pérez de Quesada was left in command of New Granada. Little is known of this brother of Don Gonzalo except that he was a courageous soldier, a tyrant to the Indians, and an inveterate seeker after gold. The booty of Cundinamarca had been some 500,000 *pesos de oro* in all, most of it taken at Tunja, but that considerable sum did not match Hernán's concept of the proper harvest from the land of El Dorado. He knew of the story of Lake Guatavitá by now, and in 1540 became the first of many who attempted to drain the lake and recover the golden objects that had been cast into it.

With great difficulty, the Spaniards dredged the muddy bottom and came up with 4000 *pesos de oro* of gold, not a sufficient yield for the effort involved. With easy self-deception Hernán persuaded himself that Guatavitá must not be the true lake of El Dorado, and from there it was an instant step to the notion that the lake of gold lay somewhere to the east of the plateau. He had, after all, explored most of the country west of the plateau and north of it, while Belal-cázar had come up from the south without finding anything.

Hernán chose to ignore the fact that Federmann had spent three years in the land east of the plateau, so that a complete reconnaissance had already been made. On September 1, 1541, a party of 270 Spaniards and 5000 Indians descended from the plateau under Hernán de Quesada's command, and marched in a southeasterly direction into the hot *llanos* of the Orinoco basin. The ingredients of the *dorado* tale called for a lake in mountainous country, and so Hernán hoped to find an unknown *cordillera* east of the plains.

The heat was ghastly and the Indians were hostile. All the horses died. Hernán compelled his men to continue on foot. It was possible to see that no mountains lay east of the plains, for jungle lowlands stretched to the limits of vision. The Spaniards went on, venturing so far east that they came close to the point that Herrera had reached in 1534, coming the other way. Then they turned back after half the men had been lost. Like walking shadows the pitiful survivors came lurching into Bogotá. They had been gone more than a year. Some were close to death.

An unwelcome surprise awaited Hernán. Alonso de Lugo had arrived, flourishing his royal grant. He notified the enfeebled younger Quesada that he now was the ruler in New Granada, and when Hernán objected, unable to comprehend how this discredited scamp had done his brother out of the kingdom, Lugo had him jailed. The citizens of New Granada, who regarded themselves as followers of the Quesadas, threatened an uprising. To get the dangerous Hernán out of the way, Lugo sent him into exile. At Cartagena he took ship for Cuba, and during the journey he was struck down by lightning.

Alonso de Lugo rapidly found himself in an untenable situation at Bogotá. Maintaining his authority over the sullen settlers by sheer terror, he confiscated estates, appropriated all the emeralds from the mines, and imprisoned or executed his most vocal opponents. When in 1544 he learned that a Spanish official was coming to investigate the abuses of his government, he gathered up his treasure and hurried down the Magdalena to the coast. Twice he was arrested en route from Santa Marta to Spain, and twice he won his freedom with bribes. In Spain, the rogue was greeted by royal favors and commissions, and held influential military and diplomatic posts in Europe till the end of his life. His cousin, Montalvo de Lugo, succeeded him as interim governor at New Granada, but shortly he was replaced by another man who was destined to forfeit his life to El Dorado.

2

Hernán de Quesada's foolish idea that the realm of gold lay east of Cundinamarca was shared by many others, for no one cared to admit that there might just not be such a golden kingdom at all. Since Cundinamarca itself had not fulfilled prior expectations, the search turned elsewhere. There *had* to be more gold. Mexico had yielded gold; Peru had yielded gold; Cundinamarca had yielded some gold, though not enough. A Spanish monk, Fray Toribio of Benevento, wrote in 1540, "Gold is, like another golden calf, worshipped by them as a god; for they come without intermission and without thought, across the sea, to toil and danger, in order to get it. May it please God that it be not for their damnation." [51]

The flood of American gold was already beginning to have its calamitous effect on the Spanish economy. A treasure fleet from Peru had arrived in Spain between December, 1533, and June, 1534, carrying 708,500 *pesos de oro* in gold and a third as much in silver. Other such fleets now sailed frequently. Little of this wealth remained in Spain. The

Spaniards had no industries and had to turn to more highly developed nations for manufactured goods. Thus Spain became a funnel that poured gold into Flanders, France, Italy, England, and Germany. Within Spain, the abundance of gold drove the prices of other commodities up. During the sixteenth century the purchasing power of a Spanish laborer's earnings declined 30%, at a time of apparently unexampled prosperity. That the treasure of the Americas could impoverish Spain is one of the paradoxes of the conquest. Too little of the bonanza went into capital investment for the development of the country; too much went to pay the debts of Emperor Charles' foreign wars and to purchase the costly goods of other lands. The crowning irony came midway through the century of treasure, in 1557, when Spain found it necessary to declare bankruptcy and default on international obligations.

Economics, though, was a mystery to the sixteenth century even more than it is to the twentieth, and gold seemed the *summum bonum*. The quest continued. From Santa Marta, from Cartagena, from Coro, from Quito, from Peru—expeditions were hatched in dizzying abundance.

The great eastward shift in the location of El Dorado began even before the ill-starred expedition of Hernán de Quesada. In 1536 one of Belalcázar's men, Gonzalo Díaz de Pineda, set out from Quito to the east upon hearing rumors of a golden kingdom in that direction. Pineda advanced for some days, harassed by Indians, and at length came to a valley of cinnamon trees. Discovering cinnamon was significant, for thus far the Americas had not given Spain a supply of spices to equal that which Portugal had in the East Indies. This cinnamon grove was more valuable than a gold mine would have been, difficult as it was for the Spaniards to realize that. Nicholas Monardes, the physician of Seville, wrote that "being tasted, it hath the same pleasantness of taste as the same Cinnamon hath, which they bring from the India of Portugal, and so there doth remain in the mouth the same sweet smell, and taste, as the same Cinnamon of the East India hath. . . . And in the meats where it is put, it giveth unto them the same taste and savor that the Cinnamon of the East India hath." [52]

Pineda gave this country the name of *Canela*, "the province of cinnamon." He brought back samples of the tree. In Monardes' description, "The trees which do bear it, are of reasonable greatness, they carry a leaf like to laurel, they be all the year green, and they never loose the leaf, which is a thing common in all the trees of the Indias. They bear their fruit unto the likeness of a little hat, that hath his cup and sides as great as a piece of eight reales of silver, which is four shillings, and some greater, he is of the color of a dark tawny, as well without as within, he is smooth in the inner part, and sharp in outer part, in the highest part of the cup he hath a stalk, whereof he hangeth in the tree." [53]

Aside from these useful botanical details, Pineda also brought back from the eastern plains a fact that had much more immediate impact on the Spaniards: the Indians had told him that if they kept marching east, "they would come to a widespreading flat country, teeming with Indians who possess great riches, for they all wear gold ornaments, and where are no forests nor mountain ranges." [54] This was a blurred echo of the old legend of Meta, the golden kingdom of the Orinoco plains. Already the city of El Dorado had begun to wander.

The absence of Belalcázar on his own expedition to El Dorado made it impossible for the men of Quito to follow up Pineda's information at once. In 1539, however, Francisco Pizarro appointed his younger brother Gonzalo as governor of the kingdom of Quito, displacing Pizarro's enemy, Belalcázar. Francisco specifically charged Gonzalo with leading an expedition eastward into the cinnamon country and to the realm of El Dorado.

Of the many brothers Pizarro, Gonzalo is probably the most attractive personality, which is not saying a great deal. He was illegitimate and informally reared; taking up a soldier's career, he became an excellent horseman and was rated as the most adept lancer among the conquerors of Peru. He was a handsome man, of a sunny and forthright disposition, having little of the craftiness that distinguished his more celebrated brother Francisco. He had the useful gift of being able to inspire lasting affection among the men who served under him, although his associates observed that he was not a highly intelligent man. An ambiguous passage in the chronicle of the Peruvian conquest written by a relative, Pedro Pizarro, describes Gonzalo as *apretado y no largo*, "tight-fisted and not generous," but an equally acceptable translation of the same words has been rendered as "a compact man, not large." [55]

Gonzalo marched north from Cuzco and entered Quito in December, 1540. The city was then under the control of the officers sent from Peru in 1537 to arrest Belalcázar. Since Belalcázar had not returned from New Granada to state his claim to Quito—he was at that moment in Spain getting a confirmation of the right to rule Popayán, or southern Colombia, from Charles V—Gonzalo had little difficulty taking possession. He spent three months at Quito, bringing its affairs into order, and then mounted the most ambitious expedition of exploration that the New World had yet seen.

The expense of the enterprise was 50,000 *castellanos*, most of which Gonzalo borrowed against the hope of finding wealth in the east. His interest in the cinnamon valley was slight. This was quite frankly a quest for El Dorado by that name, for the legend of the gilded man now circulated in full-blown state throughout South America. The chronicler Gonzalo Fernando de Oviedo explained the motives for Gonzalo Pizarro's expedition in a letter written in 1543 to Cardinal Bembo, in Venice:

"He took possession of that city of San Francisco [Quito] and of a part of that province, and from there he decided to go and search for cinnamon and for a great monarch who is called El Dorado (concerning whose wealth there are many rumors in these parts). Upon being questioned by me as to the reason why they call that monarch Chief El Dorado or King El Dorado, the Spaniards who have been in Quito . . . say that what has been gathered from the Indians is that the great lord or monarch constantly goes about covered with gold ground into dust and as fine as ground salt; for it is his opinion that to wear any other adornment is less beautifying, and that to put on pieces or a coat of arms hammered out of gold or stamped out or fabricated in any other way is a sign of vulgarity and a common thing, and that other rich lords and monarchs wear such things when it pleases them to do so; but to powder one's self with gold is an extraordinary thing to do, unusual and new and more costly, inasmuch as what one puts on in the morning every day is removed and washed off in the evening and is cast away and thrown to waste on the ground; and this he does every day of his life." [56]

The *dorado* ceremony of Lake Guatavitá, which had taken place only on the accession of a new chief, or perhaps at an annual festival of purification, had thus become a matter of daily garb by 1543! The distortions were mounting; the legend was being amplified by eager imaginations. Oviedo added, "I would rather have the sweepings from the chamber of this monarch than that of the great smelting establishments in Peru, or in any other part of the world." The historian also endorsed the fallacy that had brought

[*143*]

such disappointment at Cundinamarca: if the chief called El Dorado could afford to powder himself daily with gold dust, Oviedo wrote, then it must necessarily follow "that he must have very rich mines of a similar quality of gold."

In February, 1541, an advance party started eastward from Quito. Gonzalo followed a few weeks later with the main body of his force. There are two near-contemporary accounts of Pizarro's expedition, one by Garcilaso de la Vega and one by Cieza de León, which differ in a number of minor details while agreeing on the general outline of this unusually arduous journey. According to Garcilaso, Pizarro had with him 340 Spaniards, horse and foot, 4000 Indians laden with supplies for building bridges and boats, 4000 head of swine, a flock of llamas as beasts of burden, and about a thousand of the ferocious dogs that now accompanied the Spaniards on their extended explorations. Cieza de León credits him with only 220 Spaniards and the accompanying entourage.

What is indisputable is that this expedition was a memorable epic of human endurance. It is not easy to admire the character of the *conquistadores* in general or of the Pizarros in particular, but even with reservations for their brutality, one must support Cieza de León's encomium for his own people: "No other race can be found which can penetrate through such rugged lands, such dense forests, such great mountains and deserts, and over such broad rivers, as the Spaniards have done without help from others, solely by the valor of their persons and the forcefulness of their breed. In a period of seventy years they have overcome and opened up another world, greater than the one of which we had knowledge, without bringing with them wagons of provisions, nor great store of baggage, nor tents in which to rest, nor anything but a sword and a shield, and a small bag in which they carried their food. Thus it was that they went forth to explore that which was unknown and never before seen." [57]

Actually, Gonzalo with his swine and llamas and thousands of native bearers was setting out with a good deal more than "a sword and a shield." But those comforts were stripped from him as he went along, and still he continued on the hopeless quest. The mere greed for gold does not seem a suitable motive to impel a man to wander for years in a hostile wilderness; some impulse toward abstract accomplishment, and not simply avarice, must have informed Gonzalo Pizarro, Nicolaus Federmann, Alonso de Herrera, Gonzalo de Quesada, and others who underwent such extreme rigors on the road to El Dorado.

To reach the plains of the cinnamon country, it was first necessary to cross the Andean *cordilleras*. The passage of the eastern *cordillera*, only a few miles out of Quito, was a savage one; piercing winds and intense cold assailed the marchers, and more than a hundred Indian men and women of the party were frozen to death. From these wintry heights they descended into the suffocating heat of the jungle lowlands. *Macheteros* chopped a path a hundred miles long, and finally the expedition halted in a fertile valley called Zumaque.

To conserve their provisions, the Spaniards had lived off the land as they went, devastating the cultivated fields of the natives. This created certain hardships for a following troop of Spaniards that had set out over the same route shortly after Pizarro, for they were forced to travel through a countryside that had no food left to offer, and arrived at the main camp suffering from malnutrition. This rear force of the expedition was led by Francisco de Orellana, a man marked for an imperishable but not altogether honorable place in the annals of exploration. Orellana was from Estremadura, and in 1541 was thirty years old, five years younger than Gonzalo Pizarro, who was his kinsman. Having come to the New World in boyhood, he saw action in Central America under Cortés, then took part in the conquest of Peru, losing an eye in 1535 while fighting in Ecuador. In the first of the civil wars of Peru—between Pizarro and Almagro, in 1538—Orellana had taken Pizarro's side. The war ended with the destruction of Almagro, and Orellana received as his reward the governorship of a substantial portion of what is now Ecuador. When in 1540 Gonzalo Pizarro was named as the overlord of that region, Orellana willingly resigned his administrative posts and asked to join Gonzalo's expedition to El Dorado. The offer was accepted, and Orellana returned to his home to put his affairs in order. Unable to get ready in time for the departure of Gonzalo's force, Orellana agreed to head the smaller party following its footsteps.

Though Orellana's men arrived in poor shape, they had ample time to recuperate at Zumaque, for rains began to fall with such vehemence that for six weeks the expedition was penned up there. Gonzalo, in his terse account of his exploration, simply states, *"las aguas cargaban,"* "the rains were troublesome." A more vivid figure comes from a play by the Spanish contemporary of Shakespeare, Tirso de Molina, dealing with the adventures of the Pizarros: the rain, says Gonzalo in *Las Amazonas en las Indias*, "baptized our very souls." [58] It also rotted their gear and ruined their provisions, and turned the jungle into such a swamp that no forward progress was possible.

During this enforced halt, Gonzalo and seventy men set out on foot—for the horses could not negotiate the muck—to find the cinnamon country. "They took a route in the direction of sunrise," says Cieza de León, "having local Indians with them as guides. They started and marched for several days through dense and rugged forest country until they came to where the trees they call *canelos* grow. . . . This is the cinnamon of the most perfect kind." [59] The trees were sparsely situated, though, and Gonzalo asked the local inhabitants where he might find more extensive cinnamon plantations, as well as the open country where the civilized and wealthy cities were located. The Indians replied that they knew nothing of such wonders, for they were hemmed in by other tribes and never left their own district.

"I took measures to inform myself," Gonzalo related afterward in his letter to Charles V, and Cieza de León tells us what those measures were. He stretched some Indians on improvised torture racks made of flexible cane. When this loosening of limbs failed to loosen any tongues, Gonzalo barbecued his victims on their frames, and allowed a few to be devoured by his dogs. But the Indians still could give him no map to the home of El Dorado. The annoyed Pizarro forged on through the jungle, until a flash flood relieved him of most of his baggage and nearly drowned his men. "They saw that there was nothing but ranges of forest-clad and rugged mountains in all directions," notes Cieza de León, and "they decided to return by the way they came and see if they could not find another track which would lead them in the direction they wanted." [60] Pizarro had been gone from Quito only a few months, but already he was having private misgivings about the wisdom of this adventure. He kept them to himself, and headed back toward his camp at Zumaque displaying a public optimism that he was far from feeling.

3

On the way to Zumaque, the Spanish scouting party came to a river too wide to ford. As they halted in uncertainty, Indians in canoes appeared. The Spaniards shouted out that they came in peace, and the Indian chief, Delicola, accepted that at face value and did not attack. Gonzalo offered him combs and knives, and questioned him about El Dorado.

During the course of this parley a forest messenger brought Delicola some unsettling news: a thorough description of the havoc the Spaniards had worked in the last village, with details of the various tortures employed to wring information from its people. Delicola was clever enough to realize the mistake of that hapless village. He knew no more about El Dorado than the other Indians did; they had declared their ignorance, and had been broken on the rack for it. Delicola would invent a golden land as delectable as any Spaniard could imagine, and spin glossy tales of it, so that his dangerous visitors would hurry off to the east as rapidly as possible.

The chief showed Gonzalo a narrow place where he could bridge the river. The bridge was built, and while Pizarro went to Delicola's village, a Spanish messenger summoned the encampment at Zumaque to come forward and join the advance guard. Delicola delighted his guests with stories of the golden kingdom. However, some of the Indians panicked at the sight of the Spaniards and attacked them. They were defeated, and the leading men of the tribe were chained together, with Delicola himself at the head of the chain gang. The chief remained a prisoner while Pizarro and his second-in-command, Orellana, debated their next step.

They were inflamed by Delicola's stories of a rich and well-peopled land in the east. The wide river that ran through Delicola's territory flowed rapidly eastward, and seemed like an ideal route to follow to El Dorado. (It was the Coca River, one of the tributaries of the Amazon.) Pizarro and Orellana decided to march by land along the banks of the Coca, using Delicola as their guide.

The journey downstream was a taxing one through

swamps and creek-riven morasses. "The creeks in the swamps were so deep that swimming the horses through them was an arduous task," says Cieza de León. "Some Spaniards and horses were drowned. The Indian men carrying loads could not cross these swamps on foot. . . . When the bad places were narrow they made bridges of trees, and crossed in that manner. In this way they advanced down the river for forty-three marches, and there was not a day when they did not come upon one or two of these creeks, so deep that they were put to the labor we have described, each time. They found little food and no inhabitants, and they began to feel the pangs of hunger." [61]

The proud expedition that had set out in February from Quito was now a sorry sight. The thousands of swine had long since been devoured or lost; the gay silk uniforms were in tatters; the costly armor was ruined; the gunpowder was a soggy mass. Most of the Indian bearers were dead or had deserted. Few llamas remained. The Spaniards had even butchered their own hunting dogs. Their only source of food now lay in the occasional and widely spaced river settlements where they could find corn and guavas and an edible root known as yuca or cassava, *Jatropha manihot*. Their problems were compounded when Delicola and his chained comrades slipped away in a moment of Spanish negligence and vanished into the jungle. Now the Spaniards were without guides in the torrid and trackless rain forest.

It was clear that they could not hope to continue by land through this nearly impassable wilderness if they had to carry their own heavy gear. Pizarro decided to build a brigantine that would sail downstream, carrying the surplus baggage and the sick men. Despite the unremitting rain, charcoal was prepared and a forge set up, so that the Spaniards could make nails from the shoes of dead horses. "Gonzalo Pizarro, as became so valiant a soldier, was the first to cut the wood, forge the iron, burn the charcoal, and employ himself in any other office, so as to give an example to the rest, that no one might have any excuse for not doing the same," the account of Garcilaso de la Vega declares. "For tar for the brigantine, they used resin from the trees; for oakum, they had blankets and old shirts; and all were ready to give up their clothes, because they believed that the remedy for all their misfortunes would be the brigantine. They then completed and launched her, believing that on that day all their troubles would come to an end." [62]

The brigantine departed, deliberately slowing its downstream course so it would not get too far ahead of the men who followed it by land. Though their hunger was extreme and their strength was waning, Pizarro's men were buoyed by one hope. Delicola had told them that the entrance to the rich country lay at the place where this river flowed into another that was even larger. That confluence, the chief had said, was only ten or fifteen days' journey beyond the point where the brigantine had been built. When they reached it, the Spaniards firmly believed, they would find themselves at a large settlement that could provide food for all, and leave them, so says Garcilaso, "well supplied with provisions and rich in gold, and in all other things which they wanted." [63]

But after some weeks of further toil the promised land was nowhere in sight. Another change in plan was called for: Gonzalo and his exhausted men would make camp beside the Coca, while Orellana and seventy Spaniards would go ahead on the brigantine to find the river junction and its rich settlements. They were to load the brigantine with food and come back upstream to the camp, which would be succored by the provisions and could thus continue the march.

In high expectations Orellana's party was chosen and boarded the brigantine. The little vessel was cast loose, and the current took it and bore it rapidly out of sight. It was just after Christmas, 1541.

A cheerless Christmas it was in Gonzalo Pizarro's camp, for there was nothing to eat and the rain continued around the clock. Several days passed. No word came from Orellana. Gonzalo's fears mounted, for Orellana had taken with him all the baggage that remained, and most of the muskets and crossbows. Had the brigantine been swept to destruction in the swift river? His patience cracking, Pizarro broke camp and resumed the march downstream. "Meanwhile, not to die of hunger," writes Cieza de León, "they ate some remaining horses, and dogs, without wasting any of the entrails, skin, or other parts. . . . At this time they had come in sight of an island in the river; but facing it, on the mainland where the Spaniards had to pass, there were great swamps and bogs which they could not traverse." [64] Stymied once more, Pizarro camped and sent one of his officers down the river with a few men in canoes captured from the Indians to look for a trace of Orellana. They were gone eight days and returned reporting that they had seen nothing of Orellana, nor of a confluence with another large river, nor of a land of gold and produce.

A second scouting party went out, this one equipped for a longer stay. It was led by Gonzalo Díaz de Pineda, he who had discovered the cinnamon country five years before. Pineda's canoes went downstream until the long-sought confluence appeared. The Río Napo, an Amazon tributary much mightier than the Coca, flowed into the Coca there, the two becoming one vast river. Here they found the marks of knife-slashes on the trees, a sign that Orellana and his companions had been there. They turned upstream to explore the Napo, and after traveling thirty miles they came to a large plantation of the root called yuca, which had been abandoned by the Indians and was thick with unharvested crops. The thankful Spaniards ate well and loaded their canoes with yuca to bring back to the main camp.

For twenty-seven days Gonzalo Pizarro and his men had waited for Pineda's return, "eating nothing," says Cieza de León, "but some horse and dog-flesh with herbs and leaves of trees. They had also eaten the saddle and stirrup leathers, boiled in water and afterwards toasted." [65] When Pineda appeared with his cargo of yuca, the hungry men fell upon them and devoured the roots without bothering to wash away the earth that still clung to them. "Blessed be the Lord our God who has thus remembered us," they declared as they ate.

However, the real news Pineda had brought was chilling: Orellana had reached the confluence safely in the brigantine, and inexplicably had continued on downstream instead of returning, as agreed, with provisions. It seemed an act of incredible treachery. Gonzalo found it impossible to believe that his old comrade had betrayed him in this way, blithely sailing onward to El Dorado or even to the Atlantic without a thought for the men he had left behind. The only possible explanation for Orellana's absence, Gonzalo insisted, was that he and his men had been slain by Indians below the confluence of the Coca and the Napo.

The immediate problem was not Orellana's whereabouts but the obtaining of food. Gonzalo led his men to Pineda's yuca plantation. The captured canoes were used to ferry everyone to the western bank of the Coca, and then the expedition continued overland until reaching the yuca grove on the bank of the Napo. There they halted for eight days, ripping up yucas from the earth and eating them, soil and all. "The Spaniards were very sick and sore, wan, and wretched," reports Cieza de León, "and in such an afflicted condition that it was very sad to look upon them." [66]

The yuca sustained them. They ate the roots raw and

cooked, and ground them into meal for bread. Two Span-iards died from overeating; others were so bloated they could not walk, and when Gonzalo gave the order to march on they had to be strapped into their saddles with cord. For more than a hundred miles they followed the Napo down-stream toward the confluence, still vainly hoping to be over-taken by a returning Orellana.

But there was no Orellana. Scouts went out ahead regu-larly in search of him or at least an Indian settlement, but they found nothing. "The Spaniards were in a very bad state," declares Cieza de León. "They had eaten nothing but the yucas, which brought on a flux which wore them out; besides that they all went with bare feet and legs, for they had nothing in the way of shoes, except that a few made a sort of sandal from the leather of the saddles. The road was all through forest, and full of prickly trees: so that their feet got scratched all over, and their legs were constantly pierced by the many thorns. In this condition they went on, nearly dead with hunger, naked and barefooted, covered with sores, opening the road with their swords; while it rained so that on many days they never saw the sun and could not get dry. They cursed themselves many times for having come to suffer such hardships and privations, which they could well have avoided." [67]

In this season of despair they came to the meeting place of the Coca and Napo and camped. Shortly, a half-naked Spaniard came upon them, looking even more desperate than they did themselves. He was Hernán Sanchez de Var-gas, one of the men who had departed on the brigantine with Orellana, and he had a somber tale to tell. The worst suspi-cions were confirmed. The brigantine, said Sanchez de Var-gas, had whisked down the river to the confluence in three days—Pizarro's men, on foot, had needed two months to cover the same distance—and had made a landing at the point where Pineda had seen the knife-slashes on the trees. There they had deliberated their course, and many of the men had argued that it was difficult or even impossible to fight the current upstream back to Gonzalo's camp. Orellana had yielded to this argument, and it had been decided to keep going downstream, perhaps to the land of gold, maybe all the way to the Atlantic. When Sanchez de Vargas protested that this was a shameful dereliction, Orellana had marooned him in the jungle, abandoning him to probable death.

Gonzalo Pizarro was stunned. He denounced Orellana bitterly for his treason. No one in the camp spoke of El Dorado now. The expedition had become a disaster. The Spaniards wished merely to find some way out of this boundless, roadless, directionless jungle and return to Quito.

4

The real motives of Francisco de Orellana have been debated with intensity for more than four hundred years. Many of the Spanish chroniclers had violent words for him. To Agustín de Zárate, whose history of the discovery of Peru was published in 1554, Orellana was "a mutineer and a rebel." Oviedo offers without qualification Gonzalo Pizarro's own accusation that "Francisco de Orellana had shown the greatest cruelty that any faithless man could indulge in." Pedro Pizarro, in a work published in 1639, called it "one of the greatest iniquities of this kind that ever happened in that land, failing to keep faith with his relative, captain, and friend." [68] Later historians maintained the same tone; Prescott called Orellana's deed "repugnant both to humanity and honor," and later in the nineteenth century, the Spanish scholar Marcos Jiménez de la Espada published a study of Orellana under the title, *The Treason of a One-Eyed Man*.

This last work motivated the Chilean geographer José

Toribio Medina to make a thorough study of the documents of the Orellana voyage, relying not on chroniclers but on the writings of the men who had been with Orellana. In 1894, Toribio Medina produced an elaborate rehabilitation of Orellana's reputation which is accepted by many students today as the final word on the events. Since it is founded on the statements of men who were eager to avoid the charge that they had been traitors, it is still open to objections, but generally modern historians are inclined not to be as harsh on Orellana as their predecessors were.

The last that Gonzalo saw of Orellana and his brigantine was the day after Christmas, 1541. In three days the power of the rushing river had brought the vessel to the Coca-Napo confluence—according to Sanchez de Varga. Probably a more reliable authority is the diarist of Orellana's voyage, the hearty, indomitable Fray Gaspar de Carvajal. This sturdy friar, born in the same Estremaduran town that produced the Pizarros, was the chaplain of Gonzalo's expedition, and boarded the brigantine apparently to bring divine favor to the search for food. He was thirty-eight years old and a man of great physical strength. Like many priests of the conquest, Fray Gaspar was not averse to wielding a sword himself in times of peril.

His account of the river journey first appeared in Oviedo's *Historia general de las Indias*, which did not see print in its entirety until 1851, three centuries after it was written. Thus the Carvajal text was not available to Prescott or any of the earlier historians. A more extensive manuscript of Carvajal was published for the first time by Toribio Medina in his book of 1894, and translated into English in 1934.

According to Carvajal, the brigantine had gone downstream for nine days before halting a short distance below the confluence. Orellana had little food on board. Such provisions as remained had been left at Gonzalo's camp, since it was expected that the brigantine shortly would be at a place where food could be obtained. On the second day out, a jutting treetrunk nearly ended the expedition at once, but repairs were made to the brigantine's battered hull. Three days later, with no settlements yet in sight, the food was exhausted, and the men began to eat shoes and hides. On the first day of 1542 they thought they heard the drums of a nearby settlement, but it was nowhere in view, and the next night Fray Carvajal contributed the flour he had saved for the Host of the mass to the dinner supply. The drums were heard again after the confluence was passed. On January 3, the brigantine rounded a bend in the river and an Indian village came into view.

The Spaniards went ashore; the Indians fled, leaving a meal that had just been prepared, and the hungry explorers dined on it. Cautiously the natives returned. Orellana, who was a remarkable linguist, addressed them in a language they understood, telling them to have no fear. (According to Carvajal, Orellana "always made it a point to get to understand the tongues of the natives and made his own elementary primers for his guidance; and God endowed him with a good memory and excellent natural aptitude. . . ." [69]) Orellana contrived to win the confidence of the Indians. They brought him meat, fish, partridges, and wild turkeys, and informed him that he had come to the village of Aparia, ruled by a chief of the same name. In the name of Gonzalo Pizarro and Charles V, Orellana took formal possession of the village, probably without employing his linguistic skills to let the natives know what he was saying.

Now Orellana began to collect the provisions given him by the natives of Aparia to take upstream to Gonzalo Pizarro, in accordance with his orders. His men began to mutter that it was impossible to go upstream on the speeding river in the brigantine. Sensing mutiny, Orellana tried to persuade some of them to make the trip in canoes, but they declined even to do that. On January 4, he was presented with a petition in the elegant hand of the expedition's notary, signed by forty-nine men, with the name of Friar Gaspar de Carvajal heading the list. It began:

"We, the cavaliers and hidalgos and priests who are here with this expeditionary force with Your Worship, having become aware of Your Worship's determination to go up the river over the course down which we came with Your Worship, and having seen that it is an impossible thing to go back up to where Your Worship left Gonzalo Pizarro, our Governor, without risking the lives of us all. . . . Therefore we beseech Your Worship, and we beg him and summon him, not to take us with him back up the river." The petitioners piously added, "We hereby exonerate ourselves from the charge of being traitors or even men disobedient to the service of the King in not following Your Worship on this journey." [70]

It was a politely phrased document, but it carried a steely tone. On the following day, Orellana issued a written reply granting the petitioners their request, saying, "inasmuch as it was impossible to go back up the river again, he was ready, although against his desire, to look for another route to bring them out to a port of rescue." [71] In another decree he ordered that anyone who had in his possession clothing or other objects belonging to the men left behind in Pizarro's camp should bring them to him, under pain of being punished for theft. All these wordy documents, and a good many besides, were carefully preserved by Orellana and are still in existence in the Spanish archives; obviously he expected to have to answer eventually for his abandonment of Gonzalo, and wished to bolster his case with as much in the way of formal backing as possible. (Orellana's detractors maintain that he needed no coaxing at all to give up the upstream attempt, and had all the petitions drawn as self-serving evidence for future use.)

Once it was resolved, Orellana made ready to leave Aparia. Nothing is said about the marooning of Sanchez de Varga in Carvajal's account. Carvajal simply says that Orellana offered a thousand gold *castellanos* to any men who would go upstream to tell Gonzalo what had been resolved, and that three men had volunteered, but apparently never actually set out. Toribio Medina was unable to find the story of the marooned officer in any of the primary documents of the voyage, which is not terribly surprising if Vargas had indeed been left behind because he objected to taking part in an act of treason. The earliest reference to Vargas that could be traced was in Garcilaso's chronicle, written many years after the journey. "I do not know where Garcilaso could have got this piece of pure invention," Toribio Medina wrote,[72] but there is no certainty that the Vargas story was an invention.

The Spaniards began to build a second brigantine at Aparia. In twenty days they had a supply of nails and other materials, but chose to postpone the actual construction until later in their trip. They left Aparia on February 2 and started downstream, calling at various Indian villages and obtaining turtles, parrots, and other provisions. On February 11, the Napo debouched into an even larger river. Orellana had reached the Amazon.

It was not then called by that name. Those who had explored the gigantic river at its mouth knew it as the Marañon, from the Spanish word *marañas*, "entanglements"—a reference to the impediments found in the river. It was also called *El Mar Dulce*, "the freshwater sea," although that name was usually reserved for the Río de la Plata farther to the south. For several weeks they enjoyed a pleasant cruise down the Marañon, greeted hospitably by the inhabitants of the villages on its banks, and at the end of the month they landed at a large and particularly friendly village to con struct the second brigantine. This task kept them busy until late in April, when they entered the river once more.

"From here on," says Padre Carvajal, "we endured more hardships and more hunger and passed through more uninhabited regions than before, because the river led from one wooded section to another wooded section and we found no place to sleep and much less could any fish be caught, so that it was necessary for us to keep to our customary fare, which consisted of herbs and every now and then a bit of roasted corn." [73] But on May 12 they arrived at the villages of a region called Machiparo, of which they had learned in Aparia.

Here the welcome was less friendly. The Indians attacked before the Spaniards had had a chance to dry their gunpowder; unable to use their terrifying arquebuses, they relied on crossbows to drive the natives back. Eighteen Spaniards were wounded as they fought their way ashore to raid the turtle-pens for food. Night fell, with the brigantines surrounded by hostile Indians in canoes, and in the morning the Spaniards found that they were in the midst of a heavily populated section of the river. For two days and two nights they battled downstream through Machiparo, whose villages were nearly continuous for eighty leagues. Said Carvajal, "There was one settlement that stretched for five leagues without there intervening any space from house to house, which was a marvelous thing to behold: as we were only passing by and fleeing, we had no opportunity to learn what there was in the country inland; but, judged from its resources and appearance, it must be the most populous that has been seen, and this was just what the Indians of the province of Aparia had told us that it was, that there was a very great overlord in the interior towards the south, whose name was Ica, and that this latter possessed very great wealth in gold and silver; and this piece of information we considered to be very reliable and exact." [74]

Carvajal's "piece of information" never engendered a quest for El Dorado south of the Amazon, despite its vouched-for reliability and exactness. Having passed gratefully out of the country of Machiparo, Orellana's voyagers now entered the territory of the Omagua Indians, and here, though they did not suspect it, was the region where El Dorado was shortly going to be hunted by a new generation of questers. Carvajal helped to fire this quest with his description of an Omagua village:

"There was a villa in which there was a great deal of porcelain ware of various makes, both jars and pitchers, very large . . . and other small pieces such as plates and bowls and candelabra of this porcelain of the best that has ever been seen in this world, for that of Málaga is not its equal, because it is all glazed and embellished with all colors, and so bright that they astonish. . . . And here the Indians told us that as much as there was made out of clay in this house, so much was there back in the country in gold and silver." [75]

Orellana and a few men went inland in search of the gold of Omagua, and, Carvajal relates, "he had not gone half a league when the roads became more like royal highways and wider; and, when the Captain had perceived this, he decided to turn back, because he saw that it was not prudent to go on any farther; and so he did return to where the brigantines were, and when he got back the sun was now going down, and the Captain said to the companions that it would be well to depart at once from there, because it was not wise to sleep at night in a land so thickly populated." [76] El Dorado of the Omaguas, lying north of the Amazon, thus was left for other seekers.

A hundred leagues beyond the Omagua country was the country of Paguana, where the natives were friendly, and on June 3 the brigantines discovered the mouth of the Río Negro, the great river which links the Orinoco and Amazon basins. The Negro emptied into the Amazon from the north, and its water, writes Carvajal, "was black as ink, and for this reason we gave it the name of Río Negro, which river flowed so abundantly and with such violence that for more than twenty leagues it formed a streak down through the other water, the one not mixing with the other."

A few days afterward, the voyagers called at a village that had a curious structure in its main plaza. This was a tree trunk ten feet in diameter, on which the image of a walled city had been carved in high relief. Two fierce jaguars were shown upholding the city, and there was a hole in the hollowed core of the trunk through which offerings of *chicha*, the native wine, were poured during religious ceremonies. Like tourists inspecting the cathedrals of a foreign land, the Spaniards inquired after the uses of the shrine, which Carvajal called "a thing well worth seeing." The Indians amiably informed them that it was sacred to a certain race of warrior women who ruled this entire district. The people of the town were tributaries of these warlike women, and, in Carvajal's words, "the only service which they rendered them consisted in supplying them with plumes of parrots and macaws for the linings of the roofs of the buildings which constitute their places of worship . . . and that they had that thing there as a reminder, and that they worshipped it as a thing which was the emblem of their mistress, who is the one who rules over all the land of the aforesaid women." [77]

Orellana was about to discover the Amazons.

5

Fed on their romantic novels, the *conquistadores* were always ready to find the wonders of epic narratives coming forth in real life here in the South American jungles.

Calafia, Queen of the Amazons, was familiar to any man who had read *Sergas de Esplandián*, and Orellana's men must have known that romance well. It did not startle them at all to find a tribe of Amazons now.

The legend of the Amazons had a lengthy pedigree. Herodotus was one of the first to write of them, placing them in Pontus near the shore of the Euxine Sea, and describing their raids against Scythia, Thrace, and the coasts of Asia Minor. No men were permitted to dwell in their country, though once a year the warrior women visited a neighboring nation for purposes of procreation, slaying all male children or returning them to their fathers, and recruiting the baby girls. Their name allegedly came from the Greek *a-mazos*, "without breast," from their custom of amputating the right breast to make the drawing of the bow more convenient, but a variety of other derivations have been put forward.

Down through the Middle Ages the story of the Amazons descended along with all the other accumulated mythology of a credulous era, and by a natural process was transplanted to the New World. Columbus mentioned encountering bellicose women in the West Indies, but the real excitement over Amazons began after the publication of *Sergas*, with its account of Queen Calafia of California, about 1510. The romance went into many editions and is known to have been among the favorite reading of the *conquistadores*. One of the first Spaniards to land on the shore of Yucatán heard mention of Amazons in 1518. Cortés, when he invaded Mexico in the following year, was under official instructions to learn "where and in what direction are the Amazons." [78] The warrior women were pursued as assiduously as El Dorado later would be, and for generally the same psychological reasons. They were sought in western Mexico, in Central America, and in many other places, the explorers often persuading themselves that they had found the women they had come to find. In 1533, a rumor rocketed through Spain that seventy large vessels had docked in the Spanish ports of Santander and Laredo, "bringing ten thousand Amazon women who had come to mate with Spaniards because of the reputation for valor and virility of our men. The arrangement was that any Amazon who became pregnant would give fifteen ducats to the man concerned for his work, and she would remain to give birth. If the offspring were males, the Amazons would leave them here: if female, they would carry them away." [79] Alas, there was no substance to the report.

Juan de San Martín, one of Quesada's lieutenants in the conquest of New Granada, transferred the Amazons to the vicinity of Cundinamarca, and tacked a vestige of the El Dorado story to them for good measure by describing them as "very rich in gold." He wrote, "While in camp here in this valley of Bogotá we got news of a tribe of women who live by themselves without men among them, for which reason we called them Amazons. They become pregnant by certain slaves which they buy and if they bear males, they send them to their fathers; if females, they rear them. It is said that these women only use the slaves for becoming pregnant, after which they send them away and so, from time to time, they summon them and dismiss them. . . . [Quesada] sent his brother with some mounted men and others on foot to see if what the Indians told us was true. He could not reach these women because of the mountain ranges in the way, though he came within three or four days' journey, getting more and more news that they existed. . . ." [80]

The concept of Amazons was thus neatly linked to that other *desideratum*, a nation that possessed an abundance of gold. When Orellana's men heard that they were entering the realm of the Amazons, then, the sudden hope infected them that this strange journey might yet bring them to El

Dorado, which they had left Quito to discover some sixteen months before.

As they approached the Amazons, the voyagers found the Indians increasingly hostile. The river now was enormously wide, so that as they coasted one bank they could make out the opposite bank only as a dark line on the horizon, and the many villages along this huge waterway were inhabited by fierce and aggressive natives. When necessary to replenish food stores, Orellana pulled the brigantines in at one of these villages and stormed it, sometimes meeting with hot resistance. Carvajal's journal is a record of such landings and battles.

Sometimes there was no landing, as on June 22, when "we saw a great deal of inhabited country on the left shore. . . . We were going down the middle of the river; we wanted to go over there, but we could not because of the heavy current and the rougher waves, and there were more than at sea." [81] The next day a great deal of food was taken at a village not far downstream, and the day after that, Carvajal wrote, "We were proceeding on our way searching for a peaceful spot to celebrate and to gladden the feast of the blessed Saint John the Baptist, herald of Christ, when God willed that, on rounding a bend which the river made, we should see on the shore ahead many villages, and very large ones, which shone white. Here we came suddenly upon the excellent land and dominion of the Amazons." [82]

The natives had been forewarned, and came out in canoes "in no friendly mood" to meet the Spaniards. Orellana spoke to them, but they mocked his words and shouted back that they were going to seize the intruders and take them to the Amazons. The captain ordered his men to open fire with crossbows and arquebuses. The Indians gave way, and the brigantines approached shore so provisions could be gathered. "As we began to come in close to land," wrote

Carvajal, "the Indians started to defend their village and to shoot arrows at us, and as the fighters were in great numbers it seemed as if it rained arrows; but our arquebusiers and crossbowmen were not idle, because they did nothing but shoot, and although they killed many, they [the Indians] did not become aware of this, for in spite of the damage that was being done to them they kept it up, some fighting and others dancing: and here we all came very close to perishing." [83] The priest himself was struck by an arrow, but his thick clothing protected him from harm. Orellana led his men to the shore and onto the beach, and the engagement of arms lasted more than an hour.

The Indian warriors defending the village were men; but, says Carvajal, during the course of the battle the natives sent for the help of the Amazons whose subjects they were, and a dozen or so of these warlike women came to rally the defenders. "We ourselves saw these women, who were there fighting in front of all the Indian men as women captains," testifies Carvajal, "and these latter fought so courageously that the Indian men did not dare to turn their backs, and anyone who did turn his back they killed with clubs right there before us, and this is the reason why the Indians kept up their defense for so long." [84]

Carvajal's description of the Amazons is the most celebrated and the most controversial passage of his narrative:

"These women are very white and tall, and have hair very long and braided and wound about the head, and they are very robust and go about naked, with their privy parts covered, with their bows and arrows in their hand, doing as much fighting as ten Indian men, and indeed there was one woman among these who shot an arrow a span deep into one of the brigantines, and others less deep, so that our brigantines looked like porcupines." [85]

The Spaniards killed seven or eight of the Amazons,

breaking the back of the native resistance; but as reinforcements began to arrive from other villages, Orellana ordered
a hasty retreat. The brigantines got under way just as a
great fleet of canoes appeared. Orellana's battle-weary men
were too tired to row, so they simply let the swift current
carry them along. With them came a prisoner of war, an
Indian trumpeter about thirty years old, and Orellana at
once began to practice his linguistic skills on him in an
attempt to learn more about the empire of the Amazons.

Since no food had been obtained at the last landing, the
brigantines halted at the next village down the river, which
seemed to be unoccupied. Orellana reluctantly let a party of
foragers go ashore, Carvajal among them. Squadrons of
Indians lay in ambush; as the landing party approached
shore, the hidden warriors burst forward, launching a
shower of arrows. Most of these thumped harmlessly into
the shields of the Spaniards, but, Carvajal relates, "out of all
they hit no one but me, for they planted an arrow shot right
in one of my eyes, in such a way that the arrow went
through to the other side, from which wound I lost the eye
and [even now] am not without suffering and not free from
pain, although Our Lord, without my deserving it, has been
kind enough to grant me life so that I may mend my ways
and serve Him better than I had done hitherto. . . ." [86] The
one-eyed captain, Orellana, now had a one-eyed chronicler,
but Carvajal's wound did not hinder him from taking an
active part in the remaining adventures of the river journey.

Once again the Spaniards were forced to retreat without collecting provisions. The land, they saw, was fertile,
with groves of oak and rolling savannahs, and Carvajal,
citing the temperate climate, envisioned it planted over with
wheat. But it was impossible to make a landing now, and the
brigantines hewed to the middle of the river, zigzagging

from time to time to avoid the attacks of native canoes. They halted for the night at an island that appeared uninhabited, but did not go ashore.

The next day, June 25, 1542, the brigantines entered a maze of channel islands that likewise appeared uninhabited. Abruptly some two hundred large native vessels appeared, each carrying twenty to forty Indians. The boats were painted in gay colors, and those who manned them carried trumpets and drums, pipes, and stringed instruments, "and they came on with so much noise and shouting and in such good order that we were astonished," says Carvajal. "They surrounded our two brigantines and attacked us like men who expected to carry us off; but it resulted in just the reverse for them, for our arquebusiers and crossbowmen made it so uncomfortable for them that, many as they were, they were glad to stand off." [87] The brigantines passed through the islands and on into the open river again. Tired and hungry as they were, the Spaniards were gladdened by the obvious fertility of the district, for they were already envisioning a new empire here.

The thickly populated villages were too dangerous to enter, though, and the best the Spaniards could do was attempt to barter by putting beads and bangles into a gourd and throwing it into the water, hoping that the Indians who endlessly trailed them in canoes would take the hint and bring food in exchange. But the natives mocked at Orellana's merchandise and answered with volleys of arrows.

Stopping for the night at a quiet place between villages, Orellana found time to question his captive trumpeter about the nature of the region. He learned that a chief named Couynco ruled over all the villages for a hundred fifty leagues along the river here, but that Couynco was subject to the Amazons, who lived in the interior of the country, a seven-day journey from the river. Orellana was told that the Amazons were unmarried, and occupied some seventy villages which his informant had often visited while bringing tribute. The houses in these villages were built of stone, the Indian said, and a network of toll roads linked the Amazon settlements. How, Orellana asked, did these women perpetuate themselves, if they had no husbands? The answer he received might have come straight from Herodotus, and indeed is so close to the classical legend that one must suspect Orellana's comprehension of the native speech was colored somewhat by his knowledge of the established Amazon traditions:

"These Indian women consorted with Indian men at times," Carvajal declares the native told Orellana, "and, when that desire came to them, they assembled a great horde of warriors and went off to make war on a very great overlord whose residence is not far from that of these women, and by force they brought them to their own country and kept them with them for the time that suited their caprice, and after they found themselves pregnant they sent them back to their country without doing them any harm; and afterwards, when the time came for them to have children, if they gave birth to male children, they killed them and sent them to their fathers, and, if female children, they raised them with great solemnity and instructed them in the arts of war." [88]

Predictably, Orellana learned that these Amazons— like most mysterious Indians who lived just beyond view— were rich in gold and silver. The eating utensils of the noble Amazons were of these metals, although plebeians made do with wood and clay; in the principal Amazon city were five large temples sacred to the sun, in which were kept "many gold and silver idols in the form of women, and many vessels of gold and silver for the service of the sun." [89] The women wore coronets and crowns of gold, and rode on the backs of "camels"—an echo again of Peru's llamas. Two saltwater lakes gave them a lucrative supply of salt. "He related," says Carvajal, "that when the sun went down no male Indian was to remain in all of these cities, but that any such must depart and go to his country; he said in addition that many Indian provinces bordering on them were held in subjection by them and made to pay tribute and to serve them." [90]

Only in one major respect did Orellana's Amazons differ from the Amazons of antiquity: "These women that we are dealing with here, although they do use the bow, do not cut off their breasts nor do they burn them off," Carvajal noted, and so it was etymologically improper to call them "Amazons," as he admitted, for " 'Amazon' in the Greek language means: 'having no breasts.' " Yet Carvajal felt that it was fair to call these women Amazons anyway, since in other respects they lived as did those to whom the ancients gave that name.

Except for the dozen who fought against them at the shore, the Spaniards never actually claimed to have seen the Amazons on this voyage, and later explorers in the region were unable to find their empire. The Spanish chroniclers of the following century, who were so critical of Orellana's "treachery," regarded his claims of having found Amazons as unreliable, pointing out that among many tribes of the West Indies and the mainland it was no new thing for the women to fight alongside the men, but that was not quite the same as postulating a sovereign state of women. In 1844, Sir Robert Schomburgk, a British traveller and geographer, explored the district where Carvajal said the Amazons were to be found, and detected no trace of them, though the persistence of the story among the Indians of the Amazon basin has led many reputable anthropologists to suggest the likelihood of a female-dominated culture in the area at some earlier time, possibly even surviving into the present in one of the many unexplored recesses of the wilderness.

In the morning the Spaniards departed, hoping to leave the settled country behind and find a place where they could rest from their hardships. Soon they were in a new province, but as thickly populated as the last. Its people, who came out in canoes to attack, were extremely tall, taller even than the Spaniards, and wore their hair clipped short. They fought with their bodies stained black, which led Orellana to name this part of the basin *Provincia de los Negros*, "the province of the black men." The Spaniards were unable to land. According to their prisoner, these people were subject to a great overlord named Arripuna, whose country was rich in gold and silver and whose habits were cannibalistic.

Finally, two days later, the Spaniards effected a landing at a small village, captured it, and loaded the brigantines with all the corn they could hold. One of Orellana's men was killed by a poisoned arrow here, the first fatality since the beginning of the voyage. Another man was similarly slain in a battle several days afterward. But there was one cheering element: the rise and fall of oceanic tides could now be detected, and the voyagers knew they were not far from the sea.

The scenery was changing. For some weeks they had passed through a high savannah country, relatively cool and pleasant. Now they entered into hot, low country, and the river was broken by many islands. Orellana turned the brigantines into the channels of these islands, and never again in the trip did they reach the mainland shore on either side. They raided the villages of the islands when possible; but the prolonged effects of undernourishment had weakened them and undermined their judgment as seamen, and at high tide one evening the smaller brigantine was carelessly steered over a hidden log that smashed through the hull and swamped the boat. At once, Indians appeared from the woods. They were driven off, but by then the tide had ebbed and the damaged brigantine was left on its side, while the other was trapped on a shoal. Orellana divided his forces, half to stand off the Indians and half to try to float the smaller brigantine. He and Carvajal and another priest watched over the grounded larger brigantine. Luck was with them; the Indians did not attack again, the damaged brigantine was righted and patched, and the larger vessel was pushed free of the shoal.

For eighteen days they made port at an uninhabited island to repair the smaller brigantine, making nails and strengthening the battered hull. Food ran so low that the corn ration was counted out in individual grains. But, as Carvajal puts it, "once again, while we were in the midst of this suffering, Our Lord manifested the special care which He was exercising over us sinners." A dead tapir the size of a mule came floating down the river; Orellana sent a few men in a canoe to bring it in, and they fed on its meat for nearly a week. "The tapir had been dead for only a short time," Carvajal reports, "because it was warm and it had no wound whatsoever on it." [91] They supplemented their diet with snails and crabs.

On August 8 they were on their way again. The brigantines were in shaky condition, but the repairs insured that they would last until the sea was reached, barring further mishaps. Now the sails could be used, and the brigantines tacked from side to side, using stones as anchors whenever the tide grew too violent. Sometimes the strength of the tide was such that the boats were dragged upstream as far in an hour as they had come downstream in a whole day, the stone anchors bumping impotently along the bottom as the little vessels were pulled inland. But the brigantines somehow withstood these buffetings, and the Indians near the mouth of the river were generally docile, making no show of resistance when the Spaniards came ashore for food.

Now the sea was near. The voyagers had no pilot, no compass, no navigation charts. They prepared to navigate at sea wherever fortune might guide them and cast them. Before leaving the river, they halted for final repairs on the rigging of the boats. On August 26, they passed at dawn through the mouth of the Amazon. "This mouth of the river, from cape to cape, is four leagues wide," Carvajal relates, "and we saw other wider mouths than the one through which we went out to sea; and to the minds of experienced men, and in view of the pattern of the many islands and gulfs and bays which the river formed fifty leagues back before we got out of it, it was quite evident that there remained other mouths to the right as we came down, on which side we encountered a heavier and rougher sea, although it was fresh water, than over the whole distance that we later traversed in salt water." [92]

The weather was fortunately calm as the small vessels sailed past the large island of Marajó and into the Atlantic. For four days they travelled together, hugging the coast on a northward journey toward the Venezuelan settlement at Cubagua. On the night of August 29 they became separated, and did not find one another again until the end of the voyage. Carvajal's brigantine was driven by storm into the Gulf of Paria, which he calls "the Mouths of the Dragon," and for seven days a contrary wind kept the boat penned there, "so strong that it would make us lose in one hour what we had won in a whole day." [93] During those seven days the men manned the oars day and night without ceasing. Reaching the open sea again at last, they made for Cubagua, where they arrived on September 11, two days after the smaller brigantine had reached the same port. "So great was the joy which we felt, the ones at the sight of the others, that I shall not be able to express it," declares Carvajal, "because they considered us to be lost and we them." [94]

After a few months of rest and recuperation among the pearlfishers of Cubagua, Orellana and his men put to sea again, bound now for Spain to tell their tale to the Emperor Charles V. Orellana had a great deal to tell, for he had successfully concluded one of history's most astounding voyages of exploration, a complete traversal of the world's mightiest river from source to mouth. He had found a new inland empire potentially far more wealthy than Mexico or Peru, and he hoped to be confirmed by the Emperor as governor of this vast domain. Not incidentally, Orellana also knew that he was vulnerable to charges of having betrayed and abandoned Gonzalo Pizarro, and he was eager to set his case before the court to forestall any hostile account of his actions. He chartered a ship in Trinidad and with some of his closest companions reached Santo Domingo on November 22, 1542. Carvajal remained behind to recover from the loss of his eye, and did not go to Spain at all, returning instead to Peru, where he took part in the civil wars, then adopted a more properly clerical way of life, and ultimately became Archbishop of Lima.

Orellana remained in Santo Domingo long enough to tell his story to the historian Oviedo, who later wrote to Padre Carvajal in Lima and secured a copy of his journal. Had Oviedo's book, with its interpolated text of Carvajal, been published when it was written, Orellana's subsequent place in the history of exploration might have been less tainted by charges of treason. As it was, Oviedo's manuscript was published only in part, and Orellana was denounced furiously until the nineteenth century, when his side of the story was made public.

Damage to his ship during the Atlantic crossing forced

Orellana to land in Portugal. He was detained there by the King for several weeks, telling of his adventure and fending off invitations to enter Portuguese service. By May of 1543 Orellana was at the Spanish court. His reception there was cooler than he had expected, for the Emperor feared that most of the territory Orellana had explored belonged rightfully to Portugal by the division of the world under Pope Alexander VI. Certainly the mouth of the Marañon was clearly Portuguese, and the river that Orellana called the Amazon was indisputably the same as the Marañon. The Emperor's secretary was of the belief that Orellana's discovery was of no use to Spain.

Nevertheless, Orellana was asked to file a detailed report on his voyage, which he did, claiming the royal favor to colonize the new land. After lengthy discussion the Council of the Indies ruled that it would indeed be advantageous to Spain to take this land, since it did not appear to lie in the Portuguese sector, and moreover France was thought to be looking covetously toward that part of South America. On February 13, 1544, Orellana was granted the governorship of Spain's Amazonian province, which was called New Andalusia. His articles of agreement absolved him of any blame in the abandonment of Gonzalo Pizarro, citing his laudable intent to return upstream if it had been possible to do so. He was permitted to build two towns along the Amazon and to conquer and settle the region south from the river for two hundred leagues. (The land north of the river was thought to belong to the Welsers under their grant of Venezuela, for the extent of the distance between the Amazon and the northern coast was not yet comprehended.)

The Emperor, though, did not choose to contribute toward the financing of Orellana's colonization of New Andalusia, though he was willing to present the explorer with resonant titles, *adelantado* and governor and captain-general. Monetary difficulties kept the not very wealthy Orellana from launching his expedition for many months. The date of departure was postponed again and again, while Orellana found himself mired in ever-deepening bogs of political and fiscal trouble, but at length a rich relative came to his aid and some ships were purchased and equipped. Orellana's woes were increased when word came that the King of Portugal was preparing an expedition "for the Great River and the province of the Amazons," [95] in the belief that the new land lay in his own sector of the line of demarcation. The Council of the Indies recommended to Charles V that assistance be rendered to get Orellana out to sea ahead of Portugal, but the Emperor still stayed his hand. In desperation Orellana slashed through the final obstacles with his final resources, and on May 11, 1545, after an infinity of delays, he sailed with four ships carrying several hundred colonists, including his own wife. Economies practiced all along the way had left the fleet ill-equipped for the conquest of New Andalusia.

For three months Orellana anchored in the Canary Islands, hoping to bring his ships up to minimal standards, to recruit more colonists, and to obtain the provisions that he still lacked. The stay was a disaster; an epidemic ran through his people, and nearly a hundred died. One ship was abandoned. When the fleet was considered ready to set sail, three of Orellana's ablest captains and fifty of his soldiers remained behind, some because they were too sick to continue the voyage, some because they had forebodings of catastrophe.

The forebodings were justified. The crossing of the ocean was hellish; water ran low, and only providential rainstorms kept them all from dying of thirst. One of the ships, carrying seventy-seven colonists, eleven horses, and a brigantine that was to go up the river, was lost at sea. After some problems of navigation, the two other vessels reached the Brazilian coast and found the fresh water that told them they were near the Amazon. On December 20, 1545, the ships made port in the mouth of the river, having nearly been wrecked on shoals as they entered. The men were tired and the river was in flood, but this was a country that Orellana knew well, and he was impatient to begin its conquest. He took his ships a hundred leagues up the river and halted for three months to build a new brigantine, tearing one of the ships apart for its nails and planking. In March, the brigantine was ready. Orellana sent it up the river for food; the dogs and horses had already been eaten, and fifty-seven men had perished since the landing. Indians repelled the landing parties; the brigantine returned with heavy losses; and Orellana made the unsettling discovery that he was not even on the main arm of the river, but along some unexplored limb of the complex estuary.

The brigantine and the remaining ship set out together to find the main arm. Almost at once the ship was driven by the tide onto an island, and wrecked. Orellana left some thirty of his men on the island and went forth with the rest in the brigantine seeking the main arm. After nearly a month of futile wandering he returned to the island, and found his men gone. They had given up hope and built a leaky boat, and after many adventures upstream in search of Orellana had decided to return to the coast. The survivors of this group managed to get out to sea and piloted their boat along the coast for hundreds of miles, arriving in December, 1546, at the island of Margarita near Trinidad.

There they met about two dozen of their companions, those who had gone with Orellana in the brigantine. Orellana's wife was among them, but she was now Orellana's widow. As one member of the party reported, "She told us that her husband had not succeeded in getting into the main

branch which he was looking for, and consequently, on account of his being ill, he had made up his mind to come to a
land of Christians: and during this time, when he was out
looking for food for the journey, the Indians shot seventeen
of his men with arrows: From grief over this and from his
illness Orellana died. . . ." [96]

Seeking El Dorado, Francisco de Orellana found instead the mightiest of rivers. But his discovery brought him
only an early death and centuries of infamy.

6

During those months in 1542 when Orellana, Carvajal,
and their companions were making their river journey of
nearly two thousand miles across South America, Gonzalo
Pizarro and his abandoned followers still wandered hopelessly in the rain forest of northern Peru. They had no
inkling of the direction to take to reach civilization. The best
they could hope to do was to work their way upstream along
the Napo in the faith that it would bring them perhaps to
Quito or perhaps to one of the cities of the south that the
Spaniards held, such as Cuzco or Lima.

Pizarro sent his most experienced scout, Gonzalo Díaz
de Pineda, ahead up the river with a few men in two canoes
lashed together. Each night Pineda lit a fire to signal his
location, and Pizarro followed with his main force. They
continued in this fashion for more than a hundred fifty
miles, Pizarro by land and Pineda by river. Their only food
was wild fruit and the edible root yuca, which they had
brought from the plantation near the confluence of the Napo
and Coca. Since the land was uninhabited, it seemed that
they would certainly die of hunger once their supply of yuca
was exhausted.

Pineda discovered a village, though, where he obtained
a little food. Cutting marks on trees for Pizarro to see, he

went upriver beyond the village, and in the clear dawn beheld a range of mountains in the distance, which he thought might be the *cordillera* of Quito, or possibly the mountains north of Quito near the cities of Popayán and Cali. After eleven days of exploring this region Pineda went downstream to rejoin Pizarro, a trip that took a day and a half. He found the main party in severe straits. Hunger had taken several of Pizarro's men. Only two dogs remained uneaten, those belonging to Pizarro and his lieutenant Antonio Rivera. Most of the horses were gone. But the marchers were cheered by Pineda's news of a village ahead, and high mountains in the distance, and the possibility of a road that would lead to some land where Christians dwelled.

They followed the path Pineda had blazed up the river. As they neared the Indian village, Pizarro sent nineteen of his men to get food. They fought their way in, bursting upon the Indians like malevolent demons and putting them to flight. The rest of the Spaniards entered and rested there a while before resuming their trek. Their route, they were gradually discovering, was only a short distance to the north of the path they had taken on their outward journey. In June, 1542, just about the time that Orellana's men were engaging in combat with the Amazons, Pizarro led his footsore force into the small village at the edge of the cinnamon country where his enterprise had stayed the year before. The Indians received them in friendly fashion and gave them food.

"In talking to the Indians," Cieza de León writes, "it was found that there was a shorter way to Quito by another track, not the one they had followed, so they determined to take it. But on this track they met with several broad and very deep rivers, so that they were obliged to make bridges over some of them. Journeying in this way they came to a river which was so rapid that it took them four days to make a bridge; and whilst keeping watch at night, lest the Indians should come and attack them by surprise, they saw a great comet traversing the heavens. In the morning Gonzalo Pizarro said that, in his dreams, a dragon came and plucked out his heart, and tore it to pieces with his cruel teeth. He then sent for one Jerónimo de Villegas, who was held to be something of an astrologer, to ask him what he thought of it. He is said to have answered that Pizarro would find that the object he most prized was dead." [97]

So it befell; for while Gonzalo had wandered through the jungle pursuing the elusive phantom of El Dorado, assassins had slain his brother and his idol, the Governor-General of Peru, Francisco Pizarro. A message had been sent into the cinnamon country, bringing tidings of the revolution to Gonzalo, but the word had not reached him, and so the first tidings that he had of his brother's overthrow came when he entered Quito in August of 1542.

The return of Gonzalo Pizarro was a pathetic and moving sight. Agustín de Zárate, a Spanish official who witnessed it, wrote that "All, the general as well as the officers and men, were nearly naked, their clothes having been rotted by the constant rains and torn besides, so that their only covering consisted of the skins of animals worn in front and behind, and a few caps of the same material. . . . Their swords were without sheaths, and all eaten up with rust. Their feet were bare and wounded by thorns and roots, and they were so wan and wasted that one could no longer recognize them." [98]

This army of the walking dead numbered little more than a hundred. The thousands of Indians that had set out with the magnificent expedition early in 1541 had perished; the swine were gone, as were the dogs, the horses, and the llamas. In a year and a half of futile and immensely strenuous exertion, Gonzalo's expedition had marched in a great circle, covering almost two thousand miles mainly on foot, discovering nothing whatever, and returning naked, empty-handed, and broken in health.

Gonzalo now learned that his brother had been dead for more than a year. The quarrel between Francisco Pizarro and the faction of the executed Diego de Almagro had exploded into insurrection. On the night of June 25, 1541, according to Cieza de León, "A sign was beheld in heaven. . . . The moon, being full and bright, presently seemed on fire, and changed color, one half of it becoming blood-red, and the other half black. Then there was seen to dart from it certain shimmerings also the color of blood."[99] On the following morning, after having gone to Sunday mass, Francisco Pizarro was dining at home with his friends when a band of Almagrist assassins burst in. The sixty-three-year-old Pizarro had no time to buckle on his armor, but seized his sword and defended himself vigorously until he was cut down.

Much had happened since then. Young Diego, Almagro's son, had been proclaimed Governor of Peru and had occupied the Inca capital of Cuzco, proclaiming a revolution and the total overthrow of the Pizarros. Meanwhile a Spanish official, Vaca de Castro, had been slowly making his way to Peru at royal command to restore order to the faction-torn land. Vaca de Castro was under orders to present himself to Francisco Pizarro and do all he could to aid him; but in the event of Pizarro's death, he was authorized to take control of Peru himself.

Upon the assassination of Pizarro, one of his loyal lieutenants notified Vaca de Castro, who immediately quickened his pace toward Peru. The royal emissary was no soldier, but a wise and honest judge whose strength of character made up for his lack of martial skills in this rough land. Arriving in Quito, Vaca de Castro announced that by the

Emperor's decree he was the successor to Francisco Pizarro, and branded young Almagro and his followers as rebels. The Spaniards of Ecuador and northern Peru accepted Vaca de Castro as governor of the realm; those in the south adhered to Almagro. When Gonzalo Pizarro came out of the jungle to learn all this, he was vastly displeased at what he considered Vaca de Castro's usurpation, for he regarded himself as his brother's heir. Vaca de Castro had already left Quito to carry the civil war to Almagro; and Gonzalo Pizarro set out after him in the hope of persuading the newcomer to relinquish his control.

However, Gonzalo's grueling jungle adventure had left him too weak to move rapidly. Vaca de Castro was proceeding through the country proclaiming himself as governor, and he had the active support of the powerful Sebastián de Belalcázar. The Spaniards of Peru were choosing sides; as soon as Almagro left Lima, that city declared for Vaca de Castro and the loyalist cause, but Cuzco remained Almagrist, and the surviving members of the Inca royal family, eager to see the Spaniards destroy each other, sent weapons and armor to the outnumbered Almagro forces. In September, the loyalists and the rebels met in battle at the valley of Chupas. The fighting was brisk and brutal. The loyalist army carried the day; many men were wounded, and nearly all of these died that night of exposure to the frost. The next day, most of young Almagro's men were executed. Almagro himself, who had slipped from the battlefield hoping to take refuge with his Inca allies, was pursued and taken, and was decapitated on the same spot where his father had been put to death four years before. Vaca de Castro took up residence in Cuzco, and for the first time since its conquest Peru had a just and honorable governor.

To him at last came Gonzalo Pizarro, riding down from Quito and letting it be known publicly that he felt he had a rightful claim to the governorship. Vaca de Castro handled the bumptious Pizarro cleverly, receiving him at the official residence of the governor, questioning him about his epic journey, and gently suggesting that he now had earned a lengthy period of rest. Gonzalo was tactfully sent into exile on his country estate before he had a chance to put into action a plot he had been hatching against his rival's life. Vaca de Castro was too suave for him, and had outmaneuvered him on every count.

Gonzalo lived in fuming impatience and in rural obscurity for several years, enjoying princely revenues and waiting for a chance to supplant Vaca de Castro. Early in 1544, a royal viceroy arrived in Peru, a knight named Blasco Nuñez Vela, whom Charles V had sent to take command after he had learned of the outcome of the civil war. That good and faithful servant Vaca de Castro was relieved of his responsibilities with little more than a letter of thanks from the Emperor. The new viceroy was a rash and foolish man, and his first official acts were so stern and arbitrary that Gonzalo Pizarro sensed the time had come to rebel. He came to Cuzco and gathered an army. Once more Peru was racked by civil war, the viceroy making his base at Lima and Gonzalo at Cuzco. By October, 1544, most of the country backed Gonzalo, and as the unpopular viceroy fled to Quito, Gonzalo entered Lima to take the oath as "Governor of Peru pending His Majesty's pleasure." The following March, Blasco Nuñez collected an army at Quito with Belalcázar's aid and began to invade Peru, but was driven back by Pizarro. When Gonzalo invaded Quito, the viceroy retreated to Popayán. In January, 1546, the two armies met; Nuñez was taken and beheaded, and Gonzalo was supreme lord of Peru.

His reign was short. For a while he was master of much of the western part of South America, and during his admin-

THE CEREMONY OF EL DORADO

Blowing gold dust on an Indian chieftain after his body has been anointed with resin.

The supposed smelting and casting of gold on the shores of Manoa.

The refining and working of gold among the Peruvian Incas.

istration the fabulous silver mines of Potosí were discovered, an event that brought more wealth to Spain than had been had from all the gold of the earlier conquests. But Gonzalo had put to death the Emperor's viceroy, an unforgivable crime, and the court sent a new official to Peru to deal with him. This was a priest, Pedro de la Gasca, a man of awkward appearance but indomitable will. He arrived quietly at Santa Marta in the summer of 1546, spread proclamations of his royal powers southward toward Peru, and by skill and determination won many supporters. He assembled an army of 2000 men, the largest force of Spaniards yet gathered in Peru, and marched against the outlaw Pizarro. In March of 1548 he advanced on Cuzco. Fear took hold of Gonzalo's men, for Gasca carried the authority of God and the Emperor. Before his troops deserted entirely, Gonzalo chose to carry the attack to the loyalists. The armies met five leagues from Cuzco. Garcilaso de la Vega, one of Gonzalo's officers and the father of the historian, defected to the enemy when he saw the size of Gasca's army, and that was the signal for a general stampede to the other side. In rage Gonzalo broke his lance against his own fleeing men. He was taken prisoner and beheaded, his estates confiscated, his mansion in Lima razed. His head was displayed in Lima bearing the label, "This is the head of the traitor Gonzalo Pizarro, who rebelled in Peru against his sovereign, and battled in the cause of tyranny and treason against the royal standard." [100] Gonzalo's downfall ended the civil wars of Peru and the reign of the Pizarro family. He was forty-two years old when he died.

Gonzalo Pizarro's meteoric career thus led solely to quick grief. Overshadowed most of his life by his older brothers, attaining high rank only by usurpation, he is best known for his wholly catastrophic venture in search of El

Dorado—and even on that his portion was nothing but suffering, while his kinsman Orellana won the immortality of a great discoverer.

7

As they followed the rushing Amazon eastward, Orellana's men had learned of the alleged golden kingdom of the Omaguas, lying north of the great river. It had seemed unwise to leave the river to search for it, but Carvajal had made a note of it in his journal, and perhaps Orellana had intended to find El Dorado of the Omaguas on his ill-starred attempt to conquer the land he called New Andalusia. Unknown to any of them, however, an expedition to the Omagua country was then under way from the north.

The death of Georg Hohemut at Coro in 1540 had left the Welser grant of Venezuela without a governor. Nicolaus Federmann applied for the job, but, as we have seen, his behavior during Hohemut's administration did not incline the Welsers to think favorably of him. Instead the post was assumed on an interim basis by Rodrigo de Bastidas, the Bishop of Santo Domingo. (He is not to be confused with the man of the same name who had founded Santa Marta in 1525.)

The Bishop arrived at Coro in November, 1540, and found the colony languishing, as well it might, since its first two governors, Ehinger and Hohemut, had spent virtually all of their time in search of El Dorado. He realized that Venezuela was in need of some dramatic coup that would make it a magnet for new colonists; and the discovery of El Dorado seemed to him the most likely way to win repute for Coro. He began to mount an expedition.

As its leader the Bishop chose Philipp von Hutten, who had accompanied Hohemut on his expedition. Hutten, a relative of the great German scholar Ulrich von Hutten, also was a kinsman of the Welsers. He was a young man, noble in bearing, idolized by his men, and far less an obsessive gold-seeker than his predecessors. He had come to South America out of the highest motive of all, pure curiosity; as he wrote to his brother, "God knows it was no lust for gold that drove me to undertake this voyage, but quite another yearning that I have had for a long time now. I know I could never have died in peace, if I had not seen the Indies first, and thus I have no regrets, nor do I wish to go back on my undertaking." [101]

On his march with Hohemut in 1535–38, Hutten had heard rumors of a golden "temple of the sun" somewhere south of Coro and east of the Colombian *cordilleras*. Hernán Pérez de Quesada, at Cundinamarca, had also heard of this El Dorado in the center of the continent, and was about to launch his unsuccessful expedition from New Granada, while in Quito Gonzalo Pizarro was gathering his forces for an eastward thrust in the same general direction. So once again many men were converging on the same goal. Hutten gloomily wrote to his brother in 1541, "We expect wars not only against the Indians but also among the Christians."

The Hutten expedition left Coro in July of 1541. Gonzalo Pizarro had begun his nightmarish adventure four months earlier; Hernán de Quesada was due to set out several months later. Hutten's party included some 200 men. One of his lieutenants was Bartholomäus Welser, the young son of the banking family's leading member. The chief adviser on the expedition was Pedro de Limpias, who had been with Federmann from 1536 to 1539. Limpias had the demonic nature of the authentic seeker of El Dorado, and served to fire the enthusiasm of the otherwise rational Hutten.

Many new small settlements now existed in Venezuela, which a decade earlier could claim only the coastal towns of

Coro, Cumaná, and Paria. Hutten went by sea to the new port of Burburata, east of Coro, and marched inland to the town of Valencia and then south to Barquisimeto, the gateway to the central plains. Then the expedition headed into the unsettled region in the south.

It was hardly unexplored territory. Federmann had come this way in 1530, Hohemut in 1535, and Federmann again in 1536. Hutten halted when the winter rainy season began, making camp at a docile Indian village that Federmann had called La Fragua and Hohemut had named Nuestra Señora. Then, swinging southwest, Hutten marched toward the borders of Ecuador. As he neared the *cordillera*, he learned from the natives that Hernán Pérez de Quesada had passed that way a short while before. The Indians warned Hutten that Quesada's southeastward route was taking him into an uninhabited and dangerous region, and tried instead to get the German to go in a northeastern direction, to the land of a powerful, wealthy tribe whose chief city was called Macatoa. Hutten was shown samples of gold formed in the shape of fruit, which were said to have come from Macatoa.

Hutten assumed that this talk of Macatoa was a deliberate fraud, and decided to follow Quesada's track, with some thought of sharing the wealth of El Dorado with him if either of them made the discovery. Quesada was moving in a vague circle, going south from Cundinamarca into the tropic heat and torrential rains of the lowlands, then striking east into the heart of the continent, and finally, as his endurance waned, veering north and west to come back to New Granada. For nearly a year Hutten marched on this track. It was a journey from nowhere to nowhere; the rains came again and drove the Venezuelans to the highlands, where no food could be found. For a time they lived on a mixture of corn and ants, using corn meal as the bait to lure the ants from their hills. Grubs and beetles were the only variations on this diet. The men sickened and their skins sprouted ulcerated sores.

Quesada eventually gave up and returned to Bogotá without ever learning that Hutten had been following him. Hutten completed his loop and found himself unwittingly coming back to the village of Nuestra Señora, his starting place of a year before. At this point, Hutten himself, given a free choice, might well have opted to call the whole exploit off and go back to Coro. He had spent a year in the wilderness to no benefit, and this clear-minded young man had probably formed some sharp opinions on the subject of El Dorado, based on the not very rewarding experiences of Ehinger, Hohemut, Federmann, Ordaz, Herrera, D'Ortal, Belalcázar, and the brothers Quesada. However, he had Pedro de Limpias among his men, and the fiery Limpias, having been frustrated in his dream of the gold of Cundinamarca, was set on remaining on the march until the authentic Dorado was in his grasp. Limpias reminded Hutten of the city of Macatoa and its alleged gold. Perhaps reluctantly, Hutten authorized an attempt to find that city.

Instead of going toward the *cordilleras* in the west, as he had done before, Hutten, accompanied by forty of his healthiest men—including Limpias—now rode toward the southeast. They came to the Río Guaviare and entered the country of the Uaupés, the tribe which had given Hohemut such trouble. Now they were friendly, and supplied the Venezuelans with venison, fish, and corn. The city of Macatoa turned out to be no myth, but the actual capital of the Uaupés—a town of about 800 people, with sturdy houses and open plazas. It was not, however, the city of boundless gold that Hutten had been led to believe.

He asked the Uaupés where gold was to be found, and the Indians obligingly told him about their rich neighbors, the Omaguas, to the south. Quareca, the Omagua monarch, was said to dwell in a magnificent palace which also served as the temple of a solar cult and was filled with massive idols of pure gold, some as large as young children, at least one the size of a full-grown woman. Besides the incalculable wealth of the main Omagua city, the Uaupés said, there were other cities rich in gold, while beyond the territory of the Omaguas lay more kingdoms of great splendor and power. No tale could have been better calculated to get Hutten's party out of the country of the Uaupés and into the realm of their neighbors.

It was now the latter part of 1542. Orellana had touched on the southern border of the Omagua country a few months earlier, and had heard the same stories of gold that Hutten now was hearing on the Omaguas' northern frontier. With his forty men Hutten crossed into Omagua territory, accompanied by a few Uaupés guides.

The Omaguas belonged to that wave of Indian invaders known generally as the Caribs which had swept outward on a career of conquest from the vicinity of modern Paraguay to take first the Amazon basin, then the province of the Orinoco, and finally the isles of the West Indies. The Carib branch that became known as the Omaguas occupied the territory along the northern shore of the Amazon for several hundred miles flanking the Río Negro confluence, and northward from there to the Río Guaviare and the land of the Uaupés. They were strong in battle and tightly organized on a tribal basis, but such civilization as they had was only elementary, perhaps consisting of little more than distorted reverberations of the distant greatness of Peru. The Jesuit Cristoval de Acuña, who visited them in 1639, reported that their name means "flatheads," from their custom of binding the heads of infants for cosmetic purposes. The missionary Samuel Fritz, who spent some thirty years among the Omaguas beginning in 1686 and left the only detailed account of these now virtually extinct Indians, wrote that "they proceed little by little to flatten the tiny heads of their young children by applying to the forehead a small board or wattle of reeds tied with a little cotton so as not to hurt them, and fastening them by the shoulders to a little canoe, which serves them for a cradle." [102]

As Hutten's party entered Omagua country, they came to cultivated fields and a village of some fifty huts which the Uaupés guides explained belonged to slaves that guarded and farmed the plantations of the Omaguas. These Indians offered no resistance. Hutten advanced until he occupied a hill overlooking the main city of the Omaguas.

What he saw filled him with excitement. Down there was a city so great that he could not see its farther end. The streets were straight, the houses were well laid out and ably constructed, and in the center of the settlement was a building of great height. The Uaupés informed him that this was the palace of Quareca, the Omagua ruler, and also the temple of the sun. Within it, certainly, were the golden idols of El Dorado. From the hilltop the city looked like the abode of all wealth. It was not the first time that Europeans had misjudged an Indian city from afar; only a few years earlier, the first Spanish scouts entering the pueblo country of New Mexico had deceived themselves into thinking that the distantly glimpsed mud walls of the Zuni were the buildings of a city more fabulous than any in Moctezuma's land.

Inflamed by the imagined wonders of the city that lay before them, Hutten and his men rashly charged full speed down the hill. The Omaguas were not taken by surprise. A war drum sounded, and armed men rushed from the houses to shower the invaders with arrows and spears. Hutten ordered an immediate retreat, for his cavalry was useless within the city; they pulled back to level ground, pursued by the Omaguas, and defended themselves successfully until nightfall, when the Indians ceased their attack.

In the morning the Omaguas returned—15,000 strong, if we can believe the second-hand report of Fray Pedro Simón. The little band of Venezuelans was surrounded. Hutten was wounded and carried from the field in a hammock by the Uaupés; command of the Spaniards passed to Pedro de Limpias, who, although wounded himself, led his men with unflagging vigor. There was no thought now of conquering the city and plundering El Dorado; the Spaniards were fighting for survival and escape. Limpias hacked his way through the Omagua ranks, and his men followed. Miraculously, no Spaniard was slain in the frenzied flight from Omagua country. They fled toward the safety of the land of the Uaupés, with the Omaguas giving chase until the frontier was reached.

It was a bitter defeat for the Venezuelans, whose illusions about the wealth of the Omagua city were, if anything, heightened by the ferocity of its defenders. The weary men, many of them gravely wounded, rested in the village of the Uaupés. The chief of this tribe resorted to a grotesque method of examining Hutten's injury. An old slave of the Uaupés was outfitted in the German knight's armor and set astride Hutten's horse. An Indian with a javelin then wounded him as Hutten had been wounded. The unfortunate slave's body was opened to determine the direction of the wound; then Hutten was treated by native doctors in accordance with what they had learned from the proxy victim.

Though Hutten recovered from his injury, he was too weak to take an active part in directing the return march to Coro, and a quarrel arose between his two ranking lieutenants, Pedro de Limpias and Bartholomäus Welser. Limpias claimed the right to act as commander by virtue of his seniority, his experience in warfare, and his valor in the escape from the Omaguas. The much younger Welser pressed his own claim, based chiefly on his status as scion of the banking family. No detailed account of the conflict has come down to us; but it appears that the enfeebled Hutten sided with his German kinsman against Limpias. The soldiers divided into factions of Limpias men and Welser men. Ultimately Limpias saw that events were running against him and, with a small detachment of loyal followers, broke away from Hutten and Welser and set out for Coro on his own.

It was now late in 1543. Hutten had been absent from Coro more than two years. His progress back to the Welser colony was slow, for he was very weak and Welser, now the leader of the expedition, was not well acquainted with the region. It seems that they halted for many months at the village of Nuestra Señora. There apparently was some intention to obtain substantial reinforcements from Coro and make a second attempt to conquer the Omagua capital. But during Hutten's long absence great changes had taken place in the government of Coro.

No Germans were in control there any longer. Bishop Bastidas, the interim governor, had returned to Santo Domingo after a short stay, leaving a man named Diego de Boiça as his representative until the Welsers could supply a governor of their own. Boiça soon was forced to flee to Honduras to avoid standing trial for criminal misrule. Another Spaniard was named as governor, and brought a hundred men in from Cubagua at Welser expense to maintain order at Coro, but he died in a few months, and was succeeded by several men whose brief stays in office were marked by notable corruption. By 1544 the colony was at the point of collapse.

At this juncture a brutal, violent military man named

Juan de Carvajal seized power in Coro. (He was not a relative of Orellana's priestly chronicler, Fray Gaspar de Carvajal, nor of a monstrous old man named Francisco de Carvajal who took part in Gonzalo Pizarro's rebellion in Peru.) This Carvajal was no agent of the Welsers, and had not the slightest interest in serving their welfare; within three months after taking office in 1545, he persuaded most of the population of Coro to abandon the town and join him in a campaign of conquest aimed at New Granada. This was an open act of war against the Spanish crown, but Carvajal tempted his followers with a promise to share the gold of New Granada among them, and the men of Venezuela were hungry enough for a taste of wealth to go along. First plundering the homes of those settlers of Coro who did not wish to join the expedition, they gathered together most of the cattle of the colony and started southward along the plains.

Carvajal's expedition never got close to New Granada. Halting at the Río Tocuyo, still in Welser territory, Carvajal found a fertile valley to his liking and established a settlement. There was no gold at this place, but Carvajal saw a different path to wealth through agriculture and livestock-raising. It was to Carvajal's town of Tocuyo that Pedro de Limpias came after he had broken away from Hutten.

Limpias discovered the state of affairs and pledged himself to Carvajal's side. He reported that Hutten and his men were on their way back to Coro. That seemed a threat to Carvajal, for he had heard that a Spanish judge named Frías had come to Coro to bring him to heel. When Hutten reached Coro, he would almost certainly offer his troops to Frías to help quell Carvajal's rebellion. Therefore it was necessary to intercept Hutten and Bartholomäus Welser before they could make contact with Frías.

Hutten had left Nuestra Señora and was making his

way slowly north toward Coro, unaware of Carvajal's tyranny or Limpias' treachery. An advance force under Bartholomäus Welser was preceding Hutten, and had gone as far as Barquisimeto, north of Tocuyo. Carvajal sent one of his men there with a message instructing Welser to proceed to Tocuyo instead of to Coro. Welser let himself be persuaded to do so. A second messenger was despatched to Hutten to inform him that Welser would be waiting for him at Tocuyo.

Welser and Hutten, with their respective forces, arrived at Tocuyo to find Carvajal in command. The presence of their enemy Limpias warned them that they were in danger; but Carvajal received them in friendly fashion, provided a lavish feast, and tried to persuade them to remain at Tocuyo. Hutten insisted that he was required by duty to present himself to the imperial judge, Frías, at Coro. Carvajal's response was a calm and untroubled one.

The next day Carvajal sprang his trap. Orders were published that all of Hutten's soldiers now were to join the army of Tocuyo. Amazed, Hutten hurried to Carvajal to protest, and once more expressed his own loyalty to Charles V, the imperial judge Frías, and the Welsers.

At this Carvajal cried out to his followers, "You are witnesses that he says that his province belongs to the Welsers." The rebellion was in the open; Carvajal hoped to incite Hutten's Spanish men against their German leaders. But they remained loyal. Swords were drawn. A brief skirmish followed; three times Bartholomäus rushed toward Carvajal with upraised lance, but each time he was driven back. In the tumult few solid blows were struck, and Hutten and Welser, with their men, were able to escape from Tocuyo and make camp in the plains outside the town.

Carvajal sent priests and a Welser official as emissaries to negotiate with them. An agreement was worked out by which Carvajal promised to permit Hutten and Welser to go to Coro unmolested. They started toward the coastal city, while Carvajal and his soldiers silently followed, probably guided by Pedro de Limpias. For six days the two Germans and their men marched in confidence that Carvajal would adhere to his treaty. On the seventh evening, as Hutten and Welser slept, Carvajal overtook them and fell upon their camp. The Welser loyalists were taken into custody. At dawn, a quick trial was held, and before sunset the two German knights were beheaded with a rusty machete that had been used shortly before for chopping wood.

With the brutal executions of Philipp von Hutten and Bartholomäus Welser, German rule over Venezuela came to its end. It had become clear to the Spanish government that the Welsers could not effectively control a province populated almost entirely by Spaniards. The Spanish authorities promptly brought the ruthless Carvajal into check, and he was seized and beheaded in 1546 at Tocuyo. No attempt was made to restore the province to the Welsers. Through a succession of legal steps the German banking house was relieved of its responsibilities in Venezuela, and by 1550 the Welsers' grant was entirely revoked. They had sent to South America administrators of all sorts, from the savage Ehinger to the light-hearted Federmann to the noble and knightly Hohemut and Hutten; but all had become infected with the fever of El Dorado, and the province had been allowed to lapse into anarchy while the mad quest for golden cities proceeded.

Hutten's tragic career had produced one tangible effect on the nature of that quest. He had glimpsed with his own eyes a city in the heart of the continent that seemed resplendent with treasure, a storehouse of gold and silver. By a semantic shift, El Dorado now meant not only a man, the gilded chief, but a place, the golden city, and so the Omagua capital that Hutten had seen became known as the city of El Dorado. The goal of the quest thus formally moved eastward from conquered Cundinamarca and was established in northwestern Brazil.

[5]

THE CRUISE OF THE

TYRANT AGUIRRE

 HE MIDDLE YEARS OF THE SIXTEENTH CEN-
tury were complex ones for Spain. The flow
of treasure from the New World had been
continuous and ever-increasing, taking a
mighty rise after the discovery of the silver
mines of Potosí, yet all this wealth was weakening the mother country in many ways.
Charles V was financing exploits in Italy, France, and the
Netherlands with his gleaming American harvest. Spain's
backward industries were not growing. The Church, in possession of one-sixth of the country's land, tended to maintain
the traditional agricultural and pastoral economy to the detri-
ment of the national strength. Spain was weary after centuries of dynastic wars, religious wars, and aristocratic exploitation. The Jews, whose skill in business and industry
would have been valuable at this critical time, had been ex-
pelled in 1492. The gifted Moors had been suppressed. The
most energetic and dynamic of the Spaniards had been
drained off to the Americas by the vast colonial enterprise.
A country of no more than nine million people, as Spain then
was, could not tolerate so many strains when already handi-

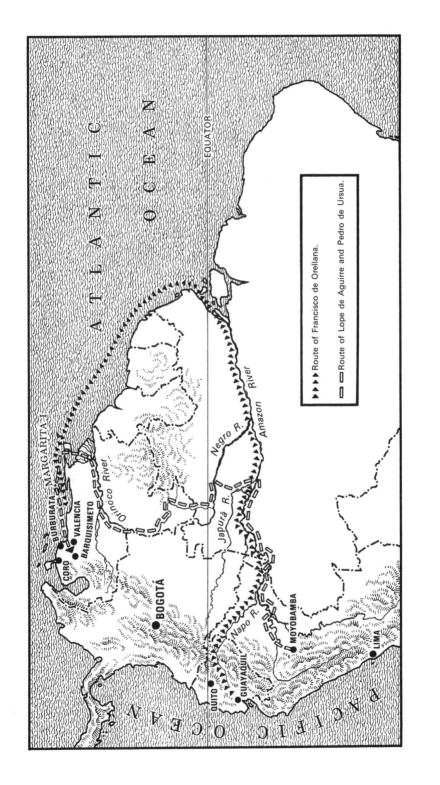

ATLANTIC OCEAN

PACIFIC OCEAN

EQUATOR

Route of Francisco de Orellana.

Route of Lope de Aguirre and Pedro de Ursua.

MARGARITA I.

BURBURATA

VALENCIA

BARQUISIMETO

CORO

Orinoco River

Negro R.

Amazon River

Japurá R.

BOGOTÁ

Napo R.

MOYOBAMBA

QUITO

GUAYAQUIL

LIMA

capped by poor internal communications, an insufficiency of harbors, and an unfriendly climate.

The impossibility of ruling over half of Europe and most of the New World had taken its toll on Charles V, too. By 1548 the Emperor's strength was spent, though he was still two years short of his fiftieth birthday, and he began to seek some way to escape from the crushing responsibilities of universal sovereignty. Piece by piece he started to divest himself of his enormous empire. In 1555 he formally resigned as sovereign of the Netherlands, giving that crown to his son Philip. That same year he turned over the Holy Roman Empire to his younger brother Ferdinand. In January, 1556, Charles abdicated as King of Spain in Philip's favor. Soon afterward, he distributed the rest of his European possessions, and in 1557 retired to Estremadura to spend the remaining two years of his life in peace, tending his garden, hunting in the woods of a local monastery, and slipping into moods of odd and mystic religious exaltation.

The Spanish throne—and with it the New World—thus passed to a very different sort of man. King Philip II, who was twenty-nine years old when his father abdicated, was Spanish-born and Spanish-reared, and something of that somber land of harsh shadows had entered his soul. Charles V was a mixture of the amiable and the ambitious, and in the end his amiability triumphed and took him to the monastery in Estremadura; but there was nothing amiable about Philip. A dark, brooding man, haunted by his high responsibilities and a sense of the innate righteousness of the monarch, intensely religious, endlessly energetic in his duties, he distrusted everyone, loved few, and lived in strange isolation from those about him. His callous suppression of the national spirit of the Netherlands made him a hateful figure there, while to the English he was loathsome first as the consort of the unpopular "Bloody" Queen Mary, and then, after her death and succession by Elizabeth, as the sinister schemer who ultimately sent the Armada of 1588 on its disastrous course of invasion.

Much of Philip's trouble stemmed from the inherent weaknesses of his father's empire. He did not have to cope with the problems of Austria and Germany, which went to a different branch of the Habsburg family, but Spain was his particular cross. He inherited a country on the verge of bankruptcy, and one of his first official acts was to default on Spain's international loans, thereby nearly causing the ruin of his father's old backers, the Welsers. Throughout his reign he juggled the currency, raised taxes, incurred new debts, went through other bankruptcies, and otherwise attempted to halt Spain's incomprehensible decay. The new ruler asked his American possessions for more gold. Now, more than ever, it was imperative to find and plunder El Dorado.

2

El Dorado had been found, of course, on the plateau of Cundinamarca; but the land of the gilded man had not produced a continuing yield of treasure, since its soil contained no precious ores. Out of Cundinamarca—which by 1539 had become Gonzalo Jiménez de Quesada's Kingdom of New Granada—came the impetus for the next stage in the quest, a search for Philipp von Hutten's El Dorado of the Omaguas.

New Granada had come close to political chaos only a few years after its founding. We have seen how Quesada went to Spain to be confirmed as its governor, only to have that prize snatched by his unscrupulous rival, Alonso de Lugo. Lugo's greed led to his quick expulsion from New

Granada; his cousin, Montalvo de Lugo, remained as his deputy. In 1545 the Council of the Indies sent Judge Don Miguel Díaz de Armendariz to the New World to oversee the entire region of what is now Colombia, for at this time the Council had lost patience with the unruly *conquistadores* in many parts of South America and was sending men of authority to restore order everywhere.

Armendariz had the title of *juez de residencia*, "inquisitorial judge," with authority over Santa Marta, Cartagena, Popayán, and New Granada. When he landed at Cartagena in 1546, he was besieged by reports of the crimes of the Lugo family in New Granada. Armendariz appointed his nephew, Pedro de Ursua, to proceed to Bogotá, displace Montalvo de Lugo, and take charge of the government of New Granada.

Ursua was then about twenty years old. He was a knight from the city of Pamplona in Navarre, one of the kingdoms comprising *las Españas*, and though accounts of his character differ, he appears to have been a man of great bravery, nobility, and honor, flawed by a headstrong nature that admitted of no advice from others. Ursua journeyed up the Magdalena to New Granada with a small force of men and entered New Granada at the city of Tunja. On his first night there, the house in which he was lodged was burned to the ground, and the charge of complicity in the arson was sufficient pretext for Ursua to order the arrest of Montalvo de Lugo. With Lugo out of the way, Ursua was formally recognized as governor of New Granada.

It was not long before he was hunting El Dorado. With 400 men he set out from Tunja in 1548, on what was ostensibly a mission to pacify the warlike cannibals on the borders of the plateau. The Chibchas, the former rulers of Cundinamarca, had been so thoroughly subjugated that they were rapidly disappearing, and the once fierce Panches had also been beaten, but such tribes as the Musos, the Chitareros, and the Laches were still troublesome. Ursua passed northeastward through the territory of the Laches, and defeated the Chitareros while simultaneously making a fruitless search for gold in that part of the plateau. He found no treasure. Establishing a city which he called Pamplona after his native town, he returned to Bogotá in 1550.

His uncle Armendariz had meanwhile run into difficulties. At the behest of the Spanish throne he had promulgated new laws protecting the natives from slavery and exploitation. When Blasco Nuñez Vela had attempted to promulgate the same laws in Peru, the entire country had erupted and Gonzalo Pizarro had taken power on a pledge to ignore the new legislation. Armendariz did not meet with rebellion, but rather with non-compliance; typical of the response of the settlers was that of Belalcázar, still ruling at Popayán, who obediently posted the new laws but instantly suspended them pending "clarification" from Spain. Armendariz soon was so deeply embroiled in disputes with the settlers that he could not effectively govern them, and he was deposed in 1549 by a royal commission consisting of three young Spanish lawyers. They sent him back to Spain.

However, the fall of Armendariz does not seem to have injured the fortunes of Pedro de Ursua. Upon his return from Pamplona, the three commissioners asked him to undertake another expedition to conquer the Musos and find El Dorado in the northwest. With 150 men he made a rapid foray into the country of the Musos. The Spaniards were well armed; it was said that half the utensils in Bogotá were melted down to make bullets for them. Ursua established a fortified camp in the midst of the grassy prairie of the Muso territory. The Indians attacked daily, but were unable to penetrate the Spaniards' defenses. An attempt by the Musos to starve the intruders out by setting fire to their own cultivated fields failed. At length the leaders of the Indians were forced to negotiate; Ursua invited the chieftains into his camp and then, in the hope of breaking the strength of the tribe, put them to death. It was, noted the chronicler Pedro Simón, "a felonious act, and unworthy of a soldier of honor like Ursua." [103]

Ursua had stained his reputation to no useful purpose, for the expected paralysis of the Musos did not result. Instead they grew more fierce. Ursua left a garrison behind and returned to Bogotá for reinforcements, but as soon as he departed the Indians drove his men out and burned the camp before their eyes. It was some years before any Spaniard entered the Muso country again.

Ursua's operations north of Bogotá between 1548 and 1551 constituted the last attempts to find El Dorado anywhere in Cundinamarca. Ursua went on in 1551 to become chief justice of Santa Marta, and took part in a campaign against the belligerent Tayronas Indians, who dwelled in the mountains just inland from the Caribbean coast. They had gold and silver, and fashioned attractive ornaments in the shape of eagles, toads, deer, bats, and crescents. Ursua marched against them with a strong force, but was cut off from his line of supply and suffered great hardships. A difficult retreat was made possible only by Ursua's personal courage; though feverish and weak, he led twelve men up a craggy hill to find a pass that his men took to escape a cul-de-sac, held the pass for several hours against an Indian onslaught, and finally brought his men down again to scatter the enemy.

Restless at Santa Marta, Ursua went next to Panamá where he joined the entourage of the Marquis of Cañete, Don Andreas Hurtado de Mendoza, who had been appointed the new viceroy in Peru. The Marquis told Ursua that he would be welcome to join his service in that country. First, however, Ursua became involved in a campaign against the *cimarrones*, a band of runaway slaves who were terrorizing Panamá. With two hundred soldiers he entered the thick forests of the Isthmus and exterminated the Negro marauders in a toilsome war lasting two years. Then, in 1558, Ursua went on to Lima to enroll in Cañete's administration.

The new viceroy had found Peru in considerable disarray. The civil wars were over, and all the Pizarros were dead but for one who was a prisoner in Spain, but the boisterous men who had conquered the Inca realm were still divided among themselves. Rebellions had been suppressed in 1552 and 1554. The Marquis of Cañete, arriving the year after the second rebellion, presided over a country simmering with discontent and infested by lawless ruffians whose naturally violent natures had been exacerbated by the long years of fratricidal conflict among the Spaniards of Peru.

Jailing all these men was impossible. Persuading them to lead orderly lives was unthinkable. One way to deal with them, the Marquis realized, was to harness their brawling energies to some project that would fire their own greed and get them out of Peru. What better solution than to drum up an expedition to find El Dorado?

A disturbance on the other side of the continent gave the viceroy his opportunity to organize the new quest. Viraratu, an Indian chief of the Brazilian coast, came into conflict with his neighbors and decided to lead his people inland up the Amazon in search of a less crowded country. Several thousand Indians in a fleet of large canoes started up the river, accompanied by two Portuguese who spoke their language. After ascending the Amazon for some days, they reached a great lake in a large plain rimmed by towering mountains. On the shores of this lake were populous villages whose inhabitants came out in war canoes to drive off

Viraratu's people. The invaders were defeated in a naval battle and fled back to the river, which they continued to ascend until they came to Moyobamba, near the Río Huallaga in Peru, a district inhabited by the Motilones Indians. Communicating with the Motilones by sign language, Viraratu related his adventures since leaving the coast of Brazil, describing the numerous villages along the great lake and the quantities of gold and silver that he believed they contained. The Motilones repeated these stories to some Spaniards, who had Viraratu taken to Lima to tell his tale to the viceroy.

"These Indians," wrote Fray Pedro Simón, "brought news respecting the provinces of the Omaguas, mentioned also by Captain Francisco de Orellana, when he descended this river Marañon after deserting Gonzalo Pizarro, in the cinnamon country. In these provinces of which the Indians spoke when they reached Peru dwelled the gilded man; at least this name was spread about in the land, taking its origin in the city of Quito. It so excited the minds of those restless spirits with whom Peru was full, and who were ever ready to credit these rumors, that the viceroy thought it prudent to seek some way by which to give employment to so large a body of turbulent men." [104]

He sent for Ursua, whose gifts of leadership had been demonstrated many times in the past ten years, and offered him command of the expedition to El Dorado. The royal treasury would finance the adventure, whose locale was to be the vaguely known country east of the Andes, already entered by Hutten and Hernán de Quesada and traversed by Orellana by river. Ursua would receive the title Governor of Omagua and El Dorado, with power to appoint officers, form settlements, and reward his companions out of the booty of the land.

Delighted with the assignment, Ursua at once began to

recruit his men. He was now thirty years old, an experienced commander and yet an unabashed romanticist as well, whose chivalry was so ingrained that he took his lady fair, Doña Iñez de Atienza, along as part of an expedition whose personnel consisted of the scum of Peru. His friends advised him not to do so, for the presence of a young and beautiful woman on such an excursion could lead only to rivalries and strife; but Ursua's tragic fault was his utter impermeability to advice.

About this Doña Iñez we have some conflicting information from the early chroniclers. The primary source of our knowledge of the Ursua expedition comes from a manuscript entitled, "A narrative of all that happened in the expedition to Amagua [*sic*] and Dorado," written by Francisco Vásquez, a soldier who took part in the enterprise. A near-contemporaneous account was composed by Don Toribio de Ortiguera in 1561, based on interviews with some of Ursua's men. The same informants who spoke to Ortiguera were consulted by Juan de Castellanos, the soldier-turned-priest who wrote that copious verse history of the exploration of the Americas. Castellanos' account of Ursua's expedition was published in Spain in 1588. (The second part of his chronicle, dealing with the adventures of the German knights and Belalcázar, did not appear until 1847.) These three accounts—Vásquez, Ortiguera, and Castellanos—were written by contemporaries of Ursua. The next chronicler, Fray Pedro Simón, was born in 1574, reached South America at the age of thirty to teach theology and the arts in Bogotá, and in 1623 began to write the first of his histories of the Americas, based on the documents of the conquerors and on interviews with the surviving members of the earlier expeditions. He based his account of Ursua largely on the manuscript of Francisco Vásquez. Some details of the story struck Simón as too horrible to relate, and he omitted them;

but these blanks were filled by another reliable historian, Lucas Fernández Piedrahita, who was born at Bogotá early in the seventeenth century and became Bishop of Panamá in 1676.

The events of Ursua's quest for El Dorado thus must be pieced together from these five primary and secondary sources, and they do not always jibe—particularly on the subject of Doña Iñez. It is generally agreed that she was the widow of a citizen of the Peruvian coastal town of Pinira, that she was unusually beautiful, and that she had become Ursua's mistress some time before he was chosen to lead the Omagua quest. Vásquez, who was there and ought to know, calls her a woman of loose character. Ortiguera agrees. Padre Simón, following Vásquez, depicts her as shamelessly promiscuous. Yet the otherwise trustworthy Castellanos portrays her as a noble and heroic woman whose devotion to Ursua was sublime, whose soul was undaunted by hardship, and whose ultimate violent death called forth this aria of lament from the chronicler: "The birds mourned on the trees, the wild beasts of the forests lamented, the waters ceased to murmur, the fish groaned beneath them, the winds execrated the deed, when Llamoso cut the veins of her white neck. Wretch! art thou born of a woman? No! What beast brought forth a son so wicked? . . . Her two women, amidst lamentations and grief, gathered flowers to cover her grave, and cut her epitaph in the bark of a tree: 'These flowers cover one whose faithfulness and beauty were unequalled, whom cruel men slew without a cause.' " [105]

Whether saint or sinner, Doña Iñez did not belong on the expedition, and Ursua's own fate would have been happier had he heeded his friends' counsel and left her in Lima. However, he committed a much more serious error—a fatal one—when he overruled his advisers and accepted in his expedition a native of Biscay named Lope de Aguirre, perhaps the single most villainous figure in the annals of the Spanish conquest.

Aguirre, who transformed Ursua's expedition into a wild orgy of bloodshed and mad cruelty, was about fifty years old when Ursua recruited him in 1559. Simón describes him as "of short stature, and sparely made, ill-featured, the face small and lean, beard black, the eyes like a hawk's, and when he looked, he fixed them sternly, particularly when angry." [106] For twenty years he had lived in Peru, employed chiefly as a trainer of horses, and had taken part in all the civil wars of that unhappy land, changing sides as it pleased his fancy. During the short reign of Gonzalo Pizarro, Aguirre was nominated to be an assistant to the public executioner, a job well suited to his sanguine nature, but he chose to go to Nicaragua instead, remaining there several years. Returning to Peru, he took part in the rebellion of 1552, was condemned to death, escaped, and participated in the rebellion of 1554. Under the general amnesty following the defeat of that uprising, Aguirre was pardoned and joined the royal forces in the final cleanup of the rebels. "He mixed himself up in so many seditions in various parts, that he could not be tolerated in the country," commented Simón. "He was driven from one province to the other, and was known as Aguirre the madman." [107]

He belonged in the legion of titanic nay-sayers, men so shaped by birth and breeding that they dedicate themselves to a nihilistic demolition of all human institutions. What furies burned within his spare frame we more rational souls can only guess at; he was of that tribe of malcontents and avengers so frequently portrayed in the Elizabethan and Jacobean drama, and to us seems more like some bombastic character out of Webster or Tourneur than a human being who once lived in the real world. Aguirre's character is amply illustrated in an anecdote from the chronicle of Garcilaso de la Vega, who related that in 1548 Aguirre was a member of a platoon of soldiers escorting Indian slaves from the mines at Potosí to a royal treasury depot. The Indians were illegally burdened with great quantities of silver, and a local official arrested Aguirre, sentencing him to receive two hundred lashes in lieu of a fine for oppressing the Indians. "The soldier Aguirre, having received a notification of the sentence, besought the *alcalde* that, instead of flogging him, he would put him to death, for that he was a gentleman by birth. . . . All this had no effect on the *alcalde*, who ordered the executioner to bring a beast, and execute the sentence. The executioner came to the prison, and put Aguirre on the beast: but all the principal people of the town went to the *alcalde*, entreating him not to execute so rigorous a sentence, and he at length consented to delay it for eight days. When they came to the prison, they found that Aguirre was already stripped, and mounted on the beast; and, on hearing that the punishment was only delayed for eight days, he said: 'I prayed that I might not be put on this beast, and stripped naked, as I now am, but now that I have come to this, I prefer to suffer at once, rather than bear the suspense of eight more days.' On saying this, the beast was driven on, and he received the lashes. . . ."

When freed, Aguirre announced his intention of killing the official who had sentenced him, the *alcalde* Esquivel. Esquivel's term of office expired and he fled to Lima, three hundred twenty leagues away, but within fifteen days Aguirre had tracked him there. The frightened judge journeyed to Quito, a trip of four hundred leagues, and in twenty days Aguirre arrived. "When Esquivel heard of his presence," according to Garcilaso, "he made another journey of five hundred leagues, to Cuzco; but in a few days Aguirre also arrived, having travelled on foot and without shoes, saying that a whipped man has no business to ride a horse, or to go where he would be seen by others. In this way, Aguirre followed his judge for three years, and four months." Wearying of the pursuit, Esquivel remained at Cuzco, a city so sternly governed that he felt he would be safe from Aguirre. He took a house near the cathedral and never ventured outdoors without a sword and a dagger. "However, on a certain Monday, at noon, Aguirre entered his house, and having walked all over it, and having traversed a corridor, a saloon, a chamber, and an inner chamber where the judge kept his books, he at last found him asleep over one of his books, and stabbed him to death. The murderer then went out, but when he came to the door of the house, he found that he had forgotten his hat, and had the temerity to return and fetch it, and then walked down the street." [108]

He admitted his crime to two young men and asked them to hide him, which they did for forty days, while the authorities of Cuzco blocked every road and searched the city for Aguirre. Finally Aguirre cut his hair and beard and stained his skin with the juice of a wild berry until it was black; then, in the clothing of a Negro slave, he went on foot before his confederates to the borders of the city, was allowed through by the guards, and made good his escape. This man, whose lunatic thirst for revenge had occupied him for more than three years, now affiliated himself with the expedition of Pedro de Ursua.

3

While the personnel of the expedition was being recruited at Lima in 1559, Ursua set up a preliminary camp at Santa Cruz de Capacoba, near Moyobamba, the terminal point of Viraratu's voyage from Brazil. Here, on a branch of the Río Huallaga, Ursua put twenty-five shipwrights and ten Negro carpenters to work building a fleet of brigantines. Leaving them at this task, he returned to Lima to collect his men. He sent his unruly brigands to Moyobamba under the leadership of his second-in-command, Pedro Ramiro, but remained behind in Lima for nearly a year trying to raise funds to supplement the treasury appropriation given him by the Marquis de Cañete. Ursua was still short of money when he came back to Moyobamba and arranged to borrow two thousand pesos from the priest there, who hoped to be named a bishop in the new lands to be conquered. But the priest, after a careful survey of Ursua's men, decided that the expedition was bound to come to evil, and withdrew his offer. That put Ursua in an awkward position. He called together a few of his lieutenants, "all fighting men and of elastic conscience," in Padre Simón's words, and told them his problem. "His friends saw no difficulty about the matter, even if a little violence was resorted to; so one night they reported that Juan de Vargas (who was then quartered in the church on account of two wounds), was dying, and one of them went for the *cura* Portillo, urging him to lose no time in going to confess Vargas. On leaving his house the *cura* was seized by Ursua's friends, and was forced to sign an order for two thousand [*pesos*] on a merchant of the town, who was the keeper of the *cura's* wealth." [109]

The main part of Ursua's force had gone ahead in the brigantines to the town of Santa Cruz, deeper in the land of the Motilones, led by Pedro Ramiro. Two of Ursua's other officers, Francisco de Arles and Diego de Frías, became jealous of Ramiro's preeminence and had him assassinated, sending word to Ursua that they had put him to death because he had attempted to rebel against Ursua's leadership. The enterprise had already begun to devour itself.

But Ursua had learned the true motives for the killing.

Making no show of anger, he went forward to Santa Cruz, greeted Arles and Frías with bland good will, and lulled their followers into a state of calm. Then he arrested the killers and ordered their execution. The culprits refused to believe that their old *compadre* Ursua would really permit the sentence to be carried out, and were greatly surprised to be led into the main plaza of Santa Cruz to be beheaded.

The first crisis had been weathered without disruption of the expedition; but three key captains were dead. Ursua felt that he had shown his strength by the firm handling of the situation, and indeed for a while his three hundred rag-tag criminals and rebels behaved less turbulently. But mutiny was afoot. While at Santa Cruz, Ursua received a letter from one of his friends, warning him once more that he had picked a band of rascals, and citing in particular Lope de Aguirre and one Lorenzo de Salduendo as men who should be dismissed from the company. The letter also repeated the suggestion that Ursua should send Doña Iñez back to Lima. Ursua did not reply, nor did he accept the suggestions.

Advance forces went out at the beginning of July, 1560. An officer named García del Arze took thirty men down the river some sixty miles to gather provisions and store them in a depot on the banks. This party traveled by raft and canoe; a second force of a hundred men under Juan de Vargas went by land. The two parties were to meet at the mouth of the River Ucayali, one of the many converging rivers of northeastern Peru that are tributaries of the Amazon.

The two advance parties missed connections. García del Arze did not wait for Vargas, but descended the Huallaga for about six hundred miles, losing some of his men, and running short of food so that it was necessary to hunt and eat small alligators. They halted at last on an island in the river, which they fortified, and held out there for three months waiting for Ursua to catch up with them. Vargas, not finding García del Arze at the rendezvous point, was inspired to make a side journey up the Río Cocamá, another tributary, in search of provisions. Leaving most of his men at the mouth of the river, he ascended the Cocamá for three weeks before he could find inhabited villages. He returned to his main camp to discover some of his men dead of hunger and the rest already plotting mutiny.

The misadventures of these two preliminary sorties might not have occurred if Ursua had followed at once with the rest of the expedition, as had originally been planned. But there were delays in completing the brigantines, and when finished most of them sprang leaks. A delay of several months ensued while canoes and rafts were hurriedly constructed. It was necessary to leave behind all but forty of the 300 horses, nearly all the cattle, and much of the expedition's baggage. Finally, with one brigantine, three small flat-bottomed boats, and an assortment of rafts and canoes, the main party embarked on September 26, 1560. "The people were in such a state of ill-humor that they almost mutinied," we learn from Simón, "and wished to return to Peru, so as to save what they had there, and this they would have done had not the governor, by his dexterous proceedings, arresting some, flattering and dissembling to others, warning and blandly admonishing the whole, put plainly before them the misery they would experience should they remain behind; adding that on the contrary, by going onwards there was hope of fortune, and the glory of being in such an expedition." [110] An expedition that had made so unpromising a start seemed certain to end in quick abortion, however.

The route trended northward down the Huallaga, veering gradually to the east as the Huallaga approached the Marañon to become the Amazon. (The old name of Marañon is still used for the westernmost arm of the Amazon.) On the second day out the flotilla lost sight of the Andes and entered flat country, in which they would remain until the end of the journey. On the third day, the brigantine ran into a bank and damaged its keel, which had to be repaired at the cost of several days' delay. But eventually the greatly overdue Ursua party came to the mouth of the Cocamá, where Juan de Vargas was waiting with his edgy, half-mutinous men. Their rafts and canoes had rotted and they had run out of food.

The arrival of Ursua was some comfort to Vargas' party, but conflicts were running strong in both groups as they met. Vargas' men and their belongings had to be divided up into Ursua's boats, producing serious overcrowding, a dangerous matter for the small vessels on the flood-fattened river. Ursua invariably maintained a spacious cabin for himself and Doña Iñez, no matter what the conditions under which the others lived, and this stirred further resentments.

The voyagers now were moving rapidly down the Marañon. In a few more days they came to the island where García del Arze and his companions had been waiting. Once more united, the expedition sped downstream and reached the first Indian villages that had been seen since leaving Santa Cruz four months earlier. "The natives were tall and strong, clothed in well woven cotton shirt-like coverings," Padre Simón's account relates. "No gold was found, which produced dissatisfaction amongst the Spaniards, seeing that they had journeyed so far without meeting with the least sign of the precious metal." [111] The Spaniards, in fact, were finding sources of dissatisfaction in almost every aspect of the journey, and were muttering of mutiny again behind Ursua's back.

A little below the island where García del Arze had stayed, the Marañon was joined by a river flowing from the northwest, and variously known to the explorers as the Canela (Cinnamon), the Orellana, and the Napo. This was, of course, the tributary through which Orellana had entered the Amazon in 1542, and from this point on Ursua was following Orellana's route. Ursua's guides—several of Viraratu's Brazilian Indians—pointed ahead to the east, saying that the land of El Dorado lay in that direction and to the north of the great river.

Ursua's organization was so informal that since the murder of Pedro Ramiro he had not appointed specific lieutenants. Now he chose Juan de Vargas as his lieutenant-general, and gave the third command post to a young man of noble birth named Fernando de Guzmán, who was to play a prominent role in the strange story that soon would unfold.

Continuing rapidly downstream, the expedition halted from time to time to extort food from the Indian villages, or to make side excursions into the provinces bordering the river. Ursua made an honorable attempt to spare the natives from abuse, forbidding his men to deal with them except through him or in his presence. Word spread that these Spaniards were trustworthy ones, and shortly the Indians were coming forth willingly and cheerfully to barter their produce for the cheap trinkets of the voyagers. It was a technique of trade that few of the Spanish explorers bothered to employ, to their great cost.

The absence of any gold thus far provoked a new attempt at mutiny, led by a man named Alonso de Montoya. He was imprisoned; but, says Simón, "Ursua was naturally merciful, indeed too merciful, and at times his acts savored of weakness. Sometimes he punished those who deserved severe castigation for their turbulence and crimes, making them row for some days in the brigantines and canoes; some of the soldiers took occasion . . . to irritate those who were undergoing punishment, by telling them that death was far

Spaniards encountering wonders on the shores of Lake Parima near Manoa or El Dorado.

Spanish scouts sent to find Manoa being slain by Indians.

SIR WALTER RALEIGH *and his men
observing the burial customs
of the Tivitivas of Guiana.*

GOLD AND GOLD-PLATED ORNAMENTAL SCULPTURE

CLOCKWISE FROM THE TOP: *Flat gold human figure* (3″), *Colombia. Gold ornament representing a human figure* (3″), *vicinity of Bogotá, Colombia. Gold human figure* (2⅛″), *Ecuador. Gold figure of a man* (1¾ x 4½), *vicinity of Bogotá. Gold figure of a man* (7″), *vicinity of Bogotá. Small triangular gold pendant representing a man* (2¼″), *Chibcha Indians, vicinity of Bogotá.*

better than such disgrace. These malicious sayings were the sparks of the burning villainy which filled their breasts." [112] Chief among the instigators was Lope de Aguirre. Convinced that he had embarked on a fool's journey, he wished to dispose of Ursua and return at once to Peru.

An Indian girl captured by one of the scouting parties confirmed that the rich province of the Omaguas was still far distant, for she had not even heard its name. Some four hundred miles from the island of García del Arze the Spaniards reached some scattered villages where the natives had pendants, earrings, and nose-pieces of fine gold, but not in any very exciting quantity. Beyond this region the country was uninhabited for nine days' voyage. The Spaniards, who in all these enterprises seemed unable to find edible food in the plenty of the tropical forest except at Indian villages, began to suffer from hunger. The leaky brigantine had gone to the bottom at last, so that they were compelled to transport themselves and all their cargo on small boats and rafts and in canoes, and that made the carrying of provisions difficult. Leaving the last village of the earring people, they carelessly neglected to load up with food, little expecting to find so extensive an uninhabited stretch ahead. As food dwindled, they ate unsatisfactorily on a diet of fish and turtles, "but in very small quantities for so large a party," says Simón, "and in some places they found none. This misery increased their weakness each day, and had it lasted a little longer they must all have died. The whole blame was laid on the governor [Ursua] for his improvidence; for had he informed himself of this long tract of desert, he might have laid in a stock of provisions." [113]

Suddenly they came upon a village. Most of its inhabitants fled when the Spaniards appeared, leaving only a few fighting men armed with blowpipes and arrows. Ursua, carrying an arquebus, boldly approached them waving a white flag, and by sign language was able to calm them and arrange for the purchase of food. The Indians provided corn, beans, roots, and turtles of several sorts, which were kept in pens at the village. The Spaniards ate with such gusto that it appeared to the natives that their stores would be devastated, whereupon they began to hide some of their food little by little each night. Ursua's men discovered this and ransacked several of their hiding places. To discourage such treatment of their hosts, Ursua had the guilty men punished, and one of those chastised was the personal servant of his third-in-command, Fernando de Guzmán. This later became a point of friction between Guzmán and Ursua.

The village, it was learned, was the first in the province known as Machiparo, which had given Orellana a hostile greeting in May, 1542. Ursua's more enlightened attitude toward the Indians resulted in a kindlier greeting, and he passed through Machiparo without trouble, collecting food and making inquiries after the Omaguas at each village. While in Machiparo, the commander sent an officer named Pedro de Galeas with some soldiers to ascend a creek flowing into the Amazon. They passed through a narrow mouth of terrifyingly black water, and entered a lake of astonishing size; Simón says that "after they had sailed in it for two or three leagues, they entirely lost sight of land; and, fearing that if they went any further, they would be unable to find the opening by which they had entered . . . they determined to return." [114] No villages bordered this lake, one of the many that adjoined the Amazon here, and so it could not be the one that Viraratu and his people had attempted to enter. But Galeas rightly concluded that Omagua country could not be far off.

While this exploration was under way, the main party became involved in a native war. Two hundred men from the neighboring province of Carari came to attack the villages of Machiparo, as the latest phase of an ancient feud. Finding the Spaniards there, the intruders withdrew; but the men of Machiparo wished to give pursuit, and asked the Spaniards to aid them. Ursua dispatched his lieutenant, Juan de Vargas, with fifty arquebusiers to accompany the warriors of Machiparo. The Machiparo canoes encircled the enemy, and Vargas' men opened fire, ignoring the pleas of the Carari braves for mercy. The result was total annihilation of the invaders. It was one of the rare instances when Spaniards allied themselves with Indians to take part in a purely Indian dispute.

Galeas now returned and described the vast lake which he had explored. Ursua conferred with the Brazilian Indians, with one of the Portuguese who had accompanied them on their westward journey, and with several of his men who had traveled with Orellana eighteen years before. They attempted to arrive at some idea of where they might be in relation to El Dorado.

Their obvious uncertainty about their whereabouts stirred new talk of mutiny. Aguirre and his confederate, Lorenzo de Salduendo, whispered that El Dorado was a myth and that their only hope was to go up the river to Peru. Ursua sent for these malcontents, and delivered what he intended as an inspiring speech. No rich province had ever been discovered without suffering hardships, he said; and even if they had to search until they were old men, that was a minor thing in comparison with the attainment of the great riches that would eventually be theirs.

These words heartened the simpler men. Aguirre, though, was convinced that his youthful commander was a dreamer whose starry quest for gold would lead them all to their doom. He began to form a conspiracy to assassinate him. Searching out one man after another, Aguirre murmured his accusations: that Ursua was a poor leader, capricious in his alternation of harshness and mildness; that he allowed Doña Iñez to make his decisions for him; that he disliked the company of his soldiers and spent all his time with his woman; that he was "an enemy of giving away and a friend of receiving"; that he had deliberately sentenced innocent men to extra hours of rowing as a punishment, so that Doña Iñez might have comfortable transportation; that he was resolved to seek for El Dorado until even the boys of the expedition had grown gray in the quest.

The conspirators agreed that Ursua would never heed their demand to return to Peru, and so would have to be slain. Since they all were of low birth and could not hope to command much authority, they sought out some highborn member of the expedition who would lead them after Ursua's death. Aguirre approached Don Fernando de Guzmán, who had the proper requisites of rank, and who was known to be at odds with the commander.

Guzmán was a shrewd choice. He was young, naive, vain, and malleable. Aguirre, burning with hatred for all authority and possessed of devilish force of personality, had an easy time of turning Guzmán's head. He praised Guzmán's merits and noble ancestry, criticized Ursua's flaws of leadership, and argued that it would be a service to God and the King to overthrow him. Moreover, Aguirre pointed out, had Ursua not violated protocol by seizing and chastising Guzmán's own servant? Guzmán agreed. "Swelled up by the wind of ambition," says Simón, "he gave them thanks for what they had offered him, and assented to all their projects."

Apparently Guzmán had been told that Ursua would not be murdered, but simply abandoned at the Indian village where the expedition now was encamped. Some of the milder conspirators also believed this. Once they were all thoroughly committed, though, Aguirre and Salduendo declared that Ursua must die; and then, as if to obscure the enormity of that crime by another far more monstrous, Aguirre went on to suggest that upon returning to Peru they should overthrow the government and make Don Fernando the lord of the country, with themselves to enjoy its fabulous riches. A mere mutiny was turning into national revolution.

There were omens of an uprising, but Ursua ignored them. Warned by friends that he should post a guard at his dwelling, he laughed the suggestion off, and declined any offer of such aid. The conspirators hatched their plans. On the day after Christmas, 1560, the Spaniards left the village where they were staying and took up residence about twenty miles downstream at another. Here, Ursua was shown a wide road leading inland, which an Indian told him was the route to a rich province, and he sent a party of soldiers under one Sancho Pizarro to investigate it. It happened that most of the men who were still loyal to Ursua were included in Pizarro's scouting party. With the commander's friends gone from the camp, Aguirre chose to strike.

It was the evening of New Year's Day. The conspirators gathered at the lodging of Don Fernando de Guzmán and sent a slave on an errand to Ursua's quarters to find out if he was alone. The slave reported that he was. The murderers set out for the Indian hut in which Ursua was staying. Aguirre himself remained in the rear; the party was led by two men who had earlier attempted mutiny, Alonso de Montoya and Christoval Hernandez de Chaves. "Entering Ursua's house," writes Padre Simón, "they found him in his hammock talking to a little page named Lorca. When they saluted the governor, he said, 'What seek ye here, caballeros, at this hour?' The reply was several stabs, which missed him. He then rose from his hammock to reach his sword and buckler, which he had at hand, when the rest of the mutineers entered, and they all made a murderous onset on Ursua, so that he soon fell dead, without being able to say more than '*Confessio, confessio, miserere mei Deus.*' The deed being done, they sallied out of the hut, and one of them, with a loud voice, shouted, 'Liberty! Liberty! Long live the King, the tyrant is dead.' " Ursua died aged thirty-five years. His river voyage had lasted three months and six days.

4

The noise of the murder aroused Ursua's lieutenant, Juan de Vargas, who hastily donned his armor of quilted cotton, seized his sword, shield, and rod of office, and rushed outside. He met the conspirators coming from Ursua's lodging. They attacked him in a group, taking away sword and shield, stripping open his armor. A mutineer named Martín Pérez thrust his sword through Vargas with such vehemence that he wounded another conspirator standing behind him. Ursua and Vargas were quickly buried in a pit dug at Ursua's hut.

The rest of the camp was in an uproar. The conspirators let it be known what had happened, and took advantage of the confusion to quell any opposition. Don Fernando de Guzmán was named the new governor, with Aguirre as his second-in-command. Ursua's stores of wine were distributed in general celebration, along with some sacramental wine that now was not likely to be used at the hearing of the mass. A wholesale butchery of Ursua's supporters commenced. Doña Iñez, whose role in these events seems ambivalent, was spared.

From this moment on, a tone of paranoia infected every aspect of the voyage. Lope de Aguirre was in control, and Aguirre saw the world through the eyes of one to whom all men were enemies. Fearing a counter-conspiracy, his first command was that no man was permitted to whisper, but must speak out loudly and plainly, on pain of death. Several soldiers spoke from habit in low voices and were instantly seized, but Aguirre was persuaded to spare them. Later he would not be so merciful.

After a night of drunken revelry, the ringleaders met and parceled out the remaining offices; Montoya became captain of cavalry, Hernandez de Chaves and Salduendo captains of infantry, and so forth. Not to seem too greedy, they allotted a few of the high posts to men who were not of their faction, such as the Portuguese guide, Sebastián Gómez, and the scout Pedro de Galeas. One man, Diego de Belalcázar, was offered the title of *justicia mayor del campo*, or chief judge, and when handed the staff of office glared at the mutineers and loudly declared, "This staff of office I take in the name of King Philip our lord, and in no other." It was a brave defiance of Aguirre; but for the moment, at least, he did not suffer for it.

Two days after the mutiny, Sancho Pizarro and his scouting party returned, having found only a pair of empty villages on the inland road. Ursua's many friends in this band were stunned to learn of the murders, but could do nothing now that Aguirre held full command. Sancho Pizarro himself acted discretion's part and pledged allegiance to Guzmán; he was rewarded with the title of sergeant-major.

The nominal head of the expedition, Don Fernando de Guzmán, called his first council of the camp soon afterward to discuss future plans. In all innocence the young knight proposed that they continue the quest for El Dorado; for, he said, if they found it they would not only be wealthy, but surely would be pardoned by a grateful king for the murders of Ursua and Vargas. He went on to suggest that they draw up a document stating why it had been necessary to deprive the governor of his life—because of his negligence, his intolerance, and his unfitness to govern, which threatened the success of the attempt to find El Dorado.

Aguirre, though he was a madman, did not share the particular madness of the seekers of the Dorado. He had no urge to chase a fantasy through the jungles when the known wealth of Peru awaited plundering in the west. He remained silent, then, as Don Fernando outlined his plans for a further quest. When the document was prepared, Guzmán asked everyone to sign it, so that it could eventually be presented to King Philip II. Guzmán signed first. Then Aguirre stepped forward and with a flourish put down his signature: "*Lope de Aguirre, the traitor.*"

Some of the men gasped in surprise at this frank avowal on a document intended for the King. Aguirre laughed. "You have killed the King's governor, one who represented his royal person, one who was clothed with royal powers," he told them, "and do you pretend that with documents concocted by ourselves, we shall be held blameless? . . . Yes, we have all killed the governor, and the whole of us have rejoiced at the act; and if not, let each man lay his hand upon his heart, and say what he thinks. We have all been traitors, we have all been a party to this mutiny." [115]

What of El Dorado, he asked. Even if they were lucky enough to find it, they would be deprived of its benefits by the power of the Spanish law. "My opinion is . . . that we should abandon these intentions of searching for these new lands; for if we discover them and people them, our lives will be sacrificed. Let us therefore anticipate the evil time, and let us settle ourselves well in a good land known to you all, which is Peru."

Several of Aguirre's men shouted approval. Only Juan Alonso de la Bandera, one of the original conspirators, objected to Aguirre's casual assumption of the name of traitor for them all, saying that the death of Ursua had been no treason, nor had any crime been committed, for under Ursua's sloppy leadership El Dorado would never have been found. His Majesty thus was better served by the death of the governor. He repeated Guzmán's theory that the King would reward and pardon those who went on to discover El Dorado, and concluded, "He who says that I am a traitor in this matter, I tell him that he lies, and I will make good my words, and I now dare him to mortal combat." [116] The hot tempers were soothed, and the quarrel subsided. But Aguirre's intentions had been openly stated. This had ceased to be an expedition in search of El Dorado.

For the moment, Aguirre did not choose to impose his will on the others. Five days after Ursua's death, the expedition proceeded downstream, some men still under the illusion that their aim was to find the golden city of the Omaguas. It suited Aguirre's purpose to go on in this direction, for he had come to the same conclusion that Orellana had reached before him: it would be impossible to struggle upstream back to Peru. They would have to take the long way around, following the Amazon or another river to the Atlantic, then coasting along the mainland around Guiana and Venezuela to the Isthmus of Panamá, making the overland journey across the Isthmus, and thence down the western coast of the continent to Peru.

The trip would require large sea-going vessels. Since the voyagers now were traveling in canoes, rafts, and a few little flat-bottomed boats, none of which was suitable for an ocean cruise, Aguirre chose a place where good timber was available and deliberately bored holes in the boats. They sank, obliging Don Fernando de Guzmán to order the construction of new brigantines in which the horses and cargo could travel. Three months passed while these brigantines were built.

The work was slowed by hunger, for the river at this point was mysteriously scant of fish, and the nearest plantation of the yuca root was on the far side of the river, three miles broad here. The men sustained themselves with wild fruit, which Padre Simón calls "sustenance more suited for monkeys than for men," and began to consume their poultry, dogs, and horses. Aguirre was pleased at this, for if the domestic animals were eaten it would be impossible to establish any permanent settlement or even to make extensive inland explorations.

He used this interlude of ship-building to rid himself of the remaining pro-Ursua men in the camp. García del Arze, one of Ursua's oldest friends, was arrested and strangled after Aguirre had persuaded Guzmán that the deed was necessary for the general security of all. Objections came from Diego de Belalcázar, the chief judge of the camp, he who had refused to recognize Aguirre's authority to confer on him the staff of office. Aguirre attempted to murder him as he slept, but Belalcázar slipped away and gained the protection of Guzmán. Several other officers fell victim to Aguirre's bloody whims at this time.

Among the dead were two of the original conspirators. A rumor circulated that these two were planning to kill Fernando de Guzmán. To strengthen his own credit with the nominal governor, Aguirre had the men seized and executed on this trumped-up charge. Though he was appreciative of this service, Guzmán had the folly to show favors to Juan Alonso de la Bandera, the man who had attacked Aguirre for claiming that they all were traitors. Guzmán raised Bandera to a position equal to Aguirre's, and then, as dissension between the two grew, Guzmán relieved Aguirre of his post of second-in-command (*maestro del campo*) and gave it to Bandera. Aguirre was given the title of captain of cavalry, and his *compadre* Salduendo received Bandera's former post, captain of the guard.

These shifts infuriated Aguirre, but he chose to hide his resentment for the moment and bowed to Guzmán's wishes. Those who were close to Guzmán had begun to suggest that Don Fernando would be better off with Aguirre dead; Guzmán lacked the courage to give the order. With Bandera temporarily in the ascendant, Aguirre went armed day and night, fearing some plot by Bandera's followers against him.

He sought to ingratiate himself with Guzmán, whose attitude toward him seems to have been a mixture of worship and terror. The weak young governor promised Aguirre that he would be *maestro del campo* again before they reached Peru, and went so far as to offer to arrange the marriage of his brother, Martín de Guzmán, to Aguirre's adolescent halfbreed daughter, who had accompanied the expedition. The offer was an estimable one, for Martín de Guzmán was of high birth and well regarded in Peru, and Aguirre indicated that he was flattered by it. Guzmán presented the girl with a rich silken robe that had belonged to Ursua; he addressed her as his sister-in-law thereafter.

Aguirre now was ready to move against Bandera, who had grown haughty in his high office and had lost popularity. Bandera and Lorenzo de Salduendo both were rivals for the affections of the late Governor Ursua's mistress, Doña Iñez, and Aguirre used this rivalry to his own advantage. First he spread a rumor that Bandera was planning to kill Guzmán and take his place as governor. When Aguirre took this tale to Guzmán, Don Fernando brushed it off, saying that he was aware of the enmity between his two lieutenants, and could hardly accept Aguirre's testimony about Bandera's intentions. Whereupon Salduendo came forward and swore that all Aguirre had said was true: Bandera was planning a coup against Guzmán and Aguirre. Don Fernando was swayed, and agreed to the death of Bandera and his chief follower, Christoval Hernandez de Chaves. The two victims were invited to Don Fernando's lodging for a game of cards. When the play was at its height, Aguirre and several armed followers entered, fell upon Bandera and Hernandez, and slew them.

Aguirre's cruise was becoming a tour down a river of blood. Yet the worst still lay ahead, crimes so extraordinary that a sixteenth-century Portuguese writer, López Vaz, was moved to pay Aguirre a strange compliment: "He was born in Biscay, a country near unto France, wherefore I believe him rather to have been a Frenchman than a Spaniard, for that in the heart of a Spaniard there could not have been as much cruelty as this man showed." [117]

5

While the brigantines were under construction, some Indians came to the camp to offer food in exchange for beads and bells. The hungry Spaniards were eager for the barter, but without Ursua's restraining influence they began to practice those gratuitous cruelties against the Indians to which they were devoted. The Indians fled, and no more came. When famine threatened, a squadron of men went into the interior to find supplies of yuca, and six were killed in an Indian ambush. Among them was the Portuguese pilot, Sebastián Gómez. The numbers of the expedition were steadily dwindling.

No one dared to oppose Aguirre now that Bandera was dead. Don Fernando was of the opinion that he himself was the commander, but the others knew who the real master was. To identify his enemies, Aguirre coaxed the pliable Guzmán into calling for formal pledges of loyalty: those men who did not wish to follow Don Fernando to the conquest of Peru were asked to stand forth and proclaim themselves. In a flowery speech, Guzmán requested the Spaniards to set him aside along with all his officers if they did not approve of his conduct of the expedition. The soldiers, guided by Aguirre, reconfirmed their oath to their youthful governor. Next Guzmán called for each man to sign a paper swearing himself to the conquest of Peru, for Aguirre had brought him around to that ultimate goal. All willingly signed except three courageous men who would not thus brand themselves as rebels against their country: Francisco Vásquez, Juan de Cabañas, and Juan de Vargas Zapata. Their weapons were taken from them; but for the moment they were allowed to live. At Guzmán's command, the chaplain celebrated mass, and while the Host was still in his hands all the loyal members of the army came up to touch it and solemnize their vows, first Guzmán, then Aguirre and the rest, joining in a declaration of war against the government of Peru.

In resonant phrases Aguirre now proclaimed his puppet, Don Fernando, to be Prince of Peru and King over all of South America. "It is absolutely necessary," Aguirre cried, "that we forswear our allegiance to the kingdoms of Spain, our birthplace; and declare that we will not obey the King Don Philip; for it is clear that no one can serve two masters." He led the way: "I say that I denaturalize myself from the kingdoms of Spain, where I was born; and if I have any rights there in consequence of my parents being Spaniards, and vassals of the King Don Philip, I give up all my rights, and I deny that he is my king and lord; and I repeat that I know him not, neither do I wish to know him, nor obey him as such; but rather, being in possession of my own liberty, I elect from this time for my prince, king, and natural lord, Don Fernando de Guzmán; and I swear and promise to be his faithful vassal and to die in his defence." [118] Aguirre kissed the hand of the flattered and proud Don Fernando, and the others followed.

Henceforward Guzmán conducted himself as though a

crowned king, insisting on the title of "Your Excellence," walking with haughty mien, giving elegant new ranks to his officers, and promising them large donations out of the treasury of Peru. He dined alone, and was served with the homage due his rank. The many decrees he issued were inscribed, "Don Fernando de Guzmán, by the grace of God, Prince of *Tierra Firme* and of Peru."

The full plan of conquest was revealed by Aguirre. The new brigantines would traverse the river to the sea, and go to the island of Margarita, opposite the Venezuelan port of Cumaná, where provisions and recruits could be obtained. Without stopping, the brigantines would make for the port of Nombre de Díos on the Isthmus of Panamá, which would be conquered in a surprise attack. The city of Panamá would then be invaded and its administrators killed; all ships in the port would be seized, and every malcontent in Central America would be invited to join in the invasion of Peru. An invincible force would descend by sea to Peru, overthrow the constituted government, and divide the vast wealth of the kingdom.

The brigantines were finished in April, 1561: two sturdy vessels with hulls as strong as those of ships of war. After the three-month delay the Spaniards embarked once more, proceeding from village to village through the Machiparo country. The territory of the Omaguas still lay ahead, and Aguirre feared that if it were entered, the dream of El Dorado would distract the men from his plan of conquest and lead them to expend their energies in futile inland explorations. So when a tributary river presented itself on the left, Aguirre arranged to have the brigantines enter it, thus leaving the Amazon and adopting a northerly route. In all the records of South American conquest, Aguirre stands out as the only man who ever went to great lengths to *avoid* finding El Dorado.

The Cruise of the Tyrant Aguirre

The exact nature of Aguirre's course is uncertain, but it appears probable that the tributary he entered was the Río Japurá, which the brigantines followed in a westerly direction for a few days through a damp, mosquito-plagued country, going thence into a network of watery channels that brought them northeast into the Río Negro, which they took until they reached the Cassaquiari Canal, the waterway that connects the Negro and the Orinoco. It was an elaborate route that had never been traveled by Europeans before, and doubtless Aguirre went much of the way by random choice, trusting to luck that one river of this maze would bring him to the Atlantic.

The voyagers halted for eight days, at Don Fernando's command, to celebrate Easter. During the holiday, one of Ursua's former officers was overheard suggesting a counter-rebellion to a companion. Word of this came to Aguirre, who, says Padre Simón, "was growing morose, because many days had elapsed since an occasion had offered to kill anyone." [119] Aguirre had the two men arrested; Guzmán ordered that they not be executed until after Easter, but the command came too late to help.

On the river again, the Spaniards encountered friendly Indians who regaled them with "a sort of wine, made from many things, and of a pasty substance," and offered them fish, turtles, and manatees. They remained at this village for a month, enlarging the brigantines and adding decks to them so that they would be safer at sea. Most of the men were idle during this period, and they devoted rather too much time to thought, so that their consciences began to trouble them about the death of Ursua and the subsequent bloodshed. Don Fernando and some of his friends privately admitted the unlikelihood of a successful conquest of Peru, and recognized the fear that they would all be severely punished when they returned to civilization. Guzmán began to toy with the possibility of ridding himself of the ferocious Aguirre and going back to the Amazon to continue the abandoned search for El Dorado. At a council of his trusted followers it was resolved to kill Aguirre at once.

But Alonso de Montoya, one of Guzmán's men, suggested that the best time to slay Aguirre was after the brigantines had resumed their voyage. A little frightened at his own plan, Guzmán accepted the argument for delay. It was a fatal decision; for Aguirre, who had some drift of what was being discussed, instantly started to consolidate his own position and to plot the removal of his enemies.

Among those who had turned against Aguirre was his own closest ally, Lorenzo de Salduendo, who now had taken Doña Iñez as his mistress. As the brigantines were being readied for departure, Salduendo made some rearrangements of the cabins so that Doña Iñez and her servant girl would have comfortable quarters. Extra mattresses were brought on board. Aguirre told Salduendo that there was no room for them, and the mattresses would have to be left behind. Salduendo stalked off in fury, exclaiming, "Am I to beg favors from Lope de Aguirre at these my years?"

Aguirre interpreted this as a veiled threat, and ordered some of his men to kill Salduendo. Hearing of this, Salduendo called on Don Fernando for protection. One of Guzmán's captains sent word to Aguirre that Salduendo was not to be molested; but Aguirre ignored the message, and Salduendo was attacked and slain in Guzmán's very presence. Then, says Simón, "the cruel beast Aguirre, now bathed in the blood of Salduendo, longed to shed that of Doña Iñez, and, calling to mind his distaste for her, and some threats of hers, he determined that she should suffer a similar punishment; so he ordered one of his sergeants, called Antón Llamoso, and one Francisco Carrion, a *mestizo* [halfbreed] to go and kill her wherever they might find her. . . . No sooner was the sanguinary command given, than the murderers went to where Doña Iñez lodged, and rushing upon her with drawn swords, took her life in such a barbarous manner that after her death, even the most hardened men in the camp, at sight of the mangled victim, were broken-hearted." [120]

Don Fernando de Guzmán upbraided Aguirre for the poor taste of killing Salduendo before his eyes. Aguirre protested that Salduendo had meant to kill Guzmán, and that all his actions were intended for his lord and master's protection. But now the days of Don Fernando himself were numbered. Troubled by Guzmán's delay in having Aguirre removed, most of those who had agreed to kill the Biscayan grew timid, and withdrew their support from the plot, knowing that if it misfired Aguirre would surely have their lives. Two of these men came to Aguirre with full details of the conspiracy against him. Aguirre took immediate action.

The Spaniards were camped on a narrow island. Don Fernando's lodgings were at one end, Aguirre's at the other, with Montoya and other supporters of Guzmán in between. At night Aguirre posted guards on the road to cut off communication from one part of the island to the other, and gathered his friends. They went first to the dwelling of Montoya and another officer and killed them. Then they withdrew to the brigantines and waited for dawn, since the moonless night was too dark for an effective attack. In the quiet of morning they came ashore to complete the slaughter. One of the first victims was the chaplain, Padre Alonso Henao, though Simón admits that the murder may have been an accident since the priest had taken the oaths of rebellion against Spain. "They then proceeded to the Prince's quarters and found him on his couch," Simón relates, "quite unprepared to be hurried out of the world. Don Fernando arose, on hearing the noise made by the entry of the soldiers, and, on seeing Lope de Aguirre among them,

said, 'What is all this, my father?' for this was the way the
Prince generally addressed Aguirre, who replied, 'Do not be
alarmed, Your Excellency.' " [121] Passing onward, Aguirre and
his men took the lives of three of Guzmán's lieutenants, and
then returned to Don Fernando, dispatching him with a
volley of arquebus fire. "Thus he fell dead at their feet," says
Simón, "bringing his rebellion to an end, a fate which he
might have averted had he taken proper precautions. He was
scarcely twenty-six years of age, of good stature, well
formed and strong of limb, with the manners of a gentleman, fine face and beard, slow to action, more kind than
otherwise, and born in the city of Seville." [122]

6

The bloodshed was over for a while. As the sun rose,
Aguirre called everyone together. He was armed head to
foot, and surrounded by eighty of his followers. Coolly he
explained why it had been necessary to send Don Fernando
and his friends to join Ursua, Vargas, Salduendo, Doña
Iñez, and the rest. Had they been allowed to live, he declared, all would surely have perished through his bad government. Proclaiming himself general, Aguirre assured them
all that he would lead them to victory in Peru.

The Aguirre faction had taken on the name of *Marañones*, a punning label drawn from the name of the river, the
Marañon, on which they had begun their cruise, and from
the Spanish word *marañas* ("entanglements" or "plots")
that described not only the river but the tenor of the expedition. Aguirre distributed the highest ranks among his
Marañones. Martín Pérez, one of the slayers of Don Fernando, became *maestro del cámpo;* Juan López, a ship's
caulker, was named admiral; Juan Gonzalo, a carpenter,

was appointed sergeant-major. No one challenged Aguirre's authority.

Fearful of conspiracies, he revived an earlier order: with death the penalty, no man could speak in private with his companions. It became similarly proscribed to go about in groups, and it was forbidden for anyone to put his hand to a sword or other weapon in Aguirre's presence.

They left the village of all this butchery and embarked up the Río Negro again. Having heard that the country of the Omaguas lay on the right side—that is, to the east— Aguirre kept the brigantines to the left, occasionally deviating onto side branches so that the *Marañones* would not be aroused by a revived dream of El Dorado. Once, low mountains were seen in the east flanking broad savannahs, and the light of mány fires could be detected, a sure sign of a large village; so fanatical was Aguirre in his aversion to the golden country that it was a capital offense even to mention the village. "They could only look and be silent," notes Simón. "The Brazilian Indian guides said clearly that those were the lands and people of the Omaguas whom they were in search of, so, to stop any investigation on this head, Aguirre immediately issued an order, under pain of death, that no one should talk with the Brazilian guides, or speak of the lands of the Omaguas." [123]

In a high plain thick with cork trees, farther up the river, the voyagers entered the country of a Carib tribe, the Arnaquinas. Like most Caribs, they were cannibals—the word "cannibal" itself is a sixteenth-century distortion of "Carib"—and were skillful with their bows. The Spaniards drove them from their village and inspected their temple, in which they found two blood-stained planks on which human sacrifices presumably had been celebrated. Aguirre celebrated a few more sacrifices of his own; a soldier named

Monteverde was put to death only because he seemed insufficiently sadistic, Simón tells us, and was given the epitaph *amotinadorcillo*, "a poor little mutineer." (Simón also reports that Monteverde was revealed as a Lutheran, and that devout man Aguirre could not tolerate a heretic in his band.) Aguirre furthermore slew Juan de Cabañas, one of the three men who had refused to sign Guzmán's proclamation of rebellion against Spain, and two of his own officers, including the sergeant-major Juan Gonzalo, on suspicion of mutiny. The tyrant now lived in a state of perpetual fear, cloistered among his least distrusted followers, and taking lives steadily as a method of attaining tranquility.

The Brazilian guides, seeing that the expedition was no longer heading toward the Omaguas, slipped away and were not seen again. The brigantines loaded up with the produce of the Arnaquinas and set sail, one under Aguirre's command, the other led by the *maestro del campo*, Martín Pérez. There were signs of a tide in the river, for they had passed from the Negro into the Orinoco and were rapidly nearing the sea. In another two weeks, the river was wide enough to contain clusters of islands, and since Aguirre had slain most of the experienced navigators of the expedition they wandered in confusion, pulled back and forth by the rise and fall of the tides. Gradually they neared the estuary. The land was low and humid here, and tempers were short. Aguirre decided to abandon the remaining Indian slaves who had come with them from Peru, and two Spaniards, somehow conceiving that they were being left behind as well, were heard plotting against Aguirre and were instantly executed.

They reached the mouth of the Orinoco and found it to be several hundred miles wide, with huge waves crashing across it. Laboring under great difficulties, the brigantines bucked the tides and emerged into the Atlantic on July 1, 1561. In the nine months since the departure from Santa

Cruz in the foothills of the Andes, Aguirre and his men had covered thousands of miles in a voyage nearly as astonishing as Orellana's in its geographical scope, and probably unsurpassed in its savagery. Ninety-four days of this span had been spent on the river, the rest encamped.

Aguirre ordered the brigantines steered for Margarita. The sea was calm and the wind was fair, and in seventeen days the two vessels came to the Venezuelan island without once being separated. They suffered so from thirst and hunger that many men were at the edge of death when Pampatar, the principal port of Margarita, came into sight. As they neared the island a violent storm came up, parting the brigantines, and they had to make for different ports. Aguirre landed at Paraguache, afterward known as "the tyrant's port," and Pérez' ship made landfall six miles to the north. As he came into port, Aguirre was consumed with suspicions directed toward two officers, one of them the Diego de Belalcázar who had mocked him after Ursua's death. Afraid that they would betray him when they went ashore, he had them executed by a cruel and characteristically Spanish means, the *garrote* or strangling-cord.

A soldier named Alonso Rodríguez was sent with several others to find Pérez' brigantine and lead its men to Aguirre. Rodríguez carried the additional order to strangle one of his companions, Sancho Pizarro, while en route, and he did not forget to carry this out. At the same time Aguirre sent an officer called Diego Tirado into the city of Margarita to beg for provisions, claiming that the *Marañones* were merely innocent sailors who had lost their way at sea and were in need of aid. The people of Margarita had been disturbed by the arrival of the ships, believing at first that they were French men-of-war; but Tirado reassured them that they were merely a band of hungry and friendly Spaniards. A delegation of soldiers from Margarita visited

Aguirre's brigantine and condoled with him over the hardships of his voyage. Aguirre, hiding most of his able-bodied men belowdecks, promised to pay for any food the Margaritans could offer, and said that he would sail for Panamá as soon as his men were strong enough to take up the journey.

Deceived by this tale of woe, the governor and several officials of Margarita came to offer their greetings to the newcomers. The official party arrived at daybreak; Aguirre met them with the greatest respect and submission at the shore, and there were warm embraces and an exchange of gifts. Aguirre requested permission for his weary men to come ashore fully armed, which was not a usual custom, so that they could take some exercise. The governor rashly granted the request. Returning to the ship, Aguirre told his men, "Mark me well, my *Marañones*, sharpen your swords, and clean the arquebuses, for they must be damp, from being at sea. You have the governor's permission to go on shore armed." [124]

The *Marañones* marched ashore as though this were a military parade, and the officials from Margarita watched them as though they were reviewing it. Abruptly the soldiers surrounded the governor's party. Aguirre smoothly declared his feeling that Margarita was planning some treachery, and told the officials that they must consider themselves his prisoners.

"This caused a tumult amongst the governor's party," writes Padre Simón, "and they went back a few paces, saying, 'What is all this? what is all this?' putting their hands to their swords, as if in defense; but this was in vain, for the traitors surrounded them, presented lances, partisans, and arquebuses to their breasts, and thus they were made prisoners; when Aguirre, his captains and soldiers, advanced and disarmed them, taking also their staves of office, and their horses. They then mounted, and took possession of the passes and roads, so that no one could go to the city and give information of what had been done." [125]

Straightaway Aguirre led his men on a march to Margarita. He mounted the governor's horse and invited the bewildered man to ride behind him; when the governor refused such an indignity, Aguirre declared, "Well, then, we will all go on foot." When they had walked a short distance they met the men of the other brigantine, headed by Martín Pérez, who complimented Aguirre for the deft way he had taken possession of the city's authorities. The road was hot, and Aguirre mounted the horse again after a while; and this time, the governor abandoned his pride and climbed up in the rear.

At noon a mounted party under Pérez burst into Margarita, shouting, "Long live Aguirre! Liberty! Liberty!" Erupting through the streets, they rushed into the undefended fort and seized it. The city was in tumult. Aguirre arrived, leading his prisoners, and put them under guard at the fort. Then he went to the main plaza, where, as in many towns of Spanish America, a wooden column called a *rollo* had been erected as an emblem of jurisdiction. Seizing an axe, Aguirre began madly chopping at the *rollo;* but it was of the dense wood called lignum vitae, or *guaiacan*, and "the steel flew from the hatchets, while the *rollo* received no particular harm, and some prognosticated that it would remain there, as representing justice, and the name of the king." [126]

Aguirre's next call was at the royal treasury. The door was smashed in, and the tyrant confiscated gold and pearls that had been set aside for the royal fifth, destroying the account books. Meanwhile his soldiers were passing from house to house, collecting silk and linen clothing, wine, food, and anything else of value. This was brought to the fort and divided among the *Marañones*. At Aguirre's orders, all canoes and boats were collected, so that no one could leave the island. The citizens of the conquered city were warned to stay in their houses and make no resistance, on penalty of death.

A night of rape and plunder ensued. The city was a prosperous one, fattened on the pearl trade, and it was ripe for piracy. Some of Margarita's own soldiers, seeing the *Marañones* enjoying the benefits of their invasion, presented themselves to Aguirre and asked to join his service. He gladly enrolled them under his banner and paid them out of government funds. "He then gave them permission to become as great villains as the rest, and this was exactly what they desired," the Simón account declares. "They joined the other soldiers, and led them to those spots, of which they knew, where the inhabitants had hidden some of their property, merchandise, clothes, jewels, and strings of pearls. They effected these robberies secretly, and divided the plunder." [127]

These new recruits informed Aguirre that a priest from Santo Domingo, Fray Francisco Montesinos, had recently arrived aboard a fine, large, and well-armed ship that was now anchored at the mainland port of Maracapana, where the *padre* was engaged in the conversion of the Indians. The vessel was just what Aguirre needed for the voyage from Margarita to Panamá, and he sent one of the brigantines, with eighteen men under a captain named Pedro de Monguia, to find Padre Montesinos' ship and bring it to the island. As he neared the mainland, Monguia contemplated the course of the enterprise thus far, and it occurred to him that having placed himself beyond the reach of the terrible Aguirre, it might be the part of folly to return. Some of Monguia's men, enjoying their life of crime, did not share this view, and as the brigantine reached Maracapana he had them disarmed.

Monguia sought out Padre Montesinos and related all that had occurred. The priest resolved to set sail at once to notify the Venezuelan authorities at the port of Burburata, and, as his route would take him past Margarita, to attempt to attack Aguirre as well. Monguia and the other ex-*Marañones* agreed to join Montesinos' crew.

Confident that Monguia would bring him Montesinos' ship, Aguirre began to lay in provisions for the voyage to Nombre de Díos and Panamá, ordering the inhabitants of the island to slaughter six hundred sheep and some bullocks and to salt down the meat. The Margaritans, already embittered by the havoc worked by Aguirre's men, and groaning under the necessity to quarter the *Marañones* in their own houses, grumbled at this. With his customary mountainous audacity Aguirre informed the citizens that "my arrival in this island with my companions is not with the object of settling here, neither to offend any of you, but rather to render you good service; for, God is my judge, that I did not intend to remain here more than four days; but my ships came in such a bad state, that it was impossible to continue my voyage with them, and, not finding here any other vessels to meet my wants, I am obliged, now that Providence has proportioned me the ship of the Reverend Father Provincial, to await its arrival, rather than build others, which would detain us here a much longer time." [128] He added that payment in full at an honorable price would be made for all that the Margaritans supplied, a promise that was believed as earnestly as it was offered.

As always when Aguirre was forced to wait in one place, his boiling hatreds overflowed upon his own men. Growing suspicious of his captain of ammunition, he hanged the man and gave his post to Antón Llamoso, one of the murderers of Doña Iñez. This led four other men to resolve to desert, for they had seen how Aguirre could turn on his own favorites in sudden bursts of irrationality, and knew that no man's life was secure near the tyrant. They slipped out of the city by night.

"When this was known to Aguirre," says Padre Simón, "he was furious and raved like a madman, foaming at the mouth with rage and passion, for he believed that if he did not give himself up to such like demonstrations, and give peremptory orders to find them, all his men would desert and leave them." [129] A reward was posted for the capture of the four deserters. Aguirre compelled the Margaritans to join in the search, on the threat of executing their governor. The island was combed, and two of the men were taken prisoner. Aguirre had them executed, pinning to the body of each the inscription, "These men have been executed because they were faithful vassals of the King of Castile." Over the corpses he said, "Let us now see if the King of Castile will give you life again."

Aguirre began to foment total anarchy. He told his men that they were to put to death all monks, bishops, viceroys, presidents, judges, governors, and lawyers whom they encountered in their campaign of conquest, "for that all these persons had entirely destroyed the Indies." [130] To this end, a monk of Margarita was seized, but Aguirre let himself be persuaded not to kill him. Aguirre added to the list of those marked for death all *caballeros* of noble blood and all unchaste women, and the list grew as his feverish mind conceived new enemies.

When a Margaritan named Alonso Pérez de Aguilar slipped through Aguirre's guard and escaped from the island, the tyrant had Aguilar's house leveled to the ground, his cattle slain, and his fields ploughed with salt. While still in this rage he turned against a kind-hearted officer named Juan de Turriaga, who had given some food to the poor, and, "as flowers are rendered poisonous by the pestilential spider, so Aguirre said of this captain that he was his enemy," [131] and ordered Martín Pérez to kill him at his own dinner table. Turriaga rose when the *maestro del campo* entered his lodging, and bowed to him in proper deference; Pérez signaled, and his men rushed forward with lances and swords. By morning, Aguirre's mood had shifted. In unexpected remorse he gave Turriaga a full military burial, with muffled drums and a parade of troops in mourning.

The failure of Monguia to return with Padre Montesinos' ship was distressing to Aguirre. Assuming that Montesinos had killed or imprisoned the *Marañones*, Aguirre vowed a dreadful vengeance against the Father Provincial, declaring that "a thousand monks should be sacrificed, with the most painful deaths," and vowing to flay Montesinos himself alive, "and make a drum of his skin, as an example to all." [132] Montesinos had in this time carried the information of Aguirre's revolt all along the Venezuelan coast from Cumaná to Burburata, and the authorities in charge were gathering forces to oppose the tyrant. Now Montesinos himself was sailing to Margarita to be the first to make war on Aguirre.

Seeing the handsome ship approach the island, Aguirre thought it was being brought to him as a prize by Monguia. But another craft from the mainland arrived, and the *Marañones* learned from its seamen that Montesinos was coming to attack. In an access of monumental fury, Aguirre seized the leading citizens of Margarita and their wives and children, put them in irons, and imprisoned them in the fort with the city officials. Word now came that Montesinos had landed at a place called Puerto de Piedras, fifteen miles from the city. Aguirre armed his men to go against the friar; and that night, as an act of terror to encourage his troops, he decided to execute the city's administrators.

The governor and several other officials were confined

in a room high in the fortress. Aguirre had them released and brought to a lower room where he told them to have no fear, for they were not in danger. After these soothing words he left them, and at midnight sent to the prisoners Francisco Carrion, another of the murderers of Doña Iñez, who entered with several slaves carrying strangling-cords. The governor protested to Carrion that only a short while ago Aguirre had given his word that no harm would come to them; shrugging, Carrion advised them to pray, and the executions took place. Still later in the evening, Aguirre summoned his men to view the bodies in the fortress. Reciting all the past crimes of the expedition, he observed that they "had added crime to crime," slaying Ursua and his lady, Guzmán, many captains and soldiers, and now four governmental officials. "Having committed so many, and such grave and atrocious crimes," Aguirre declared, "be ye sure that ye are not safe in any part of the world, excepting with me. . . . Thus I counsel you not to leave me, to sell your lives dearly when the occasion offers, and to let all be of one mind." [133]

In the morning Aguirre and eighty arquebusiers marched toward Montesinos at Puerto de Piedras. Martín Pérez was left in charge of the city of Margarita, and he and his men spent the day in drunken revelry after seeing Aguirre out of town. At Puerto de Piedras, Aguirre discovered that Montesinos had put to sea and was making for the city. Hurrying back to Margarita, Aguirre was greeted by the surprised and somewhat intoxicated Pérez. While they waited for the arrival of Montesinos' ship, Aguirre was approached by one of the common soldiers, Christoval García, who whispered that Pérez had spent the day plotting to kill Aguirre and escape to France.

The accusation was sufficient proof of guilt for Aguirre, and he sent a platoon of assassins to deal with the *maestro del campo*. Pérez was summoned to Aguirre's presence in the fort. When he entered, he was fired upon from behind, then beset with daggers and knives. Though hid-eously wounded and half disemboweled, Pérez staggered from the room and wandered about the fort, begging for confession. Finally he fell, and one of Aguirre's men cut his throat.

There followed a scene of pure horror worthy of the most febrile Jacobean dramatist. Aguirre had also heard that the villainous Antón Llamoso, now one of his closest confederates, was part of Pérez' conspiracy against him. As he stood by Pérez' ruined corpse, Aguirre said to Llamoso, "They also tell me that you were one of the party with the *maestro del campo;* how was this? Was this friendship? And dost thou hold so lightly the love I feel for you?"

Those who had just slain Pérez waited for the expected order to throw themselves upon Llamoso. But Llamoso pro-tested his innocence with a thousand blurted oaths, and then, seeing that the tyrant still was displeased, dropped to the floor beside Pérez' mutilated form.

Padre Simón relates that Llamoso "rushed upon the body of Martín Pérez, which was almost cut to pieces, and, before those who were present, he threw himself upon it, shouting, 'Curse this traitor, who wished to commit so great a crime! I will drink his blood!' and, putting his mouth over the wounds in the head, with more than demoniac rage, he began to suck the blood and brains that issued from the wounds, and swallowed what he sucked, as if he were a famished dog. This caused such horror to those who were present, that there was not one who was not turned sick at heart by the scene. Aguirre was satisfied of his fidelity, and so it turned out, for there was no one who sustained him, until his last hour, like unto this Llamoso." [134]

7

Forces were gathering in Venezuela to put an end to the nightmare exploits of the *Marañones.* Pablo Collado, the governor of Venezuela, was at Tocuyo when he learned of Aguirre's revolt. He sent word to Burburata that all women and children were to be evacuated from the city in case the tyrant should land there, and had that city and the recently founded inland town of Trujillo readied for defense. Collado passed Padre Montesinos' grim message on to Pedro Bravo de la Molina, the governor of the new city of Mérida in northwestern Venezuela. In August, 1561, Molina began to mobilize his own men, at the same time sending messengers to New Granada to spread the alert. By September, Molina's men were in Bogotá to relay an account of Aguirre's atrocities, and an army was assembled against the event that Aguirre might attack New Granada. Its command was given to the old *conquistador* Gonzalo Jiménez de Quesada, who had returned to New Granada after his long absence, and Quesada's officers included several men who had figured in the original conquest of Cundinamarca in 1537, such as Juan de Cespedes and Hernán Vanegas.

Town by town, the provinces were getting ready for Aguirre. The governments of Popayán, Santa Marta, and Cartagena were given the warning. All of Venezuela and what now is Colombia was in a ferment of military preparation. New Granada alone mustered 1500 ordinary soldiers, 400 pikemen, and 200 arquebusiers. Never had there been such a threat to the general welfare as Aguirre represented; for even Gonzalo Pizarro's rebellion in Peru had been the rational act of sanely ambitious men, while Aguirre seemed to claw the very skies in his frenzy to destroy everything.

Until Aguirre left unhappy Margarita and made his next move, no steps could be taken against him. Several courses of action were debated in New Granada, but in the end the huge army was held on the plateau to await Aguirre's plans.

Aguirre watched with displeasure as Montesinos' ship

took up a position half a league off shore at Margarita, out of range of his artillery. But Montesinos did not attempt a landing. From the safety of his vessel he sent envoys inviting Aguirre to surrender. Aguirre replied with a florid letter beginning, "Magnificent and Reverend Sir," and expressing the pious wish that it could have been possible to celebrate the priest's arrival "with boughs and flowers, rather than with arquebuses and discharges of artillery." He humbly declined the name of traitor, which he said could be applied only to far more noble souls, and begged to be excused for such violent deeds as had been necessary to commit as "we sought to find a land, miserable as it might be, to give rest to our poor bodies." He denounced Monguia and the other renegades serving with Montesinos as murderers, rebels, buffoons, and cowards, and concluded by beseeching the priest to reply to his letter, adding, "Let us treat one another well in this war. God will bring trouble on all traitors, and the King will restore the loyal to life." [135]

Some Indians carried this letter to Montesinos, who regarded it as the ravings of a madman, and replied in measured terms, warning Aguirre to abandon his road of errors and return to the service of God and King Philip. Then, seeing that the *Marañones* were impregnable in their island refuge, the priest sailed off to Santo Domingo to carry the news of the revolt to the West Indies.

Aguirre now decided to leave Margarita. Abandoning his earlier idea to sail to Panamá, he chose to make the much shorter journey to Burburata and slash a fiery trail across Venezuela and New Granada while marching inland toward Peru. During the final days of preparations for departure, many victims fed Aguirre's thirst for blood, among them several *Marañones* and a cousin of Ursua's, Martín Díaz de Armendariz, who had been a prisoner for the whole journey since Ursua's assassination. From the silk of Margarita, Aguirre had three flags fashioned: black, with red crossed swords. On August 15, 1561, mass was said at Margarita's main church, Aguirre attending in full armor. On the way to church he spied the king of spades from a deck of playing cards lying in the street, and to show his contempt for all kings he made a public show of stamping on the card, bellowing cries of disdain, and ripping it to shreds. After mass, Aguirre's pirate flags were solemnly blessed and given to his captains, "so that," according to Simón, "they might march under the flags, to follow, defend, and guard his person; . . . that they might make war upon all who opposed them; that the obstinate towns were to be sacked, but he charged them to respect the churches and female honor, but nothing else. They had full liberty to do as they pleased, for as they had made a new king, they could make new laws." [136]

Aguirre emphasized this respect for the churches by killing two priests of Margarita before departure, as well as a few more of his own men and several citizens of the island. The moment of embarkation cost the life of Aguirre's admiral, Alonso Rodríguez, for a high wave splashed the tyrant, and Rodríguez suggested that Aguirre go below, so he would not get wet. This so angered Aguirre that he drew his sword and cut off one of Rodríguez' arms, then instantly ordered the wounded man to be attended to by doctors, and shortly afterward reversed himself and had Rodríguez put to death.

The *Marañones* put to sea aboard three vessels, after forty days of devastation on Margarita. Aguirre had some 150 men at his command, including many new recruits from Margarita. He was aware that the mainland provinces had been warned and were gathering forces to oppose him.

Although it normally was a voyage of two days from Margarita to Burburata, Aguirre's ships were becalmed, and more than a week passed before they made their landing at the Venezuelan port on the seventh of September. The *Marañones* went ashore at once by the light of a merchant vessel in the port that they set afire. Aguirre hoped that the inhabitants would come forth to greet him, as they had done at Margarita, bringing gifts to appease him. But by morning no one had appeared. At the orders of Governor Collado, Burburata had been completely evacuated and all valuable property removed. Collado and a small band of soldiers were encamped at Tocuyo, and messages were going out to Mérida and the other inland settlements of Venezuela that the time had come to join forces for a concerted effort against Aguirre. Pedro Bravo de la Molina appointed a soldier named Diego García de Paredes to lead Mérida's men to Tocuyo. There it was decided for strategic reasons to assemble the entire Venezuelan army at the town of Barquisimeto, which was in open country and close to Burburata. Governor Collado named one Gutierrez de la Peña as general of this army, with García de Paredes as *maestro del campo*.

As these preparations were being made, Aguirre was exploring deserted Burburata. Only one man was in the town: a certain Francisco Martín, one of the *Marañones* who had deserted with Monguia to the ship of Padre Montesinos. Martín had repented of his desertion and slipped away from Montesinos to rejoin his old companions; and he succeeded, improbably enough, in convincing Aguirre that he had meant to be loyal all along. Martín was welcomed back into the tyrant's service. About the same time, a Portuguese named Antonio Farias was shot by Aguirre for asking, as he stepped ashore, whether this was an island or the mainland.

To discourage desertions, Aquirre had his three ships burned. The *Marañones* took up residence in Burburata, and a scouting party went out to collect horses from the countryside. These men were set upon by Indians and suffered some losses, which infuriated Aguirre. By raiding the estates of farmers around Burburata, some horses were obtained, but most of them were unbroken and it was necessary to remain in Burburata longer than planned in order to get them into useful shape. Aguirre took the opportunity to declare war formally against King Philip, proclaiming it through the streets of the town to the sound of trumpets and kettle-drums.

The next stop on Aguirre's course was the town of Valencia, a short distance from the coast. The horses were laden with guns and ammunition, and the *Marañones* marched on foot beside them. On the march, one of Aguirre's men discovered a hut that had been occupied by several of the deserters of Monguia's faction, and by chance a document was found there quoting the lengthy testimony of Francisco Martín against Aguirre. Martín made further declarations of loyalty to the master to whom he had returned, but his own words convicted him, and he was put to death.

The march to Valencia was a painful one through rough, hot, mountainous country. The horses suffered so badly that Aguirre made his men relieve the animals of some of their burdens, carrying part of the baggage on his own back. The journey lasted eight days. When Valencia was reached the tyrant himself was sick with fatigue. He was carried toward Valencia in a hammock, blazing with fever, and at one point he was so ill that he cried out to his followers to kill him, which, Padre Simón notes, "they were afterwards ever sorry they did not do."

The inhabitants of Valencia, like those of Burburata, fled upon the approach of the rebels, taking refuge among the friendly Indians who dwelled on the islands of a nearby lake. The *Marañones* seized possession of the houses, burning those they did not need for their own use. Aguirre's illness grew more severe; in a few days he was as fleshless as a skeleton, and seemed at the point of death. Then his strength returned, and he marked his recovery by several random executions of soldiers who crossed his path at poorly timed moments.

It was in Valencia that Aguirre composed the remarkable letter to King Philip II that summed up the essential nature of his character and revealed better than all his actions the boundless depths of his infamy. A priest named Pedro Contreras, who had been carried along from Margarita by Aguirre, was made the vehicle by which this strange document was released; for Aguirre offered the priest his liberty if he would bring the letter to the Royal Audience at Santo Domingo. This was done, and Francisco Vásquez, the only firsthand chronicler of Aguirre's misdeeds, inserted a copy of the text in his account. Padre Simón could not bring himself to quote such blasphemies in the narrative that he prepared from Vásquez' manuscript, and the letter remained unpublished until the eighteenth century. Aguirre addressed his sovereign in these words:

"King Philip, a Spaniard, son of Charles the Invincible! I, Lope de Aguirre, thy vassal, am an old Christian, of poor but noble parents, and native of the town of Oñate, in Biscay. In my youth I crossed the ocean to the land of Peru, lance in hand, to perform what is due from an honest man, and, during fifty-four years, I have done thee great service in Peru, in the conquest of the Indians, in forming settlements, and especially in battles and encounters which I have fought in thy name, always to the best of my power and ability, without asking thy officers for payment, as will appear by thy royal books.

"I firmly believe that thou, O Christian king and lord, hast been very cruel and ungrateful to me and my compan-

ions for such good service, and that all those who write to
thee from this land deceive thee much, because thou seest
things from too far off. I, and my companions (whose names
I will mention presently), no longer able to suffer the cruelties which thy judges and governors exercise in thy name,
are resolved to obey thee no longer. We regard ourselves no
longer as Spaniards. We make a cruel war on thee, because
we will not endure the oppression of thy ministers, who, to
give places to their nephews and their children, dispose of
our lives, our reputations, and our fortunes. I am lame in the
left foot, from two shots of an arquebus, which I received in
the battle of Chucuinga, fighting under the orders of the
marshal Alonso de Alvarado, against Francisco Hernandez
Girón, a rebel, as I and my companions are now, and will be
until death: for we now know, in this country, how cruel
thou art, that thou art a breaker of thy faith and word;
therefore, even if we received thy pardon, we should give
less credence to it, than to the books of Martin Luther.

"Thy viceroy, the Marquis of Cañete, a bad, effeminate,
and ambitious tyrant, hung Martín de Robles, a man who
had been distinguished in thy service, and the ill-fated
Alonso Díaz, who had labored harder in the discovery of
Peru, than the tribes which followed Moses; and Piedrahita,
a good captain, who fought many battles in thy service; and
it was these men who procured a victory for thee in Pucara;
for, had it been otherwise, Francisco Hernandez Girón
would now be sovereign of Peru. Do not put any faith in the
accounts of services which thy judges declare they have
performed, for they are great fables, unless they call having
spent 800,000 *pesos* out of the Royal Treasury, a service.
Chastise them for their vices and evil deeds, for evil doers
they certainly are.

"Hear me! O hear me! thou King of Spain. Be not
cruel to thy vassals, for it was while thy father, the Emperor

Charles, remained quietly in Spain, that they procured for thee so many kingdoms and vast countries. Remember, King Philip, that thou hast no right to draw revenues from these provinces, since their conquest has been without danger to thee. I take it for certain that few kings go to hell, only because they are few in number; but that if there were many, none of them would go to heaven. For I believe that you are all worse than Lucifer, and that you hunger and thirst after human blood; and further, I think little of you, and despise you all, nor do I look upon your government as more than an air bubble. Know that I, and my two hundred arquebus-bearing *Marañones*, have taken a solemn oath to God, that we will not leave one of thy ministers alive. We consider ourselves, at this moment, the happiest men on earth, because, in this land of the Indians, we preserve the faith and the commandments of God in their purity, and we maintain all that is preached by the Church of Rome. We expect, though sinners in this life, to endure martyrdom for the laws of God.

"On leaving the river of Amazons, which is called Marañon, we came to an island inhabited by Christians, called Margarita, where we received news from Spain of the great conspiracy of the Lutherans, which caused us much terror and alarm. In our company there was one of these Lutherans, named Monteverde, and I ordered him to be cut to pieces. Believe me, O most excellent King, that I will force all men to live perfectly in the faith of Christ.

"The corruption of the morals of the monks is so great in this land, that it is necessary to chastise it severely. There is not an ecclesiastic here, who does not think himself higher than the governor of a province. I beg of thee, O great King, not to believe what the monks tell thee in Spain. They are always talking of the sacrifices they make, as well as of the hard and bitter life they lead in America. Be assured that when they shed tears there, in thy royal presence, it is that here they may be the more powerful. Wouldst thou know the life which they lead here? They are engaged in trade, striving for benefices, selling the sacraments of the church for a price, enemies of the poor, avaricious, gluttonous, and proud to that degree that, at the least, every friar pretends to rule and govern all these lands. They never desire to preach to any poor Indian, yet they are possessed of the best estates. The life they lead is surely a hard one, for does not each of them, as a penance, have a dozen girls, and as many boys, who catch fish, kill partridges, and gather fruit for them? Remedy this, O King and lord, or else, I swear to thee, on the faith of a Christian, that heaven will punish thee, and great scandals will follow. I say this to let thee know the truth, though neither I, nor my companions, either desire or hope for thy mercy.

"Thy judges, too, each have 4000 *pesos* a year, besides 8000 for expenses, and, at the end of three years, each of them has 60,000 *pesos*, besides land and other property. Notwithstanding all this we should be content to submit to them if, for our sins, they did not force us to bow down and worship them, like Nebuchadnezzar. This is insufferable.

"Alas! alas! what a misfortune it is that the Emperor, thy father, has conquered Germany at such a price, and has spent, in that conquest, the money that we procured for him in these very Indies! Most excellent King and lord, Germany was conquered by arms, and Germany has conquered Spain by her vices, of which we are here well rid, and are content with a little maize and water.

"Let wars spread where they may, and where men carry them, yet at no time will we cease to be obedient to the holy church of Rome. We cannot believe, O excellent King and lord! that thou canst be so cruel to such good vassals as thou hast in these parts; and I therefore desire that thou mayst know what thy ministers do without thy consent. Near the city of the kings [Lima] and close to the sea, some lakes were discovered where fish were preserved; and thy wicked judges, for their own profit, rented them in thy name, giving out that this was done with thy consent. If this be so, for the love of God allow us to have some of the fish, for it was us who discovered the lakes. Surely the King of Castile is not in need of four hundred *pesos*, which is the sum for which these lakes are rented: and, O most illustrious King! it is not in Córdova nor in Valladolid that we ask for this property. Deign to dole out charity, my lord, to the poor men who have labored in this land; and remember that God is the same to all; that there is the same justice, the same reward, the same heaven, the same hell, for all mankind.

"In the year 1559, the Marquis of Cañete entrusted the expedition of the river of Amazons to Pedro de Ursua, a Navarrese, or rather a Frenchman, who delayed the building of his vessels until 1560. These vessels were built in the province of the Motilones, which is a wet country, and, as they were built in the rainy season, they came to pieces, and we therefore made canoes, and descended the river. We navigated the most powerful river in Peru, and it seemed to us that we were in a sea of fresh water. We descended the river for three hundred leagues. This bad governor was capricious, vain, and inefficient, so that we could not suffer it, and we gave him a quick and certain death. We then raised a young gentleman of Seville, named Don Fernando de Guzmán, to be our king, and we took the same oaths to him as are taken to thy royal person, as may be seen by the signatures of all those who are with me. They named me *maestro del campo;* and, because I did not consent to their evil deeds, they desired to murder me. I therefore killed this new king, the captain of his guard, his lieutenant-general, four captains, his major-domo, his chaplain, who said mass, a woman, a knight of the Order of Rhodes, an admiral, two ensigns, and five or six of his servants. It was my intention to carry on the war, on account of the many cruelties which thy ministers had committed. I named captains and sergeants; but these men also wanted to kill me, and I hanged them. We continued our course while all this evil fortune was befalling us; and it was eleven months and a half before we reached the mouths of the river, having travelled for more than a hundred days, over more than fifteen hundred leagues. This river has a course of two thousand leagues of fresh water, the greater part of the shores being uninhabited; and God only knows how we ever escaped out of that fearful lake. I advise thee not to send any Spanish fleet up this ill-omened river; for, on the faith of a Christian, I swear to thee, O King and lord, that if a hundred thousand men should go up, not one would escape, and there is nothing else to expect, especially for the adventurers from Spain.

"The captains and officers who are now under my command in this enterprise, and who promise to die in it, are Juan Jerónimo de Espindola, a Genoese, captain of infantry, admiral Juan Gómez, a Spaniard, [a long list of others follows] and many other gentlemen. They pray to God that thy strength may ever be increased against the Turk and the Frenchman, and all others who desire to make war against thee; and we shall give God thanks if, by our arms, we attain the rewards which are due to us, but which thou hast denied us; and, because of thine ingratitude, I am a rebel against thee until death."

"LOPE DE AGUIRRE, the Wanderer." [137]

Few kings have ever received such a message from a subject—a letter full of justified complaints and insane objections, a screed that mingled piety and blasphemy, professions of loyalty with declarations of rebellion, and shifted from one attitude to its opposite within the space of a single paragraph, sometimes within a single sentence. King Philip's reaction has not been recorded. It is likely that none of his courtiers dared to show him Aguirre's letter, though Philip, a connoisseur of the irrational, might have taken a certain melancholy delight in its blazing words.

8

At Valencia, Aguirre learned the details of the force that was being mustered against him at Barquisimeto, and heard also that the men of Venezuela had requested Gonzalo de Quesada's army to march from New Granada to reinforce them. He decided on a quick thrust at Barquisimeto before the two armies could join. After executing one of his men who had a relative in New Granada, and who thus might be unreliable in battle, and putting to death two others who seemed to lack sufficient enthusiasm for further violence, Aguirre with his less than 150 men and ninety horses headed southwest over the mountain road to Barquisimeto after a fifteen-day stay in Valencia. By order of Governor Collado, scouts had been placed along this route to monitor Aguirre's movements, and as the *Marañones* took to the road the cry came to Barquisimeto to prepare for a clash.

The Venezuelans were caught off guard. Some troops were at Barquisimeto under the command of Gutierrez de la Peña, but most were still at Tocuyo. Lacking proper information about the size of Aguirre's force, Peña decided to evacuate Barquisimeto. The inhabitants took to the woods with such property as could be carried, and Peña withdrew temporarily to Tocuyo to regroup.

The thickly forested region through which Aguirre's men were passing offered temptations to deserters. One by one, ten *Marañones* slipped away. Their disappearance roused Aguirre to nearly incoherent wrath; he foamed at the mouth, stamped his feet, and cried out against the treacherous men who "would leave me in the hour of greatest need," forcing him "to fight alone with the mountain cats and monkeys of the forests." [138] On the third day of the march they reached a mining camp where gold was being extracted; the miners fled, and Aguirre, who needed provisions more than he did gold at this stage, confiscated the contents of their granaries. After a day's rest they continued onward. Rain began to fall so fiercely that the horses slid on the mountain tracks. Aguirre launched a blasphemous tirade against the heavens for daring to drench him so, concluding, "Does God think that because it rains in torrents I am not to go to Peru and destroy the world? He is mistaken in me." [139]

The troops of Gutierrez de la Peña had left Tocuyo again and were approaching Barquisimeto from the south. Among them was a deserter from the *Marañones*, Pedro de Galeas, who had been one of Ursua's captains and who had escaped from Aguirre just as the tyrant had decided to murder him. Galeas had provided Peña with a full account of Aguirre's army, revealing that of the 140 remaining *Marañones*, only about fifty followed Aguirre by choice, and the rest would gladly desert given the opportunity to evade his wrath. Peña was cheered by this, for he had formed an exaggerated view of Aguirre's strength and did not have many men at his own disposal, the vast army from New Granada not yet having arrived.

To check on Galeas' information, Peña sent out his *maestro del campo*, Diego García de Paredes, with fourteen or fifteen men to reconnoitre the rebel camp. Paredes was a veteran soldier who had been with Pizarro at the conquest of Peru thirty years before and had since seen military action under Charles V in the Emperor's European wars. The men he led toward Aguirre were on horseback, but with poorly equipped saddles, and their only weapons were crudely made lances. Peña's remaining troops numbered about seventy, with just two arquebuses among them, one not in working order.

In a heavily wooded region near Barquisimeto the soldiers of Paredes and Aguirre suddenly came upon one another, so unexpectedly that both groups retreated at once. Paredes attempted to draw his men into position for an ambush, but the *Marañones*, regrouping after their surprise, came forward by the light of the moon and put the men of Tocuyo to flight.

Governor Collado, at Tocuyo, drew up a number of letters of pardon addressed to Aguirre's men, inviting them to desert to the royalist side and offering full amnesty for their crimes. Aguirre himself was offered the same pardon if he would abandon his rebellion. Striking an oddly medieval note, Collado suggested that if Aguirre persisted in his present course, it would be satisfactory for the governor to meet the rebel in single combat, rather than involving many men in an armed battle. Aguirre ignored the proposal, and pointed out to his men with some justice that while Collado might forgive their crimes, King Philip would not necessarily take the same tolerant approach. "Put no trust in governors, nor in their papers or signatures," Aguirre told them. "Think on the cruelties, robberies, deaths, and destruction of towns you have committed. . . . Neither in Spain, the Indies, nor any other part of the world, have there been such men as you are, who have done such horrors." He called Collado's letters "bitter fruit and gilded pills, so that under a delusive color you would swallow poison." [140]

After an eight-day march from Valencia, Aguirre entered Barquisimeto and found it deserted. The small army of Gutierrez de la Peña had dug in on the heights overlooking the town, just within arquebus range. Paredes' little band cut around to the rear, and managed to capture four horses of Aguirre's party that were laden with gunpowder, seriously depleting the tyrant's resources.

Aguirre made his headquarters in a large square building with adobe walls and turrets, in the highest part of town. He set fire to the surrounding houses, destroying them so they would not afford cover to an advancing force. Peña's hilltop camp was visible, and Aguirre watched it worriedly through the first night of his occupation of Barquisimeto. At dawn, the other royalist force under Paredes stole toward Aguirre's entrenchment, armed now with five recently obtained arquebuses; shots were fired in the dim light, and there was a moment of uncertainty in the rebel camp. Aguirre sent forty arquebusiers out to attack Paredes, but the royalists disappeared before battle could be joined.

Aguirre did not dare to leave Barquisimeto, but Peña's forces were not strong enough to drive him out. The stalemate continued for several days, while Governor Collado sent out in all directions for reinforcements. After some minor political dispute, Pedro Bravo de la Molina of the city of Mérida led two hundred soldiers toward Barquisimeto. News of their arrival soon reached the besieged *Marañones*, and Aguirre's men came to the conclusion that the end of their rebellion was near.

Very much like Hitler in his bunker in Berlin in the spring of 1945, Aguirre refused to listen to any talk of defeat, urged his men wildly on to renewed confidence, and slaughtered anyone whose faith seemed to waver. Nevertheless, on the third day after the arrival of Bravo de la Molina's reinforcements, two of Aguirre's men managed to escape to the royalists. To forestall further desertions, Aguirre chose sixty men to sally forth at night and raid the royalist camp. They were spied by sentinels, and Peña's troops gave chase, driving the sixty *Marañones* into a ravine. Seeing what had happened, Aguirre rode out on a jet-black steed, his black-and-red flag fluttering above him, and feigned a flank attack on the royalists to extricate his men. The *Marañones* were outnumbered more than two to one, but they had a great many arquebuses, and they kept up a hail of gunfire that compelled Peña's soldiers to remain at a distance. Aguirre's own horse was shot out from under him by one of Peña's five arquebusiers. In the heat of the fray Diego Tirado, one of the tyrant's lieutenants, made a dash toward the royalist forces, shouting, "Long live the King, long live the King." His desertion was a gravely discouraging blow to Aguirre's men. At Tirado's advice, the royalists fanned out widely so they would not suffer the concentrated fire of the *Marañones*, and settled down to wait for Aguirre's forces to run out of ammunition.

"*Marañones*," Aguirre cried, "is it possible that you cannot bring to the earth a few herdsmen, with sheepskin jackets and hide bucklers?" This was a reference to the deerskin armor of Peña's men. Pointing out that the enemy was armed mainly with rusty swords and crooked lances, Aguirre spurred his followers to a renewed attack and managed to get them from their *cul-de-sac* and back to their fortification within Barquisimeto. That night he upbraided them for their poor showing in the battle, accusing them of having deliberately aimed over the heads of Peña's troops.

It was clear to the tyrant now that his control was ebbing. When he proposed to have all the sick and wounded strangled, so they would not be a further encumbrance in the siege, his own closest associates vetoed the atrocious idea. Aguirre meditated on the wisdom of escaping with his followers to the coast, taking ship for some distant point, and settling beyond the reach of Spanish authority. But the royalists held a tight grasp around the rebel entrenchment. It was impossible even to go out to gather food. Nevertheless the tyrant sought a way to get out of Barquisimeto. The *Marañones* were deserting in great numbers, and those who remained refused to carry out Aguirre's orders when he demanded the execution of this man or that for suspected treachery. Under pretense of attacking the royalists, most of Aguirre's men gained his permission to go outside, and promptly joined Peña's army. At last only one man remained faithful to Aguirre: Antón Llamoso, he who had staged the grotesque scene over the body of Martín Pérez. Aguirre turned bitterly to him, and asked why he did not desert also. Llamoso simply replied that he and Aguirre had been friends in life, and that he would live or die with him.

The end was at hand. Pale and dejected, Aguirre entered the apartment of his young daughter. "Commend thyself to God, my daughter," he declared, "for I am about to kill thee, that thou may not be pointed at with scorn, nor be in the power of anyone who may call thee the daughter of a traitor." [141] While a horrified serving-maid tried to prevent the murder, Aguirre stabbed the girl to death.

The royalist troops rushed into the building. Aguirre seized his arquebus, but his hands trembled and he could not fire the weapon. Throwing down his arms, he collapsed in misery on a bed opposite the one on which his daughter's body lay. A Tocuyan soldier named Ledesma seized him, but Aguirre pushed him away, saying, "I do not give myself up to such a villain as you," and surrendered instead to Diego García de Paredes.

Paredes wished to take Aguirre into custody to stand trial; but the former *Marañones*, fearing what the tyrant might reveal about their own activities, insisted that Aguirre be executed on the spot, even before Governor Collado had arrived. Paredes, says Padre Simón, "told Aguirre to prepare himself for death, and commanded two of his own *Marañones* to shoot him down with their arquebuses. This they did at once, and the traitor fell dead at their feet. It is, however, said that having received the fire of the first arquebus in a slanting direction, he said it was not well aimed; but the second was fired at his breast, and he said, 'That has done the business,' and then fell dead." [142]

The corpse was beheaded, and the severed head was placed on display at Tocuyo in an iron cage as a warning to evil-doers. Peña, Paredes, and Bravo de la Molina were rewarded by Spain for their part in destroying Aguirre. The men who had shared his wild adventure with him drifted into the other settlements of the Americas without suffering further punishment.

What had begun as an expedition to discover El Dorado of the Omaguas had become a runaway campaign of nihilism that produced not only a thorough exploration of the two great river systems of northeastern South America, but also a bright and bloody episode in the psychopathology of the enterprise of El Dorado. Lope de Aguirre, the man who was described by a contemporary as being too cruel to be a Spaniard, left a powerful imprint on Venezuela. When the German explorer Alexander von Humboldt toured Venezuela early in the nineteenth century, he found that Aguirre's memory had survived as that of an evil spirit. At night, Humboldt reported, strange and ghostly fires danced over the plains, and "This fire, which is like the Will o' the Wisp of our marshes, does not burn the grass. The people call these reddish flames 'the soul of the traitor Aguirre,' and the natives of Barquisimeto believe that the soul of the traitor wanders in the savannahs, like a flame that flies the approach of men." [143]

[6]

MANY SEEKERS

HE GHASTLY INTERLUDE OF SLAUGHTER that Aguirre had fashioned from Ursua's expedition did not dampen the ardor of those who would find El Dorado. Since the tyrant had taken care to avoid entering the fabled golden lands, the opportunity remained for others to reap the precious harvest. Within five years of Aguirre's death, a host of new seekers presented themselves almost simultaneously for what had become as ritualistic a quest as those of the romances of chivalry.

The first was Gómez de Tortoya, a wealthy citizen of Peru and a friend of the viceroy, the Marquis de Cañete. Strictly speaking, what aroused Tortoya's greed was not the old story of the gilded man, but a tale that the leaders of the Incas had fled into the forests east of Cuzco with 40,000 followers and a huge hoard of gold. The viceroy granted Tortoya and several associates letters patent "in order to the possessing themselves of part of the great riches of the Amazonian Empire which they were informed of on a branch of the River Amarumáya." [144] Tortoya spent a small fortune outfitting his expedition, but in 1566 Cañete was replaced by a new viceroy, who ordered Tortoya to transfer his rights to a certain Gaspar de Sotelle, apparently the kinsman of the new viceroy. Sotelle was taken into Tortoya's partnership, and the combined party crossed the Peruvian Andes as far as the headwaters of the Amarumaya, known today as the Madre de Díos. They entered what is now Bolivia and cut their way through the thickly forested region occupied by the savage Chuncho Indians.

The viceroy, meanwhile, had casually given permission to a knight named Juan Alvarez Maldonado, famous for his great corpulence, to seek for gold in precisely the same district. With four hundred infantrymen and a hundred cavalry, Maldonado trekked to the Chuncho country and found Tortoya's party already there. Each group had a valid and exclusive license to exploit the territory, and after some heated discussion a battle began between the rival bands of Spaniards that lasted three days and ended with nearly all the soldiers dead. The Chunchos now swept down, slew Tortoya, and captured Maldonado.

The latter was celebrated as much for his luck as for his bulk, and his luck held true. After enduring a variety of rigors he escaped, returning to Cuzco in 1569 with a story of "a land of gold" in the forest. He reported that "all these provinces are inhabited by people clothed in cotton, and all having rites and ceremonies like those of the Incas of Peru. The Chunchos and Aravaonas . . . wear feathers and make images and things of rich workmanship and very fine clothing." [145] This helped keep alive the fantasy of a Dorado of escaped Incas in Bolivia or Paraguay, but it was not directly related except as a parallel phenomenon of delusion to the notion of El Dorado north of the Amazon.

There was no lack of seekers for that glittering prize. In the same year, 1566, that Tortoya, Sotelle, and Maldonado were jockeying for the right to loot the runaway Incas, a Dorado expedition of the orthodox kind was organized in the Peruvian town of Chachapoyas by a man of substance named Martín de Proveda. His intention was to follow Ursua's route to reach "Omagua and the provinces of the *dorado*." He cut northward through the jungle until he reached the mouth of the Napo, crossing it and going on into the cinnamon country where Gonzalo Pizarro had marched so long and with such dreadful suffering. By a steady advance, Proveda entered the country of the Uaupés, penetrating from the south what the Germans of Coro had reached from the north, and perhaps he brushed the border of the Omagua province. As usual, the Indians were willing to supply him with fanciful stories of the golden treasure that lay somewhere farther on, but he did not get far enough east to discover it. Proveda's march was a notable one, and showed high endurance; but since he was covering a region that had been explored in the past both from Peru and from Venezuela, his feat has attracted little attention. He lost most of his men on the venture, and when he had reached the village of Nuestra Señora in Venezuela he swung westward across the Colombian *cordillera*, eventually arriving at Bogotá. This huge triangular reconnaissance thus took Proveda over the routes of most of the earlier Doradists in a single march —Pizarro, Ursua, Hutten, Federmann, Hohemut, and several others.

One of his companions on this expedition was another rich man of Chachapoyas, Don Pedro Malaver de Silva, a native of Xeres in Spain. Far from being discouraged by the long and fruitless enterprise, Silva became so convinced of the existence of El Dorado that immediately upon his return to civilization he began planning his own attempt. In 1568 Silva went to Spain and petitioned King Philip II for the concession to conquer and colonize the land of the Omaguas for a space of three hundred leagues, the settled territory to be known as New Estremadura. This was granted, and

Silva was named *adelantado* of New Estremadura with the power of bequeathing his title to his son. At the same time, a rival adventurer named Don Diego Fernando de Serpa arrived at the Spanish court to press his own claim to El Dorado. In 1549, Serpa had been granted by the Royal Audience of Santo Domingo the right to explore and colonize the region between the Orinoco and the Amazon—that is, the Omagua country. Serpa had failed to take advantage of his grant at that time, but now he wished to have it revived.

Through a Solomonic decision, the Council of the Indies gave Silva the right to exploit the country from the beginning of the Orinoco plains eastward for his requested three hundred leagues, and gave to Serpa the governorship of the region from the mouth of the Orinoco westward as far as the eastern border of Silva's domain, wherever that might be. An uprising of the Moors in Granada delayed Serpa's departure from Spain; he took part in the mountain war against the rebellious Moors, while Silva sailed from Spain in March of 1569, with two ships.

Silva had no trouble raising men for his expedition. He merely repeated the things he had learned while marching with Proveda, telling people that, as Padre Simón puts it, "by the margins of the rivers called Baraguan [Orinoco] and Meta was an innumerable host of people, who were so rich that all the furnishings of their houses were of gold and silver, with a thousand other lies." [146] This so excited those Spaniards who had not yet gone to the New World that they thrust themselves aggressively on Silva, demanding to be permitted to join in the invasion of El Dorado. Men sold their property and lent the proceeds to Silva to finance the purchase of equipment. He promised to return all such loans with generous interest, just as soon as New Estremadura was safely conquered and the wealth of the golden cities could be parceled out. Some six hundred men signed up for the expedition, many of them bringing their wives and families, in the hope of gaining huge estates in New Estremadura.

The two ships of Silva's expedition called first at the island of Margarita, which had just begun to revive from the devastation inflicted upon it in 1561 by Aguirre. A disagreement arose there, and a hundred fifty members of the expedition resigned from it and went no farther. With the rest, Silva sailed across to Burburata, where his two trusted lieutenants, the brothers Alonso and Diego Braba, deserted and sailed off for Cartagena with one of Silva's ships and his entire stock of wine. This so depleted the spirits of the party that other resignations followed, and most of the married men broke away to settle at Barquisimeto, Tocuyo, or Valencia.

With about one hundred forty men who remained, Silva entered the Venezuelan plains in July of 1569, and soon found himself lost in those hot, trackless *llanos*. Now plodding through enormous swamps covered with razor-keen grass that slashed at tattered clothes and cut through to skin, now dragging themselves through baking deserts, the Silva party suffered all the hardships that such men as Hohemut and Federmann had experienced thirty years before in this inhospitable country. The gleaming, angry wasteland took its toll. The hungry, thirsty men died in steady procession, until only thirty survived, and those near the limits of their strength. After six months of this terrible privation Silva found his way back to Barquisimeto, and disbanded the expedition. He departed for Bogotá in March, 1570, and shortly was back at his Peruvian home in Chachapoyas.

Serpa's luck was even worse. He extricated himself from the Moorish wars in the autumn of 1569, and recruited four hundred men on an expedition which—like that of

Ordaz in 1531—was intended to discover El Dorado by entering the Orinoco estuary and proceeding upstream, to the west. Landing at Cumaná, Serpa marched eastward along the Venezuelan coast, stopping at the mouth of the Río Salado to found a city called Santiago de los Caballeros. He left the women of the expedition there and set out for the Orinoco. En route, an Indian war party ambushed them, slaying Serpa and most of his followers. A few survivors reached Santiago, and the town was abandoned, its settlers removing to Margarita.

2

The failure of Proveda to find anything, the hardships suffered by Silva, and the catastrophic fate of Serpa all contributed to the sublime confidence of the time that a true golden land was ultimately to be found. The location of El Dorado was quite specifically fixed now, mainly by a process of elimination: it lay south of the Orinoco and north of the Amazon, in the thickly jungled plain of southern Venezuela and northern Brazil. There was almost absolute certainty of this, for Colombia and Peru had been combed thoroughly, and no gilded king or golden kingdom had been discovered.

Don Pedro de Silva of Chachapoyas was infected with the Dorado plague in its most virulent form. He had learned nothing from his experiences on the march with Proveda in 1566, it seems, or from his own harrowing and humiliating exploit three years later, for hardly had he returned to his estate in Peru when he was sketching out a new expedition. Significantly for the future course of the quest for El Dorado, Silva now abandoned the attempt to reach the golden land from the west. An eastern approach, up the Orinoco or one of the many other rivers of the Venezuela-Guiana region, struck him as the only likely way to enter. Henceforth the mouth of the Orinoco would be the central zone for the activity of the Doradists, completing the process by which the location of El Dorado shifted from the western side of the continent to the eastern.

Silva returned to Spain and found several hundred new men who were willing to ignore the failure of his last attempt. In July, 1576, he sailed from Cádiz, and landed on the Guiana coast, about midway between the estuaries of the Orinoco and the Amazon. Marching inland, Silva searched in vain for a speedy river route to El Dorado. He was set upon by the cannibalistic Caribs, who thinned his party daily, and those who did not die of wounds perished of disease. Silva and his two small daughters were among the early victims. At last only one man survived out of the entire force: Juan Martín de Albujar, a soldier who was captured by the Indians, lived among them for ten years, and finally slipped away to turn up at Margarita and tell the somber tale of Silva's disaster. The adventures of Juan Martín de Albujar later played an important part in the planning of Sir Walter Raleigh's unhappy search for El Dorado.

3

The glow of imagined gold does not easily grow dim, and the failure of one Doradist merely cleared the way for the attempt of the next. The man who offered himself at this point was no neophyte of the quest, but one of the original members of the species: old Gonzalo Jiménez de Quesada, the conqueror of New Granada. His last moment of real glory had come in 1539, when he and Ferdermann and Belalcázar had sailed off together down the Magdalena in a comic trio of affectionate rivalry, after the defeat of the Chibchas and the transformation of the Cundinamarca plateau into the Spanish territory of New Granada. Then, as we have seen, Quesada was done out of a governorship through the intrigues of Alonso de Lugo, and spent a decade wandering Europe as a philosophically inclined exile.

In 1549, securing a royal appointment to the honorable but empty title of Marshal of Bogotá, Quesada was able to return to the New World, and by 1550 he was back in the city he had founded, Santa Fe de Bogotá. It had grown large and prosperous, and many of his old officers now were wealthy landowners. Quesada lived among them as a poor man in the early years after his return, but his wisdom and legal training made him valuable to the community, and he was highly regarded by the royal governor who had replaced the corrupt Lugos.

He was restless living as a private citizen in the kingdom he had conquered, and about 1557 he began to petition Philip II for permission to set out eastward into the *llano* country about the Río Meta, searching for the city of El Dorado. Correspondence between New Granada and Madrid moved slowly, and the years dragged past without any firm decision. Quesada's position was complicated by his simultaneous demand for the title of marquis, which had been granted to both Cortés and Pizarro. He felt that his conquest of New Granada entitled him to an equivalent honor; but while the Council of the Indies debated the double question of awarding Quesada a marquisate and licensing him to find El Dorado, the time slipped by. No answer came from Spain.

Quesada meanwhile had achieved considerable authority in New Granada, since to many of the wealthiest settlers their old general had always been the legitimate ruler of the kingdom. Though he lacked official status, he was the *de facto* governor by 1561. In that year the rebellion of Lope de Aguirre shook all of Spanish America, and, as we have seen, Quesada was named to lead New Granada's army against the tyrant. He was then about sixty years old.

It was a brilliant moment for Quesada. From the far reaches of the plateau came soldiers who had served under him in 1536, once more enrolling beneath his banner. Middle-aged planters from Tunja and Pamplona and Sogamoso squeezed their portly frames into quilted armor and climbed upon their best chargers. The younger men, too, who had heard of Quesada's ancient greatness, of his single-handed arrest of the *zaque* of Tunja and of his splendid campaign against the *zipa* of Muequetá, pledged their strength to the cause. As it turned out, Aguirre's juggernaut of destruction was halted in Venezuela, and the army of New Granada never saw action against him; but the episode focused attention on Quesada and established him firmly as the leading citizen of the kingdom.

Finally in 1568 King Philip deigned to reply to the petition Quesada had sent him more than a decade before. The old man's request had worked its way through the tortuous channels of the court, and now came a surprisingly gratifying response. Quesada was given permission to undertake the conquest of the *llanos*, and he was to be governor of a grant of land thought to be four hundred leagues wide, between the Rivers Pauto and Papamene, in which he believed El Dorado was to be found. (The Papamene, or Río Caqueta, is a tributary of the Amazon. The Pauto, a tributary of the Meta, is part of the Orinoco system.) This governorship could be left to his son, or, failing any posterity, to any heir Quesada should name. The coveted title of marquis would be his if he succeeded in conquering and settling El Dorado. In the meanwhile he was awarded the impressive appointment of *adelantado* of New Granada, though without the administrative responsibilities that usually accompanied this office.

It was satisfactory. Quesada's years of waiting had been excruciatingly long, and the discomfort had been intensified by the recent activities of Proveda and Silva. These men, both Peruvians, had been licensed by the court to explore the *llano* country just east of the Andes—a region claimed by New Granada. That was bad enough, for as a patriotic man of New Granada, Quesada was moved to protest that the explorers from Chachapoyas were trespassers. Had either Proveda or Silva actually found El Dorado in the *llanos*, the situation would have been infinitely worse. But by 1568 Proveda had gone back to Peru, giving up the quest, and the following year, much to Quesada's relief, Silva chose as the site of his ill-fated foray the eastern sector of his territory. Naturally, he found nothing. Quesada, as a Doradist of the old school, was contemptuous of those men who maintained that the golden city was to be located so far to the east. Guiana and the farther reaches of the Orinoco basin were futile places to explore, he felt. With that dreamlike clarity of conviction that marked so many of the seekers, Quesada insisted that the realm of gold lay in the broad savannahs that began at the foothills of the Andes and rolled eastward into Venezuela. It went against all established knowledge, for the *llanos* had been crossed and recrossed extensively since Federmann had first penetrated them in 1530, and while they were hardly completely explored it was most unlikely that any large and wealthy civilization had escaped notice. The geology was against Quesada too, for the Spaniards had had ample opportunity to observe that alluvial plains were much less productive of gold than mountainous country.

Yet he went, like a gaunt old Don Quixote taking arms one more time against the windmills. His exalted reputation once again drew the cream of New Granada's manhood. He was nearly seventy years old, and many of the veterans of the Chibcha conquest who joined him were even older. By the terms of his royal grant, Quesada was required to take with him five hundred armed men—reduced at the last moment to four hundred—eight priests, and a great quantity of livestock. He was obliged to set up cattle ranches in the conquered country, to build defensive forts, and to establish several towns. Within four years Quesada was required to bring five hundred married colonists out of New Granada, and to have houses ready for them when they reached El Dorado. He had to pledge to set up mills and farms, and to plant sugar cane. In other words, King Philip had not permitted him merely to sally forth, seize a few million pesos of gold, and retire. He was to create a new kingdom.

The preparations for the venture were extensive and costly. Since New Granada was a flourishing land, Quesada was able to obtain all the livestock he needed—four hundred horses, five hundred brood mares, three hundred cows, a thousand pigs—but it was necessary for him to mortgage the extensive property he had accumulated in the nineteen years since his return to the New World. Even after he had pledged his last possession to raise money to equip the expedition, he was still short of the needed amount and had to solicit a large contribution from a wealthy mineowner. The total expenses ran to some 200,000 *pesos de oro.*

It was not difficult to get men to join him, both as soldiers and as colonists. Some of the most prosperous citizens of New Granada signed up, and their resources helped make this an even more splendidly appointed enterprise than the majestic expedition of Gonzalo Pizarro nearly two decades before. One sour witness to this buoyant gathering was Juan de Castellanos, who had fought with Quesada in the conquest of Cundinamarca and now in old age was a priest inclined toward writing history in the form of endless poems. Castellanos spoke testily of this exploit of Quesada's senility, commenting, "To persuade idle and unmarried men, lazy vagabonds who neither have desire nor honest occupation, to take part in such enterprises, would be tolerable, but it is wrong to incite married men, with their wives and children . . . to follow the scent of a land abounding in riches. Thus moved by false reports, married Spanish and *mestiza* women joined this miserable expedition in which nearly all perished. I do not wish to believe that their husbands took them along to get rid of them, but rather to think that they were misled by vain promises and delusive hopes which issued in dreadful catastrophes." [147]

The expedition departed in the spring of 1569, several months before the Serpa and Silva fiascos commenced. All the inhabitants of Bogotá turned out to see the brave explorers off. Quesada marched eastward across the *cordillera*. That furrowed range of mountains had proved impermeable to Hohemut in 1536, and had been conquered by Federmann in 1539 only under the greatest hardship, both attempts coming from the west; but the men of New Granada had had thirty years to explore their frontier, and many passes into the lowlands had been found, far less taxing than the one Federmann had used.

Nevertheless the progress was slow, for Quesada had to adapt his pace to that of his shuffling herds of livestock. Camping by the River Guejar on the twentieth day of march, the explorers suffered what could have been a serious loss: sparks ignited the powder magazine, and it exploded, destroying Quesada's tent and killing a number of his men. Without gunpowder, the soldiers had to make do with crossbows and spears from then on, but they met so little opposition from the Indians that the arquebuses were not missed.

The expected rigors of an extended journey through the hot savannahs produced the expected loss of life, both to men and to livestock, but Quesada plunged forward with indefatigable determination through much the same country that had unmanned his brother Hernán in 1541. Out of the

endless plain at last appeared a town: the Venezuelan outpost of San Juan de los Llanos, five hundred miles from
Bogotá, which had been founded in 1555. This town occupied the site of an Indian village well known to seekers of El
Dorado, which Federmann had called La Fragua and Hohemut Nuestra Señora; Hutten had camped there several times
on his zigzagging journey to the Omaguas, and Proveda had
reached it a decade and a half later. Now San Juan de los
Llanos was settled by shrewd men who had seen many
Doradists come and go, and who surely were aware that no
golden city lay in the plains, else they would have been
searching for it themselves. They provided Quesada's party
with food and shelter, and doubtless offered some thoughts
on the practicality of the old man's quest. Whatever advice
they gave was lost on Quesada.

He was at least determined not to follow his brother's
futile footsteps. Instead he attempted to take what he conceived to be Hutten's southeasterly route from San Juan de
los Llanos; for Hutten had actually glimpsed El Dorado of
the Omaguas before being driven off, had he not? It was
cruel country. The sharp-edged grass, waist-high, stretched
interminably to the horizons. Mosquitoes, horseflies, and
sandflies buzzed ominously just above the rough blades, and
their bites brought fevers and swellings. Anyone rash
enough to lean against one of the infrequent trees found
himself enveloped in a cloud of wasps. Snakes coiled out of
sight under foot. In sunny weather the heat was intolerable;
when the rains came, it seemed as though flesh would rot
from the bones. Game was scarce and provisions dwindled.
Jaguars descended at night to prey on the horses.

A trail of bones was strewn across the *llanos:* animals,
dead Indian bearers, Spaniards. Discarded saddles, abandoned suits of armor, trinkets intended for trade with the
natives, all these burdens were left behind as the discomforts

mounted. Still Quesada marched on. Each night one or two men deserted, fading away silently into the grass. These stragglers invariably perished in the hopeless attempt to make the return journey alone. To discourage desertions, Quesada hanged two men who were apprehended as they tried to leave camp. The harsh measure did not have its intended effect; weighing the options of their doom, the men preferred to risk the gallows or the jaguars and set out for civilized lands rather than to continue on to certain death with Quesada.

Floods cascading over the banks of the Orinoco's tributaries forced the explorers to higher land. They found a plantation of corn and yuca and solaced their hunger, but the natives could not supply them with salt, and the lack of that vital substance was heavily felt by the Spaniards. Quesada himself carried a lump of rock salt with him, as he had learned to do on the campaign of his youth, but most of the men had to do without. Their illnesses multiplied. Some became blind, others deaf, others were covered with sores in which worms bred and fed. An intolerable itching drove several men mad, and they died in frightful agony. The downpour of rain was continual and excruciating. Quesada was forced to send his sick men back toward Bogotá under one of his officers; most of them died on the way, a few reaching San Juan de los Llanos six months after they had set out.

Quesada went onward. His captains died. His priests died. Fray Antonio de Medrano, who was keeping a chronicle of the expedition, succumbed to fever, but the chronicle was continued by another priest, Fray Pedro de Aguado. The men ate roots and herbs, the bark of trees, wild fruits, and nuts. Their courage broke at last; and, convinced that their aged general was taking them to the end of the world, they mutinied and insisted on turning back. But Quesada had lost none of the personal magnetism that had carried him to the conquest of Cundinamarca. Ringed by harried, hostile soldiers, he spoke persuasively, sketched a glowing picture of El Dorado, summoned up the shreds of his old prestige, and won their renewed loyalty. The mutiny subsided. Those men who wished to go home, he said, were free to depart, but he implored them to stay with him to the end.

Only forty-five men out of the original four hundred remained to Quesada now. He had a few horses, a few Indian bearers; all the livestock had been consumed in the searing journey through the *llanos*. Of the forty-five men, twenty chose to return. Quesada and the remainder lurched onward. They halted near the junction of the Orinoco and the Río Guaviare, where the village of San Fernando de Atabapo stands today. The time had come to admit defeat. Here was no golden city, only further wilderness and an eternal blanket of humid air. Quesada's indomitable spirit could carry him no further. They turned back.

Some time in 1572 the survivors of the expedition filed into Bogotá: twenty-five Spaniards, four Indians, and a few half-starved horses. At the head of the procession was Quesada, seventy-two years old, a bony, parched man whose inner resources had withstood the three-year ordeal with surprising power. The expedition to El Dorado, on which he had staked his entire worldly estate, had been a total failure.

The old man could not shake free from his obsession. El Dorado was out there, he insisted; he had simply taken the wrong road and gone astray. The men of Bogotá believed him. They did not regard him as a poor old madman, but listened with respect as he outlined his plans for yet another attempt at the gleaming prize. Poor and broken in health, he had no hope of leading the search in person, but there were others to be inspired with the golden dream.

He lived quietly at Bogotá, writing memoirs, sedately

coursing the plateau on a placid horse, and reminiscing with old comrades of bygone days. Though he had failed to qualify for the title of marquis, and had forfeited all his property, his life appears to have been comfortable enough, and he was still regarded as the first citizen of Bogotá.

In 1575 an Indian tribe known as the Gualies went on the war path in New Granada, burning settlements in the hot lowlands near the banks of the Magdalena. The settlers raised an army to restore order, and Gonzalo Jiménez de Quesada was named its general, for it had been proven many times that soldiers would flock to his banner on any occasion. He was so feeble that he could not ride to the war on a horse, and had to be carried in a hammock by Indians, but his generalship was unimpaired. Deploying his men skillfully, Quesada lured the Gualies into an ambush and broke their strength. Their leader was slain, and they sued for peace. Quesada himself had gathered his strength for the climactic battle, leading the charge with his lance held high.

It was the last exploit of the grand old conqueror. He found Bogotá too chilly for him now, and retired to the milder climate of a country estate west of the city at Mariquita. The only surviving letter in Quesada's hand was written from Mariquita, under the date of May 28, 1578, and signed, *"el Adelantado."* He speaks of farming matters—horses, cattle, the raising of goats—and requests a jar of honey to be sent to him. Soon he slipped into his final illness, and death came to him on the 15th of February, 1579, when he was nearly eighty. Unlike most of the Spanish conquerors, he lived into old age. But he died poor.

His will was notarized on the day he died. He was heavily in debt, so there were no cash bequests to make. He willed his library to the Convent of Santo Tomas at Bogotá, and provided a small endowment to maintain a supply of water for wayfarers on a hill called Limba, where, as the testament points out, it is hot and no well exists. Quesada had had plenty of time to learn the sufferings of a thirsty wayfarer.

The only other asset Quesada could bequeath was his governorship of the four hundred leagues of unconquered land between the Pauto and Papamene Rivers, where El Dorado was thought to lie. (That is, between the Orinoco and the Amazon.) King Philip had granted him the right to bestow this grant on any heir of his choice. Quesada had never married, and had not even left any illegitimate children, and his only surviving relative was his niece, Doña Maria de Oruña, the daughter of a Spanish colonel. Doña Maria had taken as her husband a soldier of good birth named Antonio de Berrio, who had performed valiant services during the European wars of Charles V. Quesada named Berrio as his heir, designating him as the governor of the great tract encompassing El Dorado. In 1580 Berrio, with Doña Maria and their six daughters and two sons, set sail for New Granada under the impression that they had inherited a mighty province. So they had; but when Berrio reached the New World, he discovered for the first time that that province was still unconquered and unsettled. He showed no dismay. Though he was a man past middle years himself, he showed himself willing to inherit not only Quesada's royal license but also his obsession to find the golden land. As he put it in a letter to King Philip, five years later, "On arrival in this kingdom, and learning the great news of the Dorado enterprise, and that my predecessor had spent three years and much gold in search thereof, and that he had left the charge of the enterprise to me, I judged that it was no time for me to rest, but to do as I had ever done, to serve Your Majesty." [148]

[7]

THE JOURNEYS OF
ANTONIO DE BERRIO

NEW FIGURE HAD ENTERED THE QUEST, A man not previously associated with the exploration of South America. Antonio de Berrio was not fettered by preconceptions; he knew what mistakes the earlier Doradists had made, and he did not plan to repeat them. It was pointless to look for the golden land in the Andean plateaus, or in the *llanos* just to the east of them, for half a century of investigation had exhausted those possibilities. Berrio looked instead to the region Silva and Serpa had so unsuccessfully entered a decade before, somewhere east of the *llanos* and west of the mouth of the Orinoco.

No one had really explored that area. Ordaz and Herrera had passed westward through it in the 1530's, and Aguirre on his mad jaunt had come through the opposite way, but so little was known that in 1588 José de Acosta could write, "They are ignorant of the greatest part of America, which lies betwixt Peru and Brazil, although the bounds be known of all sides, wherein there is diversity of opinions; some say it is a drowned land, full of lakes and watery places; others affirm there are great and flourishing kingdoms, imagining there be . . . the Dorado, where they say are wonderful things. . . . To speak the truth, the habitations of America are to this day unknown, except the extremities." [149] But by the time those words were written Berrio had already completed the first of his remarkable reconnaissances.

He was a tough old soldier, born about 1520 at Segovia in Spain. Sir Walter Raleigh, who came into direct conflict with him, called Berrio "a gent. well descended . . . of great assuredness, and of a great heart." [150] He saw his first military action while still a young man, fighting in Italy for Charles V. Between 1560 and 1564 he took part in the Spanish expeditions against the Barbary pirates of North Africa, then served in Germany, and in 1568 was transferred to the Netherlands, where he figured in the repression of the Dutch people under the Duke of Alba. Later that same year he was recalled to Spain to fight against the rebellious Moors of Granada, and experienced grueling guerrilla combat in the Alpujarra Mountains. During this campaign one of his four brothers was killed before his eyes; two other brothers had been slain in war earlier, one fighting against the French, the other by the Turks in the famous battle of Lepanto. Apparently he married late in life, for he was about sixty when the surprising news came that he had inherited the governorship of El Dorado from his wife's uncle, and at that time many of his eight children were still small.

After his arrival at New Granada in 1580, Berrio spent several years preparing for his expedition to the golden realm. He was not the only man eager to find El Dorado at that time, of course. One of his rivals was the youthful Agustín de Ahumada, a brother of Saint Teresa of Avila, who wrote from Quito on October 25, 1582, to the Peruvian viceroy in Lima that he was negotiating with the Royal

Audience for assistance in organizing an expedition of "up to a hundred men to go in search of a certain province that some residents of this district came upon which they found was the most populous and richest in gold ever seen; from what they tell of it and the descripton that they give, one can believe that it must be without any doubt at all the Dorado, in the pursuit of which thousands of leaders and men have been lost." [151] Despite his awareness of the earlier calamities, Ahumada buoyantly added that El Dorado was so close that "in a week of journeying one is there." Fortunately for him, he does not appear to have made the attempt.

More serious for Berrio's plans, one Francisco de Caceres of New Granada somehow gained a license from the administrators of that kingdom to search for El Dorado, even though this directly infringed on the rights Berrio held. Berrio had spent a great deal of money equipping some two hundred men and acquiring horses, ammunition, and provisions, when he found himself involved in a legal dispute with Caceres. The authorities of New Granada, regarding Berrio as an interloper, ordered him to combine his expedition with that of Caceres. When he refused, they began to license all comers to seek for El Dorado, and after six such licenses had been granted Berrio hastily departed from New Granada, hoping at least to be the first to make the discovery.

He entered the plains by way of Tunja in January of 1584, taking with him only one hundred men, of whom twenty deserted almost at the outset. Crossing the Río Pauta, a tributary of the Meta, Berrio struck off southeastward through miserable swamps at a pace that brooked no obstacles and admitted of no delays. He entered the *llanos* between the Meta and the Vichada Rivers, two of the tributaries of the Orinoco, and pressed eastward. "I crossed the plains," he told King Philip in a letter of May, 1585, "passing mighty rivers and swamps, through many lands peopled by Indians, who were idle and naked and unacquainted with metals. I journeyed on for more than two hundred leagues, and by the Grace of God and his Glorious Mother, and on Palm Sunday in the year eighty-four, I discovered the *cordillera* on the other side of the plains—the *cordillera* so ardently desired and sought for seventy years past, and which has cost the lives of so many Spaniards." [152]

Berrio knew the mythology of El Dorado well, and he had remembered what so many other seekers had forgotten: that the ceremony of the gilded man had been performed in a lake surrounded by mountains. The Andean *cordilleras* on the western side of the continent had failed to produce the golden city; therefore Berrio had gone looking for an eastern mountain range, and he had found it with striking swiftness, only a few months after setting out.

Berrio's *cordillera* was the Sierra Mapicha, east of the Orinoco in the part of Venezuela that borders on British Guiana. He was not the first European to view these mountains—Hutten had glimpsed them from a great distance in 1541—but he was the first to explore their foothills, and thereby helped to transfer El Dorado from the Omagua country to Guiana. Berrio advanced until he was less than fifty miles from the mountain range. The rainy season caught him there, and floods made further progress impossible, so he was obliged to make camp for the next four months. Indians attacked the eighty Spaniards repeatedly; in one raid, Berrio says, four thousand natives besieged them, but were driven off with heavy losses. When prisoners were taken, Berrio questioned them about El Dorado. "They all . . . agreed in one thing," he wrote the King, "that in the mountains there is a very large lake, and that on the other side are great towns and a vast population, with gold and precious stones. I asked them if there were as many people there as in the plains, and they replied that in the *cordillera* there were many places having more inhabitants in each of them than there are in all the plains." [153]

The old fantasy of El Dorado thus was restored to life in a new part of the world. Berrio waited impatiently for the floods to subside, and marched toward the mountains. Shortly he came to the river he called the Baraguan—the Orinoco—which he said was the greatest river he had ever seen in his life; "within a distance of two leagues, four other big rivers enter this one, and their entrance is hardly noticeable." [154] This unusually resourceful man built a boat to transport his men and cattle across the river, and once across spent some time pondering the best way to ascend the *cordillera*. Swamp fevers sent many of his men to sickbeds; Berrio could muster only thirteen able-bodied companions to go with him on the climb.

Advancing on foot, they scrambled over the rocky crags for ten days until they reached the outer spurs of the mountains. Weariness and the difficulty of the terrain halted them two leagues short of the *cordillera*, but Berrio found some rocks that seemed to him to contain gold ore, a sufficient confirmation of what he had learned from the Indians. Taking these, he turned back and returned to his main camp beside the Orinoco. He descended the river for about six miles in his boat, coming to a small mid-river island occupied by about a thousand Indians. Unable to land because of the strong current, Berrio "sent a canoe with one soldier and the interpreter, who understood the language, with gifts to offer peace and friendship. They accepted the gifts and sent back food, and I felt certain that this island in the narrows was the limit between the plains and the mountains, and that on the farther side lay the open road to the *cordillera*." [155]

He returned to his camp, but found too many of his men too weak to go on. With a consideration rare among this group of explorers, Berrio decided not to risk losing the valuable knowledge he had gained, and sacrificing the lives of his men and himself, by forcing beyond the limits of endurance. Instead he turned back, finding a shortcut along the Meta through a dry and populous land, and after an absence of seventeen months reached New Granada. He had lost only eight of his men, three killed by Indians, five who died of disease.

2

In the spring of 1585, Berrio petitioned King Philip for aid in launching a second expedition to El Dorado. His letter of May 24 put the distance from New Granada to the Guiana *cordillera* at one hundred twenty leagues, via the new shortcut, and he thought about three hundred men would be needed for the project. He begged the King to send orders to the Royal Audience at Bogotá, asking that body to "render me all necessary assistance in raising the men, and not permit the forming of any other expedition whatever until this one shall be concluded, in view of its importance. I have spent my all in it quite willingly." Reminding King Philip of the death of his three brothers in Spanish service, of his own advanced age, and of his many young children, the eldest only ten, Berrio asked this exclusive privilege as recompense for all he had endured. He noted further that the Baraguan was the same as the Orinoco, which issued to the sea near the island of Trinidad, and shrewdly pointed out that the settlement of Trinidad would be necessary to the proper exploitation of Guiana, since it was an ideal staging base for future expeditions.

In the summer of 1585 Berrio set out again. His intent was to reach the Orinoco and follow it downstream until he came to the far side of the *cordillera*, where he hoped to find some route to the interior of Guiana. Crossing the *llanos* with his usual briskness, Berrio reached the Orinoco somewhat to the south of his first entry, crossed it, and marched for nearly six hundred miles along the foothills of the *cordillera* without discovering a pass at which the mountains could be taken. Then he returned to the Orinoco to construct canoes and make the intended downstream journey. By this time he had been away from New Granada about two years, and his men were growing impatient. One of his captains, Gonzalo de Piña, mutinied and took most of Berrio's men with him back to New Granada. Deprived of what he considered the necessary minimum force for attempting Guiana, Berrio with his usual prudence abandoned the exploration and headed home. Although he was nearly seventy, he seemed prepared to march back and forth across South America indefinitely to gain an entry to that forbidding *cordillera*.

He reached Bogotá in 1588 and found a royal commission waiting there with a decree from Spain. Berrio was officially appointed governor of El Dorado and Guiana, and given broad powers to mount further expeditions. On March 19, 1590, the tireless Berrio set out on the third and most astonishing of his Guiana journeys. His force consisted of a hundred twelve Spaniards, two hundred twenty horses, twenty canoes, the same number of rafts, and a great quantity of munitions and supplies. Instead of the customary horde of Indian bearers, Berrio took only a few Negro slaves as his attendants.

With seventy of his men, Berrio went ahead by boat, while his lieutenant, Alvaro Jorge, led the other forty-two and all the horses by land along the riverbanks. Berrio's route was well plotted: down the Casanare River from New Granada to the Río Pauto, from the Pauto into the Meta, and thence, swept along by the current, to the Orinoco. "After he entered that great and mighty river," wrote Sir

Walter Raleigh in his 1596 account of Berrio's travels, "he began daily to lose of his companies both men and horse, for it is in many places violently swift, and hath forcible eddies, many sands, and divers islands sharp pointed with rocks. . . . After one whole year, journeying for the most part by river, and the rest by land, he grew daily to fewer numbers, for both by sickness, and by encountering with the people of those regions, through which he travelled, his companies were much wasted." [156]

Once more Berrio made his quarters during the rainy season at the base of the mighty *cordillera* that rose like a wall around Guiana, sealing off the hidden land of gold. Thirty-four of his men had already deserted, carrying off many of the horses with them; thirty more, and all the Negro slaves, died of disease at the winter camp, which most unwisely had been placed in the marshes of the country of the Amapaia Indians. According to Raleigh, "This province of Amapaia is a very low and a marish [marshy] ground near the river, and by reason of the red water which issueth out in small branches through the fenny and boggy ground, there breed divers poisonous worms and serpents, and the Spaniards not suspecting, nor in any sort foreknowing the danger, were infected with a grievous kind of flux by drinking thereof, and even the very horses poisoned therewith. . . . I demanded of those in Guiana that had travelled Amapaia how they lived with that tawny or red water when they travelled thither, and they told me that after the Sun was near the middle of the sky, they used to fill their pots and pitchers with that water, but either before that time, or towards the setting of the Sun, it was dangerous to drink of, and in the night strong poison." [157]

To escape these unhealthy conditions, Berrio led his men away from the river and eastward toward the mountains. But in four months of searching for a pass through which horses, munitions, and men with packs on their backs could travel, he found none. The illness of his men forced him to give up the search and return to the camp beside the Orinoco in the Amapaia marshes. The expedition might well have foundered at this point but for the supreme qualities of leadership that characterized Berrio. He had heard from the Indians that far down the Orinoco was a great tributary called the Caroni, near which was the country of a chief named Morequito, and there, as he reported to King Philip in 1593, "the mountains ended and the provinces of Guiana began, behind which in turn came those of . . . El Dorado and many other provinces." [158]

All the canoes and the rafts had been lost in the swirling currents and rocky rapids of the Orinoco, and so Berrio ordered the construction of four new canoes for the river journey to the Caroni. During this work the provisions ran out, and the last horses were slaughtered for food. Late in 1591 the voyagers embarked, and on the first day encountered two canoes of Carib Indians who were out on a kidnapping expedition to gather meat for their cannibal feasts. The Spaniards did not look appetizing to the Caribs, it seems, for Berrio reports that "they received me apparently with pleasure, bartering with me for provisions and providing guides to lead me to Guiana, the borders of which by the great River Caroni were more than a hundred leagues from the beginning of these [Carib] villages." [159]

Berrio's anthropophagous companions entertained him, as they traveled down the river together, with stories of the gold of Guiana. At length the mouth of the Caroni was reached. This great river rises in the mountains of the Sierra Pacaraima, along the Brazilian-Venezuelan border, and flows northward through eastern Venezuela until it reaches the Orinoco not far from the estuary of the latter river. To Berrio and to his successor, Sir Walter Raleigh, the Caroni seemed to be the gateway to El Dorado, somewhere south of the Orinoco in Guiana. (Much of what was considered Guiana in the sixteenth and seventeenth centuries is now part of Venezuela.)

Berrio learned that it was impossible to ascend the Caroni—that is, travel south along it from the Orinoco—because a mighty waterfall a short distance upstream blocked any advance. Therefore he remained on the Orinoco for another twelve miles past the confluence, and entered a land that he called Morequito, after the name of its chief. He remained there for two months.

From the chief Morequito, Berrio learned that it was only four days' journey to the great cities and riches of El Dorado. It was tantalizing, but at the moment unattainable, because, Berrio later wrote King Philip, "out of the fifty soldiers which I had, there were not fifteen in good health, and it was impossible to advance with them and also guard the canoes. For if these were lost, all was lost." [160]

When he had parted from his Carib guides near the mouth of the Caroni, Berrio had hired them to carry letters to Don Juan Sarmiento, the governor of the island of Margarita, asking for help and reinforcements. He asked these Indians to bear his news to the island of Trinidad, where he believed a new Spanish settlement had been founded; the Spaniards of Trinidad, Berrio expected, would forward the letters to Sarmiento. But the Carib messengers found Trinidad not currently occupied by Spaniards and Berrio's letters got no farther. He waited for week after desperate week for aid from Margarita, while his men grew more feeble and his provisions diminished. When no word was received, the Spaniards began to move down the Orinoco again. Sixty miles down the river they came to a province he called Barquicana, known as Emeria in Raleigh's account. The Indians here were friendly and offered Berrio shelter. "The king of this land," Raleigh relates, "is called Carapana, a man very wise, subtle, and of great experience, being little less than 100 years old. In his youth he was sent by his father into the island of Trinidad, by reason of civil war among themselves, and was bred at a village in that island, called Parico: at that place in his youth he had seen many Christians both French and Spanish, and went divers times with the Indians of Trinidad to Margarita and Cumaná in the West Indies . . . by reason whereof he grew of more understanding, and noted the difference of the nations, comparing the strength and arms of his country with those of the Christians, and ever after temporized so, as whosoever else did amiss, or was wasted by contention, Carapana kept himself and his country in quiet and plenty: he also held peace with the Caribs or Cannibals his neighbors, and had free trade with all nations." [161]

This shrewd old king thus knew the trouble that even a band of sickly Spaniards could bring upon his realm, and therefore treated Berrio with hospitality. Raleigh says, "Berrio sojourned and rested his weak troop in the town of Carapana six weeks, and from him learned the way and passage to Guiana, and the riches and magnificence thereof; but being then utterly disable to proceed, he determined to try his fortune another year, when he had renewed his provisions, and regathered more force." [162] He still had heard nothing from Margarita, and so, abandoning El Dorado for the moment, Berrio made the difficult journey through the Orinoco estuary to the sea, and headed for Trinidad. The Orinoco, he told King Philip, "goes out by a great number of arms and narrow channels—so much so that it inundates the coastline for more than two hundred leagues and the interior for more than forty leagues. The arm by which I came out faces the island of Trinidad, which is four leagues from the Main. I went to Trinidad, and as it was so important for me to see and reconnoitre it closely, I spent some days there. I found it very thickly peopled by natives of a very domesticated race, the land very fertile and with specimens of gold in the ravines. I clearly recognized that if this island were not colonized it would be impossible to settle Guiana." [163] He was aware that several previous Spanish attempts to plant a settlement on Trinidad had failed.

After three weeks exploring that island, the Spaniards in their flimsy canoes made the perilous sea journey to Margarita, where almost at once Berrio became embroiled in complications. He learned that Governor Sarmiento had never received his request for aid; but in some mystic way Sarmiento had discovered that Spaniards were sniffing for gold along the Orinoco, and had sent a force of thirty-six men under one Lucas Fajardo to investigate. While Berrio was exiting through one mouth of the Orinoco, Fajardo was entering through another. Farther inland, Fajardo fell in with some stragglers of Berrio's party, from whom he learned of the land of Morequito. Berrio's men agreed to guide Fajardo's soldiers to Morequito.

"The Indians came out [to meet them] peacefully," Berrio complained to King Philip a year later, "but the Spaniards in payment of their hospitality robbed their houses, contrary to the pledges which I had left in Your Majesty's name, and carried off about three hundred stolen souls whom they sold like Negroes." [164] Berrio was incensed when he learned this, for he had gone to some trouble cultivating the friendship of the Indians along the Orinoco, knowing that El Dorado could never be reached without their guidance. Fajardo's clumsy act of brutality, Berrio realized, was likely to antagonize the entire region—which it did, for when Raleigh and an English party arrived in Morequito's country a few years later, they found to their pleasure that the Indians were vehemently anti-Spanish in outlook and so were willing to give assistance to any strangers who proclaimed themselves enemies of Spain.

Berrio protested to Governor Sarmiento, who piously clapped Fajardo in jail upon his return to Margarita, but released him two days later. Fajardo and Sarmiento soon were deep in conspiracy against Berrio, who held the legal right to conquer El Dorado and so stood in their path to wealth. It was a sorrowful time for Berrio, who was now past seventy years of age and greatly wearied from his journey from New Granada to Margarita, which had taken him completely across the continent. He had been saddened, on his arrival at Margarita, to learn that his wife had died soon after his departure, and with this grief upon him he now found himself compelled to fight against the treacherous Sarmiento for his own claim to El Dorado.

In a dolorous letter to King Philip dated January 1, 1593, Berrio recounted his many exploits, described the machinations of Sarmiento and Fajardo, and declared, "As I was aware of this iniquity and that Don Juan [Sarmiento] denied it because I was his guest, I wished to settle matters with him so as not to lose my all; for I myself had spent a hundred thousand *pesos* of good gold in the three expeditions, and my predecessor the *adelantado* [Quesada] more than fifty thousand." Berrio had offered Sarmiento a fifty-fifty share of El Dorado, "but when he perceived that I was very old and had received news here of my wife's death, that my children and estates needed my presence, that my eldest son whom I brought with me was now fourteen years old, that I myself had intermittent fever and was very far from my home, and that any one of these considerations was sufficient to induce me to go, and that when I turned my back the matter could be settled with Fajardo—a man of ill fortune who would be content with little—Don Juan had no desire to enter into any arrangement with me and began openly to do me a thousand mean turns." [165]

3

Having come to this unhappy pass, there was not much Berrio could do save write letters—to the King, to the Royal Audience at Santo Domingo, to the Council of the Indies in Spain, to anyone in high place who might possibly be able to aid him. He let it be known that he knew the way to El Dorado, and was willing to lead an expedition there, though he was old and sick; but he had small daughters whose dowry he had spent on the quest thus far, and he needed some financial aid from the government, as well as assurance that he would have clear title to his discoveries.

Berrio remained at Margarita during this torturous period of enforced inactivity. Ostensibly he was still Governor Sarmiento's guest, and the relationship between the two was superficially cordial, though Sarmiento was taking every step to block Berrio's return to Guiana. While there, Berrio met and talked with Juan Martín de Albujar, the soldier from Pedro de Silva's expedition who had been captured by the Indians in 1576 and who had lived among them for ten years, marrying a native woman and dwelling on the banks of the upper Caroni before escaping and coming to Margarita. Martín de Albujar had been regarded with almost supernatural awe by the Margaritans, for he came upon them in the garb of an Indian chief, but spoke to them in halting Castilian and identified himself as a long-lost Spaniard. As though his true story were not fabulous enough, he embroidered on it by concocting a flamboyant tale of El Dorado, which he now poured into the willing ear of Antonio de Berrio.

Berrio later repeated Martín de Albujar's fabrication to

The Journeys of Antonio de Berrio

Sir Walter Raleigh, who set it down in his own account of the quest for El Dorado, *The Discoverie of the Large, Rich, and Beautiful Empire of Guiana* (1596). Raleigh called Martín de Albujar "Johannes Martinez," and credited him with being a survivor of Diego de Ordaz' expedition up the Orinoco—an obvious impossibility, for Ordaz' voyage had been made in 1531, some sixty years before Berrio heard Martín de Albujar's story. In Raleigh's second-hand version, Berrio learned that "Martinez" had quarreled with Ordaz and was turned adrift in a canoe that was carried down the Caroni from its confluence with the Orinoco at the city of Morequito. (More carelessness on Raleigh's part, for, as he had excellent cause to know, the Caroni flows north *toward* the Orinoco, and no canoe could possibly drift south on it.) "It pleased God that the canoe was carried down the stream," Raleigh relates, "and that certain of the Guianians met it the same evening, and having not at any time seen any Christian, nor any man of that color, they carried Martinez into the land to be wondered at, and so from town to town, until he came to the great city of Manoa, the seat and residence of Inca the Emperor. The Emperor after he beheld him knew him to be a Christian (for it was not long before that his brethren Guascar and Atabalipa [Huascar and Atahuallpa] were vanquished by the Spaniards in Peru) and caused him to be lodged in his palace, and well entertained: he lived seven months in Manoa, but not suffered to wander into the country anywhere: he was also brought thither all the way blindfold, led by the Indians, until he came to the entrance of Manoa itself, and was fourteen or fifteen days in the passage: he avowed at his death that he entered the city at noon, and then they uncovered his face, and that he travelled all that day till night through the city, and the next day from sun rising to sun setting, ere he came to the palace of Inca. After that Martinez had lived seven months in

Manoa, and began to understand the language of the country, Inca asked him whether he desired to return into his
own country, or would willingly abide with him: but Martinez not desirous to stay, obtained the favor of Inca to
depart, with whom he sent divers Guianians to conduct him
to the river of Orenoque [Orinoco] all loden with as much
gold as they could carry, which he gave to Martinez at his
departure: but when he was arrived near the river's side, the
borderers which are called Orenoqueponi robbed him and his
Guianians of all the treasure (the borderers being at that
time at war with Inca, and not conquered) save only of two
great bottles of gourds, which were filled with beads of gold
curiously wrought, which these Orenoqueponi thought had
been no other thing than his drink or meat or grain for food
with which Martinez had liberty to pass, and so in canoes he
fell down by the river of Orenoque to Trinidad, and thence
to Margarita, and so to Saint Juan de Puerto Rico, where
remaining a long time for passage into Spain he died." [166]

This jumble of fantasy, conceived by Juan Martín de
Albujar, nurtured by Berrio, and set down on paper by
Raleigh, served to do several things. It confirmed the current
suspicions that Guiana was the true land of El Dorado. It
gave the capital city of El Dorado a name: Manoa. It transferred to Guiana the legend that the Incas of Peru had
escaped into some other land with much of their wealth upon
Pizarro's invasion. It further brought to Guiana the original
tale of the gilded man of Cundinamarca. All these varied
threads were drawn together by Raleigh, who concluded his
account of Berrio's version of Martín de Albujar's story with
this notable description:

"Those Guianians and also the borderers . . . are
marvelous great drunkards, in which vice I think no nation
can compare with them: and at the times of their solemn
feasts when the Emperor carouseth with his captains, tribu-

tories, and governors, the manner is thus. All those that pledge him are first stripped naked, and their bodies anointed all over with a kind of white balsam (by them called *Curcai*) of which there is a great plenty and yet very dear amongst them, and it is of all other the most precious, whereof we have had good experience: when they are anointed all over, certain servants of the Emperor having prepared gold made into fine powder blow it through hollow canes upon their naked bodies, until they be all shining from the foot to the head, and in this sort they sit drinking by twenties and hundreds and continue in drunkenness sometimes six or seven days together. . . . Upon this sight, and for the abundance of gold which he saw in the city, the images of gold in their temples, the plates, armors, and shields of gold which they use in the wars, he called it *El Dorado*." [167]

Berrio now had the name of a city toward which he could go—Manoa. The name took its place in the mythology of El Dorado, and became virtually synonymous with El Dorado as the designation for the land of gold. Its etymology deserves some comment. Martín de Albujar did not invent the name out of whole cloth, as he did the rest of his story. He had, after all, lived for ten years among the Indians of Guiana, and probably had had some contact with or report of an Indian tribe of the upper Río Negro known variously as the Mahanoas, Managus, Manaves, or Manáos. They were itinerant traders who frequently entered Guiana to barter, and apparently Martín de Albujar adapted the name of these Mahanoas or Manáos for his golden city of Manoa. But other suggestions have been put forward. One is that Manoa is derived from *Man-iaos*, "the city of the Iaos," another Indian tribe of Guiana. By another account the word *manoa* means "lake" in the language of the Achagua Indians of Venezuela, who had a myth of a *catena manoa* or "large lake" on top of a mountain beyond their territory; in this lake, they said, was an island on which was a prodigious city of gilded buildings. However, this seems to be a secondary myth possibly acquired by the Achaguas from Spaniards who came looking for El Dorado, and does not seem to be the source of Martín de Albujar's word. Finally, the most prosaic explanation is that Berrio's informant was really a Portuguese who was telling of a "great lake," *lagoa manha*, and Berrio heard the word as "Manoa."

Manoa it was, whatever the derivation, and Berrio in his unhappy months at Margarita saw its glimmering towers by night in dreams. To his mind all was clear: the mountain lake, the golden city on its shores, the Indian aristocrats in their resplendent nakedness. But Manoa was as unattainable as any vision of a dream, for King Philip did not answer Berrio's letters, and the time slipped by.

Some time in 1592, Berrio encountered a volatile and resourceful adventurer named Domingo de Vera Ybarguen who seemed a worthy ally in his struggle with Sarmiento. Vera had a sharp wit and a persuasive tongue, and offered the vigor of youth to supplement the diminishing vitality of the aging Berrio. Taken into Berrio's confidence, Vera at once wrote to his own town of Caracas to beg aid from Don Diego Osorio, the Governor of Venezuela. Osorio responded with men and supplies, and Berrio sent them under Vera's leadership to occupy Trinidad as the base for the future invasion of Guiana. On May 19, 1592, Vera formally established the settlement of San José de Oruña on Trinidad. He had thirty men.

In the remaining months of the year Berrio dispatched several boatloads of reinforcements to Trinidad, so that in his letter to King Philip of January 1, 1593, he could report that "the whole island has been explored and an inventory of the natives compiled. . . . The land is very abundant in sulphur, maize, and sugar-cane; and the plantations consist of plantains. There is good store of potatoes, a great quantity of cotton, and gold has been found in four streams. They say that it is a very good land for ginger; but the best features are its nearness to the Main, its numerous population and its large supply of canoes. I shall depart from this island [Margarita] tomorrow with another fourteen or fifteen soldiers, which will make a total of ninety-five Spaniards. I am hoping that Don Diego Osorio may send me another twenty or thirty with whom, if they come, I shall set off from Trinidad with seventy Spaniards, leaving fifty behind to guard a fort which has been built there. With these and a number of articles for barter I shall try to penetrate into the interior of Guiana by means of the chief Morequito, whom I have in my power, and of other chiefs at the actual entrance who are my friends." [168]

In this same letter Berrio set forth his views on the location of El Dorado:

"These great provinces lie between two very great rivers, that of the Amazon and the Orinoco. The Amazon comes down from Peru, and the sources of the Orinoco flow down from Quito, gathering all the springs of the New Kingdom [New Granada] which run down into the plains, which is where I embarked. There enters into this river a large number of tributaries bearing a great volume of water. The reason why the Orinoco appears small on entering the sea, while being so great, is that where the River Caroni (which is the one that flows down from Guiana) joins with it, the Orinoco is divided into seven arms from each of which flow out a great number of channels, and each arm and channel enters the sea independently. Owing to this and to the ocean-tide the coast is inundated for many leagues, and the interior is flooded for forty leagues. This circumstance prevents any vessel from entering unless it be small and fitted with oars. Men have entered through these channels to trade, and not finding the towns near the water, have probably imagined that they were further up, and the Indians have said they were further up to get rid of them from their houses; so they have travelled without finding anything and have returned. But the Indians tell the truth, because the great towns and the riches are very much further up from the border country of Morequito; but it is not possible to enter there, and the beginning of the large towns is more than sixty leagues inland. As I have travelled down the streams and circumvented the mountains (more than seven hundred leagues by land and by water) on the three occasions when I made the entry, and have spent ten years in continuous labors, I am well informed and know the facts." [169]

Berrio was confident that, having occupied Trinidad, he could go on to reach El Dorado. He asked King Philip for two ships of not more than two hundred tons for a term of five years, to bring him necessary provisions; he requested that he be permitted to convey these goods to Trinidad without payment of Spanish customs fees; he asked an investment by the King; and he hoped that arrangements would be made for some merchant, "who is not a buccaneer but a man of courage and substance, to collect a large consignment of articles for barter, consisting of axes (which should be good ones), cutlasses, gilded knives, a number of short coats, beads . . . , trumpets, needles, headgear, bells, small mirrors, and some large and well-made ones for the chiefs." [170] With the aid of God and King Philip, Berrio proposed to enter Guiana and at long last secure El Dorado for Spain.

His letter, though, touched on the difficulties Sarmiento was creating for him at Margarita: "In ten years of wandering I have not experienced such great hardship as in the fifteen months that I have been in this island, and in all those months I have collected less than a hundred men, and these at their weight in gold—a commodity which I have lacked as my home is so far away and my estates heavily pledged. The chief difficulty is the opposition which I have encountered from Don Juan, which is such that, if the authority which I bear from the King were not so ample, he would have cast me out of the land."[171] Before he could dispatch this letter, Berrio was in new troubles, as he informs King Philip in a glum postscript. Not only was he compelled to postpone the journey to Trinidad that he was planning to take "tomorrow," but he was confronted with an unexpected source of opposition.

On Christmas Eve, 1592, there arrived in Margarita one Don Francisco de Vides, who carried a royal commission appointing him governor of Cumaná and New Andalusia. Vides had obtained the succession to the late Diego de Serpa's grant of the country around the Orinoco estuary, conditional on his successful colonization of Trinidad. Berrio had all this while been operating under the grant inherited from Quesada, which entitled him merely to the region between the Pauto and the Papamene. By a casual process of extension he had pursued El Dorado eastward into Guiana, but the harsh fact now could not be denied that Vides was the rightful proprietor of that part of the continent. Suddenly Berrio saw all that he had gained swept from his grasp. He offered to negotiate with Vides and arrive at a division of the territory; but Vides, knowing that legitimacy lay on his side, would have no dealings with Berrio.

After several days of this impasse the old soldier decided on a *coup de main:* he would find Manoa, stake a claim to it, and worry about Vides later. He crossed to Trinidad with as many soldiers as he could gather and fortified it. Then, in April, 1593, he sent his lieutenant Domingo de Vera to the mainland to make the discovery of Manoa.

Vera had thirty-five men and barter goods to the value of a thousand pesos. He landed near the mouths of the Orinoco and went upriver through the country of the friendly old chief Carapana to that of Morequito, at the mouth of the Caroni. Chief Morequito, who had in the meantime converted to Christianity, was in a bitter mood after the slave raid perpetrated upon his people by Fajardo the year before. But he greeted the Spaniards with feigned submission and offered them guides to Manoa. (According to Raleigh, Morequito had met Vides at Cumaná and was in league with him against Berrio.) When the Spaniards were properly lulled, Morequito attempted to massacre them; but the plot was detected and the Spaniards escaped.

They left Morequito and traveled inland toward Guiana, reaching after fifty miles a densely populated region of tall, good-looking Indians who lodged and entertained them affably, presenting them with deer, fowls, vegetables, fruits, and wine. However, the Indians took care to conceal their golden ornaments—because, says Berrio, Morequito had warned them in advance of the Spaniards' hunger for that metal. Making inquiries about Manoa and El Dorado, Vera learned that at one day's journey was the province of Macuraguara, beyond which was the land of Gaygapari. South of Macuraguara and Gaygapari was a great salt lake, eleven days' journey ahead, "which is called the land of Manoa, around which there are a vast number of clothed people, and towns and lords, who arrived there about twenty years ago," says Berrio, "and a multitude of people accoutred with small bows, who fought with those of the lake and have been subduing a great part of that nation. These they say are in such great numbers that, judging by the populations of the towns which were seen at the entrance of Guiana and what they say of the rest, it is understood that there are more than two million Indians. . . . They say the lake is close to the sierra which is on the right hand, extending through Guiana away from the *cordillera* which the Spaniards saw, and faces south. It is a land devoid of forest, and the whole province of Guiana is a cool land with very temperate valleys. . . . In the province of Guiana they all speak the same language. It is said that the clothed people talk a different language and are a people of many trades, and very rich in gold, which they dedicate to the numerous sanctuaries which they use in the hills and mountains." [172]

Vera thus heard, although he did not claim to have seen it with his own eyes, that a great lakeside city of Manoa lay ahead, populated by highly civilized Indians who presumably had fled from Peru to subjugate this part of the continent after Pizarro's conquest. What he apparently had picked up was a report of an authentic Indian invasion of Guiana, not by Peruvian Incas but by a gold-using tribe called the Arekunas who formerly had lived near the Omagua territory in southern Venezuela. Once more there was a seed of truth at the bottom of a version of the story of El Dorado.

Without attempting to go farther, Vera returned to Trinidad in May of 1593, carrying golden trinkets that he had gathered on his march. Berrio was delighted, and sent Vera instantly off to Caracas to show the treasures to Governor Osorio of Venezuela. Osorio, though captivated by the fine workmanship of the baubles, politely declined to send more men to Berrio's assistance. Instead he began to recruit an army to find Manoa on his own account. Berrio's one supporter in high office thus became his rival the moment any hope of success materialized. "The devil himself is the patron of this enterprise," Berrio exclaimed. [173]

He learned now that the viceroy of Peru had intervened with Vides on his behalf, ordering Vides to give all possible assistance to Berrio. This message had been intercepted by Sarmiento, the first of Berrio's three enemies. (Sarmiento shortly would cease to trouble Berrio. In November, 1593, English pirates raided Margarita and killed him. Sarmiento's father had been that governor of Margarita slain by Lope de Aguirre in 1561.) Berrio, discovering somehow that Vides was under orders to help him, wrote to him at Cumaná requesting him to honor the viceroy's command, "for the love of God." Vides replied coldly that he would not cooperate with Berrio and told him to cease his attempts to reach Manoa or face severe punishment.

Harassed by Sarmiento, threatened by Vides, now menaced by the rivalry of Osorio, the unfortunate Berrio sent his elder son Fernando, a boy of about seventeen, back to New Granada to get help. Fernando made the taxing transcontinental journey successfully and began recruiting a new expedition in Tunja. At the same time—August, 1593—Berrio dispatched one of his few other trusted associates, Domingo de Vera, to Spain to seek aid directly from the court. Early in 1594, a company of soldiers reached Berrio from New Granada. His son, remaining behind to gather others, sent word that he would soon arrive at the head of large force. Vera, writing from Spain, provided the glad tidings that he was assembling a huge expedition to conquer El Dorado. His nimble tongue had spun a tale of easy fortunes, and the Spaniards were hastening to enroll, selling their estates to finance their participation in Vera's enterprise. The old madness burned as brightly as ever. Vera reported that several thousand men had joined him, and the Spanish court had contributed a huge sum toward the success of the venture, nearly twenty times as much as Queen Isabella had given Columbus.

It seemed to Berrio that his sorrows were soon to be at an end. He had a sturdy fort on Trinidad, and now he used the reinforcements from New Granada to set up a camp on the mainland in the territory of his venerable ally, Carapana.

Before long his son would join him with more troops, and then, some time in 1595, the mighty armada collected by Domingo de Vera would sail westward toward the certain conquest of the golden land. Berrio had every reason to think that he would celebrate his seventy-fifth birthday in 1595 as a rich man.

His real troubles, though, were just beginning.

4

In October, 1594, Francisco de Vides abruptly appeared at Trinidad with a small force of men that he had collected in Cumaná. He produced his royal commission, which legitimately entitled him to possession of Trinidad, and ordered Berrio to get off the island. Since he had a larger garrison at his disposal, Berrio stood firm, and Vides withdrew in anger. Berrio was angry too, and as was his custom composed a long letter to King Philip, rehearsing all that he had suffered on Spain's behalf to find El Dorado, and attacking Vides as an interloper.

The next crisis came on February 1, 1595, when an English party led by Sir Robert Dudley arrived. Dudley was the illegitimate son of the Earl of Leicester, one of the dominant figures at the court of Queen Elizabeth. Lacking anything better to do in the fall of 1594, Dudley had decided to go on a free-lance voyage of piracy in the West Indies, as fashionable men of a later day might go on a grand tour of Europe. After a random search of the coasts of Africa, Dudley turned westward and crossed the Atlantic in three weeks, landing at Trinidad at Punta de Curiapan. He sent men ashore to look for gold. What they found was a mine of marcasite (iron disulphide), which, Dudley wrote, "glisters like gold (but all is not gold that glistereth.") [174] The Indians came forth and offered such commodities as hogs, hens, plantains, tobacco, and potatoes in exchange for the

hatchets, knives, hooks, bells, and glass buttons Dudley's
vessel carried. Then Dudley discovered that there was a
Spanish settlement on the island, commanded by Berrio and
manned by several hundred troops.

This was not the first time that Berrio had been confronted by an intrusion of the English, who then were
sworn enemies of Spain. The gleam of El Dorado had begun
to dazzle the subjects of Queen Elizabeth, with Sir Walter
Raleigh the most convinced of the Doradists, and at the
beginning of 1594 Raleigh had sent his friend Jacob Whiddon on a reconnaissance voyage to Guiana. Whiddon had
called at Trinidad, where Berrio had received him peacefully and passed along to him some stories of El Dorado.
Through some treachery—possibly engineered by Berrio
himself, although the record is unclear—eight of Whiddon's
men had been killed in an ambush by the Spaniards, the rest
escaping.

Upon Dudley's arrival, Berrio once again sent messages of friendship to the English. However, Dudley knew
of the fate of Whiddon's men and was taking no chances.
Since he was not strong enough to attack the Spanish garrison, he withdrew to the other side of the island, and plied the
Indians there with questions about the gold of Guiana. They
told him such exciting things about gold mines on the mainland that he sent the boat of his ship across and into the
Orinoco. "They found the mainland . . . full of fresh rivers running one into another, abounding with fish," wrote
Dudley, "and a land all woody, seeming to have great store
of strange beasts and fowls, and very populous." [175] In a
province called Tivitivas "the king offered to bring a canoe
full of this golden ore, and to this purpose sent a canoe,
which returned and brought my men this answer, that Ar-
mago, captain of the town of Orocoa and the mine, refused
them, but if they would come thither, he himself would

make them answer." [176] At this town of Orocoa the chief boasted that "he had a mine of gold, and could refine it, and would trade with me: for token whereof, he sent me three or four *croissants* or half moons of gold weighing a noble apiece or more, and two bracelets of silver." And he told Dudley's men "of another rich nation, that sprinkled their bodies with the powder of gold, and seemed to be gilt, and far beyond them a great town called El Dorado, with many other things." But the explorers felt they were too few to seek this golden land, particularly after their Indian guide deserted them, and they returned to Dudley.

Any plans he might have had for attempting El Dorado ended when his tired, hungry men refused to make another trip to the mainland. On March 12, they left Trinidad to tour the West Indies, terrorizing the Spanish settlements on Hispaniola and Puerto Rico, and sinking a few Spanish galleons before returning to England in May.

Berrio had weathered the arrival of Dudley with the same success that had attended his handling of the visits of Whiddon and Vides. But a few weeks after Dudley's departure, a new foe made his presence known. On April 4, 1595, after twelve days of secret reconnoitering, four English ships commanded by Sir Walter Raleigh dropped anchor off Trinidad. Berrio was caught by surprise. Hastily he sent a party of soldiers from San José de Oruña to find out what the newcomers meant to do. Raleigh's men set upon them and defeated them, killing Rodrigo de la Hoz, Berrio's nephew. At dawn on April 8, while Berrio waited in agonized suspense for some news from his scouts, Raleigh and his troops, aided by Indians, crept toward San José and attacked it. Some twenty Spaniards were killed, Berrio and his lieutenant Alvaro Jorge were taken prisoner, and the town was put to the torch.

That night Berrio sat as a prisoner aboard Raleigh's

flagship, his golden dream collapsed in ruins. Without knowing it, he and Raleigh had been on a collision course for many years, and now the moment of impact had come. Neither man would ever be quite the same again; for Berrio, who had sought the Dorado for fifteen years, now proceeded to transfer his obsession to Raleigh, and set him on his long path toward tragedy.

[8]

RALEIGH AND THE

GOLD OF MANOA

 F ALL THOSE WHO SOUGHT FOR EL DORADO, there is no more fascinating figure than Walter Raleigh, nor did any of them involve himself more painfully with the hopeless quest. Raleigh was a man of many characters—mountebank and hero, philosopher and philanderer, a dabbler in poetry, piracy, and extortion, a far-seeing statesman and a self-seeking fraud. His career is stained with many hypocrisies, and his high reputation as a seaman was based on a fabric no more substantial than the tale of El Dorado itself, but yet he was a noble spirit in his way, worthy of admiration and condemnation in equal measure. He was witty and graceful, greedy, eloquent, ambitious, willing to lie and grovel to attain the highest ends. The mighty empire that he dreamed of founding in Guiana with the gold of El Dorado was a fit enterprise for a man of such inner contradictions.

He was born about 1552 in Devon. His father was a country squire of ancient lineage but little wealth who had married three times, and Walter was one of two sons by his third marriage. Young Walter had three half-brothers, his mother's children, one of whom was the immortal Elizabethan seaman Sir Humphrey Gilbert. Apparently the family name, in the loose fashion of the day, was sometimes spelled "Ralegh," and it was that spelling that he adopted in the latter part of his life.

Of Raleigh's childhood little is known. When he was sixteen he enrolled at Oxford's Oriel College, where he was regarded as a brilliant student, but his academic career was interrupted in 1569 for several years of military service in France. Returning after this baptism of violence, Raleigh took up the study of law, and by 1575 was in residence at the Temple in London, where he wrote poems, toured the taverns of the city, and occasionally contemplated his textbooks.

His half-brother Sir Humphrey Gilbert, one of the great explorers of the day, secured in 1578 from Queen Elizabeth a charter to find a northwest passage to China and "to discover, find, search out, and view such remote, heathen, and barbarous lands . . . not actually possessed of any Christian prince or people, as to him . . . shall seem good." [177] An expedition sailed in the fall of 1579, and according to one account Raleigh was in command of a small vessel. After gales had forced the ships to return to the port of Plymouth to refit, they started out again several months later, only to meet with a Spanish fleet that attacked and dispersed them. They limped back separately to Plymouth. One of the last to arrive was Raleigh's ship, its provisions nearly exhausted. His naval career had not begun auspiciously.

The failure of the enterprise left Gilbert nearly bankrupt and he went to Ireland to recoup his fortunes, Raleigh accompanying him. In the summer of 1580, Raleigh was given command of a detachment of troops to put down a rebellion; he captured a rebel leader, sentenced him to be hanged, drawn, and quartered, and saw that the sentence was carried out. When the Spaniards sent troops to aid the Irish rebels, Raleigh took part in their capture and then in a discreditable slaughter of the prisoners. His daredevil Irish exploits led to his first public prominence. In December of 1581, he returned to London and brought himself to the attention of the two most important men of the realm, Lords Burghley and Walsingham, the Lord Treasurer and the Secretary of State. Raleigh won their interest by criticizing the English administration in Ireland and putting himself forward as an expert on Irish affairs. They made him an unofficial adviser and introduced him at court.

The pretty story of Raleigh's spreading his cloak to spare Queen Elizabeth from the mud is almost certainly apocryphal, but by the spring of 1582 he had come to stand high in the Queen's favor, and quite probably had become the newest in her long succession of lovers. The marks of her favor were quickly evident: he was given the confiscated estate of an Irish rebel, the command of an infantry company, and soon several higher titles. The Queen was taken by his good looks, his courtly manner, his ready wit, and his lofty ambitions. In an age of men who dressed with peacock brilliance, Raleigh was outstanding for his raiment of silk and velvet. He gleamed with a fortune in silver jewelry. He spoke with the natural grace of a prince of words, at a time when the English language, both spoken and written, was attaining its zenith of elegance.

Raleigh rose so fast at court that in May of 1583 Lord Burghley was writing to him on behalf of his scapegrace son-in-law, the Earl of Oxford, asking Raleigh to intercede with Elizabeth on Oxford's account. In the same year Raleigh obtained the Queen's permission for Sir Humphrey Gilbert to outfit a new expedition of discovery. Raleigh did not go on the voyage which proved fatal to his famed half-brother. But in 1584 he obtained his own patent to plant a colony in North America, and sent out a small expedition that reached the coast of that continent by way of the West Indies. It returned bearing news of a fertile new land which Raleigh christened "Virginia" in honor of his Virgin Queen.

Clad now in a knighthood, Raleigh organized a colonizing party that set out for Virginia in the spring of 1585. The story of the Roanoke colony is a dramatic one, though not particularly relevant to the enterprise of El Dorado except for the light it sheds on Raleigh's determination to plant a colony in the New World. After several years of bad luck and hardship, Roanoke was abandoned, and in 1589 Raleigh returned his patent to the crown, from whom it eventually passed to the founders of the successful Jamestown colony. The experiment was a failure, but it left Raleigh permanently convinced of the desirability of counteracting Spanish influence by building settlements in the Americas.

As his influence at court grew, so did his hunger for wealth. Between 1582 and 1592 he gathered property with unalloyed rapacity, persuading the Queen to make over to him the lands and goods of a variety of rebels and discredited noblemen. His Irish estates eventually covered twelve thousand acres (he was the first man to plant potatoes in Ireland) and his domains in England were nearly as extensive. His methods of acquiring this land were frequently unsavory, as when he obtained a manor belonging to an elderly bishop by threatening to expose the supposedly celibate prelate's secret marriage, or when he detached a substantial segment of church property from another bishopric as payment for having obtained the see for a prospective candidate.

To his credit, Raleigh was open-handed with the wealth he so sordidly obtained, making generous contributions to the work of such men as the geographer Richard Hakluyt, the mathematician Thomas Hariot, and the musician John Case. Nor did he, even while grubbing for all the privileges and properties Elizabeth could bestow on him, lose his private skepticism toward the court and its courtiers. He was capable of such savage poems as this:

> Say to the court, it glows
> And shines like rotten wood;
> Say to the church it shows
> What's good, and doth no good:
> If church and court reply,
> Then give them both the lie.

> Tell men of high condition,
> That manage the estate,
> Their purpose is ambition,
> Their practice only hate:
> And if they once reply,
> Then give them all the lie.

Surely a man who could maintain such double vision toward his own milieu and his own place in it was no ordinary person. And late in his life, when all his schemes had failed him, he included in his *History of the World* a somber reflection on the vanity of vanities: "Neither have those beloved companions of honor and riches any power at all, to hold us any one day, by the glorious promise of entertainments; but what crooked paths soever we walk, the same leadeth on directly to the house of death; whose doors lie open at all hours, and to all persons. For this tide of man's life, after it once turneth and declineth, ever runneth with a perpetual ebb and falling stream, but never floweth again: our leaf once fallen, springeth no more, neither doth the sun or the summer adorn us again, with the garments of new leaves and flowers." [178]

In the years about 1590, Raleigh's tide was high and

few suspected that he might harbor such thoughts. To his fellow Elizabethans he was a figure to be regarded with admiration and suspicion; they respected his enormous energies, his brilliance of personal and literary style, and his grasp of world affairs, while mistrusting his greed, his tendency toward sycophancy, and his erratic ways. His attempt to excel at poetry, to plumb the profound mysteries of epistemology, to become the premier landowner of the realm, to settle colonies across the Atlantic, to seduce the court ladies, and to make himself the center of all intellectual activity, all simultaneously, made him appear shallow, lacking in depth for all his vast breadth.

To the public at large—and to posterity—he was also ranked as one of the great Elizabethan explorers and admirals. This reputation was almost wholly undeserved. As an explorer, Raleigh did little at first hand, and even in his El Dorado quest he merely retraced a path already blazed for him by the remarkable and undeservedly obscure Antonio de Berrio. As an admiral, Raleigh was almost comically inept, and only through mighty overrating could he be classed with such authentic masters of the sea as Sir Francis Drake and Sir Humphrey Gilbert. His one great exploit, the attack on Cádiz in 1596, was tinged with foolishness, for he hesitated at the outset in a most un-Elizabethan way, urging a postponement of the attack until another day, and then, finally entering the harbor, timidly anchored his ship so far from those of the Spaniards that it was impossible to engage them properly. A year later, when a great English fleet set sail for Spain, Raleigh's ship brought up the rear, and he was the first to retreat to Plymouth when a storm blew up. On several further occasions in the naval war with Spain Raleigh made an early retreat, became separated from the other vessels, or suffered more than ordinary discomforts in storms. During the defeat of the Spanish Armada in 1588,

Raleigh and the Gold of Manoa

Raleigh—one of the leaders of the realm—may have helped
to plan strategy, but he remained ashore in the fighting. He
was no sailor.

His real greatness lay in his statesmanship. He conceived and nearly carried through the ambitious scheme of a
British empire in South America, which if successful would
have brought England to global dominance a century before
it actually reached that status. Though he admired the courage and endurance of the Spaniards, he had only contempt
for their simple-minded lust for gold; Raleigh saw flourishing agricultural and commercial centers, built with the cooperation of the Indians, where the Spaniards could see only
mines and treasure-troves. He loved gold too, but he recognized the futility of extracting it at the cost of the destruction of the indigenous cultures; for once the mines were
empty and all the Indians had perished in slavery, the Spaniards would have nothing in the New World, Raleigh said,
and that eventually is what happened to Spain's American
realm.

The expensive and disastrous failure of his Virginia
scheme in 1586–89 ended the first phase of Raleigh's endeavor to give his nation an American empire. Perhaps even
then he was swiftly turning to thoughts of creating an empire by conquest in the tropics of South America, since the
venture in the north had not worked. His ambitious plans
were halted in 1592 by his sudden fall from royal favor; for
he had seduced and then married one of the Queen's maids
of honor, Elizabeth Throgmorton, and the Queen turned
against him—not so much for the seduction, though that
perhaps provoked her jealousy, but because Raleigh and his
bride had dared to marry without Elizabeth's permission.
The newlyweds were locked away in a prison cell at the
Tower of London, and, as an anonymous letter of the time
put it, "All is alarm and confusion at this discovery of the

discoverer, and not indeed of a new continent, but of a new incontinent." [179]

Through dutiful flattery of the Queen, Raleigh eventually won his freedom again, but he never again held his old high place at court. The brilliance of his career was dimmed, and for the rest of his life he found the footing treacherous whenever he approached Elizabeth or her successor, King James. Thus it was in 1594 that Raleigh found himself pleading for permission to accompany an English fleet against Spain, declaring, "I have no other desire but to serve Her Majesty. And seeing I deserve nor place nor honor nor servant, I hope it will be easily granted." [180] And it was in that same year that, casting about for some dramatic and spectacular way to regain his old position of eminence with Queen Elizabeth, Raleigh resolved to make her Empress of El Dorado.

2

He knew the story of the gilded man, of course, and he knew the history of the quest for El Dorado from its beginnings in the 1530's through the adventures of Gonzalo Pizarro and Pedro de Ursua to the ill-starred attempts of Serpa and Silva. Raleigh had access to the learned Richard Hakluyt, who diligently collected, translated, and published the accounts of the Spanish explorers, and the events in South America were no secret to him. And he was aware, in 1594, that one Antonio de Berrio had crossed the continent from New Granada and had taken up residence on Trinidad while preparing to invade Guiana, which now was recognized as the abode of El Dorado.

The obsession with Guiana grew until he had made up his mind to go to sea. Lady Raleigh, aware of her husband's undistinguished seamanship, attempted to dissuade him, and when this failed she wrote to the influential Robert

Cecil, Lord Burghley's son, asking him in February, 1594, to turn Raleigh's mind from the dangerous westward voyage: if he must go to sea, she said, she hoped Cecil would employ him "in sure water towards the east than help him forward toward the sunset." [181] But by that time Raleigh had sent his friend Jacob Whiddon on a scouting mission to the Orinoco. Calling at Trinidad, Whiddon was received with seeming cordiality by Berrio, and, as we have seen, eight of his men were treacherously slain by the Spaniards.

Whiddon returned with no gold but with an abundance of tales of the wealth of the mainland, and that was enough to fire Raleigh's determination. His master plan called for colonization, not merely exploitation; but gold was a highly visible and persuasive substance, and if he could obtain a rich supply of it for the Queen, he might be permitted to carry out his larger intentions in the New World. Furthermore he saw the supreme importance of securing the gold of El Dorado before it fell into the hands of the Spaniards, for Raleigh was above all else a patriot, and in the late sixteenth century that meant he must work toward the weakening of Spain. It was the plundered gold of the Indies that had financed Spain's hostility toward England. As Raleigh wrote in 1596 after his return from Guiana, the Spanish King had repaired the damage done in his great defeat of 1588, "not from the trades of sacks, and Seville oranges, nor from ought else that either Spain, Portugal, or any of his other provinces produce: It is his Indian gold that endangereth and disturbeth all the nations of Europe, it purchaseth intelligence, creepeth into councils, and setteth bound loyalty at liberty, in the greatest monarchies of Europe." [182]

The Queen rather sourly granted permission to Raleigh to make the expedition, empowering him "to do Us service in offending the King of Spain and his subjects in his dominions to your uttermost power." [183] Significantly, the words

"trusty" and "well-beloved," part of the formula of such commissions, were omitted before Raleigh's name in this document. Raleigh's half-brother Sir John Gilbert was responsible for collecting the crew, and by September of 1594 had assembled the usual unruly mob of impressed seamen. Last-minute obstacles kept the five small vessels from sailing until February 6, 1595. The route was a traditional one, southward to the Canary Islands to stock up on provisions, then westward across the Atlantic. While at the Canaries, Raleigh enhanced his stores by a little privateering, raiding a Spanish vessel laden with firearms and a Flemish ship carrying wines.

On March 22, after having lost sight of some of his ships during the crossing, Raleigh's flagship and one other vessel arrived at Punta de Curiapan at the southwest tip of

Trinidad—the same place where Dudley had anchored seven weeks before. They moved quietly along the coast of the island, coming ashore occasionally to confer with the Indians. At Puerto de los Hispanioles, then a tiny outpost and now the large city of Port-of-Spain, Raleigh encountered Spaniards for the first time, a small garrison of Berrio's men. They were willing to trade with the English, and came aboard their ships. Raleigh relates that the Spaniards were "entertained kindly and feasted after our manner, by means whereof I learned of one and another as much of the estate of Guiana as I could, or as they knew, for these poor soldiers having been many years without wine, a few draughts made them merry, in which mood they vaunted of Guiana and of the riches thereof, and all what they knew of the ways and passages, myself seeming to purpose nothing less than the entrance or discovery thereof, but bred in them an opinion that I was bound only for the relief of those English, which I had planted in Virginia." [184] Raleigh so successfully persuaded these simple soldiers that his intent was peaceful that they evidently did not immediately send word to Berrio, at San José, that Englishmen had arrived in Trinidad.

Raleigh knew that it was necessary to destroy this Spanish settlement on Trinidad before he could attempt to reach El Dorado: "To enter Guiana by small boats, to depart 400 or 500 miles from my ships, and to leave a garrison in my back interested in the same enterprise, who also daily expected supplies out of Spain, I should have savored very much of the ass." [185] Aside from logistic considerations, he was eager to take revenge on Berrio for the slaying of Whiddon's eight men the year before. So he moved along the coast of the island toward Berrio's town. Berrio belatedly discovered the English presence at his rear, and sent some men to spy on them; but these, as already noted, were found and killed by Raleigh's troops.

Then, "taking a time of most advantage," Raleigh attacked San José: "I set upon the *Corp du guard* in the
evening, and having put them to the sword, sent Captain
Calfield onwards with sixty soldiers, and myself followed
with 40 more and so took their new city which they called S.
Joseph by break of day: they abode not any fight after a
few shot, and all being dismissed but only Berrio and his
companion, I brought them with me aboard, and at the instance of the Indians I set their new city of S. Joseph's on
fire." [186]

It was a doubly joyful occasion, for two of Raleigh's
strayed ships arrived that same day, one commanded by
George Gifford, the other by Laurence Keymis, a man
marked for an important role in Raleigh's future ventures.
While San José burned, Raleigh spoke to the Indians of
Trinidad, using an interpreter he had brought from England. They were pleased to see the undoing of the Spaniards,
and told many harrowing tales of Berrio's cruelty, "how he
had divided the island and given to every soldier a part, that
he made the ancient *Casiqui* [chiefs] which were lords of the
country to be their slaves, that he kept them in chains, and
dropped their naked bodies with burning bacon." [187] That
the Spaniards practiced these crimes was undoubtedly true,
but in view of Berrio's own attitude toward the proper handling of the Indians it seems likely that much of the cruelty
was performed without his knowledge, though Raleigh
gives him credit for instigating it.

The Spaniards had clearly left the wrong sort of imprint on the natives of the island, and they were quick to
offer allegiance to their deliverers. Raleigh writes, "I made
them understand that I was the servant of a Queen, who was
the great *Casique* of the north, and a virgin, and had more
Casiqui under her than there were trees in their island: that
she was an enemy to the Castellani [Castilians] in respect of

their tyranny and oppression, and that she having freed all the coast of the northern world from their servitude had sent me to free them also, and withal to defend the country of Guiana from their invasion and conquest. I showed them her majesty's picture, which they so admired and honored, as it had been easy to have brought them idolatrous thereof." [188]

The English ships returned to their original harbor at Curiapan, Berrio coming along as Raleigh's prisoner. The relation between the two men is an interesting and ambivalent one. Raleigh speaks harshly of Berrio's alleged atrocities upon the natives, but yet clearly held the highest esteem for the tough old man, who was then some seventy-five years of age. Raleigh wrote of Berrio that he was "very valiant and liberal. . . . I used him according to his estate and worth in all things I could, according to the small means I had." What took place aboard Raleigh's ship was something of a battle of wits. Berrio was willing enough to tell Raleigh all that he knew of El Dorado, but deliberately exaggerated the distance of the journey and its hardships, in the hope of engendering such dismay that Raleigh would abandon the quest. Raleigh had already had some intelligence of the location of Manoa from Jacob Whiddon; now, however, Berrio informed him that the golden city lay 600 miles farther inland than Raleigh believed. What was at the back of Berrio's mind, of course, was the imminent arrival of Domingo de Vera's huge expedition. Berrio wished to preserve his own life by cooperating with Raleigh, and yet hoped that he could frighten Raleigh away in time to provide a clear field for Vera.

Raleigh also knew of Vera's expedition, however, for an English captain had taken a Spanish vessel at sea the year before that had been bearing a letter from Vera to Berrio. Raleigh wished to forestall Vera at all costs, since his own future ambitions depended on obtaining the gold of

Manoa. Therefore, though inwardly chilled by Berrio's exaggerated information, Raleigh simply saw to it that the revised estimates of El Dorado's distance were "kept from the knowledge of my company, who else would never have been brought to attempt the same." [189]

Berrio was free with information about the golden realm, which Raleigh added to that which he had already assembled from the chronicles of Cieza de León, López de Gómara, and others. From Berrio came the romantic tale of "Johannes Martinez" and his visit to the Incan city of Manoa; Berrio also told of his own adventures in detail, including a frank admission of his conflicts with Sarmiento and Vides. Raleigh's relation of all this material indicates that he was a good listener and an accurate reporter, for his account matches in almost every detail Berrio's own autobiographical letters to King Philip II.

At the end of Berrio's lengthy discourse, Raleigh revealed that he still intended to make the Guiana crossing. "Berrio," he writes, "was stricken into a great melancholy and sadness, and used all the arguments he could to dissuade me, and also assured the gentlemen of my company that it would be labor lost: and that they should suffer many miseries if they proceeded: And first he delivered that I could not enter any of the rivers with any bark or pinnace, nor hardly with any ship's boat, it was so low, sandy, and full of flats, and that his companies were daily grounded in their canoes which drew but twelve inches of water: he further said that none of the country would come to speak with us, but would all fly, and if we followed them to their dwellings, they would burn their own towns, and besides that the way was long, the winter at hand, and that the rivers beginning once to swell, it was impossible to stem the current." [190] Most of these warnings, Raleigh would discover, were precise forecasts of what would happen; yet he was a desperate man, and would not be turned back by Berrio's words. He knew that the shrewd Berrio was likely to be painting the darkest possible picture, and he also believed—in error—that the Spaniard was a careless observer of the true conditions.

Leaving his ships anchored off Trinidad, Raleigh crossed to the Orinoco estuary with a hundred men and a month's provisions in an assortment of barges, ship's boats, wherries, and a cut-down galley equipped with oars. The men were ablaze with the hope for gold, and Raleigh himself had visions of winning fame as an English Cortés or Pizarro. The crossing was a painful one, for, Raleigh declares, they were "all driven to lie in the rain and weather, in the open air, in the burning sun, and upon the hard boards, and to dress our meat, and to carry all manner of furniture in them [the open boats], wherewith they were so pestered and unsavory, that what with victuals being most fish, with the wet clothes of so many men thrust together and in the heat of the sun, I will undertake there was never any prison in England, that could be found more unsavory and loathsome, especially to myself, who had for many years before been dieted and cared for in a sort far differing." [191]

3

Berrio had assured Raleigh concerning "Manoa the imperial city of Guiana, which the Spaniards call *el Dorado*, that for the greatness, for the riches, and for the excellent seat, it far exceedeth any of the world, at least of so much of the world as is known to the Spanish nation: it is founded upon a lake of salt water of 200 leagues long." [192] To ascend the Orinoco to the Caroni, to ascend the Caroni as far as this great salt lake, thence to conquer Manoa—that was Raleigh's plan.

There were problems at the very outset. Having endured the painful crossing of the Gulf of Paria, in which the outflow of the giant Orinoco sets up powerful waves that must have buffeted the small boats cruelly, the English now had to find some way upstream in the river while it was at full flood. There was no lack of possible entries, but from each mouth of the Orinoco came such a gush of speeding water that it seemed impossible to ascend, and in many places the river seemed as wide across as the English Channel between Dover and Calais. "We might have wandered a whole year in that labyrinth of rivers, ere we had found any way, either out or in," Raleigh wrote. "For I know all the earth does not yield the like confluence of streams and branches, the one crossing the other so many times, and all so fair and large, and so like to one another, as no man can tell which to take." [193] By divine grace they obtained a pilot more knowledgeable than the Indian they had brought from Trinidad. While wandering in confusion along the estuary, they came to an Indian village, and this Trinidadian pilot, a Christian Indian named Ferdinando, went ashore with his brother to seek directions. The natives captured them and attempted to kill them, but Ferdinando fled into the forest, and his fleet brother managed to return to Raleigh's ships. The English seized an old man, one of the natives who was pursuing Ferdinando, and took him as hostage. Soon Ferdinando gave his pursuers the slip and reached Raleigh's barge, but it was decided to keep the old native as an additional guide—a wise move, for despite his claims Ferdinando did not really have much knowledge of the mainland.

At the suggestion of the old man, who said he belonged to the Ciawani nation of the Tivitivas Indians, the English continued laboriously up the river they had accidentally entered, which he said would lead them to the main arm of the Orinoco. They advanced slowly, now rowing against the current, now struggling to haul their boats free of the mud flats; the river flood came in spurts, making progress difficult at high water because of the velocity, and at low water because of the shallowness. To spur his men Raleigh was forced to dissemble that their goal was only two or three days' journey ahead—"that mighty, rich, and beautiful Empire of Guiana and . . . that great and golden city which the Spaniards call El Dorado and the naturals [natives] Manoa—a country which hath more quantity of gold, by manifold, than the best parts of the Indies of Peru." [194]

Each passing day seemed to bring them no closer to that goal. Raleigh was forced to the limits of his considerable glibness in order to keep his crew from rebelling. The land through which they were traveling was hot and dry, and they had little bread to eat and less to drink, "only the thick and troubled water of the river." But on the banks were edible fruits, and in the trees fluttered "birds of all colors, some carnation, some crimson, orange tawny, purple, green . . . and of all other sorts both simple and mixed," and "it was unto us a great good passing of the time to behold them, besides the relief we found by killing some store of them with our fowling pieces." [195] The old Indian whom they had forcibly made their guide told them that if they would enter a branch of the river on their right and anchor their galley, he would bring them to a town of the "Arwacas"—the Arawak Indians—where they would obtain all the food and drink they needed. This sounded agreeable to Raleigh, and he set out at the head of a party consisting of two other officers and sixteen musketeers aboard two wherries and a barge.

Because the Indian had said the village was so near, they took no victuals; but they rowed three hours without seeing sign of habitation. The guide told them that the village was just a short distance beyond. Night fell, and the English were forty miles from their galley and "ready to give up the ghost" from fatigue. They suspected treachery, and would have hanged the guide for his perfidy, but that they feared they could never find their way back alone in the darkness. "The river began so to narrow itself, and the trees to hang over from side to side, as we were driven with arming swords to cut a passage through those branches that covered the water. . . . Our stomachs began to gnaw apace: but whether it was best to return or go on, we began to doubt, suspecting treason in the pilot more and more: but the poor old Indian ever assured us that it was but a little farther, and but this one turning, and that turning, and at last about one o'clock after midnight we saw a light, and rowing towards it, we heard the dogs of the village." [196] Raleigh found few people, for the men of the village had taken a canoe trip up the Orinoco to trade for gold and buy women from the Caribs. The English rested well, and purchased a quantity of bread, fish, and hens to bring back to the main party at the galley.

The morning revealed a handsome prospect, which Raleigh described with the skill that made him the finest of the Elizabethan travel-writers: "On both sides of this river, we passed the most beautiful country that ever mine eyes beheld: and whereas all that we had seen before was nothing but woods, prickles, bushes, and thorns, here we beheld plains of twenty miles in length, the grass short and green, and in divers parts groves of trees by themselves, as if they had been by all the art and labors in the world so made of purpose: and still as we rowed, the deer came down feeding by the water's side, as if they had been used to a keeper's call. Upon this river there were great store of fowl, and of many sorts: we saw in it divers sorts of strange fishes, and of marvelous bigness, but for *Lagartos* [alligators] it exceeded, for there were thousands of those ugly serpents, and the people call it for the abundance of them the river of *Lagar-*

tos, in their language." [197] A Negro slave in Raleigh's company, rashly diving into this river for a swim, was gobbled by an alligator before their eyes.

Raleigh returned to the other party, and they continued up the main arm of the river. The next day they encountered four canoes coming downstream, and captured them. Three carried Arawak Indians bringing bread for sale at the coast, but in the fourth were three Spaniards from the mainland outpost Berrio had set up along the Orinoco in the territory of the friendly chief Carapana. These men had learned of Berrio's defeat, and were on their way to Margarita to seek other employment.

The Spaniards scrambled ashore and escaped, but Raleigh seized the Indians and pressed them into service as guides, not without causing them some fear, for they had somehow concluded that the English were cannibals. Raleigh calmed them and assured them that he would be far more generous in his treatment of their kind than the Spaniards had been. In the canoe that the Spaniards had been using, he sent back to the coast his Trinidadian pilot Ferdinando and the old man of the Ciawanis, who would be useless here.

Under the guidance of an Arawak pilot whom Raleigh named Martin, they struggled upriver through shallow, muddy channels until, on the fifteenth day of their journey, they at last entered the main artery of the Orinoco, and at the same time caught sight of the distant mountains of Guiana. That night they anchored at the confluence of three rivers: the one by which they had come down from the north, and two channels of the Orinoco flowing from west to east. They feasted on an abundance of turtle eggs, and in the morning went westward on the Orinoco to a pleasant village ruled by a chief named Toparimaca. He offered a feast of bread, meat, and fish, and provided the English both with

Spanish wine obtained from Berrio's men and with a native wine, on which Raleigh's captains got quite high. ("It is very strong with pepper, and the juice of divers herbs, and fruits digested and purged; they keep it in great earthen pots of ten or twelve gallons very clean and sweet, and are themselves at their meetings and feasts the greatest carousers and drunkards of the world." [198]) Toparimaca graciously supplied an experienced pilot, an old man of his tribe, who conducted them on the next stage of their journey.

The Orinoco here was broad and deep, suitable for sailing vessels, and a brisk easterly wind spared the English from more rowing. In six days, after some further halts, they came to the land of Morequito. Chief Morequito himself was dead, having been killed the year before by the Spaniards after a poorly executed attempt to massacre them, and his country, which Raleigh calls the province of Arromaia, was now ruled by his uncle Topiawari, a man "being 110 years old" who lived fourteen miles from the river.

The aged Topiawari came on foot to visit the English. He spread a lavish feast of venison, pork, chicken, and parakeets, treating Raleigh to his first pineapple ("the princess of fruits," he said) and giving him as a pet "a beast called by the Spaniards *Armadilla* . . . which seemeth to be all barred over with small plates somewhat like to a *Renocero*, with a white horn growing in his hinder parts, as big as a great hunting horn." [199] After the old king had rested from his walk in a tent Raleigh set up, the English stated their purpose. "I began by my interpreter to discourse with him," writes Raleigh, "of the death of Morequito his predecessor, and afterward of the Spaniards, and ere I went any farther I made him know the cause of my coming thither, whose servant I was, and that the Queen's pleasure was, I should undertake the voyage for their defence, and to deliver them from the tyranny of the Spaniards." [200] With tactful circuitousness Raleigh brought the conversation around to the geography of Guiana. Topiawari told him that the original inhabitants of the land on the far side of the mountains had been invaded in the past when he himself had been a young man: "There came down into that large valley of Guiana a nation from so far off as the sun slept, (for such were his own words,) with so great a multitude as they could not be numbered nor resisted, and that they wore large coats, and hats of crimson color . . . and that they were called *Oreiones*, and *Epuremei*, those that had slain and rooted out so many of the ancient people as there were leaves in the wood upon all the trees." [201]

It was not hard for Raleigh to persuade himself that these Epuremei were fugitive Incas. What Topiawari was telling him matched well enough Berrio's story. With his usual political acumen, Raleigh began to see that the Indians on the borders of Guiana must be enemies of the intrusive Epuremei, and that he could turn the situation to his own advantage either by allying himself with these borderers against the rich denizens of Manoa, or else reaching Manoa and striking an alliance with the Epuremei against the frontiersmen.

The next morning the English left the Orinoco and entered the Caroni, for the confluence of the two rivers was near Morequito's town. The river's flow was high, and "we were not able with a barge of eight oars to row a stone's cast in an hour." [202] They camped on the banks, sending Indian messengers ahead by land to announce that the English had come to liberate all these provinces from the grasp of Spain. Parties of Englishmen went out in various directions to look for gold or silver mines. Raleigh himself climbed a nearby hill for a view of the great waterfall that made an ascent of the Caroni impossible. He wrote that he could "see the river how it ran in three parts, above twenty miles off, and there appeared some ten or twelve overfalls in sight, every one as high over the other as a church tower, which fell with that fury, that the rebound of waters made it seem, as if it had been all covered over with a great shower of rain: and in some places we took it at the first for a smoke that had risen over some great town." [203]

The seekers for precious ores came back heavily laden, for, as Raleigh said, "every stone that we stooped to take up, promised either gold or silver by his complexion." The expedition's surgeon brought stones that resembled sapphires, and when Raleigh showed them to Topiawari's men, he was told of a mountain on which great outcroppings of such gems could be found. It was difficult for the English to take many ore samples, since they "had no means but with our daggers and fingers to tear them out here and there, the rocks being most hard of that mineral spar . . . and is like a flint, and is altogether as hard or harder, and besides the veins lie a fathom or two deep in the rocks." [204] Raleigh took what he could, not for its own intrinsic value so much as to be able to show ore of Guiana upon his return to England, as an advertisement for the much larger expedition that he was now planning.

The Indians told him a great deal about the geography of the region that lay ahead, mentioning a huge lake called Cassipa in particular. This lake Raleigh distinguished from the even larger lake on which Manoa was situated, which he called Lake Parima, but in time Cassipa and Parima were confounded into one lake by later searchers for El Dorado.

Another contribution of the Indians was the information that in Guiana there dwelled on the banks of the River Caora "a nation of people whose heads appear not above their shoulders. . . . They are reported to have their eyes in their shoulders, and their mouths in the middle of their breasts, and that a long train of hair groweth backward between their shoulders." [205] Raleigh thus gave new life to a fable at least sixteen centuries old in his day, for Pliny the Elder (23–79 A.D.) had reported that the Blemmyae of Africa "are said to have no heads, their mouths and eyes being seated in their breasts." [206] Philemon Holland's English translation of Pliny was still six years from publication, but Raleigh may have seen the reference in the original; in any case, he was certainly familiar with that collection of medieval myths published in the fourteenth century as the purported travels of one Sir John Mandeville. Mandeville, drawing on Pliny, had spoken of "foul men of figure without heads, and they have eyes in either shoulder one, and their mouths round shaped like a horseshoe, y-midst their breasts." [207]

Raleigh was honest enough not to claim he had seen the headless men himself. "Yet for mine own part I am resolved it is true," he wrote, citing the evidence of Indian and Spanish reports and concluding "that so many people did not all combine, or forethink to make the report." [208] His insistence on the verity of this medieval tale cost him much ridicule in London when he told of it, and helped to cast doubt on the truth of his entire story, but it served to inspire Shakespeare to this passage from *Othello:*

> The cannibals, that each other eat,
> The Anthropophagi, and men whose heads
> Do grow between their shoulders.

4

It was unwise to proceed by land up the Caroni to Manoa, and impossible to pause here to mine the gold that seemed to be so abundant, and the winter rains were coming on. "I thought it time lost to linger any longer in that place," wrote Raleigh, "especially for that the fury of Orenoque began daily to threaten us with dangers in our return, for no half day passed, but the river began to rage and overflow very fearfully, and the rains came down in terrible showers, and gusts in great abundance: and withal, our men began to cry out for want of shift, for no man had place to bestow any other apparel than that which he wore on his back, and that was thoroughly washed on his body for the most part ten times in one day: and we had been now well near a month, every day passing to the westward, farther and farther from our ships." [209] They therefore turned back, calling again at the town of Morequito. Old Topiawari was summoned, and Raleigh discussed the conquest of Manoa with him, pointing out that the English were his best defense both against his earlier enemies, the Epuremei of El Dorado, and against the Spaniards who now had hopes of conquering the land. Topiawari said that it would be impossible for the Spaniards to reach Manoa without the willing cooperation of the Indians who lived between here and the Epuremei frontier, and that cooperation certainly would not be forthcoming. However, he agreed to do all in his power to assist the English in the same endeavor, even accompanying them himself.

Raleigh explained that he now was going to return to England to raise a larger force, and would come back the following year to make the attempt with Topiawari's help. The old chief asked for a garrison of fifty armed Englishmen to protect him against the Spaniards meanwhile. This force Raleigh could not spare, but as tokens of good will he left two volunteers, a man named Francis Sparrow and a boy called Hugh Goodwin. For his pledge Topiawari gave his son Caworako, whom Raleigh took to England and rechristened Gualtero, the Spanish form of his own first name.

It was a mutually satisfying treaty. Topiawari expressed eagerness to invade and punish the mighty Epuremei, with English assistance, and was careful to note that his people had no interest in the gold of Manoa, to which the English were welcome; they merely wished to recover their wives and daughters, who had been kidnapped to serve as concubines in El Dorado. The Indians begged Raleigh to return speedily, and when he asked them why, "they answered, of their women for us, and their gold for you: for the hope of many of those women they more desire the war, than either for gold, or for the recovery of their ancient territories." [210]

Topiawari concluded with a description of the gold-smelting techniques of the inhabitants of Manoa. "He told me," said Raleigh, "that most of the gold which they made in plates and images was not severed from the stone, but that on the lake of Manoa, and in a multitude of other rivers they gathered it in grains of perfect gold and in pieces as big as small stones, and that they put to it a part of copper, otherwise they could not work it, and that they used a great earthen pot with holes round about it, and when they had mingled the gold and copper together, they fastened canes to the holes, and so with the breath of men they increased the fire till the metal ran, and then they cast it into moulds of stone and clay, and so make those plates and images." [211]

The journey back to the coast was easier, for now the English were traveling downstream, but the thunder and lightning of the winter storms gave them a fearful time. They had never seen such malign weather in Europe. The rush of the river forced them onto several detours, and while navigating a side branch they heard further report of the mountain of precious stones. "We saw it a far off and it appeared like a white church tower of an exceeding height," wrote Raleigh. "There falleth over it a mighty river which toucheth no part of the side of the mountain, but rusheth over the top of it, and falleth to the ground with a terrible noise and clamor, as if 1000 great bells were knocked one against another. I think there is not in the world so strange an overfall, nor so wonderful to behold. Berrio told me that it hath diamonds and other precious stones on it, and that they shined very far off, but what it hath I know not, neither durst he nor any of his men ascend to the top of the said mountain, those people adjoining being his enemies . . . and the way to it so impassable." [212]

They went a hundred miles a day, while the storms grew ever more terrifying and the river more difficult, and after many tribulations reached the most dangerous point of all, where the river issued into the sea. They hesitated here, but "the longer we tarried the worse it was," and "after it cleared up about midnight we put ourselves to God's keeping, and thrust out into the sea. . . . And so being all very sober and melancholy, one faintly cheering another to show courage, it pleased God that the next day about nine of the clock, we descried the island of Trinidad, and steering for the nearest part of it, we kept the shore till we came to Curiapan, where we found our ships at anchor, than which, there was never to us a more joyful sight." [213]

Berrio and several fellow Spaniards had remained aboard these ships all the while as gloomy prisoners. Now, to their surprise and dismay, they saw Raleigh and his men returning from Guiana, without gold and looking somewhat the worse for wear, but undoubtedly alive, contrary to expectations. It was Raleigh's intention to go back to England to raise a large expedition for the conquest of El Dorado, but first he planned to do some privateering at the nearby Spanish ports, and Berrio was an unwilling witness of this campaign.

The English went first to Margarita, appearing there on June 16, 1595. They were unable to make a landing at the first port they chose, which was strongly defended, but succeeded in anchoring at a place called Punta de Mosquitos. Alvaro Jorge, Berrio's lieutenant, was sent ashore to negotiate for his captain's ransom. Pedro de Salazar, who had succeeded Sarmiento as governor, refused to deal with Raleigh, and after two days the English sailed away, taking Berrio with them.

They called next at Cumaná, where Raleigh later claimed he had won a decisive victory and had levied a tribute from the inhabitants. The official Spanish documents contradict this. A report to King Philip filed in the spring of 1596 tells of Raleigh's attempt to invade Cumaná at daybreak on June 23, 1595: fifteen Spaniards drove the English off, forcing some of them to swim back to their ships, and many prisoners were taken. Raleigh released Berrio without ransom in exchange for an English prisoner and sailed away. "It is said he goes to England," wrote the governor of Cumaná, "and he does not go away as pleased as he could wish." [214]

It was small favor to Berrio for Raleigh to have liberated him at Cumaná, for the governor of that city was his rival and enemy, Francisco de Vides, by whom, according to another Spanish account, Berrio "was little favored and badly received." [215] His hope was to get back to Trinidad as quickly as possible to restore his position, now that Raleigh had left him in peace.

By July 8, Berrio was out of Vides' clutches and on the island of Margarita, where the new governor, Pedro de Salazar, received him in a friendly manner. Berrio recruited ten men and sailed to Trinidad, mournfully visiting the ruins of the town of San José. From there he crossed to the mainland and went up the Orinoco to the port of Morequito. Since old Topiawari had not received the English garrison he had asked for, there was no way the Indians could prevent Berrio from returning. The Spaniards built a fort there called Santo Thomé. Shortly afterward a detachment of thirty troops arrived from New Granada, led by Berrio's son.

It was a bold and farsighted move for Berrio to occupy the Orinoco-Caroni confluence in this way. By general agreement, the Caroni was the entrance to the land of El Dorado, and with a Spanish fort blocking the route the English would have a hard time reaching Manoa, when and if they returned.

Berrio dug in at Santo Thomé. When it was sufficiently fortified, he picked twenty-eight men and sent them down the Orinoco under Phelipe de Santiago, an officer who had been with him since boyhood. The purpose was to reoccupy Trinidad, rebuild San José, and get everything ready for the long-awaited arrival of the huge expedition of Domingo de Vera, which now was due in the spring of 1596. Unhappily, Santiago picked this opportunity to desert to the service of Francisco de Vides. He went to Cumaná and faithlessly informed Vides of all that Berrio had done since his return to the mainland. Vides gave Santiago a larger force of men and sent him back, instructing him first to colonize Trinidad in Vides' name, then to drive Berrio out of Santo Thomé, and incidentally to capture Francis Sparrey and Hugh Goodwin, whom Raleigh had left behind as pledges of good will with Topiawari.

Santiago visited Trinidad briefly, then entered the Orinoco. Reaching the province of Arromaia, some of the Spaniards disguised themselves as Indians and ambushed the town where the English pledges were living. Sparrey was captured and sent to Margarita, and after a long imprisonment escaped to England to report on his adventures. The Indians hid the boy Hugh Goodwin and told the Spaniards he had been devoured by a jaguar; he remained among the natives for the next twenty years, until his discovery by Raleigh's expedition of 1617.

Going on to Santo Thomé, Santiago called upon Berrio to surrender to the authority of Vides. That bit of treachery must have shaken the old man deeply, but he answered with defiance and ordered his men to open fire. The defenders of the fort could not bring themselves to shoot at their old comrades, and deliberately aimed high; but Santiago's men did the same, and in the half-hearted battle that followed no casualties resulted. Santiago withdrew, leaving Berrio in control of the fort, and returned to Trinidad. In January of 1596 he founded a new city on the southern side, named Phelipe de Montes. Berrio thereby was deprived of his base, and was cut off at his lonely fort of Santo Thomé, deep in Indian territory and supported only by a handful of men. There, having suffered calamity after calamity, he waited out the early months of 1596 in the hope that Domingo de Vera would at last arrive with his thousands of men and deliver him from his enemies.

5

Raleigh, too, was experiencing some reverses. The high point of his voyage had come in May of 1595 at Morequito, when he had concluded his compact with Topiawari. The gold of Manoa seemed almost in his grasp. Glittering ore lay at every side; all he had to do was return to England, gather together a powerful force, and return to this place whence the friendly old native chief would guide him up the banks of the Caroni to El Dorado.

But in June, things had begun to go awry. His rebuff at Margarita was a bad omen; at Cumaná he suffered a decisive and costly defeat, and many of his men were slain, including one of his captains, Robert Calfield, and his cousin, John Grenville. Disgruntled, he sailed off to Virginia to gather supplies for the homeward voyage, but rough seas prevented a landing, and he had to head for England without provisioning.

He arrived there in August of 1595 to find that news of his exploits had preceded him, and that the general attitude was one of disappointment, for it was known that Raleigh was coming home without gold. He hastened to the court to relate his adventures. But the Queen showed little interest; the Raleigh charisma was ebbing, and he spoke with the unpersuasive urgency of a man whose words were discounted in advance, and who knew it.

The Queen's skepticism inspired matching hostility among her courtiers, for there were many who were pleased at the chance to revenge themselves on the flamboyant Raleigh now that the tides of fortune ran against him. He showed the ore samples he collected; he told all he knew of the wealth of Manoa; he spoke of Amazons and headless men; he described waterfalls and jungles; he argued in closely reasoned terms the importance to England of founding a South American empire.

All to no avail. His ore samples produced no excitement, only a barrage of slanders. Some said that it was worthless fool's gold, others that while the ore was valuable, it had been purchased in Africa and carried to Guiana to be "discovered." There were whispers that Raleigh had never been to Guiana at all, but had spent the entire time skulking in Cornwall. And even though he had not claimed to see Amazons and headless men himself, but merely relayed the stories he heard, those fanciful accounts brought ridicule upon him. No one offered support for a new Guiana voyage. Raleigh saw the bright hope of May turning to ashes by September.

He attempted to salvage the situation with his gifted

pen, and swiftly produced his famous little book, *The Discoverie of the Large, Rich, and Beautiful Empire of Guiana, with a relation of the Great and Golden City of Manoa (which the Spaniards call El Dorado)*. At once a political tract and a narrative of high adventure, it embedded a compelling tale of Raleigh's voyage in a framework of cogent argument for the exploitation of Guiana by England. When it appeared, it quickly went through three printings, and was read and admired by all—but its readers, while captivated by Raleigh's command of narrative, failed to share his views of empire.

He defended himself at the outset against the accusations of fraud. True, he admitted, his men had found valueless marcasite on Trinidad and had thought it was gold, but he had disabused them of that idea. "In Guiana itself," he wrote, "I never saw marcasite, but all the rocks, mountains, all stones in the plains, in woods, and by the riversides are in effect thorough shining, and appear marvellous rich, which being tried to be no marcasite, are the true signs of rich minerals, but are no other than *El madre del oro* (as the Spaniards term them) which is the mother of gold." [216] Citing the analysis that had been made of his ore samples in London, Raleigh showed that they were indeed gold-bearing, and answered other critics by saying, "It hath also been concluded by divers, that if there had been any such ore in Guiana, and the same discovered, that I would have brought home a greater quantity thereof: first I was not bound to satisfy any man of the quantity, but such only as adventured, if any store had been returned thereof: but it is very true that had all their mountains been of massy gold, it was impossible for us to have made any longer stay to have wrought the same: and whosoever hath seen with what strength of stone, the best gold ore is environed, he will not think it easy to be had out in heaps, and especially by us who had neither men, instruments, nor time . . . to perform the same." [217]

As for the charge that the ore had come from elsewhere, Raleigh replied, "Others have devised that the same ore was had from Barbary, and that we carried it with us into Guiana. . . . For mine own part, I am not so much in love with these long voyages, as to devise, thereby to cozen myself, to lie hard, to fare worse, to be subjected to perils, to diseases, to ill savors, to be parched and withered, and withal to sustain the care and labor of such an enterprise, except the same had more comfort, than the fetching of marcasite in Guiana, or buying of gold ore in Barbary." [218]

To those who did not see the merit of the enterprise, Raleigh addressed himself at length, and it is in this part of his work that the real distinction of his part in the quest for El Dorado can be seen. So far as exploration went, Raleigh actually did very little, merely penetrating the Orinoco as far as the Caroni, which Berrio had done before him; compared with Berrio and his epic journeys across the continent, Raleigh scarcely was an explorer at all. But only Raleigh, of all the seekers of El Dorado, saw high political ends to be gained as well as gold.

He proposed nothing less than the total supplanting of Spain by England in the New World—beginning with an alliance with the "Incas of Manoa" and going on to a complete reconquest of the continent. In achieving this he intended to turn the cruelty of the Spaniards against them. He reminded his countrymen "how the Spaniards without just title or any wrong at all done to them by the harmless Indians, forcibly invaded and wrongfully detained their countries about 100 years, committing barbarous and exquisite massacres to the destruction of whole nations of people . . . in revenge whereof their own religious men do make account that the just God in judgment will one day horribly chasten and peradventure wholly subvert and root out the Spanish nation." In one of those magnificent Elizabethan periods he asked, "Who would not be persuaded that now at length the great judge of the world hath heard the sighs, groans, lamentations, tears, and blood of so many millions of innocent men, women, and children afflicted, robbed, reviled, branded with hot irons, roasted, dismembered, mangled, stabbed, whipped, racked, scalded with hot oil, suet, and hogsgrease, put to the *strappado*, ripped alive, beheaded in sport, drowned, dashed against the rocks, famished, devoured by mastiffs, burned and by infinite cruelties consumed, and purposeth to scourge and plague that cursed nation, and to take the yoke of servitude from that distressed people, as free by nature as any Christian?" [219]

He weighed the relative advantages of attempting to conquer Manoa with the aid of Topiawari and other border chiefs, and of trying to form a peaceful alliance with the Manoans. His conclusion was that it was best to employ Topiawari as a guide to reach Manoa, but that no war should be made against the people of the golden land. Rather, all attempts should be made to gain their loyalty and join with them to drive the Spaniards from Peru. He said that according to Berrio "there was found among prophecies in Peru (at such time as the empire was reduced to Spanish obedience) in their chiefest temples . . . which foreshowed the loss of the said empire, that from *Inglatierra* [England] those Incas should be again in time to come restored, and delivered from the servitude of the said conquerors." [220] It would thus be an easy matter to convince the rulers of Manoa that the English were their saviors.

Raleigh suggested this treaty to be offered to the Manoans:

"1. First that we will defend them their wives, children and countries against the Spaniards and all other intruders.

2. Then that we will help them to recover their country of Peru. 3. That we will instruct them in liberal arts of civility behoofsful for them that they may be comparable to any Christian people. 4. And lastly that we will teach them the use of weapons, how to pitch their battles, how to make armor, and ordnance, and how to manage horses for service in the wars." [221]

What Raleigh envisioned was something inconceivable at any time in the colonialist era, and not fully realized even today: a pact between an industrial nation and an undeveloped one for joint benefit. Instead of exploiting the Indians, Raleigh would have England aid and instruct them—receiving in return not only gold but the infinite commercial advantages of intercourse with a large and friendly power in the New World. He invoked the subversive principle that "no Christians may lawfully invade with hostility any heathenish people not under their allegiance, to kill, spoil, and conquer them, only upon pretense of their fidelity," [222] and made reference to God's relationship with Adam and with Noah and with Nebuchadnezzar to establish the astonishing theory that "by the gift of God, idolaters, pagans, and Godless persons be entitled to the possession, and have a capacity to take, and an ability to hold a property in lands and goods." [223]

Having issued more anti-imperialist heresy in a dozen pages than any of his fellow Englishmen would publish in the succeeding three centuries, Raleigh added the proviso that he would request the Incas to subscribe to the tenets of the Church of England. Otherwise he planned no meddling in their ways, and saw his project culminating in a well-armed, enlightened, Christianized Indian nation that would joyfully push its Spanish oppressors into the sea and join in perpetual and mutually profitable alliance with England. It was a dazzling vision, marred only by the awkward fact that there were no Incas in Guiana on which to found the alliance, nor any city of Manoa; but Raleigh did not know that yet.

The scheme was calculated to appeal to merchants, who would see the advantages of trade over exploitation—to the religious, who would relish the idea of snatching the Indians out of Papist idolatry and turning them into good Anglicans—and to the Queen, who would become the most powerful monarch in the world by virtue of her supremacy in two hemispheres. "After the first or second year I doubt not but to see in London a Contratation house of more receipt for Guiana, than there is now in Seville for the West Indies," [224] Raleigh wrote. And, to capture the imaginations of the simple, he offered this stirring passage:

"Those that are desirous to discover and to see many nations, may be satisfied within this river, which bringeth forth so many arms and branches leading to several countries, and provinces, above 2000 miles east and west, and 800 miles south and north: and of these, the most either rich in gold, or in other merchandises. The common soldier shall here fight for gold, and pay himself instead of pence, with plates of half a foot broad. . . . Those commanders and chieftains, that shoot at honor, and abundance, shall find there more rich and beautiful cities, more temples adorned with golden images, more sepulchers filled with treasure, than either Cortés found in Mexico, or Pizarro in Peru: and the shining glory of this conquest will eclipse all those so far extended beams of the Spanish nation." [225]

No prospectus could have been more cunningly crafted. But it did not gain its end. Apathy and skepticism were the responses to Raleigh's titanic scheme. He paid the price for enthusiasm: no one believed that anything so grandiose could ever be realized. The more vociferously Raleigh applied the hard sell, the less interested England grew in

Guiana. Neither a campaign of pure bloody plunder on the Spanish model nor Raleigh's astoundingly advanced suggestion of a mutual-security pact with the Incas won any backing.

As 1595 drew to its close, Raleigh saw the only possible way of swaying public opinion: sending out a small new expedition that would go quickly to Guiana, find the exact route to El Dorado, and secure a convincing supply of gold. With that he could hope to get public support for the major enterprise that he envisioned. It was impossible for Raleigh to go himself on this venture, because he had enmeshed himself in a major English naval attack on Spain, virtually a reversed version of the invasion by the Spanish Armada eight years before. A formidable force had been gathered, with every English commander of note taking part, and Raleigh was one of the chief officers. It was a brave project that ended heroically for the English, but Raleigh's role in it was shadowed by confusion, and failed to win him the return to popular esteem that he so badly needed.

Since the war against Spain would keep Raleigh busy close to home all during 1596, he chose his lieutenant Laurence Keymis to make the Guiana voyage. Keymis, though a veteran seaman, was also something of a man of letters, sensitive by nature and capable of turning neat Latin verses —one of the many improbably literate English sea-rovers of that improbably literate era. He set sail on January 26, 1596. Raleigh instructed him to look for a route to Manoa on the Guianian coast between the estuaries of the Orinoco and the Amazon, working his way northward until he found a waterway to the interior.

Keymis carried out a careful and methodical reconnaissance of the coast, stopping at the mouth of each of the many rivers to confer with the natives. The most promising entry seemed to be via a river midway between the Amazon and the Orinoco, in the land later known as British Guiana and now the independent nation of Guyana. This was the Essequibo River, or the "Dessekebe," as Keymis called it. He wrote that "The Indians to show the worthiness of Dessekebe (for it is very large and full of islands in the mouth) do call it the brother of Orenoque. It lieth southerly into the land, and from the mouth of it unto the head, they pass in twenty days: then taking their provision they carry it on their shoulders one day's journey; afterwards they return for their canoes, and bear them likewise to the side of a lake, which the Iaos call Roponowini, the Caribs, Parima: which is of such bigness, that they know no difference between it and the main sea. There be infinite numbers of canoes in this lake, and (as I suppose) it is no other than that, whereon Manoa standeth." [226]

Keymis' contribution thus was purely speculative: the guess that Lake Parima, to which the Essequibo allegedly led, was the site of Manoa/El Dorado. He did not investigate the Essequibo himself at this point, but continued up the coast of Guiana, entering to a short distance a number of rivers that had never been explored by Europeans, and at length came to the Orinoco, which he called in Raleigh's honor the "Raleana," on April 6, 1596.

While at anchor in the Orinoco estuary, Keymis was visited by Indians from the interior, who came to trade and brought him the news that the Spaniards had returned to Guiana soon after Raleigh's departure the year before. This was disturbing information, for he had planned to go up the river to Morequito, and had not counted on finding a Spanish fort there. In talking with these Indians, Keymis questioned them about the supposed route to El Dorado up the Essequibo, which now seemed like a more feasible approach than any land march southward along the Caroni. They confirmed that the best way to reach Manoa was by the

Essequibo or one of the other rivers that ran eastward through Guiana below the Orinoco, and for good measure told him about a previously unmentioned tribe, the Amapagotos, dwelling five days' journey up the Caroni, who "have images of gold of incredible bigness, and great store of unmanned horses of the Caracas breed." [227] Keymis did not fail to inquire after the men whose heads grow below their shoulders, and an Indian "certified me of the headless men, and that their mouths in their breasts are exceeding wide. The name of their nation in the Caribs' language is Chiparemai, and the Guianians call them Ewiapanomos. What I have heard of a sort of people more monstrous, I omit to mention," he wrote to Raleigh, "because it is no matter of difficulty to get one of them, and the report otherwise will appear fabulous." [228]

To see just how strongly Berrio was situated, Keymis sailed up the Orinoco and in eight days came to Morequito. He found a Spanish settlement of about thirty houses, but the Spaniards had left the town and fortified themselves at the nearby mouth of the Caroni, thereby guarding what they believed to be the authentic gateway to Manoa. Approaching this fort, Keymis found it to be impregnable, and thus he could not carry out Raleigh's instruction that he go to the mines discovered the year before and secure liberal samplings of precious ore. "We all not without grief to see ourselves thus defeated, and our hungry hopes made void, were witnesses of this their remove," he wrote.[229]

An Indian from the town informed them of the state of affairs: Berrio had some 55 men with him, including reinforcements recently received from New Granada, and he was expecting the momentary arrival of a large new force— that coming from Spain under Vera. Keymis also learned something of the treachery of Phelipe de Santiago, who a short while before had come to Berrio's fort of Santo Thomé to take it, and, failing that, had withdrawn to Trinidad. It was encouraging to hear that the Spaniards were divided among themselves, but there was no way for Keymis to get past Santo Thomé up the Caroni to the mines. As for old Topiawari, Raleigh's ally, he was dead, and the Spaniards had slain many of his people.

The dejected Keymis withdrew to look for gold mines elsewhere. An Indian guide offered to take them overland to the reputed mountain of precious stones, some fifteen miles away, but Keymis hesitated to make the journey. (This trait of hesitation was destined to lead him to utter disaster two decades later on Raleigh's final visit to Guiana.) He reserved the mine for some future trip, noting that the Indians "have devised a fable of a dangerous dragon that haunteth this place and devoureth all that come near it. But our Indian, if when we return we do bring store of strong wine (which they love beyond measure), with it will undertake so to charm this dragon, that he shall do us no harm." [230]

After further explorations that failed to produce treasure, Keymis returned to the sea, touched briefly at Trinidad, sailed through the West Indies, and headed for England, which he reached at the end of June after an absence of five months. He brought no gold, only the unsettling news of Berrio's strong position at the mouth of the Caroni and the possibly encouraging word of the river route to Lake Parima via the Essequibo. "Thus have I emptied your purse," he told Raleigh, "spending my time and travel in following your lordship's directions for the full discovery of this coast, and the rivers thereof. Concerning the not making of a voyage for your private profit, I pretend nothing. Sorry I am, that where I sought no excuse, by the Spaniards' being there I found my defect remedyless." [231] He added, more prophetically than he knew, "My self, and the remain of my few years, I have bequeathed wholly to Raleana, and all my thoughts live only in that action." [232]

Raleigh was deep in the plans for the invasion of Spain when Keymis brought him this unsatisfactory yield. He was quick to seize on the one encouraging element in Keymis' report—the Essequibo route to Manoa. Outfitting another ship, Raleigh sent Captain Leonard Berry in December of 1596 to make further explorations of the Guiana coast. After a variety of detours, Berry's ship, the pinnace *Watte*, reached the Wiapoco River, which today forms the boundary between French Guiana and Brazil, on March 2, 1597. Going in and out of the numerous rivers, the explorers sailed up the coast, never venturing very far into the interior. They received many reports of rich kingdoms inland, but Berry evidently was lacking in curiosity, for, as Thomas Masham, one of his officers, wrote upon his return, "Seeing the country above was rich as we were informed, that their bows were handled with gold . . . we should have taken the more pains, and have fared the harder, until we had gotten up in the country which we saw with our eyes." [233] These timid voyagers came in time to the Courantyne River, in later years the boundary between British Guiana and Dutch Guiana (Surinam), and found another English ship there, captained by John Leigh, on an independent voyage of discovery. The two vessels traveled together some fifteen miles up the Courantyne. Halting at an inland port, Berry spoke with an Indian who said he lived on the Essequibo, and learned from him that several hundred Spaniards were now exploring that river—news that discouraged Berry from making any attempt of his own. The same Indian said, according to Masham, that the Essequibo "doth lead so far into the country, that it cometh within a day's journey of the lake called Parima, whereupon Manoa is supposed to stand;

and that this river of Corentine doth meet with Desekebe up in the land: by means whereof we make account to go up into the country, and to have discovered a passage unto that rich city." [234] Berry allowed himself to reason that since Raleigh would soon be coming this way in person, there was no need for him to go farther up the Courantyne himself, and so he went back to the coast. Rumors of Spanish activity farther north on the coast led him to leave Guiana at once, without having gone as far north as the Essequibo. By May he was in the West Indies, and on June 28 landed in England. Raleigh could hardly have been pleased. Berry had found another ostensible river route to Manoa—the Courantyne—but he had not explored it, nor had he entered the Essequibo at all, nor had he come home with the gold that Raleigh needed to stir public interest in his project. The press of the war with Spain compelled Raleigh to postpone his own voyage to Guiana; and, as it developed, twenty years would go by before he was free to chase the fantasy of El Dorado again.

6

Between the time of Keymis' voyage and that of Berry, a year later, much had happened among the Spaniards who sought to conquer Guiana. Berrio, holding firm in his fort of Santo Thomé at the mouth of the Caroni, had withstood the attack of the perfidious Phelipe de Santiago at the end of 1595, and had turned Keymis away early the following April. Santiago, aided by reinforcements from Berrio's enemy Francisco de Vides at Cumaná, now occupied a large base on Trinidad.

For the past two years, Berrio's associate Domingo de Vera had been in Spain, mounting an immense expedition for El Dorado. He succeeded in parting King Philip from some of his own money to finance the enterprise, and gained contributions from cities, monasteries, and private citizens. It was the grandest expedition that had ever set out from Spain to colonize the New World; Vera had six ships and more than 1500 men and women.

This unwieldy flotilla made its appearance off Trinidad on April 19, 1596. Surprised to find a hostile Phelipe de Santiago in control of the island, Vera chased Santiago's men away and once more took possession of Trinidad in Berrio's name. Then he began the cumbersome job of transporting his hundreds of colonists to the South American mainland. A messenger was sent to Berrio at Santo Thomé with the news of Vera's arrival, and Berrio prevailed on the Indians to supply forty-four canoes for this ferry service. In these Vera safely shipped 470 men to the mainland. But when the next contingent was dispatched, Carib warriors from the islands of Dominica and Grenada swept down on them and killed everyone. "This," wrote Vera to King Philip, "was the beginning of a long series of hardships." [235] Vera himself supervised the next trip to the mainland, but, he wrote, "For my sins God willed that in the crossing from this island to the mainland, a distance of three leagues, He should give me a hurricane, although I had started in good weather. Therein forty of my men were drowned and the foodstuffs and munitions were thrown into the sea." [236]

By this time it was the autumn of 1596, and the first few hundred colonists had made their way inland to Berrio at Santo Thomé. Pedro Simón tells how the newcomers looked as they reached Berrio's miserable little jungle fort: "So comely that they seemed better suited for Seville by reason of the gorgeous banners which they bore . . . and their rich and costly gala dresses, which were more appropriate for weddings or royal festivals than for the conquest of so wretched a country." [237] The banners and gala dresses soon began to rot in the jungle climate, and there were only a few hastily constructed sheds and cabins to house the hundreds of colonists.

Berrio chose his loyal lieutenant, Alvaro Jorge, to lead three hundred of these new settlers on a southward march overland to Manoa, following the route of the Caroni. Jorge was in poor health and more than sixty years of age, which may have seemed like relative youth to the 76-year-old Berrio, but which was really no age to be leading a trek through unknown jungles during the winter rainy season. After the expedition had gone ninety miles Jorge died of exhaustion, and several of his officers, newly come from Spain, started to quarrel for the command. Various factions quickly formed; while the captains disputed, the men lost discipline and began to rape and plunder the Indians. Although the natives had been friendly and hospitable up to this point, they rose in fury and slaughtered more than two hundred fifty of the Spaniards. Berrio sent one of his veterans to take command, and when he arrived he found only a handful of cowed survivors whom he led back to Santo Thomé.

When Vera reached Santo Thomé himself some months after this fiasco, he found matters in poor shape—hundreds of his colonists dead, the rest hungry, feverish, and ragged. Yellow fever was ravaging them now, and the outpost was crackling with dissension as well. Berrio, who had endured every conceivable frustration in his sixteen years of seeking El Dorado, was in a state of blazing exasperation: for here he was, camped at the very gateway to the golden land, and after sitting there for eternal rainy months waiting for Vera's big expedition to arrive, he now was presiding over a catastrophe. He greeted Vera with an ill-tempered burst of wrath. Vera, equally exasperated, blazed back at him just as angrily, and for three days the two leaders traded accusations, each blaming the other for the mishaps thus far. Finally in disgust Vera turned around and went back to Trinidad.

For eight months he sulked there and Berrio sulked at Santo Thomé; there was no communication between them, nor any attempt at reaching Manoa. The settlers at Trinidad were harried by an invasion of hungry and carnivorous insects which made small wounds that rapidly became infected and gangrenous. The same chiggers infested Santo Thomé at this time; but Vera on Trinidad at least had forges at which irons could be heated to cauterize the infections, while the occupants of Berrio's fort had to suffer their pains without such aid.

Since it was apparent that Berrio could not penetrate the interior to the promised land of gold, the men who had come out from Spain with such glowing dreams began to desert him, breaking away in groups of twenty and thirty to go downstream toward the coast and across to Vera's settlement at Trinidad. Nearly all were drowned in the Orinoco; Vera says that only three men actually survived to reach Trinidad in the first seven months. In the spring of 1597, Berrio's son Fernando, who had gone back to New Granada once more to fetch further reinforcements, arrived at Santo Thomé to find the colony in a state of collapse and his aged father close to death.

Fernando de Berrio immediately sent a message to Vera, asking him to come to Santo Thomé to discuss ways of ending the hiatus. Vera left at once. When he reached the Caroni he found that Berrio was dead, worn out by his travail and by the supreme anguish of seeing El Dorado slip from his grasp at the moment when attainment seemed so near. Fernando de Berrio was in charge, and was apprehensive about a royal warrant Vera had that entitled him to govern the colony in the event of Berrio's death. But, Vera wrote to King Philip, "I came to consider the great sagacity which he showed, his quiet demeanor, his carefulness in setting guards and other requisite precautions, and above all his very good Christian character and inclination to do well," and gave him the royal warrant, "saying that I did not wish to make use of it." [238] Fernando de Berrio now was the officially recognized heir to his father's claim of El Dorado, whatever that might be worth. Vera put himself at his service.

Together they planned a new attempt to reach Manoa. But nothing would come of it, as perhaps they sensed even as they drew up their plans. With the death of Antonio de Berrio, the heroic phase of the quest for El Dorado, with men striding back and forth across the continent in tireless ambition, was at its end. The quest was about to trickle away into anticlimax. El Dorado had been pinpointed to a highly specific site—the city of Manoa, on the shores of Lake Parima, in Guiana—and all that remained was the small task of finding Manoa. But Manoa was a fantasy of self-deluding men; and as reality impinged on that fantasy, the golden dream began to fade.

[9]

THE END OF
THE QUEST

S THE SEVENTEENTH CENTURY BEGAN, EL Dorado occupied a firm position on the map of South America. The mapmaker Jocodus Hondius put it there in 1599, in a map entitled *Nieuwe Caerte van het goudreyke landt Guiana* ("New Map of the goldrich land Guiana"). He placed a huge lake in central Guiana, between 1°45′ and 2° north latitude, larger than the Caspian Sea, and labeled it *Rupunuwini, Parima, or Dorado*. In the same year, the Dutch publisher of voyages, Theodore de Bry, issued a Latin translation of Raleigh's book, and illustrated it with a remarkable map of Guiana complete with Amazons and headless men. De Bry's map showed the Essequibo River rising from a vast inland lake, Parima, on whose northern shore was Manoa, captioned *Manoa or Dorado, regarded as the largest city in the entire world*. Lake Parima and the city of Manoa would remain on maps of Guiana as late as 1808, with Manoa placed sometimes on the western shore, sometimes on the eastern, sometimes on the north. Yet the lake and the golden city eluded the best efforts of many discoverers in those two centuries.

There were skeptics, of course. Writing about 1601, the Spanish geographer Antonio de Herrera, discussing the possible sources of the Río de la Plata, remarked that "others say it cometh from the Lake of the Dorado," but noted, "there be opinions that there is no Dorado." [23]

One who did not share that opinion was Sir Walter Raleigh, but he was in no position to make good on his belief in the Dorado's reality. When Leonard Berry returned from his unsuccessful voyage in 1597, Raleigh was entangled in the politics of Queen Elizabeth's court. Two younger men had emerged as powers at that court: Robert Cecil, son of the old and influential Lord Burghley, and the Earl of Essex, the latest lover of the Queen. Raleigh viewed these men as rivals—Essex had once challenged him to a duel, and Cecil had become the Queen's secretary of state over Raleigh's opposition. Since the aging Elizabeth delighted in keeping her courtiers in uncertainty, the tense relationship between Raleigh, Essex, and Cecil underwent many shifts, and in 1597 even took the form of a triple alliance. But Cecil's star was rising and Essex' was descending, and Raleigh, long out of favor himself, benefited from his complex association with them.

It could not last; Essex was already on the disastrous course that would lead to his execution by Elizabeth in 1601, while Cecil, foreseeing the death of the childless Queen, had begun to curry favor with her likely successor, Scotland's King James Stuart, at Raleigh's expense. It was impossible for Raleigh to gain backing for his Guiana project at this time, for he did not know from one day to the next whether the ever more powerful Cecil was his ally or his enemy. He spoke of himself at this point as "mad with intricate affairs and want of means." [240]

Despairing of his native country, Raleigh turned in 1598 to Sweden, an unlikely sponsor for an expedition to

South America. That summer he became friendly with James Hill, a diplomat about to depart for the court of the Duke of Sudermania, afterwards King Charles IX of Sweden. At Raleigh's suggestion, Hill broached the Guiana idea to the Duke, and wrote to Raleigh on September 25, 1598, to say that "the Duke will send twelve ships for Guiana, and join with him [Raleigh] in any other order. If Sir Walter will send his meaning unto me, I will inform his Excellency, and write him his Grace's answer. For victual, men and ships will the Duke provide. . . ." [241] In October, Raleigh's half-brother Sir John Gilbert was busy assembling half a dozen ships to accompany the Swedish flotilla, and the following month the news of Raleigh's intended return to Guiana reached the court of Spain, where it caused great apprehension. King Philip was uncomfortably aware of Raleigh's grand plan for driving the Spaniards out of the New World by an alliance with the Indians of Guiana, and he more than half thought it would succeed. The Council of the Indies recommended immediate fortification of Trinidad, and Philip agreed.

Evidently Raleigh was planning to reach Manoa via the Essequibo or Courantyne, judging by the fact that Sir John Gilbert was collecting a fleet of pinnaces, light and small enough for river navigation. However, for reasons unknown the Swedish project collapsed. Raleigh maintained an active interest in a Guiana voyage during the next few years, but the rapidly shifting political situation at home left him in too precarious a position to think seriously of the venture. His alliance with Robert Cecil was at an end, and Cecil, aided by his friend Sir Henry Howard, had taken complete control of the heir apparent, James Stuart. Together they persuaded the gloomy Scottish monarch that Raleigh was a dangerous man who must be removed from public life.

The End of the Quest

On March 24, 1603, Queen Elizabeth died, and the crown passed to the Stuart dynasty. King James journeyed toward London a few weeks later to take possession of his new capital, and Raleigh, unaware of the intrigues woven around him, came forth to meet and greet the King at Windsor. James was cool, and for good reason, since he shortly ordered Raleigh seized and imprisoned in the Tower of London on a trumped-up charge of treason. It would be twelve years before he regained his freedom.

2

Others were drawn to El Dorado at the outset of the new century. In December of 1597, two Dutch ships commanded by Jacob Cornelisz and Marten Willemsz sailed west, reaching Guiana the following February. They meant to look for the gold mine of which Raleigh had written. Their quest began at the River Cayenne, and they worked their way northward, joined by the vessels of two of their countrymen, until by late July they were in the Orinoco. They called upon Fernando de Berrio at Santo Thomé and learned, according to a report filed in 1598, that "they are about 60 horsemen and 100 musketeers strong, who daily attempt to conquer the auriferous Weyana [Guiana], but cannot conquer the same either by the forces already used or by any means of friendship, since the nation named Charibus [Caribs] daily offer them hostile resistance with their arms, which are hand-bows, and they shoot poisoned arrows therewith, which are so poisonous that if anyone is hit by them so that blood flows, he must perforce die within twenty-four hours unless a remedy is immediately applied, and all his flesh would drop from his bones." [242]

Somewhat surprisingly, young Berrio treated the Dutchmen with courtesy, even though they were sailors of a nation that had only recently rebelled and won its independence from Spain. He permitted them to sail past Santo Thomé up the Caroni to the great waterfall in search of gold, and even sent one of his miners along as a guide. No gold was found, and the Dutch departed for Trinidad at the end of August. On their way back to Europe in October, 1598, they met one of the pinnaces that Raleigh was regularly sending to Guiana at this time to maintain his contact with the Indians of the coast pending his anticipated return.

The next event of significance was the arrival of Francis Sparrey in England in 1602. This was the man whom Raleigh had left as a pledge with the Indians of the Caroni seven years earlier; captured by the Spaniards, he had been imprisoned for some time in Spain, finally making his escape. He was regarded as the leading expert on El Dorado in England, since he had lived among the Indians for several years, and he published a brief description of Guiana in which he told of a journey he had made toward Peru on the Orinoco. Taking one river and another, he got as far west as the Río Papamene, but lost his way and had to return. Sparrey claimed that he had obtained gold from the mines of Manoa, but that it had been taken from him by his Spanish captors.

Sparrey served to keep England's interest in El Dorado alive. With Raleigh a prisoner, other men seized on the idea of colonizing Guiana. In 1604, Captain Charles Leigh sailed in the *Olive Plant* with forty-six men and boys. He had previously visited Guiana briefly, in 1602, and now he selected the Wiapoco River, the modern Oiapoque, as the most suitable site for a colony where he could trade with the natives, search for gold mines, and plant flax, cotton, and sugar.

The Indians welcomed the English—for, thanks to Raleigh, the English were popular in Guiana—and concluded a treaty with them whereby the Indians would provide the colonists with food in return for being defended against a hostile tribe. But soon Leigh's men, troubled by the hot, damp climate and the diseases it bred, began to quarrel among themselves, and a few took advantage of the good nature of the natives in such a way that the Indians turned against them. After a year, Leigh had to write to his brother and financial backer in London, Sir Oliph Leigh, for a relief mission bringing provisions, commodities for trade, and skilled craftsmen. The new ship arrived in the fall of 1605, but Captain Leigh died of fever the following March and the colony broke apart, some of its members joining a Dutch slave-trading enterprise and some going south to the Cayenne River, where the French had founded a colony in 1604. (The French were not interested in El Dorado at all, but simply planned to grow tobacco in Guiana.)

The exploitation of Guiana, which as late as 1595 had been entirely a Spanish matter, now was rapidly taking on an international character, and the more that was heard of growing flax and tobacco and of trading in slaves, the less was said of El Dorado. But Fernando de Berrio still clung to Santo Thomé at the mouth of the Caroni, and he clung as well to his father's golden dream. The Dutch who visited him in 1598 reported that he had built a road "through the rocks and hills of the mountains of . . . Worinoque, which road is about 1600 *stadien* long, and so broad that they can march five horses abreast through it, and they think by these means to conquer the country." [243] The younger Berrio established an outpost about fifty miles inland from Santo Thomé, called Los Arias, and in December of 1600 used it as the base for an unsuccessful expedition toward Manoa.

For ten years Berrio concentrated on other matters. It was easier to remain at Santo Thomé, doing business with the ever-increasing numbers of traders who came by, than it was to chase into the jungle after El Dorado. He planted tobacco and sold it at high prices to Dutch and English traders, in defiance of Spanish law, which required all New World colonists to confine their commerce only to the mother country. In 1610, Berrio made another half-hearted attempt to find El Dorado, and when nothing came of it he returned to the tobacco trade with such zeal that the Council of the Indies reprimanded him for his violation of the commercial regulations. He ignored the reprimand, and in 1612 the governor of Venezuela, Sancho de Alquiza, was ordered by Spain to deal with him.

Alquiza came to Santo Thomé in February of that year. He found only some forty residents, but they were doing a thriving trade with eighteen foreign ships. The Orinoco was full of English and Dutch vessels who knew the routes of the river better than any of the Spaniards. Alquiza removed Berrio from office and prohibited further commerce with the enemies of Spain. Three years later, Berrio turned up before the Council of the Indies, pleaded his father's great services to the homeland, and won a pardon and the promise of eventual reinstatement at Santo Thomé. He settled on his estates in New Granada, remaining there until 1619. Some years later, while en route to Spain again to protest some further political reverse, his ship was captured by Moorish pirates, and the last official mention of him is in a memorandum of the Council of the Indies to the King in May, 1623, recommending "that Martín de Mendoza y Berrio, nephew of Fernando de Berrio, be ransomed from captivity at Algiers, where his uncle had died." [244] In that way did the association of the Berrio family with Guiana and El Dorado come to its end.

3

Another attempt by the English to found a colony in Guiana was made in 1609. Its guiding spirit was Sir

Thomas Roe, afterward England's Ambassador to the Great Mogul of India, and one of the investors in the scheme was Raleigh, who put up £600 even though he was still a prisoner in the Tower. With one good-sized ship and one pinnace, Roe sailed from Plymouth on February 24, 1609, and reached the Amazon estuary in April. He explored that river to a distance of several hundred miles inland, then returned to the coast and worked his way northward, entering each river by canoe. In thirteen months of such explorations Roe came as far north as the Wiapoco River, which he believed would take him to El Dorado. He made a determined effort to ascend the river, negotiating thirty-two rapids along the way, and then, according to an anonymous contemporary Spanish report, "he found a level and uniform country without any more rapids, and afterwards a very deep and broad river, and they would have voyaged onward by it, and by it arrived at the great city of Manoa, of which there is so great fame, but since the savages who live on the banks of that river had fled . . . their cassava-root victuals and all other provisions failed them, the which compelled him with his company to return without passing further." [245]

Roe was under instructions from King James not to venture into the Orinoco, which the King conceded was legitimately Spanish property, and in view of the fragile *entente* with Spain that James was trying to create, Roe had no desire to risk his own head by committing an act of aggression against that country. Therefore he made no attempt to find El Dorado via the Orinoco, nor did he try the Essequibo route. In February of 1611 he called at Trinidad and sent a letter to Robert Cecil, now the Earl of Salisbury and the most powerful courtier in the realm, expressing his disappointment with his voyage and his doubts of El Dorado: "Your Honor shall find nothing new nor strange here," he wrote, though he indicated a belief that if England wished to run a chance of war with Spain, Santo Thomé could easily be captured from its current master, the lazy, avaricious Fernando de Berrio. Although he was skeptical of any golden city in the interior of Guiana, Roe felt that it would be possible to mine gold around the Caroni—a far less romantic hypothesis than the vistas of El Dorado that other men had conjured up.

Almost simultaneously with Roe's, a second English voyage to Guiana was launched, this one under the leadership of Robert Harcourt. Harcourt, born in 1574, belonged to an old and distinguished English family, and after a few genteel years at Oxford became interested in founding colonies in the New World. In 1607 he obtained from King James "his gracious letters patents for the planting and inhabiting of all that tract of land, and part of Guiana, between the rivers of Amazones, and Dessequebe, situate in America, under the Equinoctial Line." [246] With three ships and ninety-seven men all told, Harcourt left England on March 23, 1609, less than a month after the departure of Roe's expedition.

He let the trade winds drive him across the Atlantic to the Amazon estuary, then hugged the coast until he reached the mouth of the Wiapoco on May 17. The Indians were friendly, and Harcourt cemented the relationship by speaking of Raleigh and explaining that he had come to take the place of that great man. They agreed to supply his colony with food if he aided them in their battles against the voracious Caribs.

When the winter rains ended, Harcourt moved some of his settlers from the coastal marshes to more suitable farming land in the interior, and they planted sugar, cotton wool, and tobacco. Once the colony seemed firmly established, Harcourt and some of his men went to look for El Dorado. This was in July, 1610. Although Harcourt's primary purpose was agriculture and trade, he could not resist the allure of Manoa.

So, he relates in the book he published in 1613, "I began to travel abroad in search of those Golden Mountains, promised unto us before the beginning of our voyage (by one that undertook to guide us to them) which filled my company so full of vain expectation, and golden hopes, that their insatiable and covetous minds (being wholly set thereon) could not be satisfied with anything but only gold." [247] Evidently some Indian sojourning in London— there were a number at that time—had volunteered to lead Harcourt to El Dorado; but, he writes, "Our guide that vainly made those great promises, being come unto the wished place to make performance, was then possessed with a shameless spirit of ignorance, for he knew little, and could perform nothing. What other intelligences (of mines already found) I had from other men in England, and from the master of my ship, who had been heretofore in those parts, I found them by experience false, and nothing true concerning mines, that was in England reported unto me." [248]

The frustration and disappointment produced by their failure to strike gold brought Harcourt's men to the edge of mutiny, but he managed to pacify them. For all the contempt of their gold-seeking that he expresses above, Harcourt himself seemed to share the fever of his crew, however; he continued to search for mines and for the city of Manoa. One day an Indian presented him with a crescent in gold-copper alloy, and several images and plates of gold. "All which things," he wrote, "they assured me were made in the high country of Guiana, which they said did abound with images of gold. . . . These things I showed to my company to settle their troubled minds, which gave much contentment to the greater part of them, and satisfied us all that there was gold in Guiana. Shortly after that my Indian Anthony Canabre brought me a piece of a rock of white spar, of which this country is full. . . . I made trial of a piece of spar . . . and I found that it held both gold and silver, which (although it was in small quantity) gave me satisfaction that there be richer mines in the country to be found: but the best lie deeper in the earth, and we had not time nor power to make search for them." [249]

Though the hope of finding raw gold was thus thwarted, Harcourt still entertained the possibility of discovering Manoa, with its wealth of gleaming treasure. He left his brother Michael in charge of the colony and sailed up the Wiapoco, but waterfalls blocked his advance, and he came back with nothing more than a rumor of "a nation of Caribs having great ears of an extraordinary bigness, hard to be believed." [250] Next he sailed farther north along the coast with the intent of finding some other river route to Manoa, but at the Cayenne River his pinnace suffered an accident that forced a long delay for repairs. During this interval, he went with nine other men in the ship's boat to the Marowyne River, and struggled upstream against the rapids for a hundred twenty miles until "we met with such shoale rocky stream, and great overfalls, that there to our grief our journey ended." [251] Since it was now time for Harcourt to return to London to secure fresh capital and new colonists, he commissioned his cousin, Unton Fisher, to prosecute the search for Manoa in his stead. Fisher went 300 miles farther up the Marowyne before running out of provisions, but was drowned on the way back. As for Harcourt, he encountered extensive problems in London and did not reach Guiana again until 1627, by which time his original colony had long since disbanded. He died in 1631, apparently at his new colony in Guiana.

4

During these years when other men nibbled at the frontiers of El Dorado, Sir Walter Raleigh languished bitterly in the Tower of London. The charges that had led to his arrest in 1603 were flimsy ones, made convincing only by the glibness of Raleigh's enemies at court. His troubles began with a Catholic plot to seize King James and compel him to grant a more favorable position to the Church of Rome in England. Raleigh was not involved in this, but several of his friends were, and by an intricate maneuver the King was persuaded of Raleigh's complicity. When he was questioned, Raleigh denied that he was part of the plot—which was true—but made the mistake of denying also that he knew anything about it, which was false. He had had some inkling of what was being schemed.

Suddenly Raleigh realized that he was in very serious trouble, and he grew so despondent after his arrest that he attempted suicide in the summer of 1603. He recovered, but wrote in lament to his wife, "I am now made an enemy and a traitor by the word of an unworthy man. . . . Woe, woe, woe, be unto him by whose false hand we are lost. He hath separated us asunder. He hath slain my honor; my fortune. He hath robbed thee of thy husband, thy child of his father, and me of both." [252]

He now was caught in the same millstones that had ground so many of England's greatest men to powder in the last fifty years—the savage intrigues of the court—and Raleigh, who had profited most flagrantly from the downfall of others, now had to watch his estates and honors being confiscated and his property parceled out to his destroyers. He came to trial late in 1603 at Winchester—London was in the grip of plague—and among his judges were Robert Cecil and Sir Henry Howard. Raleigh was charged on four counts: conspiracy to deprive the King of his government, to raise up sedition within the realm, to further the cause of "the Roman superstition," and to deliver the kingdom to foreign enemies. Specifically, Raleigh was accused of treasonable dealings with King Philip of Spain and others to gain his ends.

He pleaded not guilty—serving as his own lawyer, after the custom of the day. He was not permitted to call or question witnesses, or even to interrupt the course of the prosecution's case. The attorney-general, Sir Edward Coke, read a lengthy and impassioned attack on Raleigh's malice and treasons. Raleigh denied all charges. No witnesses for the prosecution were brought forward; the one man who had made the lying statement that Raleigh was part of the plot could not be produced, for his bald untruths would seem too shameless in the courtroom. Realizing that he was condemned in advance of the trial, Raleigh maintained an icy dignity, breaking it only near the end, when Coke began to recapitulate the "evidence" and Raleigh attempted to correct him.

"Thou art the most vile and execrable traitor that ever lived," said Coke in annoyance at the interruption.

"You speak indiscreetly, barbarously, and uncivilly," Raleigh snapped.

"I want words sufficient to express thy viperous treason."

"I think you want words indeed," Raleigh replied, "for you have spoken one thing half-a-dozen times." [253]

The verdict was reached in fifteen minutes: guilty. Raleigh threw himself on the King's mercy, confident that James would not dare have him put to death after such a mockery of justice. The lord chief justice addressed Raleigh, reminding him, "It is best for man not to seek to climb too high, lest he fall," and reproving him for his covetousness. The sentence was a ghastly one: to be hanged and cut down alive, then disemboweled, beheaded, and quartered. The other conspirators against King James received the same penalty. However, the punishments were quickly commuted to simple beheading. The first execution was held on December 6, 1603; Raleigh's was scheduled for seven days later. He wrote a groveling letter to James begging for pardon, and then a noble one to his wife, expressing resignation at his fate. But the King did not have the courage to send a popular hero like Raleigh to the scaffold. The sovereign ordered that the execution be suspended—not commuted—and Raleigh was sent to the Tower of London to await the pleasure of the crown.

It was, Raleigh knew, a possible term of life imprisonment—though he might be taken out and beheaded any time at James' whim. Late in December he entered the Tower. He was almost fifty-two, vigorous and healthy, at the peak of his powers. When he emerged, more than a dozen years later, he would be an old man, weary and ill, pathetic in his desire to restore his high place. He had risen from obscurity to dazzling fame between the ages of thirty and forty—the lover of the Queen, the founder of American colonies, the master of enormous estates. From 1592 onward, the course had been downward, and now, after a decade of decline, he found himself a miserable prisoner under sentence of death. The titles and ranks he had accumulated during his swift rise were taken from him, and only that property remained which he had been able to convey to other members of his family.

He was the Tower's leading tourist attraction. Daily he took his exercise on the walls of the grim old fortress, and Londoners gaped at him from below. Foreign dignitaries asked to visit him, which created an awkward situation for

King James. The King's son, Prince Henry, remarked, "Only my father could keep such a bird in a cage."

It was a foul cage at first, damp and rat-infested. After a year in a cell—spent in writing endless appeals for freedom—Raleigh was given the freedom of the Tower garden, and was allowed to build a small house in which he later conducted chemical experiments. Friends visited him; his wife lived in the prison with him for a while, and his second son was born at the Tower. He occupied himself with literary and scientific projects. From time to time he requested that King James free him to undertake an expedition to Virginia or Guiana. Guiana continued to fascinate him. He was certain that it held, if not a golden city of Manoa, then at least rich mines of gold.

Laurence Keymis fanned this belief into a raging blaze. Raleigh's old lieutenant visited him in the Tower and reminded him of the gold mine on the Caroni that he had learned of in 1595. Keymis swore that it was genuine and that he could find it again. To Raleigh the mine became an indisputable reality. In one of his many letters on the subject, to Viscount Haddington in 1609, Raleigh wrote asking Haddington's help in launching a new Guiana expedition, and declared, "If I bring them not to a mountain (near a navigable river) covered with gold and silver ore, let the commander have commission to cut off my head there." [254] In another letter he said, "I am contented to adventure all I have (but my reputation) upon Keymis' memory." [255] These requests came to nothing, and Raleigh had to content himself with vicarious participation, as an investor, in Sir Thomas Roe's disappointing expedition of 1609.

When the command of the Tower passed to one of Raleigh's old enemies, his special privileges were withdrawn, and his situation became more and more one of harsh captivity. Now it became more important than ever to end what seemed a permanent incarceration. Raleigh said little of El Dorado, knowing that somber King James was not the man to grow enthusiastic over the hope of finding a fabulous city that explorers had hunted for eighty years in vain. Rather, he used as bait the gold mine near the Caroni that Keymis was so sure he could locate. He felt that the Spaniards could be driven out of Santo Thomé, and the mine worked to the great profit of England. Gold, nothing but gold, was all that Raleigh offered James—no alliance with the "Incas of Manoa," no fanciful schemes for a South American empire, merely an abundance of the yellow metal.

However, James was taking a pro-Spanish attitude in an attempt to end the hostility between England and Spain that had prevailed since the middle of the previous century. The powerful, ambitious King Philip II had died in 1598, and Philip III, his successor, was weak and overly pious, leaving the administration of his realm to clever grandees who sought accommodation with England. Spanish gold liberally bought English sympathies; and King James himself, no strong monarch, listened to his bribed courtiers and was willing to deal with Spain. Though he coveted the gold of Guiana, James recognized the region around the Orinoco as a Spanish sphere of influence. As the Spanish ambassador to James' court, the sinister Count Gondomar, pointed out to him, an English expedition to Guiana would amount to an act of war against Spain.

So Raleigh's requests went unheard. He busied himself in scholarship. Prince Henry, the heir to the throne, became his pupil, and Raleigh wrote a ponderous *History of the World* for him. Henry favored Raleigh's Guiana scheme, and did all he could to sway his father; but the boy's death in 1612 deprived Raleigh of his most influential supporter, and it began to seem to him that he would never have his freedom again.

Other deaths were more advantageous to Raleigh: Robert Cecil's that same year of 1612, and Henry Howard's in 1614. He had outlived his chief enemies, and scarcely any reason for his continued imprisonment remained. Through bribery Raleigh now obtained the intercession of the current court favorites, and in March, 1616, his cousin George was able to write, "Sir Walter Raleigh is enlarged out of the Tower, and is to go his journey to Guiana, but remains unpardoned until his return; he left his mansion in the Tower the 19th day of this month." [256]

5

It is impossible to fathom the motives by which King James let himself agree to send Raleigh to Guiana. He was deeply under the influence of Count Gondomar, and the Spanish ambassador was irate at the idea of the expedition; yet, over Gondomar's furious protests, James let Raleigh go.

James and Gondomar were in the midst of delicate negotiations designed to bring about a marriage between James' heir, Prince Charles, and a daughter of Philip III of Spain. Not since the 1550's, when the future Philip II was the consort of England's Queen Mary, had relations between the two countries been so cordial. A word from the ambassador at this time should have been enough to quash the Raleigh project. In August of 1616, Gondomar angrily told James that it was absurd to profess friendship with Spain and at the same time countenance an armed invasion of the Spanish Empire. He made it clear that Spain laid claim to the whole of Guiana, and expressed his fear that Raleigh—whose name still was anathema in Spain—would turn pirate and raid the thriving towns of the Spanish Main. Raleigh was known to be raising an armada more than sufficient to his purpose, and Gondomar saw it as a voyage of war. He went so far as to offer to permit Raleigh to go to Guiana with a Spanish escort and mine all the gold he pleased, but he could not permit the sailing of this belligerent-looking English fleet.

King James listened to all this, and licensed the expedition nevertheless. Perhaps he felt that Raleigh could bring him so much gold that it was worth daring the anger of Spain. Or—and James was a devious man—it may well be that he hoped Raleigh would commit some act of war against Spain that would allow James in one stroke to dispose of him for good with a clear excuse and to win new favor with Spain through the punishment. Raleigh's commission was craftily designed along this line. He was ordered to carry out his explorations without setting foot on Spanish territory or inflicting "the least injury in the world" upon a Spanish vassal. Raleigh agreed to these terms; but they were impossible conditions, for how could he explore the Orinoco without trespassing on Spanish territory, and how could he take Santo Thomé without injuring Spanish vassals? On the face of it, Raleigh was going forth to commit a knowing trespass that would certainly open him to serious charges. Perhaps he hoped to bring back so much treasure that James would overlook the prohibited trespass. What James' motives were are beyond easy comprehension, though from later events the implication cannot be resisted that he was maneuvering old Raleigh into his grave.

In the first weeks of his freedom, Raleigh wandered London in wide-eyed wonder, simply observing the city. He was followed by a keeper, for he had not won a complete pardon, merely the royal permission to sail to Guiana. The old sentence of death imposed in 1603 remained on the books, though Raleigh had the expectation that it would be lifted on the successful conclusion of his voyage. Borrowing money from all his friends, he put his own remaining capital into the project as well, and raised more than £30,000 in short order. A handsome new ship, the *Destiny*, was built for the enterprise, and others were purchased. By the spring of 1617, he had assembled seven ships of war and three pinnaces at Plymouth, and a company of 90 "gentlemen adventurers" and 318 seamen. The sailors had been recruited by Keymis, who had offered a share in the profits to every man. They were a rough, brutal bunch of cutthroats; Raleigh could do no better, now.

In May, while Gondomar frantically attempted to halt the departure, Raleigh issued his orders to his men. Though he was frayed and worn from his long confinement, only a shadow of his former self, he struck a tone of firm authority. He told his roughneck sailors that "you shall take especial care that God be not blasphemed in your ship," and required them to praise Him every night "with singing of a psalm at the setting of the watch." [257] Theft and drunkenness were prohibited, and no man was to do injury to a native, or to eat any unknown fruits in Guiana. "You shall not sleep on the ground," he decreed, "nor eat any new flesh till it be salted, two or three hours, which otherwise will breed a most dangerous flux, so will the eating of over fat hogs or turkeys: you shall also have a great care, that you swim not in any rivers but where you see the Indians swim, because most of the rivers are full of alligators: you shall not take anything from any Indian by force, for from thencefore we shall never be relieved, but you must use them with all courtesy." [258]

The ten vessels sailed on June 12, 1617. Soon after, they were joined by four more large ships, one commanded by Keymis, so that now Raleigh's company numbered nearly a thousand. A fierce gale immediately scattered the ships and drove them back into port. The crew, who Raleigh had discovered consisted of "the scum of men," was unruly at the outset; one of Raleigh's officers wrote of "continual quarrels and fighting amongst our own company with many dangerous hurts." [259] The ships regrouped and went to sea again, and just west of the Scilly Islands they were beset by storms once more. This time one vessel foundered. A third attempt to put to sea was also unsuccessful, as though the gods of the wind were trying to force Raleigh to stay in England. The fleet was blown into harbor at Cork, and remained there from June 25 until August 19, waiting for the contrary winds to subside. The best summer sailing days thus were lost.

Finally at sea, they found provisions running low, and some of Raleigh's captains wanted to confiscate the stores of four pirate ships encountered off the French coast. But Raleigh knew that he had to be on his best behavior lest he be called to account by King James, and he would not permit the act. On September 6 they reached the Canary Islands and negotiated with the Spanish authorities to come ashore and stock up on food and water. Through a misunderstanding, the islanders thought Raleigh's men were Barbary pirates, and set upon the landing party, killing fifteen. Still bending over backwards, Raleigh banned any retaliation.

While provisioning in the Canaries, Raleigh's force was struck by an epidemic of fever and dysentery. By September 22, fifty men aboard the flagship alone were unfit for service. Raleigh ordered an unscheduled stop at Brava, one of the Cape Verde Islands, to take on fresh meat in order to check the disease. Leaving Brava they were hit by a hurricane; one pinnace sank and the rest were driven out to sea, where after eight days the weather reversed itself so ungratefully that they were becalmed. The sick men began to die by the dozens. Forty-two men of the *Destiny* perished. Raleigh himself grew so ill that for four weeks he was unable to take solid food.

The fleet limped across the Atlantic in this way, alternately buffeted by storms and gripped by deadly calms, and on November 11 came to Cape Wiapoco in Guiana. Raleigh had not seen Guiana for twenty-two years—not since the swaggering old days when he had captured Antonio de Berrio, made treaties with Indian chiefs, and pried golden ore from the banks of the Caroni. On November 14 the vessels dropped anchor in the mouth of the Cayenne River, after a voyage that had lasted four times as long as it should have. Raleigh was extremely feeble; his men despaired of his life.

They rested at the Cayenne estuary for three weeks, while provisions were brought to them by Indians whose chief had gone to England to visit Raleigh and who had spent two years with him in the Tower by way of companionship. Then, on December 4, they sailed northward along the coast toward the Orinoco and planned the journey inland.

Raleigh had recovered from his ailment, but he was still so weak that he could not lead the exploring party in person. Its command went to his nephew, George Raleigh, and Laurence Keymis was assigned the responsibility of guiding a party to the mine near the Caroni of whose existence he was so sure. The question of what to do if the Spaniards of Santo Thomé offered resistance was discussed at length. Raleigh, as all his men knew, was under royal orders not to attack Spaniards. Therefore he instructed Keymis to attempt to get around Santo Thomé and onward to the mine, which supposedly lay three miles beyond the town, without bloodshed. Keymis was to maintain a strong line of communication between the miners and the ships in the Orinoco. If the Spaniards chose to attack, George Raleigh was authorized to repel them, but otherwise there was to be no violence. Raleigh would remain opposite the Orinoco estuary with the ships, in harbor at Punto de Gallo, Trinidad, and he guaranteed the inland party that he would remain there even if a hostile Spanish fleet appeared: "You shall find me at Punto Gallo," he told them, "dead or alive. And if you find not my ships there, you shall find their ashes. For I will fire with the galleons, if it come to extremity; run will I never." [260]

Even if Raleigh had been well, he probably would not have been permitted by his captains to go with them up the Orinoco. With the crew a surly, mutinous lot, there was the real possibility that some other officer left in charge of the support fleet at Trinidad might be overthrown by the men, who would sail off on a voyage of piracy leaving Keymis and the inland party marooned. Raleigh alone was considered to have sufficient power of leadership to prevent such a rebellion. So he remained behind as five of the ships, provisioned for a month, entered the river with three hundred fifty men on December 10.

It took three weeks to reach the main arm of the Orinoco that led to Santo Thomé. During this trip two of the ships were disabled and had to be abandoned. The Spaniards knew of their coming, and harassed them with gunfire from the banks, while Santo Thomé itself got ready for invasion.

The town had prospered in the past decade, largely because of Fernando de Berrio's policy of trading with the Dutch and English tobacco ships, and though its population was still small it now consisted of a number of substantial houses where the elder Berrio's bamboo huts had been. As noted earlier, Fernando de Berrio had been removed from office in 1612 for his violation of Spanish commercial regulations, and now was in residence on his estates in New Granada. Santo Thomé was under the administration of Diego Palomeque de Acuña, a relative of Count Gondomar.

The town lay between the English and the mine, and a collision between Keymis' party and the Spaniards was inevitable, despite the command of King James and Raleigh's eagerness to obey it. Keymis actually had two mines in mind, but evidently had not made his intentions clear to Raleigh. The first lay on the right bank of the Caroni, about three miles south of the confluence with the Orinoco. Raleigh and Keymis had been there together in 1595, when no Spanish fort at Santo Thomé yet existed, and had collected samples of ore that some judged valuable when they were brought to England. When Keymis returned to the Orinoco early in 1596, he found Berrio's Santo Thomé blocking his approach to the Caroni, and after withdrawing had learned of a second mine, fifteen or twenty miles inland—the one supposedly guarded by a dragon. He had not actually visited this mine himself.

Apparently it was the second mine whose fabulous riches, wholly imagined by Keymis, had inspired this entire expedition. But Keymis did not dare to lead his party to an unknown mountain in the jungle until he had first gone back to the known source of ore on the Caroni and mined it. He could not reach that mine without passing Santo Thomé; and so an invasion of the Spanish town was necessary. According to one theory, Keymis had received word from within Santo Thomé that the town was on the verge of rebellion against the unpopular Palomeque de Acuña, whose strict rule was odious after the laxity of Fernando de Berrio, and Keymis had been told that all he need do was arrive before Santo Thomé and its inhabitants would overthrow Palomeque and permit the English to enter peacefully. This theory is borne out by Spanish documents which show that Santo Thomé actually was about to expel or assassinate Palomeque at the time of Keymis' arrival. However, nothing in the English side of the record indicates any documented evidence that Keymis knew of this—so his approach to

Santo Thomé could only have been the prelude to armed attack, against the wishes of King James and of Raleigh.

On the afternoon of January 2, 1618, the English force led by Keymis and George Raleigh landed on the Orinoco bank about five miles from Santo Thomé. According to the affidavits of several of the officers, Keymis refused to attempt to reach the mine until the town had been taken. A force of soldiers was disembarked and made its way slowly under cover of gathering darkness toward the town, guided by Indians. The ships went ahead and anchored under the walls of the town. Though Santo Thomé was now at the mercy of their guns, the ships did not open fire, and even when a Spanish mortar bombarded them, they held their peace. They were there to blockade, not to attack.

All during the evening Keymis was marching toward the town—spending seven hours to cover four and a half miles of jungle bordering the Orinoco. What his exact plans were is uncertain; since the thirty or forty Spaniards in Santo Thomé now were held prisoner there by the artillery of the English ships, he could simply have gone around the town to the mine unhindered. Alternately, he may have been expecting the overthrow of Palomeque and the voluntary surrender of the town in the morning. Certainly he was in a firm strategic position. But Keymis, for all his gifts as a Latin poet, was no leader, and he stumbled now into a fatal blunder.

The English foot party, without realizing it, had come within half a mile of Santo Thomé, and Keymis had still given no clear indication to his men whether he planned to attack the town, would go around it, or was anticipating its instant capitulation. Suddenly a Spanish reconnaissance party led by one Gerónimo de Grados came upon them. Grados had left Santo Thomé with ten men earlier in the evening to keep watch on the movements of the English through the jungle, and Keymis marched his force right into Grados' party unawares.

Grados immediately gave battle, and many of the English, thinking they had been ambushed by a large body of Spaniards, fled into the forest. For a moment all was confusion and panic. Then an English officer, to rally the bewildered men, gave a loud shout and rushed forward in a wild attack on the town.

This officer was young Walter Raleigh, the elder son of Sir Walter—a gallant and reckless man of lively spirit, with all his father's buoyant enthusiasm and none of his father's streak of overweening ambition. "Come on, my hearts, here is the mine you must expect, they that look for any other one are fools," [261] young Raleigh shouted as he charged toward nearby Santo Thomé. Most of his men—the unruly blackguards who formed the bulk of Raleigh's personnel—failed to follow him. A Spanish soldier named Arias Nieto cut him down, and with his dying breath Raleigh's son urged the others to go on.

The English had discovered by this time that only a handful of Spaniards opposed them. They put their foes to rout and burst into Santo Thomé. By one in the morning, the town was in their hands. Aside from young Raleigh, only two other Englishmen were killed; there were three Spanish fatalities, including Nieto and Governor Palomeque. Santo Thomé was taken—but at the highest possible cost, for young Walter Raleigh had been his father's chief joy, and Keymis had no idea how he was going to break the news to the old man who waited with the ships off Trinidad.

The Spaniards slipped off into the forest as Keymis took possession of their town. The badly shaken Keymis now had no excuses for not proceeding to the mine; but by the light of morning he saw new things to fear. The surrounding countryside seemed terribly unfamiliar to him. He began to doubt that he could find the mine that he had visited only hastily, twenty-three years before. This oversensitive man pictured himself marching out at the head of his band of roughnecks, wandering for days in the jungle, and finally being forced to admit he did not know where the mine was. That would be unthinkable.

So Keymis announced to his men that there would be a short delay before they commenced mining operations. While they waited, he left Santo Thomé secretly one night accompanied only by a few officers, and marched to the place where he remembered having found ore with Raleigh in 1595. He gathered some rock samples and took them back, but the party's assayer told him that they were worthless.

He was close to total despair. A logical next step would have been to leave a garrison at Santo Thomé and make an overland search for the dragon-guarded mountain of precious stones said to be fifteen or twenty miles away, if not to make a more intensive hunt for the mine up the Caroni. But the frightened Keymis had visions of Spanish reinforcements coming up the Orinoco to cut him off while he was lulling the distant dragon. Unable to bring himself to return to Sir Walter Raleigh without gold, he ordered a frantic search for treasure in Santo Thomé itself. That produced nothing, but some friendly Indians told him of another gold mine, six or eight miles up the Orinoco west of the confluence with the Caroni. The Spaniards of Santo Thomé had retreated in that direction, which led Keymis to suspect that they might be trying to guard a rich mine. Remaining at Santo Thomé himself, he sent two boats upstream to investigate.

The Spaniards hiding in the jungle, thinking that the English were launching an attack on their place of refuge, prepared another ambush. Gerónimo de Grados and nine armed men hid along the bank of the river, and opened fire when the boats drew near, killing two and wounding six. The English retreated in alarm, without finding the mine.

Next the tormented Keymis sent three well-armed launches in the same direction under the command of George Raleigh. One boat stayed in midstream, and the other two surveyed the right and left banks. The Spaniards did not attack. But no gold mines appeared, even though the launches traveled for three weeks and got three hundred miles up the Orinoco. Then they admitted the futility of the effort and went back.

Keymis remained dug in at Santo Thomé for all of January and half of February, waiting in vain for someone to find some gold for him—anywhere. He saw belatedly that it had been a tactical error to drive the Spaniards out of the fort, for now they were free to rove the forest as guerrillas, picking off his men whenever he sent exploring parties to look for mines. It would have been wiser to keep them besieged and impotent in their fort while he surveyed the jungle at his leisure. Instead, the English were the ones penned up in Santo Thomé, with all the drawbacks of that position. But there was nothing that Keymis could do about that now.

Early in February he found the courage to send a message to Raleigh informing him of the death of his son. The news reached him on February 13. Keymis spoke of Walter's "extraordinary valor and forwardness . . . when some began to pause and recoil shamelessly," [262] but left a clear implication that if the young man had not been so rash as to try to enter Santo Thomé single-handed, he would not have died. The news that Walter's death had been needless, that he had been one of only three casualties out of hundreds of men, deepened Raleigh's grief. He sank into a mood of bitter misery that could not have been raised had Keymis come back to him festooned with all the gold of El Dorado.

But Keymis had found no gold, and the men in Santo Thomé were demoralized by the failure. His weak leadership had led them to the edge of mutiny. The Spaniards, camping in the nearby jungle, were so bold in their harassments that it was growing difficult for the English even to gather food. At length Keymis gave the order to set fire to Santo Thomé and return to Trinidad. Ironically, he had been within a few hundred yards of a rich mine all the time —not of gold, but of mercury. A decade later the Spaniards would strike quicksilver just outside the town.

Keymis was a pitiful figure on the downstream journey, regarded with contempt by his fellow officers for his atrocious mishandling of the expedition, and eyed with anger by his mutinous rabble of a crew, who could well calculate their share of nonexistent profits. Worst of all, the confrontation with Raleigh lay ahead: and Keymis would have to explain how he had come to let the life of young Walter be placed in such jeopardy, as well as how he had failed to find the mine of which he had spoken for more than twenty years.

On March 2, the expedition returned to Trinidad and Keymis came before Raleigh. The first rush of Raleigh's sorrow was past, and he had had two weeks to compose himself; so he greeted Keymis in a mood of black calm, rather than in open anguish. But he had no kind words for his old friend. According to a letter Raleigh wrote to his wife three weeks later, "I told him that he had undone me, and that my credit was lost forever." [263]

Keymis attempted to explain why he had not reached the mine, but his fumbling and patently false excuses only made the matter worse. Instead of admitting that he had lost the way, he blurted that with young Raleigh already dead, and Sir Walter presumably at the point of death from his fever, he had felt it was folly to enrich "a company of rascals." It had seemed to him that if he uncovered the mine it would only be for the benefit of the Spaniards, who would work it after lack of provisions had forced the English to withdraw, and thus he had not attempted to open it. He hoped that Raleigh would forgive him for this and would defend his actions in any official inquest that followed.

Raleigh replied that he would not accept Keymis' excuses; Keymis would have to justify his course himself to the backers of the expedition. "I would not favor or color in any sort his former folly," Raleigh declares in his account of the meeting. "He then asked me, whether that were my resolution; I told him it was; he then replied in these words, 'I know then, sir, what course to take,' and went out of my cabin up into his own, into which he was no sooner entered but I heard a pistol go off. I sent up (not suspecting any such thing as the killing of himself) to know who shot the pistol; Keymis himself made answer, lying on his bed, that he had shot it off, because it had been long charged, with which I was satisfied. Some half an hour after this, his boy going into his cabin, found him dead, having a long knife thrust under his left pap through his heart, and the pistol lying beside him, with which it appeared he had shot himself; but the bullet, lighting upon a rib had but broken the rib, and went no further." [264] Even in his suicide poor Keymis had made a botch of things.

6

Even in this moment of double tragedy, Raleigh could not free himself from the golden manacles of his obsession. He suggested at once that he lead a second expedition to Santo Thomé to find the mine; for two authentic ingots of gold had been taken from the Spaniards, as well as documents indicating the presence of nearby mines. Shattered as he was, he still saw gold as the key to his future fortunes. If he could bring even a basket of gold-bearing ore to King James, something might yet be salvaged from this terrible voyage. But the men who had just come from the Orinoco were in no mood to return. They felt that a Spanish fleet would soon arrive to drive them off, and insisted on an immediate withdrawal. Raleigh yielded, and they began to cruise northward through the West Indies.

On March 12, 1618, they dropped anchor off the island of Nevis. Two of Raleigh's ships had already deserted him at Grenada to go on a voyage of piracy. While Raleigh hesitated at Nevis, other vessels broke away for the same purpose. He crossed to the adjacent island of St. Christopher and remained there for ten days, at the end of which time he had only five ships left. He sent one back to England, with "a rabble of idle rascals, which I know will not spare to wound me, but I care not," [265] and told the captains of the other ships to rendezvous with him at Newfoundland. What he planned to do at that point is not clear, but it seems as if, having reached that northern land, he intended to persuade his men to go all the way back to Guiana, or else perhaps make a raid on a Spanish treasure fleet—a wild act that might have caused war and certainly would have made him an outlaw.

From St. Christopher on March 22, Raleigh wrote to his wife to break the news of their son's death. He gave her a copy of an official report to the government that he had written the day before, setting forth every detail of the fiasco and relating how in the assault on Santo Thomé "my son having more desire of honor than of safety was slain, and with whom, to say the truth, all respects of the world hath taken end in me." [266] The accompanying note to his wife declared, "God knows, I never knew what sorrow meant till now. . . . My brains are broken, and tis a torment to me to write." [267] He did not conceal his bitterness toward Keymis, whose mismanagement had undone him. He concluded, "I am sure there is never a base slave in the fleet hath taken the pains and care that I have done, hath slept so little, and travailed so much. . . . God in heaven bless you and strengthen your heart." [268]

Slowly he headed toward Newfoundland. His other ships, preceding him, engaged in numerous acts of piracy, one of them robbing four French vessels of their cargo of dried Newfoundland cod and taking the fish off to Italy for sale. As he approached Newfoundland, Raleigh learned that his own men were planning to follow that example. To circumvent them he changed course and ordered an immediate return to England, without a landing at Newfoundland. A mutiny followed, and Raleigh was placed in mortal danger; but the mutineers were driven off as they attempted to enter the harbor of St. John, and had to come to terms with him. Raleigh agreed to put the mutineers off in Ireland, where they would not be punished. With the remnants of his crew, he continued on to England, and landed at Plymouth on June 21. A year and nine days earlier he had set sail for Guiana with a great armada; now he returned with one ship, and that depleted by mutiny.

His fate was already sealed, for he had tolerated Keymis' wanton invasion of a Spanish settlement in contravention of his orders, had failed to prevent his men from becoming pirates, and—worst of all—had found no gold. The word of his voyage had preceded him, and Count Gondomar was screaming for vengeance. On June 9 King James had issued a proclamation expressing his "utter mislike and detestation of the . . . insolences and excesses" of Raleigh's expedition, and calling for punishment for those guilty of "so scandalous and enormous outrages." [269] An order was out for Raleigh's arrest, and James told Gondomar that his punishment could be carried out in Madrid if the Spaniards wished the pleasure of executing their arch-enemy themselves.

Raleigh was tired and heartbroken, and he scarcely attempted to defend himself. He made a half-hearted feint at escaping to France, but neglected to take advantage of a sure opportunity to find refuge there, and allowed himself to be made a prisoner. His journey to London in custody took him past one of the great estates that had once been his, and he stared at it as though that lost splendor had been only a fitful dream. A second and equally half-hearted effort to escape to France failed, and early in August Raleigh was again a prisoner in the Tower of London.

Gondomar demanded his death. James, who had been willing to risk a breach with Spain if Raleigh could bring him gold, now had no scruples at healing that breach by giving Gondomar Raleigh's head. It would not be necessary to put Raleigh on trial, for the death sentence of 1603 still stood; but even James hesitated to invoke it after a lapse of fourteen years.

Royal commissioners interrogated Raleigh in the Tower and filled many pages with an account of Keymis' activities at Santo Thomé. Depositions were taken from members of Raleigh's expedition and from those to whom he had told his plan for escaping to France. It seemed that Raleigh had entertained some fleeting idea of persuading France to launch its own El Dorado expedition under his command.

The royal commission reported to King James on October 18 that Raleigh was undoubtedly guilty of many crimes, but that it would be poor procedure, though legal, to execute him on the 1603 charge. Though no new trial was necessary, they recommended some sort of formal hearing at which Raleigh's recent offenses could be made known—

largely for purposes of soothing public opinion—after which the death penalty could be carried out. Four days later, Raleigh was brought before a special commission of jurists and heard the King's accusations of "an hostile invasion of the town of Santo Thomé (being under the obedience of our said dear brother the King of Spain) and by killing of divers of the inhabitants thereof, his subjects, and after by sacking and burning the said town . . . maliciously broken and infringed the peace and amity, which hath been so happily established, and so long inviolably continued, between Us and the subjects of both our crowns." [270] There were subsidiary charges of piracy and treasonable dealings with the French.

Raleigh's defense was straightforward: "That Guiana be Spanish territory can never be acknowledged, for I myself took possession of it for the Queen of England, by virtue of a cession of all the native chiefs of the country. His Majesty knows this to be true, as is proved by the concession granted him under the great seal of England to Harcourt." [271] But it was too late for Raleigh to draw attention to the contradictory nature of King James' Guiana policy, nor did the pleas of his thirteen-year-old son Carew win him any mercy. The charges were made and Raleigh gave his answers, denying all guilt. Then the lord chief justice called him forward to ask if there were any reasons why execution should not be carried out.

He replied that "the judgment which I received to die so long since, I hope it cannot now be strained to take away my life; for that since it was His Majesty's pleasure to grant me a commission to proceed in a voyage beyond the seas, wherein I had power, as marshal, on the life and death of others, I presume I am discharged of that judgment. For by that commission I departed the land and undertook a journey, to honor my sovereign and enrich his kingdom with gold, of the ore whereof this hand hath found and taken in Guiana; but the voyage, notwithstanding my endeavor, had no success but what was fatal to me, the loss of my son and wasting of my whole estate." [272] At this point he was interrupted; the lord chief justice reminded him that this line of argument was irrelevant, and after a sober and sympathetic review of Raleigh's virtues and faults, concluded with the words, "Execution is granted."

There were no appeals possible. El Dorado had brought Raleigh to his death as surely as it had slain Ursua, Ehinger, and so many others, the difference being that Raleigh met death in an unfriendly homeland and not in some remote jungle. His friends visited him on his final night, and lastly came his wife, and at dawn he was alone when a priest came to him to help him compose his mind. Raleigh was more serene than the priest. At eight in the morning on October 29, 1618, Raleigh was led forth to die. King James had gone back on his word to Gondomar: the execution would not take place in Madrid, but at Westminster. By way of diverting public attention, James had chosen the day of the Lord Mayor's parade, hoping that most of London would attend that; but the spectacle of witnessing the death of the last great Elizabethan hero took precedence over any parade, and the area around the scaffold was thronged.

As Raleigh came forward, he spied a bald old man in the crowd. Smiling, Raleigh tossed him his own cap, saying, "You need this, my friend, more than I do." He ascended the scaffold and asked permission to make a final speech. To refuse the request would have been to spoil the drama of this carefully staged occasion. Raleigh was allowed to speak.

His voice was weak from illness, and he suffered from fits of trembling that he hoped would not be mistaken for the quiverings of fear. Apologizing to those who might not be able to hear his words, he launched into a forty-five-minute speech, defending his actions, denying the charges against him, and insisting that he would have brought back ample gold had not Keymis' foolishness betrayed him.

"In all the time he was upon the scaffold," wrote an eye-witness, "there appeared not the least alteration in him, either in his voice or countenance; but he seemed as free from all manner of apprehension, as if he had been come hither rather to be a spectator than a sufferer." [273] When he had done speaking, he embraced the friends who stood about him, and the scaffold was cleared of all but the headsman, the priest, and the victim. The golden city of Manoa had never seemed more remote. Yet after the torment of his woeful last voyage to El Dorado, death must have seemed an attractive release from that hopeless quest.

Many witnesses recorded Raleigh's jaunty last moments; he went out with his old insouciance, knowing that it would serve his name well to make a good exit. A spectator named Thomas Lorkin wrote how after the scaffold was cleared "he takes up the axe, and feels the edge, and finding it sharp for the purpose, *this is that*, saith he, *that will cure all sorrows*, and so kissing it, laid it down again. After that he went to three several corners of the scaffold, and kneeling down desired all the people to pray for him, and conceived a long prayer to himself. Then he began to fit himself for the block, without permitting any help and first laid himself down to try how the block fitted him. After rising up, the executioner kneeled down, and desired him to forgive him, which, with an embrace, he professed he did; but entreated him not to strike till he gave a token, by lifting up his hand; *and then fear not*, saith he, *but strike home*. So he laid himself down to receive the stroke, and the hangman directed him to lay his face toward the east. *No matter how the head lie*, answered he, *so the heart be right*. After he had lain a little while upon the block, conceiving some prayers to himself, he gave the watchword, and the executioner, it seems, not minding it, he called aloud unto him, asking him why he did not strike. *Strike, man*, said he; and so, in two blows, was delivered from his pain." [274] Another witness entered in his journal for the day, "Sir Walter Raleigh had the favor to be beheaded at Westminster, where he died with great applause of the beholders, most constantly, most religiously, most christianly." [275]

7

The judicial murder of Sir Walter Raleigh removed the last of the larger-than-life Elizabethans, and eased a small king's fears of having such a great-souled, unpredictable, wayward genius at liberty in his kingdom. As one biographer of Raleigh puts it, "James killed his troublesome servant in a mood of frightened exasperation." [276] With Raleigh's passing the last of the compulsive Doradists was gone as well. Though other men would search the jungles of South America for golden cities, none were possessed by the same sublime, quasi-mystic assurance that they would reach their goal. Trading concessions were becoming more important than the allure of Manoa. The seeds of what would become Dutch, French, and British Guiana had been planted along the coast.

Manoa and Lake Parima remained on the maps, though, and continued to draw seekers. In 1637 two Franciscan lay brothers, Fray Domingo de Brieva and Fray Andres de Toledo, revived a century-old folly when they started from the eastern slope of the Andes in search of El Dorado and the Temple of the Sun, taking the route of Gonzalo Pizarro and Francisco de Orellana. Accompanied only by six Spanish soldiers and two Indians, and with no gear other than the clothes on their back and a small dugout canoe, they journeyed down the Napo and the Amazon, collecting provisions from the Indians as they went. Miraculously, they encountered no hardships or dangers, and after three months arrived at Pará, near the mouth of the Amazon. They had seen no cities of gold.

Their appearance in Brazil motivated the Portuguese to attempt the reverse journey, up the Amazon from Pará to Quito. A large fleet sailed upstream in July, 1637, commanded by an experienced captain named Pedro Teixeira. The Portuguese ascended the river with great skill, and Teixeira, leaving his fleet at a camp on the Napo, continued on with a small party to Quito, experiencing none of the difficulties suffered by Gonzalo Pizarro. The Spanish authorities gave the Portuguese explorers a friendly reception, but did not really welcome the idea of outsiders roaming Spanish territory, and instructed Teixeira to return immediately to Brazil. Two Spanish Jesuits were appointed to accompany him and make careful observations of all the Portuguese saw and did, to be forwarded to the Council of the Indies. Christoval de Acuña, one of these Jesuits, kept this journal, the most detailed account of the Amazon basin since that of Orellana's chronicler Carvajal.

On this return trip, the Portuguese revisited a village they had seen on the way up, which they called the Village of Gold because the natives were wearing golden ornaments. Acuña asked the natives where their gold came from, and "that which they said to me respecting the mines whence this gold is taken, is what I relate here. Opposite this village, a little higher up on the north side is the mouth of a river called Yurupazi, ascending which and crossing a certain district by land, in three days another river is reached called Yupura, by which the Yquiari is entered called also the river of gold. Here at the foot of a hill, the natives get a great quantity; so that by heating it, they make plates, which they hang to their ears and noses. The natives, who communicate with those who extract the gold, are called Managus." [277]

Acuña's Managus are the same Indians known to other explorers as the Manáos or Mahanoas—and it is not a great stretch of the imagination that turns gold-using Manáos tribesmen into the golden city of Manoa. The Portuguese obtained a fair quantity of gold from these Manáos of the Amazon basin, trading iron knives and tools for it, and probably never suspected that here, and not in Guiana, was the supposedly fabulous city of Manoa for which Berrio and Raleigh had searched so long.

Others continued to look for Manoa in Guiana. In 1655 a native of Ghent named Mathias Matteson, who had been Teixeira's pilot on the Amazon voyage of 1637–39, set out from Santo Thomé with sixty Spaniards and four hundred Indians to find the golden city. He did what Berrio and Raleigh had never quite succeeded in undertaking: he followed the Caroni upstream to its sources, entering the vast plateau of eastern Venezuela known as *La Gran Sabana* and approaching Guiana's Mount Roraima. According to the theory of Manoa, the great inland salt lake of Parima should have been there, but Matteson did not find it. Six years later he led a Dutch expedition westward along the Essequibo and explored another previously unknown interior sector of Guiana with similar results.

The Bohemian missionary Samuel Fritz, who spent much of a long lifetime in the Amazon region, detected a continued Portuguese interest in an earlier El Dorado, that of the Omaguas, in the late seventeenth century. Fritz, who was born in 1654, was chosen by the Jesuits of Quito to bring the gospel to the Omaguas and other tribes of the Amazon. Going among them alone, he met with a warm reception and lived a Schweitzer-like existence among these tribes for decades. He encountered the Manáos, whom he called Manaves and described as "a tribe of unconverted

Indians. . . . [They] are very brave and feared by other neighboring tribes, and offered resistance for years to a Portuguese troop. Their arms are bows and poisoned arrows; they grow no hair in order, say they, that they may have nothing to be laid hold of in battle; they go nude; their foreheads as far as the ears they smear with a black resin of the nature of balsam. Their lands lie in the northerly direction upon a stream called Jurubetts, to which one arrives by the river Jupura." [278] Fritz confirmed Acuña's observation that these Indians dealt in objects of gold; "they do not themselves extract the gold," he noted, "but they go to the river Jurubetts navigating the Yquiari, where they obtain it by barter, and this is the river much famed for its gold amongst these tribes." [279]

Father Fritz encountered Portuguese along the Amazon, for that nation had taken possession of Brazil and was engaged in a dispute with Spain over the boundary between their respective spheres of influence. The Portuguese claimed that Fritz was trespassing on their territory and made some trouble for him, even imprisoning him as a spy for nearly two years when he came to Pará to seek medical attention, but eventually he prevailed and was allowed to continue his missionary work. When the Portuguese made a clearing in the forest near Fritz' mission and told him they intended to settle there, he commented in his journal, "I doubt not that they would do so because of their craving to make slaves of the Indians from here upwards, in addition to which they imagine that from here they can find a gate of entrance to El Dorado, that they dream is not very distant." [280] Fritz did not attempt to disabuse them of this fancy, and in time they learned the illusory nature of their plan the hard way.

The delusion of a Guianian Manoa persisted into the eighteenth century. Each mapmaker showed it on its lake:

De Laet in 1630, Blaeuw in 1640, Sanson in 1656, Heylin in 1663. The French cartographer Delisle omitted the lake on his map of 1703, but inserted a legend, "In this region some place the lake of Parima and the city Manoa of the Dorado." Later in the eighteenth century, some maps began to give Lake Parima a subsidiary name, *Mar Eldorado*, the Golden Sea. (The Spanish article "*el*" was starting to suffer an erosion of meaning, so that it became possible to speak of "the Eldorado" or "an Eldorado" in unabashed redundancy. What had originally signified "the gilded one" was coming to mean "a place of treasure," without grammatical reference to its underlying Spanish sense.)

Since the lake was on all the reputable maps, obviously it had to be real. In 1714, the Dutch West India Company sent secret instructions to its man in Guiana, Pieter van der Heyden Resen, ordering him to outfit and dispatch an expedition "to seek exact information, but in a careful and as guarded a manner as possible, concerning the nature and location of the towns of Lake Parime [*sic*], and especially also concerning Manoa o Eldorado, or the Golden City, in what manner it may be reached, of what disposition the people there are, and how the same must be treated, according to which they will be able to regulate their acts as far as possible. When the aforesaid persons shall have arrived at the chief town of Lake Parime, and also at the Golden City, they will have to act with great caution, and the one who is entrusted with the command and direction will have to inquire for the chief of that place, and endeavor to see and to speak with him, if such may be done, and otherwise address himself to the other great men. And he shall then represent to the same and make them believe that they have come there as friends, in order to deal in friendship with those people, and to establish a trade with them, with promises to bring them only such goods as they desire, and to that end offer them, as a proof and commencement, the goods which they have brought with them, and if they desire those goods, the same shall be sold to them, or exchanged for gold and silver, and for no other moneys than for gold and silver alone, and they shall endeavor to obtain from them as much of that mineral as can be got in a friendly manner." [281]

Unfortunately for historians, Commander van der Heyden Resen carried out his orders in so careful and guarded a manner that the archives of the Dutch West India Company offer no clue to the success of his attempt to trade with Manoa. But the records for 1722 tell of the first arrival of Indians called *Maganouts* at the Dutch trading posts, and since these Indians are later referred to in the same records as *Magnouws* and *Manoas*, it appears that van der Heyden Resen had reached, if not the city of Manoa, then at least the gold-using Manáos.

The Spanish interest in El Dorado waned notably in the eighteenth century; Spain herself was in severe decline and heading toward the collapse that would strip her of most of her overseas empire in another hundred years, and the rampaging *conquistadores* had given way in South America to timid bureaucrats. In 1722 and again in 1730, certain priests of Venezuela sent memoranda to the King, describing the riches of El Dorado in great detail and offering precise instructions for reaching it, but no expeditions were forthcoming. Something of the old spirit, though, was revived by a German, Nicolas Horstman, a few years later.

Horstman, like Pieter van der Heyden Resen, was sent out by the Dutch West India Company to find Parima and El Dorado. He left the Dutch coastal base of Essequibo (later transferred to British control) on November 3, 1739. The Dutch officials at Essequibo had high hopes that Horstman, a surgeon by profession and an unusually intrepid and capable man, would succeed in reaching the golden city. But

Horstman never returned to Essequibo, and it was nearly three years before the Dutch found out what had happened to him. Setting out ambitiously with two soldiers, passports in Dutch and Latin, and four halfbreed creoles to serve as guides and interpreters, Horstman had ascended the Essequibo River—Keymis' route to El Dorado—until he came to another river running southward. Following this, he was brought to the Río Negro, and thence to the Amazon, finishing his travels at the Portuguese coastal base of Pará. There he simply enrolled in Portuguese service without bothering to notify his former Dutch employers of his travels. Only when his four creole guides, who had been imprisoned by the Portuguese, escaped and returned to Essequibo did the Dutch West India Company learn the story.

The Dutch administrator at Essequibo, Laurens Storm van 's Gravesande, was angered and disappointed. He wrote to the West India Company's home office to declare, "This unexpected conduct of the aforesaid Nicolas Horstman (who was a Protestant) and showed himself to be a great lover of such undertakings, and moreover had all the outward bearing of an honorable man, has greatly astonished me, and I shall leave it to Your Honors' consideration how necessary it will be that these two dishonorable cheats [Horstman and one of his soldier escorts, who also deserted] should be got hold of in order that they may be punished rigorously as an example to others." [282]

Horstman was never "got hold of" by the Dutch, but the diary of his journey was somehow obtained by the French geographer and explorer Charles Marie de la Condamine, who copied it and published a synopsis of it in his account of his own travels, issued in 1745. La Condamine asserted that Horstman had actually found the mysterious Lake Parima, but that he found in it "little resemblance to the picture he had formed of the Golden Lake." [283] Early in the twentieth century, C. A. Harris, the chief clerk of the British Colonial Office, unearthed la Condamine's complete extract from Horstman's diary, which had been filed in the Bibliothèque Nationale at Paris, and it turned out to have considerable geographical importance of a negative sort.

La Condamine had headed the manuscript "*Extract from the Journal of Nicolas Horstman, Surgeon of Hildesheim, in Westphalia, come from Río Esquive, on the Coast of Surinam, to Pará, by the Río Negro, written in bad Portuguese, but just as he wrote it.*" Below was Horstman's own heading: "*Journey which I made to the Imaginary Lake of Parima, or of Gold, in the Year 1739.*" [284] He described his trip up the Essequibo, passing one dangerous cataract after another, and making side journeys to look for gold mines and mountains of sapphires and emeralds. The best he found was an outcropping of pretty crystals of no particular commercial value. On the 11th of May, 1740, he noted, "we . . . entered the great lake, called by the Indians Amucu, in which we proceeded constantly over reeds, with which the lake is entirely filled, and it has two islands in the middle." It was his opinion that this was the alleged Parima; but there was no golden city here. After a search of several days he left the lake via another river, and spent fifteen days in fruitless quest for a silver mine of which the Indians had told him. Continuing southward, Horstman came on June 24 to the River Parima, which had evidently lent its name to the mythical lake. This river had an interesting feature: "in it there stands a mountain which has a great lake on top, which I went to see, and I found fish in the said lake of the same sort as are in the same river, but the water is black in the lake and white in the river." [285] A mountain lake fit the description of the place at which the original ritual of the gilded man was performed, but there were no settlements here, and Horstman journeyed on to the Río

Negro, arriving on July 16 at a village called Aracari, where, "after having passed such great dangers and difficulties of sea and wild Indians . . . I was robbed and pillaged by a Carmelite friar, a missionary of the said village." [286]

Enough information about Horstman's trip filtered back to the Dutch settlement to indicate that there was a River Parima, but no Lake Parima, and that the one large inland lake to be found, Lake Amucu, was not the site of El Dorado. Yet the hardworking administrator at Essequibo, Storm van 's Gravesande, could not bring himself to give up the fantasy so easily. When some Spaniards explored the Guianian hinterland in 1748, Storm acquired by subterfuge a copy of their map, and wrote excitedly to his superiors at The Hague in November, 1749, that the map was "of no small advantage for us—that notorious Lake of Parime, of which so much has been written for and against, by many believed to exist, by others held as a fable, having now at last been discovered and found, and even, according to the map, situated within our jurisdiction." [287] Not surprisingly, he soon discovered that the Spaniards were in error. But he remained optimistic about El Dorado. Since Horstman had shown himself to be a scoundrel by deserting to the Portuguese, it was clearly an error to believe anything he might say on the subject of the non-existence of Lake Parima. In a despatch of 1764, Storm reported that two of Guiana's rivers, the Massaruni and Cuyuni, "have their source in a large lake or inland sea, as the Indians call it, which lake is enclosed by high mountains, inhabited by vast numbers of Indians, who, through fear of the Spaniards, allow no strangers to come into their country, it being related that already two detachments of Spaniards sent into those parts to make discoveries have been beaten and massacred. Whether this lake is the lake of Parima or that of Cassipa is not yet known." [288]

But El Dorado had already passed into its proper realm. Voltaire had published his *Candide* in 1759, and one of the many fanciful places visited by his innocent hero in the course of his violent education was the land of Eldorado. Voltaire appropriately placed his golden kingdom in Guiana, and got Candide there, accompanied by his valet Cacambo, by a river journey as awesome as any undertaken by Berrio or Orellana: "They drifted for some leagues between banks which were sometimes flowery, sometimes bare, sometimes flat, sometimes steep. The river continually became wider; finally it disappeared under an arch of frightful rocks which towered up to the very sky. The two travellers were bold enough to trust themselves to the current under this arch. The stream, narrowed between walls, carried them with horrible rapidity and noise. After twenty-four hours they saw daylight again; but their canoe was wrecked on reefs; they had to crawl from rock to rock for a whole league and at last they discovered an immense horizon, bordered by inaccessible mountains. The country was cultivated for pleasure as well as for necessity; everywhere the useful was agreeable. The roads were covered or rather ornamented with carriages of brilliant material and shape, carrying men and women of singular beauty, who were rapidly drawn along by large red sheep whose swiftness surpassed that of the finest horses of Andalusia, Tetuan, and Mequinez. 'This country,' said Candide, 'is better than Westphalia.'" [289]

They had arrived in Eldorado, which is to say Utopia. The children there amused themselves with quoits of gold studded with emeralds and rubies, which they discarded like ordinary playthings at the end of their game. The houses were like European palaces. At the inn where Candide stayed, soups garnished with parrots, condors, and hummingbirds were served in dishes of rock crystal, by boys and girls garbed in cloth of gold. Attempting to pay for his lodging with two large pieces of gold he had found by the wayside, Candide was met with laughter; the "stones from our highways," he was told, had no value in Eldorado, and all inns were run free of charge by the government.

An old man informed Candide that "the kingdom where we are now is the ancient country of the Incas, who most imprudently left it to conquer part of the world and were at last destroyed by the Spaniards. The princes of their family who remained in their native country had more wisdom; with the consent of the nation, they ordered that no inhabitants should ever leave our little kingdom, and this it is that has preserved our innocence and our felicity. The Spaniards had some vague knowledge of this country, which they called Eldorado, and about a hundred years ago an Englishman named Raleigh came very near to it; but, since we are surrounded by inaccessible rocks and precipices, we have hitherto been exempt from the rapacity of the nations of Europe who have an inconceivable lust for the pebbles and mud of our land and would kill us to the last man to get possession of them." [290] There were no priests in Eldorado, said the old man; rather, every citizen was a priest. But there was no need of prayer, since God had granted the people of the happy land everything they could desire, so their religion consisted solely of giving thanks.

Candide and Cacambo were conducted to the royal palace, where the King of Eldorado greeted them with a warm embrace and invited them to supper. While the meal was being prepared, they toured the town, and saw "the public buildings rising to the very skies, the market-places ornamented with thousands of columns, the fountains of rose-water and of liquors distilled from sugar-cane, which played continually in the public squares paved with precious stones which emitted a perfume like that of cloves and cinnamon. Candide asked to see the law courts; he was told that there were none, and that nobody ever went to law. He asked if there were prisons and was told that there were none. He was still more surprised and pleased by the palace of sciences, where he saw a gallery two thousand feet long, filled with instruments of mathematics and physics." After a pleasant dinner with the King, Candide obtained permission to depart. The request was granted, and the monarch placed at their disposal a "machine" to float the travelers over the mountains surrounding the kingdom, which were ten thousand feet high and more than ten leagues broad. "Ask anything else of me you wish," he said. "We ask nothing of your Majesty," replied Cacambo, "except a few sheep laden with provisions, pebbles, and the mud of this country." Laughing, the King said, "I cannot understand the taste you people of Europe have for our yellow mud; but take as much as you wish, and much good it may do you." Off to civilization floated Candide and Cacambo, laden with gold and precious stones on the backs of sheep. But the sheep died in the wilderness beyond the mountains, and the two wanderers straggled into Surinam bowed under the weight of their treasure, of which they were soon relieved by men of sharper wits.

Voltaire had placed El Dorado in the right context: never-never land, where children play quoits with golden rings. But in 1772, the governor of Spanish Guiana sent a detachment of soldiers led by an officer of artillery named Nicholas Martenez to find and occupy El Dorado and Lake Parima. The Portuguese of Brazil regarded this excursion as an invasion of their territory, and sent a counter-expedition of their own to repel Martenez. The Spaniards were ambushed, and from this last of all official ventures toward the golden city only one man, Antonio Solís, returned alive.

8

In the nineteenth century, that period of great scientific achievement and global exploration, the time arrived to spike the myth of El Dorado for good. The task was undertaken by the formidable Prussian scientist Alexander von Humboldt, who recognized all knowledge as his province. Humboldt, born in 1769, studied a host of sciences in his university days, specializing, if such a man could be said to have specialized at all, in geology and mineralogy. When he was twenty-three he obtained an appointment to the department of mines of the Prussian government, and while in the civil service found time to carry on experiments in mining technique, in the stimulation of frogs' nerves by electricity, and in the physiology of animals. The death of his mother in 1796 provided him with an inheritance that freed him from the need to serve the bureaucracy. He resigned in February of 1797, intending to travel and make scientific observations throughout the world.

After pursuing his studies in the capitals of Europe, Humboldt met a botanist named Aimé Bonpland in Paris, and discussed a joint expedition with him. They decided to go to Algiers, join the spring pilgrimage to Mecca, and go on to Egypt to see the ruins of ancient grandeur. But the ship that was to take them to Africa was shipwrecked off Portugal before they boarded it, and then their visa was canceled because of political instability abroad. Humboldt and Bonpland went to Madrid instead. A series of interviews with government ministers brought Humboldt an audience with the Spanish King; the young German proposed a survey of the royal possessions in South America, which no foreign scientist had been permitted to tour since the journey of la Condamine more than half a century earlier. The

King agreed, and Humboldt and Bonpland received royal letters of recommendation that gave them access to Spanish territory everywhere.

They sailed for Cuba in June, 1799—beginning a five-year tour of the New World in which they would cover more than six thousand miles on foot, muleback, and by boat, surveying the topography and making extensive collections of flora and fauna. All of Central America, most of the West Indian islands, and the whole of South America except for Brazil, Patagonia, and Tierra del Fuego were at their disposal. This vast empire was divided into various kingdoms whose political structure had been organized in the sixteenth century, and there had been little change since that time; the Spaniards still ruled as absolute conquerors, the huge Indian populations had no role in government and little right to own property, and an air of torpidity hung over everything.

Humboldt spent the first eighteen months of his stay in Venezuela, whose territory then was much more extensive than it is today. He had the opportunity to retrace much of the country through which the seekers of El Dorado had gone, and since the theme of the golden city appealed to Humboldt's imagination, he devoted a good deal of his time to analyzing their routes. His travels began at Cumaná in July of 1799, and he proceeded inland toward the *llanos*, those vast savannahs in which Federmann and Hutten and the rest had consumed so many years of their lives. "The traveller sees before him," Humboldt wrote, "steppes receding until they vanish in the far horizon. Neither hill nor cliff rises, like an island in the ocean, to break the uniformity of the boundless plain; only here and there broken strata of limestone, several hundred square miles in extent, appear noticeably higher than the surroundings. . . . Here, no oasis recalls the memory of earlier inhabitants; no carved stone, no ruined building, no fruit tree, once cultivated but

now wild, speaks of the art or industry of former generations." [291] Earlier travelers had looked for golden kingdoms
here; Humboldt collected electric eels and puzzled over their
inexplicable immunity to their own current.

Traveling southwestward, Humboldt and Bonpland
arrived in March of 1800 at the Río Apure, a tributary of
the Orinoco, and began an extensive reconnaissance of the
entire Orinoco basin, making the trip in a large sailing canoe
with four Indian oarsmen and one pilot. During rainstorms,
they huddled in a cabin near the stern, under a roof of
leaves; ox hides stretched over wooden frames served Humboldt as a table for his observations; at night, they camped in
hammocks along the banks, lighting fires to keep the jaguars away. They went down the Apure and up the Orinoco
against fierce rapids, past the confluence with the Río Meta,
then by a devious route to the Río Negro, and down that
river to the Brazilian border, and back to the mouth of the
Cassaquiari, which unites the Orinoco and the Negro. An
attempt to reach the sources of the Orinoco was thwarted by
hostile Indians. At last they arrived at the tiny outpost of
Esmeralda, in the mountains near the source of the Caroni—
the very place where Lake Parima and the city of Manoa
had been thought to be. It was a Spanish penal colony,
priestless and infested with mosquitoes, and its inhabitants
were at a loss to understand why two foreigners should have
gone to such great lengths to get there. Humboldt prowled
the surrounding mountains and found open veins of rock
crystal in the granite—the "emeralds" and "diamonds" that
the Indians had described to such men as Keymis. Humboldt had studied his mythical geography well, and he made
every effort to find the lakes variously known as Parima,
Cassipa, and Rupunuwini, and the inland salt sea.

There were many rivers here—the Caroni, the Para-
gua, the Branco, the Cuyuni, and numerous others, most of

them emptying northward into the Orinoco. These rivers frequently overflowed their banks during the winter rains. Humboldt found no great salt lakes, nor even any unusually large fresh-water ones, though he obtained ample information about Horstman's Lake Amucu, several leagues broad and containing two small islands. He concluded that Lake Parima, the inland salt lake, was nothing more than the *River* Parima at its flood stage, and the River Parima was identical with the River Branco shown on some maps. "The Laguna Rupunuwini, or Parima of the voyage of Raleigh and of the maps of Hondius," Humboldt wrote, "is an imaginary lake, formed by the lake Amucu and the tributary streams of the Uraricuera [a section of the Parima/Branco river system], which often overflow their banks. . . . Slight local circumstances, joined to the remembrance of the salt lake of Mexico . . . served to complete a picture created by the imagination of Raleigh and his two lieutenants, Keymis and Masham." [292] There never had been a Lake Parima, merely a winter inundation that temporarily flooded huge tracts of land in the interior of Guiana. The city of Manoa, of course, was no more genuine than the lake on whose shores it was said to be situated.

Having punctured the terminal myth of the tale of El Dorado, Humboldt went to the source of all the frenzy —Cundinamarca, the plateau of the gilded man. He started up the Río Magdalena early in 1801, with the river in full spate against him, and after a 300-mile cruise lasting forty-five days came to the tableland on which Bogotá was located. Humboldt and Bonpland crossed and recrossed the Andean *cordilleras* for many months, and did not fail to visit Lake Guatavitá.

Humboldt knew the story of the gilded man, and comprehended the process of delusion whereby El Dorado had slipped eastward from this plateau into Guiana. Visiting the sacred lake, he reported seeing "on its banks the remains of a staircase hewn in the rock, and serving for the ceremonies of ablution." [293] Humboldt also noted "vestiges . . . of a breach, which was made by the Spaniards for the purpose of draining the lake."

That gave him an idea. He computed quickly that if a thousand Indians a year had made an annual pilgrimage to the lake for a century, and if each worshipper had, as some accounts said, thrown five golden trinkets into the water as tribute to the resident deity, then there were upwards of 50,000,000 golden images in the thick ooze at the bottom of the lake. Humboldt reckoned that this amount of gold would have a monetary value of some $300,000,000. (When he reported his theory, M. de la Kier of the Royal Institute of Paris revised Humboldt's estimate of the cash value of the horde to $5,600,000,000!) It would be profitable, then, to drain the lake and recover some of this treasure.

He was not the first to conceive such a scheme. Hernán Pérez de Quesada, dredging at Guatavitá in 1540, had recovered gold worth 4000 *pesos de oro*. Forty years later, a rich merchant of Bogotá named Antonio Sepulveda journeyed to Spain to get a royal license to sift the lake, promising a fifth of the proceeds to the crown. Sepulveda assembled a squadron of Indian laborers and had them cut a section out of the encircling wall of earth and stone, fifty feet high, that rimmed the lagoon. After months of work, they chopped down to water level, and enough of the lake poured through the opening to expose several feet of black mud around the edges. (This was the "breach" noticed by Humboldt.) Sepulveda found many gold trinkets and an emerald as large as a hen's egg, but it was necessary to lower the lake still further to get at the real wealth of Guatavitá.

His capital gave out, though, and the project had to be

abandoned. He died soon after; most of his gold was confiscated in the King's name. However, the gentlemen of Bogotá remained convinced that the scheme was a worthy one, and in 1625 formed a syndicate for draining the lake. The task proved too much for them. They recovered some gold, but not enough to pay the cost of the labor involved. The same result was reached by another dredging syndicate in 1677, and there were further attempts every generation or so through the eighteenth century.

Humboldt, of course, did not propose to grub for Guatavitá's gold himself. Money interested him so little that he consumed not only his income but his principal on his travels, and nearly went bankrupt later financing the publication of the many volumes of his scientific reports. He simply suggested that it might be lucrative to investigate the depths of Guatavitá, and thereby touched off a craze. Speculators moved in on all the lakes of the former Chibcha domain. One man built a 400-foot tunnel to carry off the water of his lake, but it collapsed, killing his workers. Another hired a huge mob of Indians as a bucket brigade, hoping to empty a lake through unremitting toil. (It did not work.) Despite the crude engineering techniques of these operators, some important finds were made, the most interesting coming from Lake Siecha, a small body of water near Guatavitá. It was a small group of figures of men on a raft, 9½ centimeters in diameter and weighing about 260 grams, all of gold. This unique piece seemed clearly to show the gilded chieftain, surrounded by priests and nobles, as he rowed out onto the sacred lake to enact the *dorado* ceremony.

The application of modern methods was required, and in 1912 an English firm that called itself Contractors, Ltd., appeared in Bogotá with $150,000 worth of equipment. Their plan was to pump the lake dry. Armies of laborers dragged giant wood-burning pumps onto the plateau, and soon the water of Guatavitá was spurting forth. Within weeks, the water level was down forty feet, and it had been a dry season to begin with, so the level had been low when work had commenced. All that remained was to shovel out and screen the gold-filled muck.

A curious thing happened. Once exposed to the sun, the mud became hard as rock. It was impossible to get anything loose. And while the workers struggled with picks and axes, the lake slowly filled again. Contractors, Ltd., had recovered $10,000 worth of gold, but it had cost them $160,000 to do it. They fled away, and the abandoned pumps rotted, and the sanctuary of the gilded man remained inviolate.

9

Though Humboldt had settled the question of Lake Parima and a Guianian Dorado, some doubters remained— for mankind's capacity for self-delusion is boundless. A map published in France in 1806 still showed Parima and Manoa, as though in defiance of Humboldt's findings. As late as 1844, a New Yorker named J. A. Van Heuvel published a scholarly and reasonable book entitled *El Dorado*, in which he argued, "It appears indubitable that there is an extensive tract inundated, separate from the lake Amucu, on the table-land between the Essequibo and the Oronoke, on which passes the *Cordillera* of Parima." [294] Though he admitted that this body of water was a "temporary inundation," not a lake, he insisted that its existence should not be denied, and even argued for the likelihood that its shores, during the season of flooding, were occupied by a populated and prosperous Indian civilization which could easily have been distorted into the Manoa of Berrio and Raleigh.

Only after the interior of Guiana was relatively well explored did the fantasy die away. Richard Schomburgk, who traversed Guiana many times with his brother Robert between 1835 and 1859, wrote of how, at break of day, he hastened from a native village "in order to be able to gaze across the wide, wide savannah undisturbed. I stood there upon ground to which many a legend and myth was attached—at my feet the '*Mar de aguas blancas*,' the '*Mar del Dorado*,' the Lake 'with gold-bearing-shores,' and the 'Golden City of Manoa.' . . . The small inland Lake of Amucu, the . . . extensive inland sea, in which the great rivers of South America, the Essequibo, the Orinoco, and the Amazon were said to have their source . . . lay before me. But in vain did I look for its 'gold-bearing shores,' for the 'golden imperial city of Manoa'; my eye rested only upon the dark rushes and giant grasses which enclosed its marshy shores and its waters, looking now so unimportant in the dry season of the year." [295]

And in 1878 the English traveler Everard im Thurm came to the same place, and looked out at a misty plain with mountains in the distance, lighted by the sun in such a way that "the whole seemed a city of temples and towers, crowned with gilded spires and minarets. The level plain at my feet was the so-called Lake Amoocoo or Parima, and the glittering cloud city was on the supposed site of the fabled golden City of El Dorado or Manoa. . . . The so-called lake is almost throughout the year a dry plain, on which lines of aeta palms mark the courses of streams, the overflowing of which in very wet seasons makes the 'lake.' Even as I looked at it that morning, the last of the mist melted, and the city once more went out from my sight, as it has from the belief of the world." [296]

Men had turned to other "eldorados," more substantial than the South American fantasy. The nineteenth century saw gold discovered in California, in Australia, in the Yukon, in South Africa. New gold rushes called forth the old metaphors, but this time there really was gold in the hills. Even Guiana finally yielded some authentic gold, though it was no Klondike. The annual world production of gold at the turn of the twentieth century was nearly 15,000,000 ounces; twice as much gold was discovered between 1851 and 1900 as in all the years from 1492 to 1850.

In these great gold rushes, of course, many men were devoured by fate and gained no fortunes. Yet at least they were chasing real metal, not the feverish fantasy of a golden city. The quest for El Dorado was an epic of human folly, really, a case history in the power of man to bemuse himself with myth. But it called forth noble deeds and led to the exploration of a mighty tract of unknown land.

It began on the plateau of Cundinamarca, with a gilded man rowing to the center of a sacred lake and diving, a flashing bright streak, into the holy waters. Studies carried out by a group of Colombian archaeologists and published in 1954 offer some clue to the origin of this ceremony that inspired so grand and foolish a quest. The archaeologists discovered that several thousand years ago, at a time when man already dwelled in the Andean *cordilleras*, a great meteorite plummeted from the sky at Guatavitá and buried itself from sight. A blazing mass of white-hot stone, a golden streak coursing like mighty lightning across the sky, a sudden descent, a roar as of thunder—surely it was some potent god coming to the world to take up his residence in the lake. And perhaps it was in emulation of this fiery descent that the gilded man of Cundinamarca, his body shining with the dust of the brightest of metals, took his ritual plunge in the sacred waters.

Bibliography

Primary Sources

Cieza de León, Pedro de. *The War of Chupas*, translated by Sir Clements R. Markham. The Hakluyt Society, London, 1918.

——— *The War of Las Salinas*, translated by Sir Clements R. Markham. The Hakluyt Society, London, 1923.

Díaz del Castillo, Bernal. *The True Story of the Conquest of New Spain*, translated by A. P. Maudslay. The Hakluyt Society, London, 1908–16. Five volumes. Abridged edition, Farrar, Straus and Cudahy, New York, 1956.

Fritz, Father Samuel. *Journal, 1686–1723*, translated by Dr. George Edmundson. The Hakluyt Society, London, 1922.

Garcilaso de la Vega. *The Incas*, translated by Maria Jolas from the French edition of Alain Gheerbrant. The Orion Press, New York, 1961.

Harcourt, Robert. *A Relation of a Voyage to Guiana*, edited by Sir C. Alexander Harris. The Hakluyt Society, London, 1928.

Hakluyt, Richard, editor. *The Principal Navigations Voyages Traffiques and Discoveries of the English Nation*. Modern edition, James MacLehose and Sons, Glasgow, 1903–05. Twelve volumes.

[*409*]

Harlow, V. T., editor. *Colonising Expeditions to the West Indies and Guiana*, 1623–1667. The Hakluyt Society, London, 1925.

Monardes, Nicholas. *Joyfull Newes out of the Newe Founde Worlde*, translated by John Frampton. Modern edition, Constable and Co., Ltd., London, 1925. Two volumes.

Purchas, Samuel, editor. *Purchas His Pilgrimes*. Modern edition, James MacLehose and Sons, Glasgow, 1906. Twenty volumes.

Raleigh, Sir Walter. *The Discoverie of . . . Guiana*, edited by V. T. Harlow. The Argonaut Press, London, 1928.

——— *Ralegh's Last Voyage*, edited by V. T. Harlow. The Argonaut Press, London, 1932.

Sarmiento de Gamboa, Pedro. *History of the Incas*, translated by Sir Clements R. Markham. The Hakluyt Society, Cambridge, 1907.

Simón, Fray Pedro. *The Expedition of Pedro de Ursua and Lope de Aguirre*, translated by William Bollaert from *Primera parte de las noticias historiales de las conquistas de Tierra Firme*. The Hakluyt Society, London, 1861.

Storm van 's Gravesande, Laurens. *The Rise of British Guiana*, compiled by C. A. Harris and J. A. J. de Villiers. The Hakluyt Society, London, 1911. Two volumes.

Toribio Medina, José, editor. *The Discovery of the Amazon According to the Account of Friar Gaspar de Carvajal and Other Documents*, translated by Bertram T. Lee. The American Geographical Society, New York, 1934.

SECONDARY AUTHORITIES

Arciniegas, Germán. *Germans in the Conquest of America*. The Macmillan Company, New York, 1943.

Babcock, William H. *Legendary Islands of the Atlantic*. The American Geographical Society, New York, 1922.

Bandelier, A. F. *The Gilded Man*. D. Appleton and Company, New York, 1893.

Bibliography

Bayle, Constantino. *El Dorado Fantasma*. Consejo de la Hispanidad, Madrid, 1943.

Bolton, Herbert E. *Coronado: Knight of Pueblos and Plains*. University of New Mexico Press, Albuquerque, 1949.

Cunninghame Graham, R. B. *The Conquest of New Granada*. William Heinemann, London, 1922.

Dominquez, M. *Eldorado, Enigma de la Historia Americana, Era el Peru de los Incas*. Talleres Graficos Rodriquez Giles, Buenos Aires, 1925.

Easby, Dudley T., Jr. "Early Metallurgy in the New World." *Scientific American*, Volume 214, Number 4, April 1966.

——— "Pre-Hispanic Metallurgy and Metalworking in the New World." *Proceedings of the American Philosophical Society*, Volume 109, Number 2, April 9, 1965.

Edwards, Edward. *The Life of Sir Walter Raleigh*. Macmillan and Company, London, 1868. Two volumes.

Elton, G. R., editor. *The New Cambridge Modern History, Volume II: The Reformation 1520–59*. Cambridge University Press, Cambridge, 1962.

Friede, Juan. "Geographical Ideas on Venezuela." *The Americas*, Volume 16, pp. 145–59, 1959.

Hagen, Victor W. von. "The Search for the Gilded Man." *Natural History*, Volume 111, Number 7, September 1952.

Hamilton, E. J. *American Treasure and the Price Rise in Spain, 1501–1650*. Harvard University Press, Cambridge, 1934.

Haring, C. H. *The Spanish Empire in America*. Oxford University Press, New York, 1947.

Herodotus. *The Persian Wars*, translated by George Rawlinson. The Modern Library, New York, 1942.

Herrmann, Paul. *The Great Age of Discovery*. Harper & Brothers, New York, 1958.

Holmes, William H. "Ancient art of the province of Chiriqui, Colombia." Smithsonian Institution Bureau of Ethnology, Sixth Annual Report, 1884–85. Government Printing Office, Washington, 1888.

———— *The Use of Gold and Other Metals among the Ancient Inhabitants of Chiriqui, Isthmus of Darien.* Smithsonian Institution Bureau of Ethnology, Bulletin Number Three. Government Printing Office, Washington, 1887.

Humboldt, Alexander von. *Personal Narrative of Travels to the Equinoctial Regions of America, During the Years 1799–1804,* translated by Thomasina Ross. Henry G. Bohn, London, 1853. Three volumes.

———— *Views of the Cordilleras and Monuments of the Natives of America,* translated by Helen Maria Williams. Longman, Hurst, Rees, Orme and Brown, London, 1814. Two volumes.

Hyams, Edward, and Ordish, George. *The Last of the Incas.* Simon and Schuster, New York, 1963.

Jeffries, Zay. "Gold." *Proceedings of the American Philosophical Society,* Volume 108, Number 5, October 20, 1964.

Kellner, L. *Alexander von Humboldt.* Oxford University Press, London, 1963.

Kirkpatrick, F. A. *The Spanish Conquistadores.* Adam and Charles Black, London, 1963.

Leithäuser, Joachim G. *Worlds Beyond the Horizon,* translated by Hugh Merrick. Knopf, New York, 1955.

Leonard, Irving A. *Books of the Brave.* Gordian Press, New York, 1964.

Letts, Malcolm. *Sir John Mandeville: The Man and his Book.* Batchworth Press, London, 1949.

Mandeville, Sir John. *Travels,* edited by Malcolm Letts. The Hakluyt Society, London, 1953. Two volumes.

Meggers, Betty J., and Evans, Clifford. *Archeological Investigations at the Mouth of the Amazon.* Smithsonian Institution Bureau of American Ethnology, Bulletin Number 167. Government Printing Office, Washington, 1957.

Newton, Arthur Percival. *The European Nations in the West Indies 1493–1688.* Adam and Charles Black, London, 1933.

————, editor. *Travel and Travellers of the Middle Ages.* Routledge & Kegan Paul, London, 1926.

Bibliography

Nuñez, E. B. *Orinoco*. Editorial Elite, Caracas, 1946.

Parks, George Bruner. *Richard Hakluyt and the English Voyages*. The American Geographical Society, New York, 1928.

Parry, J. H. *The Age of Reconnaissance*. Weidenfeld and Nicolson, London, 1963.

Penrose, Boies. *Travel and Discovery in the Renaissance*. Harvard University Press, Cambridge, 1952.

Pliny. *Natural History*, translated by John Bostock and H. T. Riley. Henry G. Bohn, London, 1855. Six volumes.

Prescott, William Hickling. *The Conquest of Mexico*. The Modern Library, New York, no date.

——— *The Conquest of Peru*. The Modern Library, New York, no date.

Raasveldt, H. C. *Los Enigmas de la Laguna de Guatavitá*. Instituto Geológico Nacional, Bogotá, 1954.

Reichel-Dolmatoff, G. *Colombia*. Frederick A. Praeger, New York, 1965.

Schuller, Rodolfo. *The Ordaz and Dortal Expeditions in Search of El Dorado*. Smithsonian Institution, Washington, 1916.

Silverberg, Robert. *Empires in the Dust*. Chilton Books, Philadelphia, 1963.

——— *Frontiers in Archaeology*. Chilton Books, Philadelphia, 1966.

——— *Lost Cities and Vanished Civilizations*. Chilton Books, Philadelphia, 1962.

Skelton, R. A. *Explorers' Maps*. Routledge & Kegan Paul, London, 1958.

Southey, Robert. *The Expedition of Orsua and the Crimes of Aguirre*. Hickman and Hazzard, Philadelphia, 1821.

——— *History of Brazil*. Longman, Hurst, Rees, Orme, and Brown, London, 1822.

Steward, Julian H., editor. *Handbook of South American Indians*. Smithsonian Institution Bureau of American Ethnology, Bulletin Number 143. Government Printing Office, Washington, 1946–59. Seven volumes.

Thurm, Everard M. im. *Among the Indians of Guiana.* Kegan Paul, Trench & Co., London, 1883.

Van Heuvel, Jacob A. *El Dorado.* J. Winchester, New York, 1844.

Voltaire. *Candide.* The Modern Library, New York, no date.

Waldman, Milton. *Sir Walter Raleigh.* John Lane the Bodley Head, London, 1928.

Winsor, Justin, editor. *Narrative and Critical History of America.* Houghton, Mifflin and Co., Boston, 1886. Eight volumes.

Zahm, J. A. *The Quest of El Dorado.* D. Appleton and Company, New York, 1917.

Sources of Quoted Material

1. Raleigh, *Discoverie*, 22.
2. Bandelier, 2.
3. Prescott, *Peru*, 829.
4. Cunninghame Graham, 5.
5. Leonard, 10.
6. Purchas XVIII, 87.
7. Holmes 1888, 35.
8. Prescott, *Peru*, 830.
9. Kirkpatrick, 50.
10. *ibid*, 52.
11. Bernal Díaz, 74.
12. Easby 1965, 89.
13. *ibid.*
14. Prescott, *Peru*, 822.
15. Penrose, 153.
16. Steward V, 72.
17. Raleigh, *Discoverie*, 18.
18. Garcilaso, 152.
19. *ibid*, 123.
20. Purchas XV, 71.
21. Kirkpatrick, 304.
22. Herrmann, 224.
23. Monardes I, 28.
24. Purchas XVIII, 137.
25. Humboldt, *Narrative*, III, 40.
26. Bandelier, 41.
27. *ibid*, 42.
28. Friede, 155.
29. Bandelier, 43.
30. *ibid*, 45.
31. *ibid*, 49.
32. Cunninghame Graham, 176.
33. *ibid*, 1.
34. *ibid*, 18.
35. *ibid*, 21.
36. Kirkpatrick, 315.
37. Purchas XVIII, 139–40.
38. Kirkpatrick, 311.
39. Raleigh, *Discoverie*, 11.
40. Garcilaso, 209.
41. Cunninghame Graham, 79–80.
42. *ibid*, 135.
43. Purchas XVIII, 149.
44. Zahm, 10.
45. Leonard, 76.
46. *ibid*, 30–40.
47. Cieza de León, *Las Salinas*, 263.
48. *ibid*.

49. Cunninghame Graham, 172.
50. Bandelier, 55.
51. *ibid*, 30.
52. Monardes II, 4.
53. *ibid*, 3.
54. Cieza de León, *Chupas*, 55.
55. Toribio Medina, 46 n.
56. *ibid*, 391.
57. *Chupas*, 57.
58. Prescott, Peru, 1074.
59. *Chupas*, 59.
60. *ibid*, 61.
61. *ibid*, 65.
62. Raleigh, *Discoverie*, liv.
63. *ibid*.
64. *Chupas*, 68.
65. *ibid*, 70.
66. *ibid*.
67. *ibid*, 73.
68. Toribio Medina, 81.
69. *ibid*, 72 n.
70. *ibid*, 254.
71. *ibid*, 256.
72. *ibid*, 76 n.
73. *ibid*, 189.
74. *ibid*, 198.
75. *ibid*, 201.
76. *ibid*, 202.
77. *ibid*, 205.
78. Leonard, 46.
79. *ibid*, 56.
80. *ibid*, 57.
81. Toribio Medina, 212.
82. *ibid*.
83. *ibid*, 213.
84. *ibid*, 214.
85. *ibid*.
86. *ibid*, 216.
87. *ibid*, 218.
88. *ibid*, 220.

89. *ibid*, 221.
90. *ibid*, 222.
91. *ibid*, 230.
92. *ibid*, 445.
93. *ibid*, 477.
94. *ibid*, 234.
95. *ibid*, 157.
96. *ibid*, 151.
97. Cieza de León, *Chupas*, 291.
98. Bandelier, 62.
99. *Chupas*, 109.
100. Prescott, *Peru*, 1218.
101. Herrmann, 228.
102. Fritz, 48.
103. Simón, xxiv.
104. *ibid*, 3.
105. *ibid*, xxxvii.
106. *ibid*, 230.
107. *ibid*, 233.
108. *ibid*, 234.
109. *ibid*, 7.
110. *ibid*, 18.
111. *ibid*, 23.
112. *ibid*, 27.
113. *ibid*, 29.
114. *ibid*, 32.
115. *ibid*, 49.
116. *ibid*, 56.
117. Hakluyt XI, 246.
118. Simón, 70.
119. *ibid*, 78.
120. *ibid*, 87.
121. *ibid*, 93.
122. *ibid*.
123. *ibid*, 97.
124. *ibid*, 117.
125. *ibid*, 118.
126. *ibid*, 120.
127. *ibid*, 123.

128. *ibid*, 126.
129. *ibid*, 128.
130. *ibid*, 129.
131. *ibid*, 132.
132. *ibid*, 133.
133. *ibid*, 138.
134. *ibid*, 150.
135. *ibid*, 153.
136. *ibid*, 158.
137. *ibid*, 188–94.
138. *ibid*, 196.
139. *ibid*, 198.
140. *ibid*, 208.
141. *ibid*, 227.
142. *ibid*, 228.
143. Humboldt, *Narrative*, I, 164.
144. Raleigh, *Discoverie*, lxiv.
145. *ibid*.
146. *ibid*, lxvi.
147. Zahm, 94.
148. Raleigh, *Discoverie*, 91.
149. Purchas XV, 59.
150. Raleigh, *Discoverie*, 15.
151. Leonard, 23.
152. Raleigh, *Discoverie*, 92.
153. *ibid*.
154. *ibid*.
155. *ibid*, 93.
156. *ibid*, 27.
157. *ibid*, 28.
158. *ibid*, 99.
159. *ibid*, 96.
160. *ibid*.
161. *ibid*, 30.
162. *ibid*.
163. *ibid*, 100.
164. *ibid*.
165. *ibid*, 101.
166. *ibid*, 20–21.

167. *ibid*.
168. *ibid*, 101–102.
169. *ibid*.
170. *ibid*, 104.
171. *ibid*, 102.
172. *ibid*, 107–8.
173. *ibid*, lxxxiv.
174. Hakluyt X, 205.
175. *ibid*, 208.
176. *ibid*.
177. Waldman, 11.
178. Raleigh, *Discoverie*, xxxv.
179. Waldman, 73.
180. *ibid*, 93.
181. *ibid*, 94.
182. Raleigh, *Discoverie*, 9.
183. Zahm, 147.
184. Raleigh, *Discoverie*, 13.
185. *ibid*, 14.
186. *ibid*.
187. *ibid*.
188. *ibid*, 15.
189. *ibid*.
190. *ibid*, 34.
191. *ibid*, 16.
192. *ibid*, 17.
193. *ibid*, 36.
194. Zahm, 164.
195. Raleigh, *Discoverie*, 40.
196. *ibid*, 41.
197. *ibid*, 42.
198. *ibid*, 46.
199. *ibid*, 50.
200. *ibid*, 51.
201. *ibid*.
202. *ibid*, 53.
203. *ibid*, 54.
204. *ibid*, 55.
205. *ibid*, 56.
206. Pliny I, 405.

207. Mandeville, 142.
208. Raleigh, *Discoverie*, 57.
209. *ibid*, 59.
210. *ibid*, 62.
211. *ibid*, 63.
212. *ibid*, 66.
213. *ibid*, 69.
214. *ibid*, 131.
215. *ibid*, 123.
216. *ibid*, 7.
217. *ibid*, 8.
218. *ibid*, 9.
219. *ibid*, 140.
220. *ibid*, 78.
221. *ibid*, 146.
222. *ibid*, 141.
223. *ibid*, 142.
224. *ibid*, 4.
225. *ibid*, 71.
226. Hakluyt X, 459–60.
227. *ibid*, 465.
228. *ibid*.
229. *ibid*, 466.
230. *ibid*, 469.
231. *ibid*, 479.
232. *ibid*, 481.
233. Hakluyt XI, 9.
234. *ibid*, 11.
235. Raleigh, *Discoverie*, 109.
236. *ibid*.
237. *ibid*, xcii.
238. *ibid*, 111.
239. Purchas XIV, 549.
240. Raleigh, *Discoverie*, c.
241. *ibid*, ci.
242. *Ralegh's Last Voyage*, 129–30.
243. *ibid*, 357.
244. *ibid*, 361.

245. *ibid*, 13.
246. Harcourt, 51.
247. *ibid*, 106–7.
248. *ibid*, 107.
249. *ibid*, 108.
250. *ibid*, 109.
251. *ibid*, 117.
252. Waldman, 155.
253. *ibid*, 169.
254. *Ralegh's Last Voyage*, 103.
255. Raleigh, *Discoverie*, civ.
256. Waldman, 195.
257. *Ralegh's Last Voyage*, 121.
258. *ibid*, 125–6.
259. *ibid*, 52.
260. *ibid*, 57.
261. Waldman, 206.
262. *Ralegh's Last Voyage*, 60.
263. *ibid*, 244.
264. *ibid*, 80.
265. *ibid*, 82.
266. *ibid*, 239.
267. *ibid*, 243.
268. *ibid*, 245.
269. *ibid*, 87.
270. *ibid*, 246.
271. *ibid*, 249.
272. *ibid*, 303.
273. *ibid*, 313.
274. *ibid*.
275. Raleigh, *Discoverie*, xxxviii.
276. *Ralegh's Last Voyage*, 98.
277. Fritz, 40.
278. *ibid*, 61.
279. *ibid*, 62.
280. *ibid*, 77.

281. Storm van 's Gravesande, 186.
282. *ibid*, 202.
283. *ibid*, 167.
284. *ibid*, 171.
285. *ibid*, 175.
286. *ibid*.
287. *ibid*, 249.
288. *ibid*, 466.
289. Voltaire, chap. XVII.
290. *ibid*, chap. XVIII.
291. Kellner, 37.
292. Humboldt, *Narrative*, III, 38.
293. *ibid*, 45.
294. Van Heuvel, 38.
295. Storm van 's Gravesande, 183.
296. Thurm, 36–7.

INDEX

Index

Index

Gilded man, the, 4–5
  and Ehinger, 47, 52
  and Quesada, 92
  and Raleigh, 294
Gold, 5, 6–8
  of Mexico, 27
  of Peru, 34
  of Cundinamarca, 137, 403
Gómara, Francisco López de, 33
Gómez, Sebastián, 226
Gondomar, Count, 367–8, 370,
    382, 383, 385
Gonzalo, Juan, 232, 234
Goodwin, Hugh, 330, 334
Grados, Gerónimo de, 375–6,
    377
Grenville, John, 336
Grijalva, Juan de, 23
Guaiac, 42, 43, 44
Gualies Indians, 277
Gualtero, 330
Guasca, Lake, 99
Guatavitá, Lake, 4, 99, 107
  ritual at, 100, 122–3, 143
  attempts to drain, 137, 404–
    05
  Humboldt on, 402–03
Guerra, Christoval, 15
Guiana, 282
  Vera in, 300
  as El Dorado, 284, 288, 299,
    314
  explored, 401–02
Guzmán, Fernando de, 214, 216
  and Aguirre, 218, 224, 225,
    229
  made governor, 220–1
  and El Dorado, 222–4
  made Prince, 227–8
  death of, 231–2
Guzmán, Martín de, 225

H

Haddington, Viscount, 366
Hakluyt, Richard, 310, 314
Harcourt, Michael, 362
Harcourt, Robert, 360–2
Hariot, Thomas, 310
Harris, C. A., 394
Henao, Padre Alonso, 231
Henry, Prince of Wales, 366,
    367
Henry the Navigator, Prince of
    Portugal, 8, 11
Henry VII of England, 12
Henry VIII of England, 41
Herodotus, 162, 168
Herrera, Alonso de, 58–9, 60–2,
    63, 64, 68, 138
Herrera, Antonio de, 354
Heyden Resen, Pieter van der,
    391–2
Heylin, 391
Hill, James, 355
Hispaniola, 13, 14, 44
*Historia de la Conquista de
    Nueva-España*, 33
Historia de Venezuela, 83
Historia general de las Indias,
    155
*Historia Natural y Moral de las
    Indias*, 34
History of the Conquest of Peru,
    16
History of the World, 17, 311,
    367
Hohemut, Georg, 67, 80, 132,
    184, 186
  and El Dorado, 68–73, 74,
    75, 264
Holland, Philemon, 329
Holy Roman Empire, 26, 27
Hondius, Jocodus, 352

Index

Index

Simón (*Continued*)
on food, 224
on Guzmán's death, 231–2
on Monteverde, 234
concerning Margarita, 236–7, 238
on Llamoso, 243
death of Aguirre, 260–1
on Santo Thomé, 348
Situa, 100–03
Slavery, 48
Sogamoso, 108
Solís, Antonio, 398
Solís, Juan de, 28, 29, 38
Solomon, King, 7
Sorocotá, 104
Sotelle, Gaspar de, 263
South America, 5
settlement of, 19, 45
exploration of, 13–15, 54, 399–404
political structure of, 44, 45
Spain, 7
becomes a nation, 8–11
and Indians, 16–18
effect of gold, 37–8, 139–40
and New World political structure, 44–5
bankruptcies, 199
and New Granada, 269
and England, 312, 342, 367–8
and El Dorado, 392
Spanish Armada, 119, 312
Sparrey, Francis, 330, 334, 356
Speyer, Georg von
see Hohemut, Georg
Spira, Jorge de
see Hohemut, Georg
Sudermania, Duke of, 354
Suma Paz, 77
Surinam, 346
Syphilis, 42–4

T

Tamalameque, 49, 50, 51, 82, 84–5, 88
Tayronas Indians, 202
Teixeira, Pedro, 388–9
Tenochtitlán, 23–25
Teresa, Saint, d'Avila, 280
Teusacá, Lake, 99
Throgmorton, Elizabeth, 313
Thurm, Everard im, 406
Tinca, 104
Tirado, Diego, 235
Tivitivas Indians, 322
Tocuyo, 244, 266
Aguirre at, 247, 255, 256, 257
death of Aguirre, 261
Toledo, Fray Andres de, 387
Toparimaca, Chief, 325, 326
Topiawari, Chief, 326, 330–1, 345
Tora, 88, 89
Tortoya, Gomez de, 262, 263
Toscanelli, 12
Toynbee, Arnold, 94
Treason of a One-Eyed Man, The, 154
Trinidad, 45, 55, 56, 60, 284, 288
settlements, 290, 299, 350
Berrio on, 296, 298, 299, 314, 334
Vides on, 303–04
Whiddon on, 315
Raleigh on, 317, 321
Santiago on, 335, 345
Vera on, 348–50
Dutch on, 356
Trujillo, 66, 244
Túmbez, 31
Tundama, Chief, 112

Index